1990

WILLIAM JAMES'S

RADICAL RECONSTRUCTION OF PHILOSOPHY

WILLIAM JAMES'S

RADICAL RECONSTRUCTION OF PHILOSOPHY

Charlene Haddock Seigfried

State University of New York Press

Published by
State University of New York Press, Albany

© 1990 State University of New York

For information, address State University of New York
Press, State University Plaza, Albany, N.Y., 12246

Library of Congress Cataloging-in-Publication Data
    Seigfried, Charlene Haddock, 1943-
    William James's radical reconstruction of philosophy / Charlene
Haddock Seigfried.
    p.   cm.
    Includes bibliographical references.
    ISBN 0-7914-0401-3. —ISBN 0-7914-0402-1 (pbk.)
    1. James, William, 1842-1910.   2. James, William, 1842-1910-
-Methodology.   I. Title.
B945.J24S443   1990
191—dc20
                                                          89-48392
                                                          CIP

10 9 8 7 6 5 4 3 2 1

For H.H.S. and K.E.H.S. and all the other Haddocks in my life

"It seems to me that a general upheaval is setting in from innumerable directions in philosophy, and that the ultimate result will be a new landscape and new perspectives, with many of the old oppositions ('idealism' & 'realism' e.g.) *aufgehoben*, and with a general settling of the ground onto a much more *practical* basis. The beginnings will be abstruse and clumsy, but little by little light will be made" [ERE, 212].

Contents

Acknowledgments

I would especially like to thank John J. McDermott, H. S. Thayer, and Andrew Reck, who have over the years encouraged my research and writing on William James. Thayer's writings and suggestions, in particular, have been most helpful. Many members of the Society for the Advancement of American Philosophy have also provided encouragement and suggestions and the meetings have been an invaluable resource. My greatest booster and severest critic remains, however, Hans H. Seigfried, without whom this book would be much diminished. Concentrated work on the book was made possible by a semester at the Purdue Center for Humanistic Studies in Fall 1987. I also gratefully acknowledge permission to reprint the following articles, usually in revised form:

"James's Reconstruction of Ordinary Experience," *The Southern Journal of Philosophy*, 19:4 (1981), 499-515.

"On the Metaphysical Foundations of Scientific Psychology," in Michael H. DeArmey and Stephen Skousgaard, eds., *The Philosophical Psychology of William James*. Washington, D.C.: University Press of America, 1986, 57-72; © Center for Advanced Research in Phenomenology, Inc., 1986.

"William James's Phenomenological Methodology," *Journal of the British Society for Phenomenology*, 20:1 (1989), 62-76.

"Poetic Invention and Scientific Observation: James's Model of 'Sympathetic Concrete Observation,'" *Transactions of the Charles S. Peirce Society*, 26:1 (1990), 115-130.

"William James's 'Natural History' Methodology: Empiricist or Phenomenological?" *Frontiers in American Philosophy*. College Station, Texas: Texas A & M University Press, 1990.

Abbreviations of
the Works of William James

The Works of William James. Edited by Frederick H. Burkhardt, Fredson Bowers, and Ignas K. Skrupskelis. Cambridge: Harvard University Press. The original date of publication is given in parentheses.

PP	*The Principles of Psychology*, 3 vols., 1981 (1890)
PBC	*Psychology: Briefer Course*, 1984 (1892)
WB	*The Will to Believe*, 1979 (1897)
TT	*Talks to Teachers on Psychology*, 1983 (1899)
VRE	*The Varieties of Religious Experience*, 1985 (1902)
PM	*Pragmatism*, 1975 (1907)
MT	*The Meaning of Truth*, 1975 (1909)
PU	*A Pluralistic Universe*, 1977 (1909)
SPP	*Some Problems of Philosophy*, 1979 (1911)
ERE	*Essays in Radical Empiricism*, 1976 (1912)
EPH	*Essays in Philosophy*, 1978
ERM	*Essays in Religion and Morality*, 1982
EPS	*Essays in Psychology*, 1983
EPR	*Essays in Psychical Research*, 1986
ECR	*Essays, Comments, and Reviews,* 1987
MEN	*Manuscript Essays and Notes*, 1988

Also abbreviated in the text:

MS	*Memories and Studies.* Westport, CT: Greenwood Press, 1971 (1911)

CER   *Collected Essays and Reviews.* New York:
        Russell & Russell, 1969 (1920)

TCW   Ralph Barton Perry, T*he Thought and Character of
        William James,* 2 vols. Boston: Little, Brown, 1935

Introduction

"He belongs essentially among the lighter skirmishers of philosophy. A sketcher and popularizer, not a pile-driver, foundation-layer, or wall-builder. Within his class, of course, he is simply magnificent. It all goes with his easy temperament and rare good-nature in discussion" (TCW, I, 812).[1]

This quote could easily pass as a familiar assessment of William James, that is, magnificent as a man, but rather weak as a philosopher. But then, it is commonly understood that he did not reckon himself as more than a gifted lecturer and popularizer, although he did defend his own more tentative style against pedantic system builders and logic choppers. This book, however, is written as a deliberate refutation of such an assessment. The opening quote, in fact, is not a comment on James at all, but one made by him in a letter to Dickinson S. Miller in 1900 about Josiah Royce, the most erudite expounder of absolute idealism in America (TCW, I, 811ff).[2] Royce is criticized precisely for his lack of cogent reasoning, despite the appearance of "closeness and exactitudes of ratiocination" (810). This is partially hyperbole to express James's relief in being able to dismiss the technicalities of a formidable thinker as of no lasting threat to his own position, but it also reveals the philosophic methods and goals which he held in high esteem and hints at his own ambition to be a foundation-layer.

It is obvious that James envisions a new understanding of foundations when he praises Royce by commenting that fertility is better than perfection (TCW, I, 810). Royce is nonetheless found wanting because "the subject is not really vital to him" (812). Although unfair, this remark nonetheless shows that James's criterion for philosophy is an engaged understanding and transformation of the human condition. But this existentialist understanding of philosophy as vocation should not lead to underestimating his commitment to intellectual integrity. Despite the tendency of critics to reduce his philosophy to the supposed voluntarism of *The Will to Believe*, Ralph Barton Perry is correct in asserting that "it is evident

1

that James did not permit himself to give way to the moral motives until his logical scruples were satisfied" (798).

1. The Center of James's Vision

In chapter 7 I argue that the admonition to grasp the center of the writer's vision is the indispensable guiding principle of James's interpretive practice.[3] He also believed that a person's character could be summed up by the particular mental or moral attitude in which they felt themselves most intensely alive and active. Around 1878 James revealed his own self-image in a letter to his wife, Alice: "Now as well as I can describe it, this characteristic attitude in me always involves an element of active tension, of holding my own, as it were, and trusting outward things to perform their part so as to make it a ·full harmony, but without any *guaranty* that they will . . ., and which, although it is a mere mood or emotion to which I can give no form in words, authenticates itself to me as the deepest principle of all active and theoretic determination which I possess."[4] Many of James's characteristic themes are foreshadowed in this early self-assessment: the tension between ideal organization and recalcitrant experience; the goal of such organization expressed as a harmony, rather than as absolute transparency; the precarious character of all our attempts to understand the world; the restoration of the inarticulate feeling, as a genuine aspect of experience, to its proper place in philosophizing; and the positing of a common root to both our activity and our reflective theorizing, which are not antithetical but interdependent.

In this book I try to reconstruct the center of James's philosophic vision, with all its perplexities, insofar as this center can be derived from the textual evidence of his published and unpublished works.[5] Since it is acknowledged to be my reconstruction, James as the authoritative controller of the true meaning of the text is de-centered. Nevertheless, aspects of the texts which have so far been ignored become apparent when his complex relation to his own writings are explicitly incorporated into the context of interpretation. At the same time I also try to reconstruct the reconstruction to overcome the limitations of the original text that arise from those unexamined assumptions which prevented him from working out some of its radical implications.

His organizing center is taken to be the establishment of a secure foundation in experience which would overcome both the nihilistic paralysis of action and the skeptical dissolution of certain knowledge brought on by the challenge of scientific positivism. Just as Wittgenstein and Heidegger later rediscovered, the process of searching for foundations becomes itself the issue, and the very thoroughness of the attempt to establish an unproblematic foundation provokes reflections which lead to radically reconceptualizing how we appropriate the world.[6] This perspective is then itself reconstructed into a more coherent position, bringing out the interpretive structures employed but not explicitly developed until now and demonstrating how James's uncritical but brilliant analysis of specifically human interactions in the world needs to be modified in light of his own findings.

I therefore disagree with Daniel W. Bjork's conclusion, expressed in the "Epilogue" of his *William James: The Center of His Vision*, that this center was "the ability to visualize his own mind in relation to its experience."[7] This reading makes of James a postmodernist — not a "philosopher of modernity," as Bjork says — who dissolves all stability into "a noncommittal world of fluid, adjustable relationships" (267). To sustain this interpretation he takes James's philosophy of pure experience as ultimately a return to a "big blooming buzzing confusion," and therefore underestimates the role of James's pragmatism and moral interest in encouraging "appropriate human action." The outcome of such an interpretation is predictable. He cannot then distinguish between James's position and Skinnerian behaviorism. Throughout this book I argue for an interpretation of James's angle of vision that leads to very different conclusions.

My reconceptualization of James's writings and methodology provides a fresh approach to many of the recalcitrant problems raised over the years in the secondary literature. The longest controversy has been over his theory of truth. Gerald Myers is only the latest to take up Bertrand Russell's objections and argue that "by today's standards, pragmatism is not a genuinely technical theory of meaning or truth."[8] I challenge the basis of this objection by showing that James had already undermined its presuppositions and developed a theory of meaning and truth consistent with the finite and intentional character of knowledge.

James's lack of a systematically developed methodological approach has also led many to conclude that he did not present evidence for his positions. Some go even further and argue that he deliberately opposed the traditional philosophical insistence on rigorous proof as an aberration of over-intellectualism. But by reconstructing the structures of argumentation that he followed but never systematized it becomes obvious both that he held himself accountable to standards of proof and that he was not in principle opposed to ratiocination, but only to its excesses. At the same time the limitations of rationalism are demonstrated and variant procedures for arriving at justifiable results are developed and defended.

This reconstruction of James's philosophy takes issue with those who interpret him as a realist, a tradition which stretches from Perry to Edward Madden, Peter H. Hare, and Chandana Chakrabarti.[9] Among the standard beliefs I challenge is that James is best understood as a realist, that his pragmatic theory of truth is a version of the correspondence theory, that his pragmatism can be fully developed apart from his metaphysics of radical empiricism, and that he was always a pluralist and firmly opposed to theoretical unification. I likewise take issue with the variant tradition that, with Richard Rorty, approvingly stresses his "floating, ungrounded conversations," or with Gerald Myers and Ellen Kappy Suckiel, disapprovingly characterizes his position as "subjectivistic to an unacceptable degree."[10]

Both Myers and Suckiel equate any constructivist explanation of the objects of experience with subjectivism and base this critique on an appeal to externally existing objects. I show how one can use James's position to undermine this naive realism and to demonstrate that objectivity requires a constructive interpretation of the appropriation of the objects of experience once it is understood that their essential characteristics cannot be passively abstracted. Missing from the literature altogether or underdeveloped are the analyses I provide of his transformation of the natural history methodology, of his unique development of concrete or — as they are now called — phenomenological structures of human interactions in the world, of his interpretive strategies and poetic style, and of the centrality of his critique and reconstruction of rationalism to all his other positions.

2. Between Misinterpretation and Over-literalness

Interpreters of Nietzsche and James run into the same problem: any discursive recounting of their arguments must justify itself against the more allusive literary style of the original. Before James's arguments can even begin to be evaluated, his goals and interpretive structures must first be identified, since they are neither explicitly developed nor reflected upon in the writings themselves. The critic must develop James's position beyond what is explicitly written in any given text because James takes so much for granted. To become clear about issues in particular passages requires a general familiarity with all his writings. Consequently, an isolated quote from James can be used to prove almost anything. This is arguably the case with any text but is especially true of James because of his style of letting meanings emerge in the course of a discussion, rather than beginning with precise definitions or proceeding by way of defense of explicit theses.

Further complications arise from his deliberate suppression of parts of works transferred to new settings and his practice of drawing on his earlier explanations without acknowledgement. The interpretive structures he does utilize are neither usual in philosophical writings today nor are they reflectively analyzed. It is therefore incumbent on anyone trying to understand his philosophy to recognize and reconstruct these structures as a precondition for evaluation and further development. The involvement of the reader with the text is therefore more obvious than in more straightforwardly polemical writings, but until recently, not much attention has been paid to either James's interpretive structures nor to those of his interpreters. This lack has hampered a thorough reconstruction of his position.

When the issue of the appropriateness of the interpretation to the text does arise, it has frequently been misconstrued as being one of literal versus reconstructive interpretations, or of letting the text speak for itself versus letting one's own present-day interests structure the presentation. Fidelity to the text is construed a a literal interpretation, but this too often obscures the employment of contemporary philosophical interests and conventions. Often isolated passages are made to yield arguments about truth, belief, or the good, without any attempt to situate the passage in relation to the chapter, the book, or his other books. Sometimes James's intentions are ignored, along with his other writings, since it is assumed that the meaning of any given text is — or ought to be — transparently evident to anyone who can read English. Not surprisingly, James's arguments are then found to be inadequate. Attempts to develop a more plausible explanation of positions found to be defective in some way is understood as going beyond, and therefore distorting, the original text. To let one's own interests and philosophical position deliberately intrude on the presentation of the text is thought to be even more distortive, since the alternative — forcing the text to satisfy a current standard of philosophical discourse — is not even recognized as transformation rather than reproduction.

These attempts to strictly demarcate what is found in the text from the presuppositions, beliefs, and retrospective historical knowledge we bring to it reproduces the naively realist assumption that we can strictly demarcate facts from interpretations. This belief in an unproblematic access to being as such has been under attack at least since Hume and Kant, and the arguments refined in regard to texts already beginning with the hermeneutical theories of Dilthey and Schleiermacher and brought back to center stage by the French poststructuralists. But for the present case it is enough to point out that the pragmatic method was developed by Charles S. Peirce, William James, and John Dewey in response to the recognition of the problem that what we intuitively experience as being the case does not guarantee that it is so in reality. In Peirce's words, what we take to be reality could simply be due to tenacity, authority, or metaphysical assumptions. Furthermore, they all disclose the interests and unexamined assumptions operative in the funded character of experience on which we must draw in any determination of empirical facts. Thus it is odd indeed for philosophers working within the pragmatic tradition to assume that there is one self-evidently true meaning for any given passage of these writers, one which can be determined outside of any interpretive framework. Unless, of course, these critics are drawing on the assumptions of a different tradition than the one that they are explaining.

This is the case with Myers, for instance, who says that he turned to James after studying Moore, Russell, Wittgenstein, Ryle, and Ayer to get "a historical perspective on contemporary arguments in philosophical psychology."[11] But in reading James for his philosophy of mind the need for an interpretive analysis to recover his meaning became obvious. It also quickly became evident that "a full-scale critical study" was needed, both because James's positions cannot be accurately conveyed in isolation, and because he was interested in explicating James — not just in using him to clarify his own position. But this would not preclude evaluating James's views, and this intention is said to distinguish his book from Perry's more sympathetic and uncritical approach in *The Thought and Character of William James*. Later, in a footnote, after having carefully weighed the evidence for and against the claim that James's pragmatism was ultimately too subjective, he says that "a careful but sympathetic reading of James's pragmatic writings can rebut the charges, but not without making assumptions beyond his literal words" (563, n59). Myers's unsympathetic reading of James from the perspective of contemporary understandings of the philosophy of mind does not cohere well with this sense that he is just recounting James's literal words.

Henry Samuel Levinson, on the other hand, defends a version of literalism that attempts to recreate the original historical period. Although he characterizes his approach as a "philosophical reconstruction." by this he means showing "James in his own world, not ours."[12] He thinks that by situating James within his historical period and in relation to his other works on the topic he can avoid altogether abstracting from the texts only what is conformable to the assumptions and terminology of a later and different school of thought. His view of historical criticism is drawn from William A. Clebsch and Murray G. Murphey in that he takes presentism to be "by far the greatest sin" in the study of history (298).

Levinson denies that his interpretation is either mediated through alien beliefs or answers current religious concerns. His principle of the philosophical interpretation of historical figures is to take care to see them "as different and as distanced from us" (283). I agree with him that interpretation should be sensitive to the *Sitz im Leben* of the text, without recourse to which we will mistake our own context of meaning for the original. However, Levinson thinks he can do more, that he can recover the original meaning intact, unmediated by his own interests. He says, for instance, that sensitive criticism would seem to eschew even such "sound *reconstruction(s)*" of James's theory of truth as H. S. Thayer's claim "that James's work contains an implicit distinction between cognitive truth and pragmatic truth" because it is "one that James himself failed to make" (296). But on this criterion of strict interpretation, of not pointing out assumptions that the original text does not explicitly make, Levinson's own interpretation falls as short of a neutral interpretation of the text as Myers's does. He cannot even speak, for instance, of "distinguishing James's second-order, normative methods of appreciation from the ways in which the subjects of his study evaluated things" without using terms and making assumptions beyond James's own universe of discourse (216).

Horace Kallen, in commenting on the unfinished state of what was posthumously published as *Some Problems of Philosophy*, warned that James was still experimenting with a great plan that he had in mind. Therefore, interpreters of his work had "a hard way to steer between mis-interpretation and over-literalness."[13] But interpretation of texts involves continual renegotiation of the proper balance of contextual integrity and reconstructive activity. James would undoubtedly be pleased to know that he is not an easy philosopher to put into words, since he held that language could never capture the vibrant sense of lived experience, much less any particular person's unique angle of vision. Nonetheless, it is evident from his earnest efforts to communicate directly and dramatically, to catch and hold the attention of his audience, that he took pains to be understood. It is only when we take direct aim with our conceptual shotguns and think that we have at last hit the exact target of his thoughts that we become aware in our efforts to make all the writings cohere that something always escapes (VRE, 360). That we are always caught between misinterpretation and over-literalness seems congruent with James's emphasis on the creative space opened up by the irreducible ambiguity of interpretation.[14]

It is therefore my contention that a literal recounting of James's position is impossible. His writings cannot be read for long — five minutes will do — without encountering contradictions. The problem is exacerbated when a particular theme is systematically explored because it soon becomes apparent that exact definitions consistently adhered to are not a high priority for him. Rorty points out a related problem in that "the pragmatists keep trying to find ways of making antiphilosophical points in nonphilosophical language." There is a good reason for this procedure, "for they face a dilemma: If their language is too unphilosophical, too 'literary,' they will be accused of changing the subject; if it is too philosophical it will embody Platonic assumptions that will make it impossible for the pragmatist to state the conclusion he wants to reach."[15] Nonetheless, this lack of an obviously technical vocabulary contributes to the opacity of the texts and forces the interpreter to be more creative in appropriating them than many philosophers are comfortable with. If one does not give up at once in exasperation, then there is nothing to do but to try to make sense of the writings. Consequently, much of the secondary literature on James consists either in trying to resolve the inconsistencies or in throwing up one's hands at the impossibility.

My own strategy involves both trying to sympathetically retrieve his center of vision, that is, to recapture the way he saw his own work as a guide to interpreting its various parts, and then to critically reconstruct his project to bring out its strengths and avoid its weaknesses. A successful retrieval cannot be determined by comparison to James's actual intentions, however, or by just capturing the literal meaning of the texts, since neither of these is available to us without interpretation. Appeals made to the written evidence of his intentions, including his own reflections on his writings, are therefore tempered by the evidence of the interrelationships set up within the texts themselves. The unit of organization, for instance, is often that of the essay, or chapter, rather than that of the book.

Both the interpretation of the text and its critical reconstruction ought to be judged by two hermeneutical principles. One is sympathetic comprehensiveness, that is, how well they can make sense of the whole output of the published works in comparison with other interpretations. The other is the pragmatic criterion of fertility, that is, their success in bringing out promising aspects of the texts heretofore ignored and in eliciting creative appropriations of the text which answer developing interests. I take James's injunction to grasp the center of a writer's vision to mean to identify those driving passions that mark a body of work as the output of a particular author over time and to rework them into principles capable of providing thematic unity to the works.

James tends to emphasize now one aspect of his thought and now another, with no systematic treatise organizing them — apart from a few manuscript pages published posthumously as the opening chapters of an unfinished book called *Some Problems of Philosophy*. Nonetheless, this double strategy of retrieval and critical reconstruction has been employed to demonstrate both the lifelong project he was working through and its lasting significance. James's avoidance of a systematic presentation of issues should not obscure the thematic continuity that emerges when the context of interpretation is enlarged. Nonetheless, I am not arguing that its anti-systematic character will dissolve as illusory in light of my explanations. Even after my reconstruction its deliberate non-systematicity remains, since it is integral to James's insistence on the ambiguity at the heart of interpretation. Its resistance to a systematic explanation stands as evidence of the futility of reaching a finally comprehensive and unrevisable interpretation. "But is n't [sic.] fertility better than perfection?" (TCW, I, 810).

I think that James's project can best be made available for reflection and evaluation by reconstructing it as a defensible, coherent position. My first strategy involves a close textual analysis using James's reflections on his work as a guide. It seeks to identify the textual relationships which order each speech, essay, and book as units of organization. The second strategy involves reconstructing his position, emphasizing the inner coherence that can be achieved in hindsight by ignoring the limitations of James's personal odyssey. It draws on his total output as understood from within the larger pragmatic tradition of which he was a part and which extends into the present. It is hoped that each strategy will illuminate the other.

I concur with James's insight that beyond the question of whether such a project of retrieval and reconstruction is true or false to the texts themselves or to his intentions, there is the still more important question of the status of such attempts to order the many into one. The ordering process itself is taken to be a precondition for whatever meaning and value we want to derive from close analysis and textual interpretation. Pragmatically, therefore, my interpretation of James will be successful if it works, that is, if it revivifies the original texts and provides a basis for reevaluating the claims made in them, invigorates contemporary discussions, and suggests future plans of action. Given the renewed worldwide interest in pragmatism, the times are ripe for such a reassessment.

3. Framing the Larger Project

The secondary literature on James is divided on whether his writings are best grasped as a series of brilliant insights, their very disconnectedness being seen as evidence of his anti-rationalistic, anti-systematic, anti-foundationalist stances, or whether his writings form a unified whole, even though the coherence has to be sought despite often contrary appearances. Robert Giuffrida, Jr., for instance, in criticizing Levinson says: "To impute so much underlying unity, though, to the work of a committed pluralist like James' might have caused the latter some consternation."[16] By contrast, Ralph Barton Perry was one of the earliest to testify to the coherence and Elizabeth Flower concurs: "The fact is that James' work is all of a piece." Her reason for interpreting it this way is the same as mine: "A more persuasive reason, however, for taking his work to be a whole lies in the coherence of problem and outlook that is then exposed."[17] This book supports those who hope to profit from developing the inner coherence of James's angle of vision. The obvious anomalies in his thought are not thereby forced into a false conformity. They provide an opportunity for discovering some of the hidden assumptions that prevented James from satisfactorily resolving the issues over which he struggled for a lifetime.

As a heuristic device I will treat James's writings as falling into three stages. These are used only as rough guides, and the texts assigned to each stage can figure in more than one. There are certainly many other ways to organize the material. These stages were chosen because they reflect three major crises in James's life. Unfortunately, they do not neatly correlate with a systematic presentation of his position. Aspects of radical empiricism which he was willing to acknowledge only late in life, for instance, are already extensively developed in his earlier writings. But the stages do seem to emerge from James's reflections on his own work. These reflections are of more than biographical interest because they seem to exaggerate rather than dispel the contradictions raised by a close reading of the works. The effort to relate James's interpretation of his writings, which emphasizes perplexity, to my own interpretation, which seeks coherency, yields unexpected insights. The internal logic of textual development imposes interpretive constraints and opens up possibilities independently of how James saw them. In fact, many of the most attractive aspects of the positions developed in his writings are precisely the ones whose consequences he shrank from following up, often for reasons that we may no longer find cogent.

The textual analysis describes the new beginning in philosophy which James inaugurated, reveals its strengths and exposes its shortcomings, and consequently suggests the reconstruction necessary for a critical, post-Jamesian philosophy. The framework is developed out of texts suggesting that James underwent three crises, that is, the coming to a head of some psychological/intellectual trauma. He handled these crises by turning away from the formulation of the problem that was causing trouble and adopting a new strategy that was expected to resolve or dissolve the original quandary. These crises mark significant shifts in the direction his investigations took. They both throw light on the nature of the earlier struggle and provide a framework for understanding his subsequent moves. The first and last crises bracket his productive years. The earliest one, which antedated his scholarly career, took place off stage, as it were, and is recorded in his diary and letters. The last crisis, by contrast, is publicly attested to in the last book he published before he died. The middle crisis, also publicly announced, marks his turn away from predominately psychological genres to predominately philosophical ones.

According to Perry, the first crisis involved both a "desperate neurasthenic condition" and "morbid mentality" in the years prior to 1872 and a spiritual crisis exemplified by James's diary recording of February 1, 1870, in which he says: "Today I about touched bottom, and perceive plainly that I must face the choice with open eyes: shall I *frankly* throw the moral business overboard, as one unsuited to my innate aptitudes, or shall I follow it, and it alone, making everything else merely stuff for it? I will give the latter alternative a fair trail" (TCW, I, 322). Perry says further that "the crisis of April 1870 was a turning point but not a cure" (324). John J. McDermott emphasizes the importance of this crisis for understanding James's philosophy. He points out that Perry was referring to a diary entry of April 30, 1870, in which James explicitly says: "I think that yesterday was a crisis in my life." He peered into the abyss opened up by the possibility that free will might be an illusion and decided that his "first act of free will shall be to believe in free will."[18]

The seriousness of the crisis is evident from James's statement that only his resolve stood between himself and suicide. The parameters of such a "creative life unsupported by certitude" are said by McDermott to be developed through such early essays as "The Sentiment of Rationality," "The Dilemma of Determinism," "The Will to Believe," and in the formulation of the active self in the *Principles of*

Psychology.[19] I would add to this list the early essays in *Collected Essays and Reviews, Psychology: Briefer Course,* and *Talks to Teachers.* These are collectively designated as the early writings.

Both Perry and McDermott develop the meaning of this crisis for understanding James's philosophy. My own formulation is found in the first chapter, which draws on the early works, and emphasizes that he overcame nihilism, that is, despair over the meaninglessness of life, by asserting the right to believe. He accepted the challenge of skepticism and laid the groundwork in experience for a philosophical reflection which would eventually be fully justified. His empiricist commitment to brute facts as multifarious, observable, and testable, his idealist preoccupation with the dignity of each person and the creation of an ordered system, and his evolutionary interests in emergence and variety, all converged in his psychology. Not only was his psychology developed as an experimentally verifiable science, but also as a new, non-speculative basis for philosophy.

The second crisis is developed in the second chapter. In the works leading up to 1895 he had established the fundamental fact: 'knowing-things-together,' which is an empirical synthetic unity of consciousness, and the methodology — phenomenological description empirically verified — which unifies his early writings. For lack of recognition of the legitimacy of such a new beginning, he turned away from developing a metaphysically neutral, descriptive science of psychology. He was now free to bring out into the open and explicitly examine those metaphysical issues ruled out of bounds as long as he had deliberately located his works within the scientific genre.

Although he continued to argue strenuously for the irreducibly subjective aspect of human cognition, the natural history scientific method was inexplicably exempt, and he never reflected on what it would mean for science to "keep metaphysical and so-called epistemological inquiries" in psychology books (CER, 399; EPH, 88). Instead, he continued to distinguish in his works between the experiential data of verifiable fact and the metaphysical explanations developed to explain and extend them. He sidestepped the issue of justifying his practice of presupposing the facticity of his phenomenal findings by turning with renewed emphasis to the pragmatic method for settling disputes. This is a method for verifying factual claims by further experimentation and is explicitly indifferent to origins. But his intent in applying the pragmatic method is still to undermine skepticism by both disproving false claims and adding to the known facts of human experience, thus contributing to the eventual harmonious unification of self and world. The middle works developing pragmatism and leading up to the third crisis include *Pragmatism, The Varieties of Religious Experience,* and the early essays of *Meaning and Truth.* In addition, the articles which were largely written in 1904-1905 and posthumously re-issued as *The Essays in Radical Empiricism* make more explicit and develop further his metaphysical position.

The third crisis of 1908-1909 is detailed in the fifth chapter of *A Pluralistic Universe.* The title of the chapter, "The Compounding of Consciousness," indicates that the crisis was brought on by the same problem with which he had been wrestling since the beginning. It is expressed both "in the form of a direct personal confession" and as disclosing "the vital knot of the present philosophical situation" since "the times are ripe, or almost ripe, for a serious attempt to be made at its untying" (PU, 84-5). The problem with which he struggled for years, "covering hundreds of sheets of paper with notes and memoranda" was "how can many consciousnesses be at the same time one consciousness?" (94). In his "post-humian and post-kantian state of mind" he took up and rejected the various forms the issue had taken since *Principles* (95). His solution was to give up "intellectualistic logic," which "has an imperishable use in human life, but that use is not to make us theoretically acquainted with the essential nature of reality" (96). He explicitly embraced anti-rationalism only when he could justify the move.

It would be more accurate to say that he was acknowledging the reconstructed rational strand that already comprised a significant portion of his writings. Having worked out a metaphysics of radical empiricism and having finally decided that the value for life, that is, practical rationality, should over-rule intellectual or aesthetic rationality, James rejected classical foundationalism (see ERE, 42). He fell back on "raw unverbalized life as more of a revealer" (PU, 121). Only at the end was pluralism justified on its own terms, rather than as subject to eventual unification, and the pragmatic method adopted as indispensable, rather than as merely preparatory to future, exact, confirmation.

Since James never ceased to criticize rationalism throughout his writings, what must be made clear is why the third crisis arose in the first place. It is my contention that the third crisis, although significant as a turning point for James's understanding of his own position, is misleading if understood as revealing a shift to a different basis of explanation not already present in the early and middle writings. The crisis reveals the extent to which James, appearances to the contrary, had still held to a solipsistic understanding of personal experience and still made a strict demarcation between concrete and metaphysical analyses. In arguing for this conclusion the mutual illumination of the textual and critical approaches will be most apparent because this interpretive strategy clears up an anomalous situation often encountered in reading James. This involves the recognition by the reader that an earlier passage already incorporates a solution to a puzzle only explicitly solved in a later text or, more often, the original puzzle is discarded as unsolvable because of what turns out to be some seriously flawed assumptions still being held.

James was apparently still bewitched by the empiricist insistence on understanding the object as always the object of 'my' experience alone, therefore rendering both the reference to objects in the world and to the objects of other person's experiences problematic. In the early essay, "Knowing Things Together," for instance, he seems to have already disposed of the problem by arguing against any presence-in-absence between knowing and the object represented or between knowing and its present object. But on closer reading it turns out that he had only bracketed the issue so that he could proceed on a phenomenal level: "Whether such qualities be truly ultimate aspects of being or only provisional suppositions of ours, held-to till we get better informed, is quite immaterial for our present inquiry" (CER, 377-8; EPH, 75). It seems that his realist assumption of independently existing objects led him to take the Berkeleyan idealist identification of knowing and object known as taking place wholly within the knowing subject, which left the Kantian 'thing-in-itself' still to be brought into the knowing relation. Having finally removed the brackets by taking the phenomenal level as the *"only complete kind of knowledge,"* the caveat no longer holds (CER, 498). But then we are in a better position to understand the earlier texts than James was when he wrote them and can, by exposing the inconsistencies, begin to formulate a more coherent position.

What is needed to justify James's rejection of traditional rationalism and his replacement of it with a reconstructed rationalism is a fuller exposition of what I will hereafter call his 'full fact.' It turns out that the best formulation of his founding fact of 'knowing-things-together' had already been given in his middle period in *The Varieties of Religious Experience* (1902): "A conscious field *plus* its object as felt or thought of *plus* an attitude towards the object *plus* the sense of self to whom the attitude belongs...is a *full* fact, even though it be an insignificant fact; it is of the *kind* to which all realities whatsoever must belong..." (VRE, 393). Hints for what a Jamesian philosophy that is consistent with his reconstructed rationalism would consist in can be found scattered throughout his works, but come to the fore especially in those written around the time of his third crisis, which includes *A Pluralistic Universe* and *Some Problems of Philosophy*, as well as the earlier *The Varieties of Religious Experience* and *Essays in Radical Empiricism*, where he explicitly develops his own metaphysics.

4. Critique and Reconstruction

Central to James's new beginning in philosophy is the assumption that there is such a thing as neutral, pure description of phenomena and that such a description of mental life discloses the pervasiveness of a 'knowing-together' that can serve as an indisputable basis for philosophical reflection. But what are the consequences for the fundamental assertion that we 'know-things-together' if it can be shown that the assumption of a neutral, pure description is untenable? I will argue that the assumption cannot be supported and that James's lack of clarity on this issue leads to many false dilemmas. But the way he raised the issue and his exploration of alternate ways of maintaining it, enriches rather than impoverishes his overall work and much can still be learned from the attempt, especially since the belief in pure description is still tenaciously held by those fearing unmitigated relativism if it is abandoned. Secondly, I will argue that the fundamental fact can still be maintained, not as an absolute foundation, to be sure, but as a legitimate starting point for reflection.

There are many reasons why James maintained the possibility and desirability of pure description. One is that the positivist understanding of science went virtually unchallenged in scientific circles at the time. It is true that William Whewell had earlier opposed John Stuart Mill on the possibility of descriptive neutrality, but James sided with Mill and quotes him frequently, even going so far as to dedicate *Pragmatism* to him.[20] This contrasts with his references to Helmholtz, Poincaré, Duhem, Mach and others on whose rationalist position he drew whenever he wanted support for the contrary thesis that individuals contribute creatively to the object known. That he failed to successfully bring these two perspectives together weakens his position, but it will be shown how this can be done.

James explicitly linked neutral, pure description with science as positivistically understood. This is evident, for instance, in a letter he wrote (February 1, 1885) to Thomas Davidson about the newly organized American Society for Psychical Research. He said that whatever theoretical bias members have is irrelevant, as long as they do such a thorough job "as to constitute *evidence* that will be accepted by outsiders, just what the *phenomenal conditions of certain* concrete phenomenal occurrences are...I'm sure that the more we can steer clear of theories at first, the better."[21]

James had serious reservations about the positivist understanding of science. This did not, however, prevent him from agreeing with some of its tenets, such as the legitimacy of pure description, and he also often sided with scientific positivism for strategic reasons. Because of its technological success and scientific discoveries, the authority of science in the latter half of the nineteenth century was so great that intellectuals who wanted to be taken seriously had to come to terms with it.[22] Philosophers, for that matter, are still in the era dominated by science. From Kant's striving to set philosophy on a secure basis by following the lead of science to Husserl's attempt to found philosophy as a strict science to the current esteem accorded philosophers of science, philosophers have been aware that they have to demonstrate the legitimacy of their discourse in relation to standards set by science or resign themselves to second-class status.

James also recognized the implicit imperative to reconcile his beliefs with scientific findings and methodology and this struggle is evident throughout his writings. But he likewise recognized the strategic advantages to be gained by a public alignment. In the same letter to Davidson, for instance, he said that the society had a policy of choosing scientific men as officers, not because they are necessarily better judges of truth, but because the general public thinks them so. Moreover, he agreed that "what we want is not only truth, but evidence." Despite these precautions, he feared that even scientists would be discredited when they subscribed to "'spiritual' manifestations. But how much easier to discredit literary men, philosophers or clergymen! . . . 'Facts' are what are wanted."[23]

Another motive for defending pure description can be found in James's loyalty to the empiricist philosophical tradition. Its main strength for James was its insistence that all philosophizing begins with actual experience. That experience is accessible and describable are unshakable pillars of this empiricist position. But if this were all he meant his concrete descriptions would neither be structured analyses nor would they continue to be of so much interest. His own understanding of pure description considerably moves beyond the model of the simple observational report characteristic of both classical empiricism and positivism. I take it as consisting of an original synthesis of the careful description insisted on by Louis Agassiz as being the necessary requisite for the success of the newly emerging science of natural history and of description as the 'seeing-into' at the heart of Ralph Waldo Emerson's romantic, poetic vision of the world.

The best artists and the best scientists both rely on careful, exact description. In his notes for *Talks to Teachers*, 1899, James says that "you can't make a *good* artist or architect or a *good* naturalist out of a bad visualizer" (TT, notes, 209). He expands on this by saying that in the constitution of experienced objects thought fuses with sensation, so that the object results half from the outer world and half from within us; he gives the tracing of figures in cloud formations as an example. This explication draws on Royce's and Emerson's higher visions of inner significance. This artistic vision which sees in objects a higher reality not visible to the ordinary person is also the model on which he draws to explain genius, whether scientific or artistic. Genius is the ability to 'see' aspects of reality which are not apparent to more mundane perception.

In order to understand where the belief in pure, neutral description goes wrong, such concrete or phenomenal description must be distinguished form concretely based interpretive analysis. I will be arguing that James had original insights into both, but did not sufficiently develop them into a coherent theory which would enable him to avoid obvious inconsistencies. In reconstructing such a theory it becomes evident that concrete or phenomenal description attempts the impossible, namely, an unmediated, pure, objective description of things as they are, of reality as it is. Such an unproblematic access to being is impossible in principle because of what concrete analysis discloses. All seeing is 'seeing-as.' Seeing is not passive but always constrained by interests. The context of knowing is the full fact of self-thing-world. Finally, experience always consists of more than what can be explicitly grasped.

In the following chapters, I draw on James's analyses of passive versus interested perception, of the framework of interests operative in all rational thinking, and of the finite and temporal dimension of beliefs about reality. It is just because such concrete analyses reveal that no description or observational reports can ever claim the legitimacy of immediate access to reality as such, but only of reality-for-us, that the pragmatic method is developed as a way of testing these 'mediated' descriptions.

Therefore, the objectivity of the descriptive report demands disclosure of the interests operative in any given case. These particular interests are then related to those aesthetic and practical interests that characterize the human situation. But it is not enough to trace the interests operative in any descriptive claim. Because all descriptive affirmations necessarily originate in individuals, even though they are structured through the funded character of experience, their cogency must be tested by checking them against other centers of interest with which they have to do. These centers are both individual and institutional. Although theoretically no one's interests are any more authoritative than anyone else's, in actuality some interlocking centers of interest dominate others. How to redress the balance and bring them into actual harmony while preserving the unique values and angles of vision of each is a task worthy of all our efforts and one which James never ceased to urge.[24]

Finally, I would like to forestall misunderstanding over my use of the term 'phenomenology.' I certainly do not mean to imply that James is best seen as a forerunner to the phenomenological movement and that whatever does not conform to the later movement should be discarded. In fact, I take many of his divergences from it to be salient criticisms. James is best understood within the pragmatic movement, which is both highly original and related to many other intellectual trends. Peirce, for example, also developed a phenomenological analysis independently of the continental movement.

James uses 'experience' and 'phenomenon' interchangeably.[25] By linking phenomenology with James's less well-known expression, 'concrete,' I mean to remind the reader that his concrete analyses do form an interconnected set of propositions and not just a pastiche of disconnected insights. But to fill in what 'phenomenological' means, beyond a vague gesture, requires developing James's project of bracketing metaphysical analysis until he could describe "the living facts of human nature." He consistently appeals to his concrete findings whenever he cites evidence for a position. This methodological procedure loses its salience when understood as a simple appeal to an isolated fact or set of facts. It becomes convincing only to the extent that the appeals refer to an interconnected set of beliefs about what constitutes the human condition.

James's pragmatic phenomenology is less clearly developed than the later versions. It is also only one aspect of his long-range project, which cannot simply be reduced to his concrete analysis. Moreover, his pluralism and inherent suspicion of any description not subject to continual revision also aligns him with Nietzschean and post-structuralist suspicions of a univocal understanding of the nature of being-in-the-world. In his pragmatic method he also goes beyond such suspicions to developing justifiable plans of action.

Part One

Overcoming Nihilism and Skepticism

Chapter One

Beginnings

"The union of the mathematician with the poet, fervor with measure, passion with correctness, this surely is the ideal" (CER, 138).

William James was not a philosopher's philosopher[1]. He did not presuppose that the reader is a professional, acquainted both with the history of philosophy and the latest articles in an area of specialization. He was something much more rare: a unique combination of iconoclast and visionary. Not only has he "aroused an admiration for philosophy in minds that never admired philosophy before" (as originally said by James of Herbert Spencer), but he has also offered a fundamentally new orientation to those already engaged in it (MS, 131-2; EPH, 117). Like Friedrich Nietzsche, he philosophized in a new mold, and those who fail to recognize his radical critique of the usual way of doing philosophy and facilely accuse him of failing to fulfil the very standards that he has called into question inevitably miss the point of his critique and reconstruction.

He called the whole philosophic enterprise into question by insisting that unless it got back in touch with individual experience it would continue to lose its credibility as a guiding force in human life and dwindle into the merely academic exercise it has now largely become. Like Nietzsche and Karl Marx, he helped inaugurate — long before Martin Heidegger — the end of philosophy as traditionally understood. But no tradition is simply disproved; rather, its issues are made to seem less compelling in comparison with a new configuration of expectations, beliefs, and practices which appear more promising. In this chapter James's announcement of his reconstruction of philosophy is discussed, his motivations are explored, and the outlines of his new approach are given.

James did not turn to philosophy after abandoning psychology, as the usual periodization of his writings suppose.[2] His philosophical interests predated *The Principles of Psychology*, published in 1890. In this chapter I develop the broad outlines of his philosophical project which are evident in these early works, dating primarily from the 1870s. James is more often suggestive than programmatic, but persistent themes can be traced. His approach to philosophy is distinctive from the beginning, and he identifies very early the problems his further research is meant to solve. He also introduces and explains terms which recur in his later writings without explanation. His writings become more coherent once it is recognized that he develops and employs a specialized vocabulary. This thread of continuity is lost when his later works are taken in isolation.

The first and last sections of this chapter investigate James's 1898 announcement of his new philosophy. By working backwards from his first public declaration of his pragmatic philosophy, it becomes possible to recognize earlier moves towards a distinctive philosophical perspective. The earlier formulations, in turn, shed light on the later ones.

1. Between Trail-blazing and Perfectly Ideal Discourse

In his inaugural lecture on pragmatism, delivered before the Philosophical Union at Berkeley in 1898, James sketches out a "perfectly ideal discourse" that introduces some of the main elements of his new approach (PM, 257-270). He does not just introduce and apply "the principle of practicalism." It is difficult to credit Myers's belief that "when James delivered 'Philosophical Conceptions and Practical Results' . . .[he did not] betray any awareness that he was moving toward something momentous."[3] This assessment hardly does justice to James's emotionally charged language exuding a sense of mission, to his claim that the pragmatic principle has successfully solved the most vexing problems of metaphysics, and to his insistence that he, not Kant, is continuing the critical method in philosophy. As a matter of fact, this is one of the few essays where James brings together the various strands of his overall project and clearly expresses his intention to begin philosophy anew.

James argues that theory should start at that point where "every human being's practical life would begin," rather than being generated out of academic debate (PM, 257). The goal of such a "perfectly ideal discourse" is the same one given in 1879, namely, the synthesis and reconciliation of all human motives, interests, and desires.[4] Since interests are broadly classified into the aesthetic and the practical, their satisfaction involves not only solving mental conundrums but also facilitating emotional and moral well-being. Therefore, joy and power are as appropriate philosophical goals as is the traditionally recognized one of clarification. Theory is taken to be the reflective ordering of human experience, one which is guided by that very experience. By making articulate what is already dimly felt, all that would otherwise be evanescent in human experience can be solidified and possessed.

Even though philosophy should aim at such an ideal discourse, James emphasizes that his actual talk necessarily falls short. He compares philosophers to poets because both are path-finders who seek to articulate what others can only feel. Though their idioms differ, their function is the same, that of blazing a trail through the otherwise dense forest of human experience. However, following Kant's lead, the classical American pragmatists all insisted that a critical examination of the historical record reveals that only the scientific method can provide a sound basis for truth claims. How does James's understanding of philosophy as poetic cohere with this pragmatic insistence on the priority of scientific method?

James does say that the pragmatic method is derived from "reflection upon the hypotheses by which science interprets nature," but in his inaugural address he emphasizes that the scientific method itself must be understood in relation to the human way of being in the world (PM, 269). He draws on the power of metaphor to enable us to see the familiar in unfamiliar ways in order to encourage his hearers to reinterpret both science and philosophy as human endeavors. He deliberately undercuts the late nineteenth century infatuation with the progress of science by calling attention to the precarious and tentative character of the trails we blaze to transform the world into a human place. Trails presuppose a wilderness; they do not create the myriad places of the forest, the ferny dells or filtered moonlight, nor the secret hiding places of animals. Therefore, experience can never be reduced just to these marked trails. Such markings, though, do give us a sort of ownership, a means of using and enjoying determinate experience.

The pathfinder is aware both of the immensity of the forest and the paths not taken. Because experience is organized one way does not negate other paths, nor does it confer necessity on the one developed. For centuries Aristotle's logic was thought the only possible path of correct reasoning. Many others have now been created, without obliterating his. Poets and philosophers also know that no matter how much is said, much more is always left out. There exists a tremendous incentive to finally break through to the center where the truth must reside, but each time it seems within one's grasp it recedes behind the next hill.

James's metaphors of enclosure clash with those of receding horizons, just as our search for ultimate truths is continually thwarted by unforeseen occurrences. One can seem to be circling nearer and nearer to the truth and yet know that every day brings new vistas, each with its own horizon. James's philosophical perspective emphasizes this sense of incompleteness in time, of almost attaining but never finally resting in absolute certitude. Finitude, temporality, and struggle, the "ever not quite," are marks of philosophical integrity. Limitless power, eternal truth, smug certainty, and resting in some absolute are all delusions. Truth, as such, is elusive, and ever seems attainable with just a little more effort, but death always overtakes us before we find the goal. "So we fall back on the preliminary blazes — a few formulas, a few technical conceptions, a few verbal pointers — which at least define the initial direction of the trail" (PM, 258).

Philosophizing fluctuates between the two poles of pathfinding and perfectly ideal discourse. James preferred trail-blazing. His most characteristic remarks explicitly recognize that any particular conceptual analysis unsatisfactorily substitutes for experience and would someday be superseded. But for most of his life he was also aiming at the ever-elusive center of truth and believed he was circling closer. The tension between these two concepts of the task of philosophy generates both powerful insights and unresolved ambiguities. Both approaches are uniquely developed by James, but his use of traditional formulations often obscures his break with the tradition.

Perfectly ideal discourse, for example, includes the traditional philosophic goals of transparency and total comprehension, but also joy and power. It includes the synthesis of all human desires and interests, the starting point in individual practical life, and the articulation of our felt sense of life. These expressions distinguish James's ideal goal from more traditional expressions of the aim of philosophy and certainly from the modernist preoccupation with epistemology. His philosophical goal is an actually achieved harmony of self and nature rather than the closure of a self-contained, purely intellectual, system. His ideal discourse differs significantly from such traditional goals as "achieving the absolute," the "final explanation of all that is," and the disclosure of the "first principles and final causes of all things." Unfortunately, James often used these traditional formulations of the goals of philosophy as equivalent to his own. Sometimes he merely added his terminology to the traditional one and sometimes he substituted his own meanings while retaining the old words. Consequently, he did not sufficiently reflect on the transformations required by his radically different analysis.

His trail-blazing also differs from the skepticism of what he calls Hume's "idealistic empiricism" and the reductive "naturalistic empiricism" of Comte and Spencer (EPH, 346-347). However, he accepts as a defining characteristic of all varieties of empiricism, including his own, the claim that being must be taken for granted and can never be ultimately explained. ["Therefore the 'Relativity of Knowledge' is no imbecility of our understanding, but results from the essence of being"](EPH, 344). He also believes that the defining characteristic of the philosophic enterprise is the drive to make articulate the inarticulate, to finally explain clearly all that is. Many of his explanations will return to this puzzle of the opacity of being and the human drive for transparency. He formulates and develops it as an issue of unification, calling it the problem of "the one and the many," which is also metaphorically expressed as the weaving together of phenomenal multiplicity into a finally satisfactory pattern. The model of philosophy as harmony, both aesthetic and practical, is offered as a more promising approach than the traditional one which relies on the metaphor of transparency on the one hand and totality on the other.

2. Reducing the Reductive or Overcoming Nihilism

What does James mean by "the essence of being?" In his last work, published posthumously as *Some Problems of Philosophy* (1909-10), "The Problem of Being" is clearly identified as the question of why there is something rather than nothing (SPP, 25-26). He quotes Schopenhauer as saying that wonder at the inexplicableness of being characterizes intelligent humanity and that it is this brooding on the fact that the non-existence of the world is just as possible as its existence that keeps metaphysical speculations going (26). There are no rational solutions to the problem of being because "from nothing to being there is no logical bridge" (27). Although rationalistic philosophers have tried to "reduce the mystery," the opacity of facticity remains just as inscrutable as ever. For all schools of philosophy facts must just be accepted as given, since "the question of Being is the darkest in all philosophy" (30).

From his very earliest writings he calls into question the rationalism which grounds both idealism and empiricism, until at last he finally also gives up the attempt to explain being. This turn away from the metaphysics of being leads directly to radical empiricism and pragmatism. Just because the ultimate questions must remain beyond our grasp, the proximate ones become that much more imperative. Although we cannot explain how our finite experiences come into being, we can explain how "phenomena come and go" as long as we stay *"within experience"* (SPP, 29-30). James's most original contributions to rethinking philosophy can be found in the writings where he analyzes experience as it phenomenally appears. The vast majority of his writings explore this "concrete" level of experience. But many of his perplexities arise when he reverts to a metaphysical perspective and explicitly questions the relation of his concrete analysis to being as such.

In his earliest writings the young James has not yet abandoned the philosophic quest for ultimate answers. And in his last work he still regrets the fact that his analyses of the human condition have not transcended the phenomenal level and grasped being itself. In fact, despite his frequent criticisms of various philosophers' claims to having disclosed the essence of being and despite the impression he gives of not accepting a metaphysical ghost or double behind and causing the phenomenal appearances, I am arguing that he himself never ceased trying to bridge the gap between phenomena and the reality of which it is supposedly an appearance.[5] What makes his philosophy radical is that, despite his own largely traditional metaphysical presuppositions, he nonetheless manages to thoroughly undermine the grounds of any such metaphysical synthesis.

James's search for a perfectly ideal discourse motivates his pathfinding. The ideal discourse does not function as a preliminary set of principles from which necessary conclusions can be deduced. Instead, he blazes one trail after another through experience to arrive at such a transparent grasp of reality only to find at the end of his life that they do not converge into the high road of metaphysical disclosure. His own excursions have instead demonstrated that the metaphysical quest is just one historically developed way of blazing a trail through the wilderness and not a very promising one at that. There is an unresolved tension in James's writings between the radically empiricist turn he takes which sets him off in a new direction and the traditional categories and understanding which still provide the horizon of his thinking and into which he tries to fit his excursions. The recognition and exploration of this tension provides a means for explaining the many anomalies which keep cropping up in the texts and for stripping away the encrustations that continue to hamper the recognition and further development of the novel core.

The Schopenhauer passages on the mystery of being were first quoted in 1879 in "The Sentiment of Rationality."[6] In this article James questions whether the ground of rationality is itself rational and concludes that it is not. He takes the lasting truth of empiricism to be its recognition that the ground "of Being is left logically opaque to us, a *datum* in the strictest sense of the word" (CER, 125-128; EPH, 57-59). Already in 1875 he had stated that "all philosophic reflection is essentially skeptical at the start" (CER, 5).[7] This contrasts with ordinary, everyday thinking in which we common sensically take reality to be just as it appears to us. While attended to, every representation is taken as what is absolutely given. It is only in the light of further reflection that ordinary experiences can be called into question and "reduced" to something less than what they immediately appeared to be.

James calls "the reductive" this process by which reflection undermines the self-evident nature of immediate experience and shows that it is already interpreted through unexamined assumptions. By the reductive he means this skeptical challenge, which is a constant feature of self-conscious reflection. Philosophy is motivated by the search for foundations, that is, establishing "a position from which one could *exorcise the reductive*, and remain securely in possession of a secure belief" (CER, 6). Common sense and philosophy are alike in their efforts to establish a stable conception of things, a world in which we will know what to expect.

James's term 'reduction' means the opposite of what is usually referred to by this or similar terms in philosophy. It should not be confused, for instance, with Kant's transcendental deduction or with Edmund Husserl's transcendental reduction of the world of ordinary experience to that of the world as an object for pure consciousness. All such attempts to secure a firm foundation in being, which would withstand any further challenges, is for James the second move, that is, reducing (for example, by recourse to necessary truth) the reductive (that is, the skeptical challenge which reduces — calls into question — our native sense that we objectively grasp real objects as they are). Reduction means for James just the skeptical challenge to the self-evident truth of the world of appearances by reducing them to a supposedly more real level, such as the atomic particles out of which they are constructed or the substances that underlie appearances in Aristotelian metaphysics. The skeptic then again reduces these newly secured real objects by calling them also into question and so on ad infinitum. It is this never-ending skeptical reduction of reality to something supposedly more real, but which is in turn shown not to be the ultimate reality, that James wants to oppose by appeal to a finally unreducible reduction. He wants to stop such reductions, but not by utilizing reduction itself as a method.

James argues that every time a secure foundation is claimed in being, it can be reduced by raising the question of why there is any being at all, and why it is necessarily given as just this being and no other. This possibility of nonentity is the ultimate reductive of being. Common sense thinking refuses to consider the reductive, preferring unexamined belief, but philosophers are driven to overcome it and create elaborate systems in order to do so. It is always possible for the less curious to take being as given, as a surd, and exorcise the reductive by the simple expedient of refusing to wonder about it and simply act. System-building is said to characterize the response of idealists, while acquiescing in the opacity of being and getting on with life is more characteristic of empiricism (CER, 128ff; EPH, 59ff).

Although not himself one, James shared the annoyance of many nineteenth century Hegelians at this peremptory closure of the infinite aspirations of humanity. Why every generation should be drawn again and again to ask the ultimate questions, when the answers are ruled out beforehand, sets experience against reason and poses a problem as intractable as the one ruled out of bounds. In this clash of experience's demand with reason's veto, Kant had erected impassible barriers between transcendent reality and empirical phenomena. Hume, too, had denied that the intellect can ever fathom the ultimate springs and principles of the universe and must be satisfied with beliefs only. Although not thoroughly discredited, religious and metaphysical beliefs had been severely questioned by Comte and positivist scientists. It is worth noting that James, who is most often caricatured as the unabashed proselytizer for the right to believe, begins his intellectual career expressing scorn for those who relinquish the possibility of ever solving the ultimate problems and who settle for comforting belief or cowardly agnosticism. But James harkens back to the Scottish common sense realist position in insisting that skepticism can be avoided without falling into dogmatism. Skepticism is akin to nihilism, that is, the loss of meaning in life, in its removal of justifiable grounds for action. If no course of action is any more reasonable than any other, then only the fool acts with impunity; the conscientious person becomes paralyzed. Dostoevsky's *Notes From Underground* vividly dramatizes this loss of the will to action in the face of endless possibilities, all equally compelling and therefore none.

James's early psychological crisis of despair, which was overcome by the sheer force of willing, has been well documented.[8] This early overcoming of nihilism by positing a will to live is given as a predisposing source of his doctrine of the will to believe. But as the later doctrine makes clear, there must be sufficient grounds for belief. His summoning up of inner resources to break the grip of despair did not itself illuminate the basis for accepting the meaningfulness of life.

In positing life and action in the face of meaninglessness, he was gradually released from the paralyzing effects of nihilism, but not from its source. This accounts for his uncharacteristic vehemence against those who are not bothered by the lack of secure beginnings: "Renouvier and Hodgson, the two foremost contemporary philosophers, promptly say that of experience as a whole no account can be given, but do not seek to soften the abruptness of the confession or reconcile us with our impotence" (CER, 133; EPH, 62).

James's demonstration in "The Sentiment of Rationality" that no foundation in being could in principle be impregnable to subsequent doubt did not lessen his determination to avoid skepticism. It instead led to his earliest philosophical project: "to reduce the reductive," that is, to find such a firm foundation, which would somehow be immune to reflective doubt (CER, 129ff; EPH, 60ff). It is not clear from the text how changing the nature of the foundation from insight into being to identifying the belief needed for action could halt further doubt. James seemed to think that by suspending doubt long enough to act we would learn some facts of the human condition and could then by reflecting on them arrive at an irreducible foundation. What makes this project puzzling is that he also took the ability to wonder or doubt to be constitutive of the human condition.

3. Theoretic Rationality

James's radically empiricist or pragmatic philosophy cannot be understood outside his dismantling of traditional rationality and replacement of it by "living acts of reasoning" or "the full concrete act of thought."[9] He argues in "The Sentiment of Rationality" that no philosophical system has demonstrated its own rationality. This is so whether rational grounding means an absolute, unshakable foundation in reality for epistemological claims or an indubitable set of premises from which all other propositions can be deduced. This is no historical accident but is due to the reflective character of consciousness. Any claim can be reduced by questioning its legitimacy one step further. James's realism leaves him vulnerable to this skeptical reduction, as is evident from his characterization of the noumenal as something which lies ready to mock any world we represent to ourselves as being the case (CER, 130; EPH, 60). Furthermore, the fortuitous character of being robs it of the necessity needed to demonstrate the claimed coalescence of knowing and being. No formal propositional system can guarantee a necessary access to being because all formal systems are necessarily limited. They are not only less than what is, but what is can only be appropriated according to our needs and interests.

But although rationality cannot be grounded rationally, that is, necessarily or irrefutably, there are nonetheless sufficient grounds for its pursuit. What is thus warranted is one of the fundamental drives of human beings, i.e., a particular sort of striving which is part of our being in the world, and not any given rational system as corresponding with reality. With John Dewey we can thus see that James radically reconstructs rationality in this early work. This reconstruction is central to his project of ending philosophy as an abstract intellectual pursuit of a perfect theory or logical system and beginning it anew as a reflective endeavor to harmonize self and world in pursuit of a better future.[10]

Philosophic systems are said to owe their being to "the craving for consistency or unity in thought, and the desire for a solid outside warrant for our emotional ends" (CER, 22-23). This "craving for a consistent completeness" is aesthetically pleasing (CER, 28). Any system of philosophy, to be successful, must meet these two great aesthetic needs of our logical nature: unity and clearness (CER, 99; EPH, 41). Unity, more often called 'simplicity,' is a drive to unify the chaos, to order the multiplicity of the sensible world. Our idea of the universe is not completely rational until each separate phenomenon is conceived as fundamentally identical with every other. Theoretic rationality is often simply identified with this search for principles of unification. "This criterion of identity is that which we all unconsciously use when we discriminate between brute fact and explained fact. There is not other test" (CER, 106; EPH, 46).

But if this process of simplification is to avoid being merely speculative, it must be joined with the other great aesthetic need, that of clarity. This does not refer to the Cartesian tradition of clear and distinct ideas, but to the empiricist tradition of ideas as vivid sense impressions. Before disparate phenomena can be unified in an ordered system, they must be accurately identified, their essences determined. This means identifying the imbedded character in it and in the maximum number of other phenomena. "The living question" is "to stand before a phenomenon and say *what* it is" (CER, 109; EPH, 48). This insistence on establishing the data of perception to avoid the sterility of merely metaphysical entities marks the initial "phenomenal ground" of James's own position (CER, 115; EPH, 51).

Such determination of essences should not be confused with the Aristotelian account. In one of the first of the many characterizations of his realism, James connects the identification of essences with the characteristics that attract our interest, rather than with the unique, unchanging characteristics abstracted from objects. Thus, essences are a function of our interests, vary with them, and are not discoverable apart from them. Since, for James, "realism is eternal and invincible in this phenomenal sense," disputes over whether he is a realist or not miss the point insofar as they fail to take account of his critique of traditional realism and reconstruction of its meaning (CER, 115; EPH, 51).[11]

The will-o-the-wisp of an absolute coalescence of being and being known, thus far unattainable in any philosophy or theoretic system, can nonetheless be experienced as a not-yet-criticized absolute harmony of the oneness of self and reality. Common sense, mysticism, and poetry all exhibit this characteristic absolute living in the moment that does not require any outside justification, the moment being sufficient unto itself. The promised ecstasy of this oneness with being exerted a powerful, lifelong influence on James. Because the sufficiency of the present moment needs no justification, the highest rationality is indistinguishable from mysticism (CER, 85; EPH, 33). And since James's ideal philosophic goal of harmony is attainable in practice, the possibility that it may also be attained theoretically must be left open. In fact, keeping open the possibility that there is an all-encompassing explanation for life is a fundamental motive of his own philosophizing. He goes so far as to call it the only motive worthy of the practical person.

As a bulwark against nihilism he deliberately chose to believe that the world has meaning, that our own actions make a difference, and that the moral seriousness of concerned persons is not a colossal joke. Since we all live "on the perilous edge" of the meaninglessness of existence, he also insisted that such beliefs are insufficient. We require a solid warrant for our puny claims against the immensity of the void being opened up daily by the sciences.[12] Human significance shrinks with every disclosure of the vast extent of the universe, from the far reaches of inter-stellar space to the inner space of atomic structure. Therefore, if the mystic and poetic denial of irrationality could be turned into "a systematized method [, it] would be a philosophic achievement of first-rate importance" (CER, 134; EPH, 63).

But if it should ever be agreed "that the mystical method is a subterfuge without logical pertinency . . ., that the Hegelian method is fallacious, that the idea of Nonentity can therefore neither be exorcised nor identified, Empiricism will be the ultimate philosophy" (CER, 134-135; EPH, 63). This is not the empiricism to which James aspired because it acquiesces in an inexplicable brute facticity. Such irremediable meaninglessness undercuts any hope for ever satisfying "the emotion of ontologic wonder." As a reductive to idealist claims to having already unified the chaos, such empiricism was a handy ally, but as being the final word on the question, it was also a specter to overcome.

Thus, while James was determined to justify ontologic wonder, he realized that the task seemed impossible as long as one remained within the conditions set up by theoretic rationality. But rather than solve the problem of rationality by providing rational grounds for it, he instead dissolved the problem by pointing out that treating theoretic rationality in isolation "violates the nature of our intelligence" as fundamentally practical (CER, 136; EPH, 64). This provided the subject matter for his second essay on "The Sentiment of Rationality" (1882), which develops its practical aspect.[13]

4. Practical Rationality

Even before the first essay on "The Sentiment of Rationality," James had already refused to identify rationality just with the theoretic drive for simplicity, for the total explanation of all that is. This purely aesthetic drive must be reconciled with an equally urgent drive which motivates thinking, that of attaining a valid warrant for our beliefs. Anticipating the objection that explaining the nature of rationality in terms of drives is too subjective, James argues that even positivism cannot consistently eliminate all reference to the subject. Positivists like George Henry Lewes, "weary of the infinitely receding chase after a theoretically warranted Absolute...return to their starting-point and break off there, like practical men, saying, "Physics, we espouse thee; for better or worse be thou our Absolute!" Although skepticism can always have the last word, "at a certain point most of us get tired of the play, resolve to stop, and assuming something for true, pass on to a life of action based on that" (CER, 10). Common sense, too, "contents itself with the unreconciled contradiction, laughs when it can, and weeps when it must, and makes, in short, a practical compromise, without trying a theoretic solution. This attitude is of course respectable" (17).

Even rigorous scientists admit that their systems are founded on beliefs, not on absolute foundations. Helmholtz, for instance, says that the assumption of fixed laws in natural science is an intellectual postulate, not a proven fact (CER, 31-2). As Renouvier also says, there is no certitude, but only doubt if we leave the "narrow standing-point of the present moment in consciousness" (33). There is no certitude, only persons who are certain. The sole firm foundation thus far available to us is that provided by some belief, that is, a moral attitude. Whether we are right or wrong in our beliefs can "only be reached *ambulando* or at the final integration of things, if at all" (35). Such beliefs are legitimate until proven wrong because they are necessary preconditions for action.

James agreed with Lewes on the absoluteness of our common sense knowledge, but only in its own sphere. He could not yet go so far as to affirm that the world is "the world *as known*, but *for us* there *is* no other world" (CER, 8). As long as we stay on the common sense phenomenal level, the skeptical reductive can be held at bay. Such an attitude is respectable intellectually, as even scientists admit in their acknowledgement of the beliefs at the basis of their disciplines. We must have sufficient grounds for our actions, and rightly take as good ones as we can get. "Although the consistent pyrrhonist is the only theoretically unassailable man, it does not follow that he is the right man. Between us and the universe, there are no 'rules of the game.' The important thing is that our judgments should be right, not that they should observe a logical etiquette" (10). This sounds like the anti-rationalism of his last period, but only marks the beginning of his reconstruction of rationalism to include all the motives for thinking.

Traditional rationalism provides insufficient grounds for action. But it is incongruous, at least, and perhaps inconceivable, that the theoretic demand for simplicity and concomitant absolute justification should stand in diametrical opposition to action, which is a necessary condition for the possibility of human life. Therefore, James defended both the legitimacy of acting on less than absolutely certain grounds and the legitimacy of the demand for a comprehensive, unshakable foundation. He saw his philosophical task as reconciling both the aesthetic and the practical demands of human rationality, although he did not yet know how. He suspected, however, that the reconciliation would be effected through a thorough examination of the conditions of human rationality as it operates in everyday life.

Despite the absence of such a firm foundation, we must nonetheless act, but this necessity does not preclude the possibility that eventually such a foundation might be established. Meanwhile, actions should be grounded in the various worlds of belief, recognizing the unavoidable element of risk. But the necessity of belief for action magnifies rather than diminishes the legitimacy of the motive of ontologic wonder, which strives for an understanding of the whole universe. Ontological wonder can only be satisfied by the final unification of the various worlds of lesser extent, including the common sensical, the mystical, and the scientific.[14] This drive to unify our many subjective beliefs into an objective universe was at the center of what James called the problem of the one and the many, the phrase which summarized for him the philosophic enterprise.

This unstable equilibrium of the aesthetic and practical demands of thinking held until his final crisis of 1909 (PU, 96ff). James found intolerable the dilemma engendered by our rational aesthetic demand for a secure warrant for our beliefs, one grounded in a totally comprehensible universe, and the practical necessity of acting without such a warrant. He finally resolved the conflict by denying the legitimacy of the aesthetic rational demand. Adopting Henri Bergson's terminology, he understood his decision as succumbing to anti-rationalism. What I prefer to call his thoroughly pragmatic, post-modern rationalism could only be embraced when a substitute had been found for the role of aesthetic rationalism as a reductive to the threat of the nihilism of a meaningless world. Only after his understanding of his own philosophic position had sufficiently matured into a full-blown radical empiricism could it replace the purely aesthetic understanding of rationalism as the reductive of nihilism.[15]

The seeds of his later pragmatic rationalism were sown already in his early explanation of the practical aspect of rationality. The rationalism he eventually rejected is only the traditional one limited to what he called the aesthetic aspect. And even then, the value of the drive for simplicity and clarity was not denied, but only the possibility of their demands ever being fully and finally met. Therefore, claims could neither be absolutely grounded in any transparent and purely rational system, nor could appeals to aesthetic rational demands alone provide sufficient justification for rejecting other demands, particularly not those beliefs necessary for action (Cf., VRE, 359). The correlative practical aspect of rationality is never denied.

Although both the British empiricist and continental rationalist traditions appeal to the practical aspect of mentality, neither tradition directly derives its understanding of rationality from its practical basis. Hume, for instance, turned to the demands of everyday life as a way of escaping the demands of reason, which must remain forever dissatisfied. Kant, on the other hand, produced critiques of both pure and practical reason. But as the post-Kantian romantic philosophers argued, although Kant legitimated both on their own terms, he did not succeed in satisfactorily demonstrating how they were related. James argues that as long as theoretic rationality remains theoretical, the skeptical undermining of any secure foundation in being is irrefutable. Furthermore, on aesthetic rational grounds alone, many other long-standing philosophical disputes are unresolvable.

In the second essay on "The Sentiment of Rationality," in what looks in hindsight like an anticipation of Stephen Toulmin's and Thomas Kuhn's positions on the indeterminacy of observation, James says: "There is nothing improbable in the supposition that an analysis of the world may yield a number of formulae, all consistent with the facts" (WB, 66). Just as the physical sciences can give examples of different theories that equally explain the observed data, there are also divergent explanations for understanding the world as seen from different points of view, each consistent within itself and harmonious with the data. But these systems, equally satisfactory to purely logical analysis, still have to be accepted or rejected by our "aesthetic and practical nature" (WB, 66). What are the tests of rationality used?

The first is taken from the empiricist analysis of a feeling of rationality as a feeling of familiarity. Custom, which acquaints us with both the antecedents and consequents of a thing, makes the otherwise unfamiliar predictable and thus the relations of things appear rational. There is one particular relation of greater practical importance than all the rest and that is the relation of a thing to its future consequences (WB, 67). The first practical requisite for a conception to be rational is, therefore, that our expectancy must be satisfied. Every novel or unclassified experience is a mental irritant which is relieved only when its future consequences are understood. The utility of the emotional effect of expectation can be demonstrated according to the biological theory of natural selection. The unfamiliar elicits a feeling of anxiety and heightened alertness which is more conducive to the survival of an animal in strange surroundings than indifference or contentment would be. "All curiosity has thus a practical genesis" (WB, 68).

The second demand of practical rationality is that its explanations satisfy our desires and support our active tendencies. It is not sufficient that uncertainty is banished from the future, but the future must also be defined *"congruously with our spontaneous powers"*(WB, 70). Feelings disclose the world. Like the senses, our emotions both anticipate and respond to objects in the real world. Fear, loathing, love, and surprise are not merely subjective states; otherwise, they could safely be ignored. "Any philosophy which annihilates the validity of the reference by explaining away its objects or translating them into terms of no emotional pertinency, leaves the mind with little to care or act for" (WB, 71). Just as aesthetic rationality demands for its fulfillment that the universe and the knower are congruous, that knowledge corresponds to reality, so practical rationality demands for its satisfaction that the doer and the universe are congruent, that our emotional and active propensities are answered in the character of the real world. These postulates of aesthetic and practical rationality are central to James's radical reconstruction of the philosophic project.

To understand the intellect only or primarily in its theoretic aspect distorts its fundamental character of being built out of practical interests. The evolutionary view of cognition provides an antidote to this traditional philosophical bias toward abstract systems by showing that cognition is a fleeting moment in a larger motor phenomenon. No one doubts that cognition in lower animals is anything more than a guide to appropriate action. Unless action of some sort ensues, there is no evidence of that acting for a purpose which most broadly defines intelligence. But all cognition is incomplete until it is discharged in action. That human intelligence engages in theoretic activity far in excess of what is needed to act only demonstrates that the discharge can be postponed. Beginning already with perception, "utility wholly determines which parts of our sensations we shall be aware of, and which parts we shall ignore," as Helmholtz's work on the eye and the ear already demonstrated (WB, 72).

The idealists and romantic writers subordinated thought to action, particularly to right moral action. James often quoted Emerson and Royce to this effect, as well as Tennyson, Fichte, and Schelling. But such claims had been for some time under attack by those who appealed to the clear-sighted, factually-based reasoning of science and who characterized such merely wishful thinking as the residue of unsubstantiated mythological or mystical beliefs. For an argument to be taken seriously, therefore, meant being able to appeal to strong scientific evidence in its support: "One runs a better chance of being listened to to-day if one can quote Darwin and Helmholtz than if one can only quote Schleiermacher or Coleridge" (WB, 91). Thus, while still appealing to the idealist tradition to support the claim that theoretic rationality is dependent on practical rationality, the arguments that James developed at length were often taken from the latest physiological investigations at the basis of the new, experimental psychology.

The doctrine of reflex action, for example, had been extended by physiologists to cover every sort of organic action (WB, 91ff). Actions are explained as discharges from nerve centers, which are themselves responses to incoming stimuli carried along the sensory nerves. These reflex actions have their source in incoming sense impressions and such impressions are always expressed in actions of some kind. James modified the doctrine to reflect the fact that there is more involved than a simple stimulus-response model can accommodate. The structural unit of the human nervous system is actually a triad, with incoming sensations awakening the reflective processes of the brain, which in turn are discharged via the nervous system into motor responses. This inter-dependent action loop is thwarted if cognition does not result in directed action. Physiological evidence thus supports two claims fundamental to Jamesian philosophy, namely, that reflection is literally grounded in the sensed world and that its function is to guide action. "The willing department of our nature, in short, dominates both the conceiving department and the feeling department; or, in plainer English, perception and thinking are only there for behavior's sake" (WB, 92). This is no crude behaviorism, but part of his project of critiquing abstract rationality and reestablishing the links of thinking with concrete experience.

Edward H. Madden finds James's recourse to the physiologist's relfex-arc concept unconvincing as a defense of the theist's teleological view of nature because of the "attenuated and metaphorical sense" in which he uses it (WB, xix). I agree that none of James's defenses of theism will convince the unbeliever. James himself calls his application of the reflex-arc thesis to theistic doctrine only one of its "possible speculative consequences" (92-93). But by quoting James's admission in a letter that he sacrificed "accuracy to effectiveness" and by emphasizing his "strangely metaphorical use of the reflex-arc concept," Madden by implication seems to sweep away any recourse to the reflex-arc concept by James and to reduce his use of it to that of a mere rhetorical device (xix-xx). But it is clear from the essay that James regarded the reflex-arc concept as "fundamental and well established" in physiology and "the great achievement of our generation" (91ff.).

Even though in private correspondence he may have retracted its application to theism, there is no evidence that he considered its extension "far beyond the limits of psychology" as anything less than his usual practice of reconstructing "the strictly natural-history point of view" into a method of philosophical analysis. The primary use James made of the reflex-arc is even clearer in the letter to Hodgson cited by Madden. In it James admits sacrificing accuracy to effectiveness, but he defends the decision as a way of calling attention to his main contention: "If I had made a true analysis of mind proper, into its extremes of impression and purpose with conception and decision swinging between them, and not adopted the ready-made triad of reflex-action with its copulation of heterogeneities, I should probably have made no impression at all."[16]

Philosophies which deny the reality of the world as perceptually grasped can be dismissed as irrational. This claim is based on an understanding of perception as involving anticipation of action, either as a response to expected stimuli or to forestall unwanted consequences. Any philosophy, if it is not to be "radically alien to human nature," must assume that "the inmost nature of the reality is congenial to *powers* which you possess" (WB, 73-75). Although no particular "over-belief" so far developed systematically by various philosophers has been so convincing as to exclude all rivals, this lack of success does not abrogate the function such over-beliefs play, which is to provide a warrant for our actions. The continued attractiveness of both idealism and materialism to different persons provides some evidence that disputes about which explanation is right may never be resolved, but that *some* foundational warrant is necessary seems ineradicable from human thinking.

Since beliefs were merely subjective according to the positivist metaphysics underlying science, they were denied any role in the determination of objective laws. But James was interested in determining the conditions under which science takes place and not in adhering to a positivist ideology. He argued that the exclusion of beliefs is impossible in practice and undesirable as a methodological prerequisite. Not only scientists, but everyone who thinks rationally, engages their whole person: "intellect, will, taste, and passion co-operate just as they do in practical affairs; and lucky it is if the passion be not something as petty as a love of personal conquest over the philosopher across the way" (WB, 77). James returned to the "living facts of human nature" to show that even the most careful thinkers, who have the highest standards of objectivity, cannot construct their systems without the help of personal preferences and beliefs.

A belief means holding that something is the case when doubt is still theoretically possible, and includes the inclination to act even when the outcome is not certified beforehand. It is an absurd abstraction from actual thinking to imagine that scientists and philosophers remain paralyzed before inconclusive evidence. The blind conviction that the evidence lies along one path rather than another and persistence in pursuing a hunch until it pays off characterize successful intellectual projects. The outcome determines the sagacity of hypotheses, not the elimination of all subjective beliefs before proceeding.[17] The proliferation of hypotheses and the determination of their fitness in solving the problem being investigated is analogous to the Darwinian evolutionary model of spontaneous variations which are afterwards selected by their success in securing the survival of offspring. Beliefs are therefore working hypotheses. As such, "belief (as measured by action)" not only does, but must, "continually outstrip scientific evidence" (WB, 80).

5. On Mind Corresponding to Reality

But why cannot the philosopher or the scientist simply get it right the first time, and thus obviate the need for believing anything not verified by the senses? It has been argued that if the intent is to understand the world as it is, even if such understanding is a prelude to action, then it should be fairly simple to decide when any given claim or proposition coincides with the reality intended. One can just 'look and see.' James undermines this naive view in "Remarks on Spencer's Definition of Mind as Correspondence," (1878) and reaffirms its rejection in the last chapter of *The Principles of Psychology* (1890) (CER, 43-68; EPH, 7-22). It should be noted both that the question arises in the context of biological theory and that the critique also applies to philosophical theories of the correspondence model of truth. This linkage of evolutionary biological theory with questions of knowledge and truth, as well as of being, is more explicit in these early articles than in the later ones, where it is often taken for granted. The purposive character of mind, which is further elaborated throughout *Principles*, is appealed to in defense of the claim that theoretic rationality is dependent on practical rationality.

Mental evolution is said by Spencer to be characterized by the "adjustment of inner to outer relations" (CER, 44). The correspondence of ideas with outward fact is said to be definitive of the nature of mind. This correspondence is further clarified: "Right or intelligent mental action consists in the establishment, corresponding to outward relations, of such inward relations and reactions as will favor the survival of the thinker, or, at least, his physical well-being" (CER, 49; EPH, 11). James objects to Spencer's claim that the mind simply reflects passively whatever is put before it. He points out that Spencer's account actually distinguishes between "mental action pure and simple, and *right* mental action" (CER, 50; EPH, 11). Furthermore, it proposes a teleological criterion, namely, the subjective interest consisting in the survival of the organism. This is not something already there to be pointed out, but involves a particular interpretation of the relation of an organism to its environment, one sufficient to qualify as a mental, as opposed to a merely reactive, response.

Against Spencer's claim that an objective, passive correspondence is the relevant criterion, James argues that the relevant interests are actually subjective in two senses. Firstly, they spontaneously arise from the organism because the animal's interest in survival is brought to, not found in, the situation. Thus, the so-called correspondence is not to any existent thing, but to a desirable future or set of future occurrences. Secondly, such interests exhibit "teleology," by which James means the determination of goals to be sought by adopting appropriate means. They are not subjective in the sense of being solipsistically apart from whatever is thus grasped, however. The subjectivity of mental activity is already within and a part of the world to be known. Furthermore, Spencer, by appealing without further qualification to "existent outward relations," that is, to the world as a pre-existent totality, fails to come to grips with the problem of reference implicit in all correspondence models, namely, identifying the reality (CER, 58; EPH, 16). Without the determination that survival shall be the mark of successful mental action, there is no independently recognizable reality to use as a basis for claiming that the criteria for correspondence have been satisfied.

James is not defending the subjectivity of organisms, as such, and even says that he could express all that Spencer does but "in non-mental terms" (CER, 51; EPH, 12). What he is pointing out is that Spencer cannot satisfactorily explain mental evolution, when it does occur, without bringing in some notion of "subjective spontaneity." We can see that in James's earliest critique of a correspondence model of survival as a criterion for the presence of mentality he has already developed the basis for his later criticism of the correspondence model of truth. This basis consists in calling attention to the context of the human being in the world within which determinations are made. The problem is not so much with the correspondence model as with the positivist assumptions that such models operate somehow on their own and that the human dimension can be safely ignored as an unwarranted intrusion on an otherwise objective explanation. By drawing our attention to the context of this human dimension, which makes possible our formal and informal ordering of experience, James directly attacks the false objectivity not only of the usual way of thinking of scientific models but of any models whatever. Besides demonstrating the mistakes that follow from ignoring the human dimension of experience, he has also started characterizing such a way of being, including the relation of beliefs to action and the teleological structure of knowing.

These teleological interests both designate what is aimed at and provide the criterion for whether the goal has been met. Thus, mental cognition of reality includes what, on reflection, is later distinguished as cognitive and volitional. But the interest in self-preservation, whether on the part of the cognitive organism or as designated by the scientific observer, is only one of many cognitive interests, and not even the one most characteristic of human beings. All such interests are equally subjective and yet provide access to reality: "The social affections, all the various forms of play, the thrilling intimations of art, the delights of philosophic contemplation, the rest of religious emotion, the joy of moral self-approbation, the charm of fancy and of wit — some or all of these are absolutely required to make the notion of mere existence tolerable" (CER, 53; EPH, 13).

James continues by arguing that Spencer is either explaining how we do think or how we ought to think. In the former case he is trying to determine the constitutive laws of thought, and error and nonsense, myth and metaphor, must be included, not excluded, as Spencer claims. In the latter case he is developing a regulative law of thought (CER, 57; EPH, 15). Few would quibble that right thinking is thinking in correspondence with reality. But philosophers of different schools are notoriously at odds in their determinations of reality. As against the passive mirroring of nature, which science once supported, Spencer claims that survival is the test of a correct correspondence. James turns Spencer's own arguments against him to show that his criterion is a subjective, teleological determination and not one read off from experience. Thinking, in fact, is teleological through and through.

Every individual exercises the equivalent of a "private categorical imperative" that determines what correct thinking shall consist in for him or her. But these warrants are only postulates and not yet grounded objectively, for each of these subjective beliefs "must depend on the general consensus of experience as a whole to bear out its validity" (CER, 60-61; EPH, 17). The only criterion for what is objectively real is the coerciveness of sensations over thought, not necessarily at each moment, but, as Peirce held, in the long run. Interests are thus the only real a priori elements of thought (CER, 50; n1, EPH, 11, n1). When our hypotheses are enacted they can transform the world and help bring about that which they intend. Mind is thus properly characterized by spontaneity and not by passivity. These conclusions, derived from an analysis of Spencer's evolutionism corrected by reflections on Darwinian evolutionary theory, are reiterated in physiological terms in "Reflex Action and Theism."

6. Discerning the Initial Direction of the Trail (CER, 409; PM, 258)

In the inaugural essay with which this chapter began, James recommended Peirce's "principle of practicalism," according to which the purpose of thought is to produce belief and that of belief is to produce habits of action (CER, 410; PM, 258). In so doing James called for a radical reordering of the priorities of philosophers at the very time when the new professionalism sweeping the disciplines was reinforcing the reduction of the role of philosophy to the discussion of epistemological issues that could be settled on the level of abstract thinking alone. To this new isolationism he opposed the pragmatic principle according to which clarity of meaning must be sought in terms of directed action and not in logical coherency alone or in textual referentiality. James extended the Peircean principle to locate meaning in "some particular consequence, in our future practical experience" (CER, 412; PM, 259). We take a particular meaning to be true if it successfully foretells the experiential outcome of acting on it. But whether one outcome is also better to accomplish than another is not decided by this instrumental truthfulness of means to ends, anymore than it is by traditional truth models.

It is a notorious truism that logical arguments alone have never settled any important philosophical dispute. We are scarcely closer to resolving any major issue raised in the Platonic dialogues than when Plato first enunciated them. But if, as "a sovereignly valuable rule of method for discussion," we would apply the pragmatic principle to concrete cases, James believed that we would at least begin to head "in the true direction for the trail" (CER, 412; PM, 259). Since the use of rational thinking alone, with its exclusively aesthetic, logical criteria, has failed to definitively settle disputes or to arrive at certainty, then the time has come to see what the employment of rational thinking as practical can accomplish. Truths can be initially judged by each person directly on the basis of concrete facts and the conduct that follows from acting on such facts, and these findings can then become available for further reflection and revision. But for such individually affirmed truths to become part of the reflectively established "funded character of experience" they must additionally satisfy the criteria he later develops in *Pragmatism* and calls the marriage function or the "rich and active commerce" of experiences (PM, 34-39). He had already hinted at this social context of truth determinations in the Spencer article, where he said that "to the individual man, as a social being, the interests of his fellow are a part of his environment" (CER, 53; EPH, 13).

James next applied the pragmatic principle to the recalcitrant philosophical problem of the existence of God. He wanted to demonstrate that the traditional way of posing this question in metaphysics, namely, whether God is the first cause of all things, renders the question an idle one and makes it impossible to decide between the materialist and deistic hypotheses. But by placing ourselves "in the real world we live in," it becomes obvious that the issue of God's existence is meaningful only insofar as it is tied to the theistic belief in his providence (CER, 418; PM, 262). By a careful examination of the way he arrives at this conclusion it becomes possible to see that the determination of "concrete fact" and of "conduct consequent upon the fact" requires an understanding of "the living facts of human nature," or of what is later called by Heidegger a phenomenological analysis of *Dasein* and Being-in-the-world.

The problem with interpreting the text in this way is that James did not reflect on his own method nor call it anything else than applying the pragmatic principle in concrete cases. Once it is recognized in what his numerous appeals to the concrete consist, it becomes evident that 'concrete' is a technical term, but one which he himself never methodically introduced. His naive assumption that he was just applying the pragmatic principle in a straightforward way and that any unbiased person would spontaneously interpret the principle the same way, once they understood it, was based on his belief that he was just disclosing those facts of experience that are available to everyone. This had the unfortunate effect that he never systematically explained the origin of his pragmatism in a concrete analysis of experience, even though a careful reading of his works reveals that he constantly appealed to it. He selected different aspects to emphasize, depending on the problematic. Since he thought he was appealing to concrete facts that were available to anyone who cared to look and reflect on their own experience, it never ceased to amaze him when his critics failed to understand him.

In the present case, for instance, he does not indicate that he is going to demonstrate that both temporality and the objective reference of feelings characterizes being human. He simply backs into it. After explaining what he means by temporality and the rationality of feelings and demonstrating that they represent irreducibly human modes of encountering the world, he applies this insight to solving the problem of proving the existence of God. Since he thinks in terms of discovering facts, not in terms of a reflective analysis of how we find ourselves always already active in the world, he never even uses the word, 'temporality,' even though his whole argument stands or falls depending on whether he has satisfactorily demonstrated that it is an inalienable mode of being human.

Why would James "start off with an impossible case," if his intent were simply to prove the existence of God as a demonstration of the worth of the pragmatic principle (CER, 414; PM, 260)? After all, the pragmatic principle was conceived as a turn to real possibility to replace the bankruptcy of such intellectual games involving impossible cases. The strength of the principle consists precisely in its appeal to practical consequences and differences of concrete fact, not in solving purely mental puzzles. He does so in order to demonstrate that the future is the horizon within which human thinking and action take place. Take away the future and "the debate between materialism and theism becomes quite idle and insignificant" (PM, 261). In context James actually argues that if no future actions can be deduced from either hypothesis, then the choice between them becomes insignificant, but this claim is dependent on temporality being a characteristic mode of being human. In fact, this is how he approaches the issue.

The impossible case with which he starts out to demonstrate the scope of his principle is to imagine that this moment is the absolutely last moment in the world (CER, 414; PM, 260). If there is literally no future beyond the present moment, then the pragmatic principle could not be applied because there would be no possibility of any difference of fact or conduct to ensue upon the adoption of some belief as true. This imagined lack of any future would also render senseless our impassioned philosophical and religious debates. For something to have significance it is not enough that it have an intellectual content; it must also be felt. This is because meaning is not just an intellectual category. The only meaning we know is human meaning; we can only speculate about the possibility of some other meaning. And humans are not disembodied spirits, but sentient beings. As such, we have access to the world through our feelings.

How would we respond to a world in which this moment were literally our last? Our feelings would lose their rational significance, which consists in the irreducible role they play in our judgments, namely, that some belief of ours is worth acting on. The debate over the existence of God is significant, for instance, because of the concomitant belief in his providence. This is shown by pointing out that when we imagine that there is no future, "most of us...[would] feel as if a terrible coldness and deadness would come over the world" (CER, 414; PM, 260). This change of feelings, from the facts of the world feeling "solid, warm, and altogether full of real significance," in our usual frame of mind, and then feeling "as if a terrible coldness and deadness would come over the world" when we imagine that it is at an end, is reasonable only for a consciousness like ours that is prospective. If our consciousness were purely retrospective, then this violent alternation of feelings "would be absolutely senseless and irrational" (CER, 414-415, PM, 260).

The unstated assumption is that in the normal course of events, that is, in our experiential living in view of the future, feelings play a fundamental role in rational thinking. If we only had a past but no future, then no emotions would attach to either the theistic or materialistic alternative and the problem would be "purely intellectual." Insofar as philosophy is defined solely as an intellectual activity, and it has usually been throughout history, then James's reproach of a metaphysical problem being purely intellectual sounds ludicrous. What else could a metaphysical problem be? To understand the force of James's response it is necessary to understand the concrete analysis of being human that underlies it. This includes his critique of rationality and his emphasis on temporality as a mode of being human, the teleological character of the human organization of experience, and the place of feeling in cognizing what is real.

James says that metaphysical disputes from which no definite consequences follow are ignored by both the ordinary person and by positivist scientists. This should come as no surprise. What is unexpected in his argument is the claim that metaphysicians should adopt the same criterion. James attacks Spencer's scientific materialism, for instance, because it renders the universe meaningless, and he accounts for Spencer's mistaken belief on the grounds that he developed only the aesthetic side of the argument and neglected its practical side (CER, 419-422; PM, 262-263). The role that belief in God plays in his own philosophy is then succinctly expressed: it is to be "a permanent warrant for our more ideal interests,...a fulfiller of our remotest hopes."

The reasoning process is as follows. In a world with no future it does not matter whether God made the world or not, since on either hypothesis the actual facts would remain unchanged. In such a world there is no point in settling the issue because it would not make any difference to its actual constitution. We would therefore lose interest in the issue. Its settlement would have no value for us and would arouse in us no particular feelings. This state of affairs is directly comparable to that of persons, scientists included, for whom the god question is irrelevant. They have no interest in it because for them nothing follows one way or another from settling it. It is a merely academic or purely speculative question.

Therefore, if the question is still meaningful for metaphysicians, if it still has any significance, then that significance must arise from the fact that they expect the settlement of the issue to make a difference in the actual state of affairs. Only in a world with a future can anything change. In returning from our imagined state of affairs to "the real world we live in," we can now become aware of the importance to ourselves of our living towards the future, of the sense of incompleteness in time of any given state of affairs to what it will be, and of the significance that attaches to our beliefs and subsequent actions in view of the changes they can make in the world. "In this unfinished world the alternative of 'materialism or theism?' is intensely practical" (CER, 418; PM, 262).

To say that something is practical, therefore, is to place it within the horizon of the future, to recognize our temporality. Practical beliefs are those whose enactment brings about observable changes in the constitution of the real world we live in. Purely intellectual beliefs are those held for reasons other than their future consequences. For a belief to have practical significance also means that those "concrete attitudes of hope and expectation" that characterize our humanity are not thwarted (CER, 423; PM, 264). Chief among these is the one Kant identified as the postulation of a kingdom of ends, or as James puts it, the hope in the eventual triumph of "an eternal moral order" where the lack of reward for moral goodness and lack of success in transforming this world into a moral realm is finally remedied.

James never falters in his conviction that this belief is a necessary condition for moral action, but his published writings can be read without this being immediately obvious. This is partly due to the fact that this conviction is usually tacked on to other arguments as an application to religious questions of the central position he is defending. Therefore it can easily be overlooked or ignored, since its plausibility does not undermine the independently developed arguments. But it is also due to the fact that his defense of an eternal moral order is in direct contradiction to the main body of his work, just as his defense of a future time beyond time is at odds with his insistence on the finitude of humanly experienced temporality. He recognized, for instance, that not all people need to postulate such an ideal final kingdom in order to act morally.

Thus, although he expressed his own beliefs in Kantian terms, he also denied that by a necessary condition he meant universally necessary. In the article on Spencer, for instance, he says: "The truth appears to be that every individual man may, if it please him, set up his private categorical imperative of what rightness or excellence in thought shall consist in, and these different ideals, instead of entering upon the scene armed with a warrant — whether derived from the polyp or from a transcendental source — appear only as so many brute affirmations left to fight it out upon the chess-board among themselves" (CER, 60; EPH, 17). How he avoids relativism or the triumph of mere brute force without appealing either to a reductionist materialism or to transcendental arguments is given in the next sentence: "They are, at best, postulates, each of which must depend on the general consensus of experience as a whole to bear out its validity." But since we are in the process ourselves and not outside it, this means experientially, day by day,—"not by any *a priori* definition" but "*ambulando*"— drawing on what has already been verified, but willing to revise these findings in light of new evidence. These decisions do not give us the certainty that a priori arguments do, and therefore we are always at risk, but we cannot escape this finitude except by taking "a moral holiday" in a leap of faith. However, we deceive ourselves if we mistake such aids to action for infallible disclosures of reality.

James tried again and again to defend those beliefs which allowed him to escape nihilism within these restrictions which he himself set up. But he is more convincing in his appeals to the features of our being in the world than in his appeals to a postulated metaphysical underpinning. This is illustrated, for instance, in his essay on "The Moral Philosopher and the Moral Life," where he spends the first four sections convincingly arguing against dogmatic ethics and for including each person's contribution in the determination of defensible ethical judgments. These judgments should be developed out of reflections on our own experiences and a willingness to accommodate the needs of others, since all of us are similarly situated and no one has a privileged access to the good (WB, 141-159). But then, in the fifth and final section, he takes back this ethics developed in light of our finite temporality by saying that "the chief of all the reasons why concrete ethics cannot be final is that they have to wait on metaphysical and theological beliefs" (159).

These two aspects of his thought do not cohere, but each is developed with an eye to the other. Therefore, his long-range project comes into clearer focus by paying attention to his struggle to develop a metaphysics which is genuinely experiential. He defended his own need for metaphysical over-beliefs. If his arguments are not finally convincing for those who do not feel such a need, then he wanted to know how they avoid nihilism. The crucial test is whether a moralism unsupported by any outward guarantees can avoid the despair that seems the obvious outcome of any sensitive response to the rampant suffering and evil that is daily brought to our attention. In the same fifth section he says: "It would seem, too — and this is my final conclusion — that the stable and systematic moral universe for which the ethical philosopher asks is fully possible only in a world where there is a divine thinker with all-enveloping demands" (WB, 161).

But he also says that there is no content to these demands; we must still struggle in ignorance and therefore, as to "which course of action is best," the ethical philosopher "is on no essentially different level from the common man" (WB, 162). His concrete, phenomenological answer to skepticism is motivated by his need to avoid nihilism. But although his defense of his pragmatic phenomenology is related to his defense of his experientially based metaphysics, they are independently argued. His concrete methodology does not depend on his unreconstructed metaphysical postulates, but his methodological procedure is correct in proposing that these postulates must themselves be justified by the criteria set up by his radically empiricist pragmatic method.

It can be objected to James's translation of speculative beliefs into practical formulations that people often feel very strongly about purely speculative beliefs, such as whether God is one or many. A Jamesian analysis would either point out that those who feel strongly about such beliefs also believe that practical differences do result from holding them or that they have distorted the normal relationship of beliefs to action. Disconnecting beliefs from action leads to predictably bad results, such as spending time on scholastic distinctions that could be better spent changing inhuman conditions. As evidence for the temporal character of human experience and consequent linking of the issue of God's existence with providence, James points to the fact that in this real world of ours some people, at least, have intense feelings about the existence of God and would feel devastated if it should turn out that he or she does not exist. Only on the assumption that feelings are cognitive does this make sense. But in the inaugural lecture this claim and others, such as that belief in an eternal moral order is a necessary incentive to moral action, are simply assumed, not demonstrated. The cogency of his arguments is not the present issue, but the fact that in defending these religious applications James begins filling in the details of his radically empiricist turn to practical rationality.

Like the issue of temporality, his development of the role of feeling in human experience is part of his concrete analysis of being human which is found throughout his writings but not systematically developed in any one place. He even obscured some of the connections in cutting and pasting articles together. When he transferred to *Pragmatism* (51-56), for instance, the few pages (CER, 415-424; PM, 261-264) from the inaugural lecture that illustrate how the principle of practicalism solves the metaphysical dispute over the existence of God, he retained the feature of temporality but dropped the related feature of the significance of feeling as a characteristically human access to reality. He therefore obscured the fact that he was drawing on a concrete analysis of being human in determining when an outcome is practical. The two paragraphs on feeling (CER, 414-415; PM, 260) immediately precede the transferred pages. Without them it is no longer clear what constitutes the essential "future detail of experience" that is then only alluded to, and we are left with merely a future difference of conduct, emptied out of the context of signification that the appeal to feeling adds.

This failure to explicitly characterize his procedure means that crucial aspects of his reconstruction of philosophy were not followed through to their logical conclusions, even by James, as we have seen in his confusion of a finite temporality with a future that stretches beyond time and of a categorical imperative with a hypothetical. He can be credited with ultimately finding a path out of skepticism and of blazing a trail out of nihilism, but this conclusion depends as much on who walks the trail as on the trail itself. Because he did not clearly mark the path and sometimes even unwittingly obscured it, an ideal discourse has to be constructed to elaborate the features of the trail and make them available for criticism, use, and further development. James's perfectly ideal discourse and my reconstructed one both converge and diverge as wilderness paths sometimes do.

Chapter Two

Founding Level of Meaning: Towards an Experiential Grounding of Both Science and Metaphysics

The program sketched out in the early articles is announced and developed in *The Principles of Psychology* and in the articles defending his new approach to psychology written during the 1880s and 1890s. In this chapter I argue that *Principles* was conceived as an integral part of a larger project and not just as a book inaugurating a new science of psychology. The contradictory statements found throughout his monumental work of genius have long prevented it from being given a consistent interpretation. The exploration of the motivations and hidden assumptions behind the convolutions of the text provides a means of explicitly identifying the structures of his insistent but seldom clearly formulated program.

James's early struggle against nihilism led him to seek a founding level of meaning that would be impervious to skeptical assault.[1] Since skepticism arises out of a reflection that undermines what had once been taken for granted, its overcoming involved turning toward the pre-reflective moment of credulity. James hoped to forestall the corrosiveness of the questioning intellect through the careful explication of this pre-reflective experience. The immediate task was to demonstrate the inadequacy of British empiricism and Continental idealism because they both led to skepticism, and to develop a more accurate description of lived experience. The long-range goal was the development of sound epistemological and metaphysical systems built on such a firm foundation which would "exorcise" skepticism once and for all. He also used his concrete findings as an independent check on systematic explanations. They provided the means for identifying the failings of other philosophical positions and for justifying his own. This project was most clearly stated in the 1895 article, "The Knowing of Things Together," where he explained the purpose of his *magnum opus* (CER, 371-400; EPH, 71-89).

51

On one level James shared the characteristic empiricist failure to question the testimony of the senses and the veracity of intuitions. Consequently, he neglected the subjective conditions which structure observation and description. These historical, psychological, cultural, linguistic, and logical conditions make it impossible to straightforwardly appeal to a pristine level of pure experience and unproblematically accurate description. This blindness does not cohere with his detailed exploration of these very same conditions in stressing the teleological character of human cognition. Nonetheless, he did not rethink or reject his unexamined assumption of the possibility of pure seeing and accurate description, even when it came into direct conflict with his concrete development of selective interest.

These tensions produced a dynamic quality in James's thought, but they also ultimately prevented him from arriving at a satisfactory resolution. Insofar as philosophers share this empiricist bias they also either do not question or explain away this contradictory juxtaposition of "pure seeing" and predisposing structures of meaning.[2] James constantly pointed out the structures of interpretation which prevented others from accurately describing the facts of experience. The radical potential of his writing can be retrieved by using his own insights to challenge the neutrality of his descriptions.

In his late writings James's ideal is a pluralistic conjunction of contributing insights and methods, not their combination or replacement by a more inclusive view. But even in his early writings his postulation of an eventual metaphysical synthesis would somehow not supercede the individual contributions. It is just this refusal to transcend the contributions of individual sciences, personal experiences, artistic endeavors, and religious revelations that allowed James to unmask the will to domination hidden in conceptual schemas. But it also makes presenting James's writings as a unified body of thought difficult. He actually had to transcend the limitations of merely local organizations of experience in order to demonstrate why the contributions of each were legitimate. However, since he did so operationally rather than theoretically, any attempt to make explicit what is only implicit in the texts can always be accused of distorting the original spirit. Moreover, there is no dearth of pithy Jamesian sayings against systematization and transcendence, even conceptualization, to back up the accusation. The attempt is well worth the risk, however, because the interpretive principles James used without ever organizing them systematically are essential to legitimizing his claims by making them available for discussion and evaluation. They are also among his most original and lasting developments and are enhanced rather than undermined by a sustained presentation.

1. Cracks in the Positivist Model of Science

Daniel J. Wilson points out that the late nineteenth and early twentieth century debate over the relation of science to philosophy was characterized by "an inability to define precisely and consistently what science or its methods were."[3] James was no exception, but his initial education in science placed him in a favorable position to evaluate it, both as a participant and as a critic. However, this does not make it any easier to recognize what he meant by science, which must be derived from scattered references.

James had written *Principles* on the assumption that a metaphysically neutral, phenomenal description of human experience was both possible and desirable.[4] It was metaphysically neutral in that it did not derive its first principles from any philosophical system. It began with basic facts and therefore did not need to provide reasons for its starting point. James also thought that his psychology did not presuppose any particular set of values beyond an adherence to objective observation and description. In short, its method of phenomenal description was modeled on that of the natural sciences. In the preface to *Principles* he says that "the reader will in vain seek for any closed system in the book. It is mainly a mass of descriptive details, running out into queries which only a metaphysics alive to the weight of her task can hope successfully to deal with" (PP, I, 6-7).

But even within the acknowledged limits of "psychology as a natural science," no "solid ground" had yet been established (PBC, 400). Unlike the positivists, for James the restriction to elementary assumptions and data made the findings of empirical psychology particularly vulnerable to metaphysical criticism, rather than less so. On the "mere descriptive level" some classifications and generalizations had been made, but no propositions had yet been formulated which functioned like laws, that is, from which consequences could be causally deduced. To become such a strict science, in fact and not just in name, the limited findings must be reconsidered in wider connections and translated into other terms. But this meant that scientific psychology must be reconstructed metaphysically. The assumptions of psychology are only provisional and revisable and need to incorporate philosophic considerations of significance and truth. Provisional beginnings are typical of the particular sciences. The "Science of all things" was still, for

James, philosophy or metaphysics (9). Until and unless the interests of wider scope envelop those of lesser extent, the sciences cannot provide the absolute grounding promised by our understanding of science as such.

Since *Principles* can provide only partial and provisional data, and the *"full* truth about states of mind" cannot be known without bringing in a theory of knowledge and rational psychology, of what use are its findings? James answered that "incomplete statements are often practically necessary" (PBC, 10). Empirical psychology is indispensable but only provides a provisional point of view which will be totally transformed when taken up into the whole body of philosophy (14). But epistemology and rational psychology also have first to be re-thought in light of the new empirical findings of laboratory psychology. In order to justify this hermeneutical circle, it has to be made clear in what the practical necessity and indispensableness of the partial insights of empirical psychology consist and precisely how they are related to epistemological and metaphysical analysis. If empirical psychology can provide only a provisional and revisable basis for reflection, then the secure basis being sought must be found in a reconstructed or philosophical psychology. Furthermore, it must be shown how it came about that James, while intending to write a strictly scientific psychology as a prologue to a philosophy which would draw on its empirical findings, actually produced an original concrete analysis of the human condition as a basis for both philosophical and psychological reflection.

Despite James's intentions in *Principles* to stick to practical psychology and ignore metaphysical difficulties, it is obvious that he could not or would not eliminate metaphysical considerations.[5] Rather than assuming, as Andrew Reck does, that James meant to assert the essential incompatibility of psychology and metaphysics, I am arguing that he deliberately set out to reconcile them, but only after carefully distinguishing the parameters of each by reinterpreting them.[6] The intrusive metaphysical passages attest to a larger project of which *Principles* is only the first step. This long-range project involved founding psychology as a strictly phenomenal science, indifferent to either empirical or idealist philosophical presuppositions, in order to provide an experiential basis for developing a non-speculative philosophy. However, he could not altogether prevent his goal of a psychologically based philosophy from intruding on the immediate project of developing an appropriately neutral psychology. This was because the precise relationship between the philosophic drive for ultimate explanations and the scientific drive for fidelity to immediate facts had not been worked out.

In this early period James is not easy to place philosophically. At the time, for instance, he sympathized both with Berkeleyan idealism and scientific positivism, although he also rejected tenets of both positions. Likewise, despite his painful awareness of the incompatibility of German idealism and British empiricism, he was nonetheless committed to fundamental presuppositions of each. A lesser man, in the interest of consistency, would have chosen among these alternatives and continued their unproductive hostility. James, however, was equally convinced of the importance to life of a systematic philosophical world view, epitomized by idealist philosophies; of the necessity for adherence to individual experience characteristic of Scottish common sense philosophy and of British empiricism; and of his duty as a man of science to respect the increasingly atomistic and quantitative scientific world view. He can be numbered among those troubled nineteenth century thinkers "who feel in their bones that man's religious interests must be able to swallow and digest and grow fat upon all the facts and theories of modern science, but who yet have not the capacity to see with their own eyes how it may be done."[7]

He nonetheless carefully weighed the contributions of both science and metaphysics, despite the absence of any theoretical solution to their antagonistic interests. He thus avoided both the unsatisfactory expedient of simply denying the opposite position (as the positivists and many religious ministers did) and the temptation of a merely verbal solution, such as he called Hegel's reconciling *Geist*. This also accounts for the groping character of his writings, trying first one, then another approach. This procedure has the virtues of its vices. James's experimental method lacks the rigor and incisiveness attainable when a clearly stated thesis guides each subsequent development. But it is also open to unexpected findings and full of insights that yield promising results when vigorously pursued. However, his practice of tailoring the evidence offered to what is needed to correct the biases of the particular audience being addressed leads to a less desirable outcome. He neglects and postpones the difficult task of rethinking incompatible presuppositions of his scientific and metaphysical positions.

In *Principles* James explicitly adopts "the *psychological* point of view, the relatively uncritical non-idealistic point of view of all natural science, beyond which this book cannot go" (PP, I, 263). And yet, as early reviewers already pointed out, philosophical speculation keeps intruding.[8] Philosophical considerations are not even absent in the abridgment, *Psychology: Briefer Course*, (1892), which he shortened precisely by eliminating all matters extraneous to a strictly scientific point of view.[9] He says in the last chapter, for instance, that psychology is incompetent to deal with the question of free will (PBC, 392). But halfway through the same chapter he appeals to the momentous spiritual consequences which would follow from settling the question of whether we are free or determined as the motivation for examining the conditions under which the feeling of volition and effort arises (PBC, 373). He even ends the chapter with a section on the "ethical importance of the phenomenon of effort" (PBC, 392-394).

The most persuasive explanation of this seemingly contradictory behavior of asserting allegiance to a positivist model of science while practicing an evolutionary, philosophical psychology is that James was attempting to found psychology on a new basis and had not yet worked out all the implications of such a radical project. James recognized that dichotomizing science and metaphysics was unsatisfactory, but programmatically adhered to this division in a sustained attempt to undermine the anti-metaphysical bias of positivist science. He did this by denying any constraints on psychology derived from metaphysical speculation. But even though he rejected the Comtian anti-metaphysical bias, he heartily embraced the empirical bias of positivism with its emphasis on experimentation. His first goal was to detach the success of experimental psychology from its anti-metaphysical bias by neutralizing it by limiting it to experimentally based laws and regularities. His second goal was to use these purely factual results as a fitting basis to construct a new and better metaphysics. This dual project led him both to uphold the science-metaphysics split to accomplish the first goal and to transgress that split when necessary to point out the benefits to be gained in pursuing the second goal.

Rather than attributing the lapses against his own stated framework of a strict separation to mere ambivalence, this dual goal can account for them. This Kantian limitation of the scope of psychology precisely in order to make room for efficacious, free choice is explicitly adopted in *Principles* (PP, II, 1179).[10] But, unlike Kant, he argued that the exercise of free choice would be phenomenally accessible.[11] He denies in *Briefer Course*, for instance, that psychology as a strict science can legitimately exclude investigating the philosophical problem of free will by claiming that its protocols of verification are inappropriate. To do so would be equivalent to denying the legitimacy of such inquiries. James argues that psychology deals with human consciousness, and if free will never appears among the other phenomena being investigated, then it would seem reasonable to conclude that it does not exist at all (PBC, 392). He rejects this conclusion as absolutely unacceptable.

Lest there be any doubt as to his intentions, the larger project appears in print a few years after *Principles*. In "A Plea for Psychology as a 'Natural Science'" James most clearly sets out his view of the relation of philosophy and science to the newly emerging discipline of psychology.[12] He consciously presides over the birth of psychology as a science, out of "a mass of phenomenal description, gossip, and myth," clarifying the polemical intent of his recently published *Principles*: "I wished, by treating Psychology *like* a natural science, to help her to become one" (CER, 316-317; EPS, 270). The article is a straightforward plea for a strict separation of a scientific psychology from a philosophical psychology, with scientists foreswearing philosophical pronouncements and philosophers refraining from imposing their standards on scientific psychology.

But by keeping in mind the audience for which the article was intended and by recalling James's characterization of science and philosophy, a less straightforwardly separatist interpretation becomes more plausible. As if in corroboration James himself retracts such a sharp separation a few years later when he reluctantly admits in "The Knowing of Things Together" that such a strict dichotomy is impossible in practice (CER, 399; EPH, 88). My thesis is that James's immediate goal was indeed to free psychology from philosophical presuppositions which were preventing its development as an experimental science, but his original contributions to the emerging science of psychology involved bringing philosophy and biology together on a new basis which he hoped would eventuate in a synthesis of philosophic, biological, and psychic discoveries.

"A Plea for Psychology" was a reply to George Trumbull Ladd's attack on *Principles*, entitled "Psychology as So-called 'Natural Science.'"[13] Ladd's article was the occasion for the reply, but it is clear that in responding to him, James was addressing the entire philosophic community. He asks hypothetically in one place, for instance, "Why should not Professor Ladd, why should not any 'transcendental philosopher,' be glad to help confirm and develop so beneficial a tendency as this?" (CER, 322; EPS, 274). He also characterizes scientists, both in the article and in *Principles*, as having little "aptitude or fondness for general philosophy," nor, presumably, for anything which James, as a philosopher, would care to say to them (CER, 320; EPS, 273). The intended audience, therefore, was the philosophical community, which was understandably reluctant to relinquish even a part of its traditional subject matter, especially an area as central as psychology. It is important to recognize the intended audience in order to clarify what they were being asked to forego and what was being promised in its stead.

James argued that psychology should legitimately be considered a natural science insofar as it takes as its subject matter that limited aspect of mentality which is wholly accounted for in our natural history. As a natural science, psychology seeks the practical prediction and control of such temporal events falling within the ordinary course of nature. The biological study of human nature undertaken by psychologists, physiologists, and natural scientists — James even includes psychical researchers — is credited with yielding many promising new facts. Such researchers should not be forced to justify their findings on philosophical grounds. There is more practical betterment for humanity to be gained by sharply differentiating psychology as a strict science, the proper sphere of "men of facts, of the laboratory workers and biologists," from philosophy, the study of "the more metaphysical aspects of human consciousness" (CER, 318-322; EPS, 271-273).

Eventually philosophers should be able to take up the results of such scientific research and construct a comprehensive world view. But a premature imposition of such philosophic concepts as the soul or transcendental ego on psychology could only inhibit but not prevent the emergence of an independent science of psychology. More importantly, such an imposition would distort the understanding of those very "facts of experience" which philosophy needs if it is to avoid sterile speculation (CER, 320-323; EPS, 273-274). James was both a Comtian positivist and a British empiricist in his insistence that theories emerge from, and are a generalization of, facts, and that disputes about first principles can only interfere with a "harvest" of natural laws.

James saw his own original contribution to psychology in designating and arguing for an "undivided 'mental state'...as the fundamental datum" for the science of psychology (CER, 324; EPS, 275). He thus shrewdly supported the birth of the new psychology as a positivist science by insisting on its limitation to observable temporal events, while undercutting its positivist philosophy by designating as its proper focus a continuous, undivided mental state, rather than a series of disconnected sense data. Furthermore, he proposed developing a well defined and limited program of investigation for psychology as a science, namely, that of correlating such mental states with brain states. Thus, both philosophers and biologists can become psychologists, but only insofar as they each "forego ulterior inquiries" and provisionally take the mental state as the ultimate psychological phenomenon. Scientific psychology should be free to develop unconstrained by philosophical presuppositions as long as it recognizes its own limitations and forswears metaphysical pronouncements. As a natural science psychology should not engage in metaphysical reconstruction (PP, I, 141). One movement James hoped to counteract in scientific psychology by this disavowal of metaphysics is the reduction of mental states to physiological states.

James, then, wanted to assist at the birth of psychology as a phenomenal science by clearing "metaphysical entanglements" from its path. Given this state of affairs, if forced to choose between a theoretical, philosophical psychology and a factual, scientific psychology, he said that he would unhesitatingly choose the latter on humanitarian, pragmatic grounds because science promises the most relief for suffering humanity. However, he firmly believed that philosophers would have the last word and that, contrary to Comte, the limited understanding definitive of science will never be finally satisfactory, but will contribute to a more inclusive philosophic understanding of the world as world.[14]

Thus Reck's statement that in *Principles* and *Briefer Course* James proposed a strict separation between science and metaphysics needs to be qualified in light of all of James's early writings. It cannot be straightforwardly concluded that such a separation is either desirable or possible. The fact that James did not himself adhere to this strict separation in his psychological writings and that he afterwards explicitly repudiated such a possibility must be taken into account, especially in view of the reconstruction of James's more comprehensive project. It should be recalled that, traditionally, psychology and metaphysics had been compatible, for example, in scholasticism and Scottish common sense philosophy, but with Darwinism, positivism, and the development of a mechanistic, laboratory based psychology, the old synthesis no longer held. In supporting the new science James had to pronounce the old synthesis dead, but his intent was to prepare the way for a new union of psychology and philosophy, one developed on a firmer foundation.

2. Clash of Philosophical Goals: Ultimate Comprehension and Ecstatic Union

It would be impossible to recognize, let alone verify, this claim about James's long-range project from reading *Principles* in isolation from his other works. Since in it he took positivism as the model of science, and rationalism as the model of metaphysics, each unalterably opposed to the other's presuppositions, his insistence on a clear separation which would avoid unproductive animosity must have seemed the better course of action. But James's own practice of psychology and philosophy was already evolving towards joining the experimental and humanistic disciplines in a unique synthesis rendering such a rigid separation impossible. Although his paradigm of science mostly reflected the ruling positivist model of the day, it also differed from it in significant ways that he was careful to point out. Likewise, he spoke of philosophy in predominantly traditional terms in his psychological writings, but he was already developing his own original approach to it in his other writings. Unfortunately, he was not yet aware of the systematic possibilities of his own practice. Since the temptation is to read back (or make more explicit) the more original James into his earlier, somewhat inchoate stage, it is important to recall this strict dichotomy between positivist science and rational psychology that framed his early thinking about psychology.

In *Principles*, for instance, James sometimes uses the word, 'philosophy,' elliptically, to stand for transcendental philosophy or philosophical idealism. There are a loose set of characteristics, however, which can be ascribed to philosophy in the sense in which James used it in these early works in which he deliberately tried to stay within the conventions for scientific writings. Philosophy in this broader sense treats questions "in their widest possible connections, amongst the objects of an ultimate critical review of all the elements of the world" (CER, 321-322; EPS, 273). Its method is the Kantian one of showing how our experience of the material world, or any world, is possible (CER, 318; EPS, 271). Its goal is ultimate rationality (CER, 318-319; EPS, 271).

Only in his later works does he reject this traditional philosophic rationalism, both idealist and empiricist varieties, with an explicit feeling of being relieved of a great burden. In direct contrast to the unlimited aspirations of philosophy, natural science is distinguished by its deliberate limitation of subject matter and goal, namely, that which leads to practical effectiveness. Science, as science, is necessarily limited ("a mere fragment of truth broken out from the whole mass") and thus employs unexamined assumptions (CER, 317; EPS, 271). It seeks to find "definite 'laws' of sequence" built on such assumptions, rather than on first principles (CER, 318; EPS, 271).

But it is equally important to recognize that James was already moving away from these dichotomies. His own original philosophy was developed alongside more traditional views. The confusion is compounded by the fact that he used traditional terms even when giving them new meanings because of his usual practice of seeking a common ground with others rather than stressing differences. It is therefore not surprising that some philosophers defend him as still adhering to the usual models of philosophy and others stress his radical break with the tradition.[15] It is extremely difficult to disentangle the two strands because James himself most often did not. The strategy adopted to deal with this confusing state of affairs is to point out just what the distinctively Jamesian positions are and also to point out the more traditional framework within which he often worked. This requires making the two approaches clearer and more sharply delineated than James himself did. It has not usually been recognized that until the very end of his career James still sought to establish the first cause and final outcome of all things. The methods he developed to accomplish these metaphysical goals, however, were often strikingly at odds with their fulfillment.

In the original essay called "The Sentiment of Rationality," James argued that the purpose of reasoning is to lead to a satisfactory conclusion, passing from a state of restlessness or uncertainty to a calm acquiescence in the truth or vision of the good, a goal expressed long ago by Plato and Aristotle and in his own time by Emerson and Royce (CER, 83-86; EPH, 32-34). Three versions of this final state attracted him because they embodied such an ideal of untroubled assurance. They also repelled him because they reached the end illegitimately, not having secured an unchallengeable warrant or justification. The three are religious mysticism or poetic lyricism, philosophical idealism, and common sense or ordinary understanding.

Mystics and poets find "the peace of rationality" in which everything is explained, related, and made clear and simple "through ecstasy when logic fails," thus abolishing the opposition between knowing and being (CER, 133-134; EPH, 62-63). This is the goal stated in terms which seem to answer James's own deepest needs. But such a poetic, mystical goal could no longer be believed in solely on authoritative religious grounds or through merely artistic sentiment. The scientific temper of his time, like our own, demanded that philosophical explanations satisfy the same rigorous standards that scientific hypotheses do. Although turning away from such mysticism as a satisfactory course of action in his early years, James nevertheless left open the possibility of raising it to a "systematized method."[16] However, he presciently quotes the eccentric mystic, Benjamin P. Blood: "The disease of Metaphysics vanishes in the fading of the question and not in the coming of an answer" (CER, 134-135, n1; EPH, 63, n27). Towards the end of his life James identified his own abandonment of the search for total rationality with Blood's mysticism, but, ironically, only after decades spent developing a rationale for doing so![17]

Despite his frequent criticism of it, he was likewise attracted to the idealist philosophical goal. In 1885 he suspected that an "idealist escape from the quandary may be the best one for us all to take" (CER, 281). He himself could not take that path, but by the time of *A Pluralistic Universe* (1909), although he still objected to the systems and faulty foundations of Fechner, Royce, and Hegel, he also still allied himself with their idealist visions (PU, 94). Furthermore, in his day late nineteenth century idealism, like Scottish common sense philosophy before it, was the philosophical tradition explicitly defending the efficacy of human effort in shaping a world consistent with human dignity.

Common sense attitudes differ from the other two states mentioned in not being an ultimate goal, but "a perfectly definite halting-place of thought."[18] Common sense is the provisional state *par excellence* in that it accepts the world as it appears, with no attempt to reconcile incongruities when this involves simply dismissing an aspect of the dilemma that is as irreducibly important as the one retained. Like positivism, it refuses to examine its own assumptions, but unlike positivism, it does not turn this inadequacy into a dogma. By ruling out feeling as constituting "the 'unscientific' half of existence" scientists adopt a monistic reductionism which ignores rather than grapples with the central problem of reconciling the totality of human experience (See PP, I, 138). Common sense cannot theoretically construct such a synthesis either, but at least stubbornly insists on the multi-leveled richness of experience. Although James was plainly sympathetic to the common sense view, he thought of it as an uncontroversial place-holder for the human dimension of experience which would give way, in time, to a thorough-going metaphysical reconstruction (PP, I, 141).

The appeal to common sense plays an interesting mediating role, being neither science proper nor metaphysical speculation.[19] Unfortunately, it is infected with the same unadmitted, bifurcated notions of science and metaphysics. He says that "common-sense, though the intimate nature of causality and of the connection of things in the universe lies beyond her pitifully bounded horizon, has the root and gist of the truth in her hands when she obstinately holds to it that feelings and ideas are causes" (PP, I, 140). In other words, common sense, like some idealist philosophies, believes in the efficaciousness of mental realities. However, James argues that the importation of this belief into science should not bother scientists because positivist science insists on remaining "impartially *naif*" by not admitting its own philosophic underpinnings. Scientists can therefore have no objection to such an undeveloped philosophical presupposition as the one put forward by common sense. And even if positivist science should adopt a more critical attitude, then a thorough reconstruction "will probably" also preserve the common sense view, but will have reasonable grounds for so doing (141). He is no doubt assuming that a more reflective science will coincide with his own concrete scientific model.

James thus somewhat disingenuously argues that since he is deliberately adopting a scientific, that is, non-speculative, point of view, and since common sense is obviously non-speculative, then an appeal to common sense is not ruled out by scientific methodology. An appeal to idealist philosophy, on the other hand, would be ruled out. Without any more substantial defense, he says that he will therefore use the language of common sense throughout *Principles* (PP, I, 147). But under cover of the appeal to common sense James smuggles in a scientific psychology which is stubbornly metaphysical. By this sleight of hand he banishes metaphysics as a debatable scientific topic only to import it throughout his scientific psychology. The chameleon-like common sense allows him to surreptitiously advocate both metaphysically neutral and engaged science, opposing common sense sometimes to science and sometimes to (idealist) metaphysics. As an ally of metaphysics opposed to science, for instance, he says that common sense has always believed in the soul (181). Does this mean that, in adhering to common sense throughout the book, he will use the soul as an explanatory mechanism? No, he explicitly denies that he does so. Yet he does not banish it either, but leaves room for it as an hypothesis. But common sense is also on the side of science against metaphysics in that it is incurably dualistic and "for Absolute Idealism, the infinite Thought and its objects are one" (262).

Of the two philosophic drives which James earlier identified, "consistency or unity of thought," and securing an objective warrant for individual emotional ends, the second was clearly overriding and remained so throughout his life. The first, however, was also a motivating force during what, for convenience, I have called the early period. This period ended in 1894-1895 with the rejection of his cherished project of establishing a new psychology as an experiential foundation for a new philosophy (CER, 399-400; EPH, 88). He never really rejected the earlier project when he turned to explicitly philosophical problems. He transformed the scientific method in order to add to the "harvest of facts" as a precondition for developing an experientially based metaphysics.

He was still seeking unity in his middle period, which I date roughly from 1895 to 1908, when in the Hibbert lectures, published in 1909 as *A Pluralistic Universe*, he acknowledged overcoming a deep intellectual crisis by giving up rationalism.[20] In this second period he also argued strenuously against the first philosophic drive, but only insofar as it was taken for the whole of philosophy. He did not himself abandon it. Only in the last period of his life did he explicitly reject a unified vision as one of the two proper goals of philosophy and commit himself to the pluralistic rejection of one all-encompassing explanatory system. Even then, however, he did not totally reject the possibility of such a vision as a desirable consumation in the sense of the first of the three goals mentioned earlier, that is, poetic or mystical ecstasy. What he finally abandoned was the possibility of ever providing a rationale for such a vision. He felt a great sense of relief in being able to accept the mystical feeling of oneness with the universe — the ultimate goal of rationalism — without having to provide a rational justification for it. Philosophy would have to be satisfied, as philosophy, with a piecemeal and irreducibly pluralistic understanding of reality.

He understood realism as an injunction to remain on the phenomenal level of experience. This followed from its two premises: (1) that no single explanation could in principle exclude explanations stemming from other interests and (2) that brute facts are ultimately opaque. Despite this allegiance to realism, his project through the middle years consisted in working through philosophic problems, which precisely meant adopting the "aesthetically pleasing intellectual style...to which philosophies owe their being," namely, "the craving for a consistent completeness" (CER, 28; 115; EPH, 51). What distinguished James from avowed system builders was that he was content to lay the groundwork on which others — or himself at some later date — could erect a system true to actual experience. When he criticized system building he was criticizing such aberrations as premature closure, before all the relevant facts were known, and conceiving the boundaries of systems so narrowly that some aspects of reality were illicitly excluded.

A perfect system would account for phenomenal experiences, including their scientific correlates, as well as satisfy all our needs. He thought that systems had so far de-realized rather than corroborated our immediate experiences. The "beyond" of such an ultimate principle of belief (typically thought of by James in personal, religious terms) would mean just these crude here-and-now experiences, rather than being an alternative to them (see PP,II, 944-945. It was not until late in life that he abandoned the philosophic project as heretofore understood, leaving the second philosophical drive — securing an objective warrant for our needs — as the sole business of philosophers.

3. Overcoming the Split between Science and Metaphysics

James thought that only by carefully restructuring the domain of science could he negate its denigration of metaphysical problems as unwarranted intrusions. This explains how he could argue that psychology ought to be a strict science, despite his predilection for metaphysics before, during, and after *Principles* and his antipathy for the anti-metaphysical bias of positivist science. He clearly abhored the "mechanico-physical" scientists' assumption of "a purposeless universe, in which all the things and qualities men love, *dulcissimi mundi nomina*, are but illusions of our fancy" (PP,II, 1260). Positivism's denial of sentimental facts and relations butchers those very "aspects of phenomena which interest" human beings the most (PP,II, 1259-1260). He gave as the reason for not giving a *psychological* account of free will, for instance, the argument that science "must be constantly reminded that her purposes are not the only purposes, and that the order of uniform causation which she has use for, and is therefore right in postulating, may be enveloped in a wider order, on which she has no claims at all" (PP,II, 1179).

Since James was concerned to restrict the claims of science so that metaphysics could be taken more seriously, why did he nonetheless spend so much time, and take so much pride in, helping psychology become just such a positivist science? Hints can be found in the early articles developed in the last chapter. Positivism, like common sense, occupies "a middle ground," and in its indifference to metaphysics, it can provide a neutral phenomenal basis on which a metaphysics more in touch with human experience can be constructed. Common sense and all living thought takes the world to be objectively as experienced. It is only in reflection and dissection of such spontaneous thought that doubt enters in. In trying to reduce this reflectively generated uncertainty philosophers seek a better basis for belief. Positivism represented a refusal to question its own foundations and so could be used as a point of departure, a descriptive beginning anew, in order to exorcise the endless search for foundations.

Although commentators rightly stress James's sympathetic preference for empiricism, in the light of which his tolerance of positivism is explicable as challenging idealist absolutism, he viewed the refusal to rest in a false absolutism as but a stage in the quest for ultimate meaning. It may well be that no satisfactory explanation of being and non-being can be given, leaving mysticism as the only solace for ontologic wonder. But ontologic speculation can only view such an outcome as a defeat, however emotionally satisfying such a leap of faith might be (CER, 133ff; EPH, 62ff). In the absence of any ultimate theoretic grounding which can legitimately exercise a veto over our actions, an account of warranted belief leading to appropriate action is especially needed. The choice must be one in which a person's entire nature —"intellectual, affective, and volitional"— is exhibited (CER, 32).

It is this most characteristic Jamesian insistence on slighting none of the interests of persons in either theory or practice that makes his rejection of the possibility of excluding metaphysical considerations from the science of psychology a foregone conclusion. He says in 1895, speaking of *Principles*: "I have become convinced since publishing that book that no conventional restrictions *can* keep metaphysical and so-called epistemological inquiries out of the psychology books" (CER, 399; EPH, 88). What is difficult to understand is how he could ever have thought otherwise.

It should by now be clear that the identification of science with positivism and of metaphysics with speculative rationalism, joined with the historical circumstances surrounding the birth of psychology as a science form the womb of philosophy, led James to propose a strict separation of scientific psychology and philosophy. It should be equally obvious that this stricture did not apply either to the most lasting parts of his own psychology or to his evolving philosophy, the former not being reductively positivistic and the latter not being speculative. In the same passage in which he repudiates the "child of my genius," that is, his psychology, which was stubbornly functional in order to avoid metaphysical difficulties, he nonetheless defends the legitimacy of his offspring, which he says has been misunderstood as well as despised. At the very moment of giving it up by repudiating the false dichotomy it was based on, he says: "My intention was a good one, and a natural science infinitely more complete than the psychologies we now possess could be written without abandoning its terms" (CER, 399; EPH, 88).

But he does not methodically reflect on which terms he has in mind. In rejecting the strict separation of metaphysics and science, for instance, he does not reject their distinctiveness. With little explicit help from James, we are forced to reconstruct from his practice of it the "more complete" science of "concrete experience" that he was struggling to develop. In fact, he only abandoned the issue from the point of view of psychology as "a mere natural science" restricted to an uncritical acceptance of data, preferring to attack the same central problem — the nature of that unique manyness-in-oneness which constitutes mental states — from the critical viewpoint "of metaphysical reconstruction" (CER, 400; EPH, 88: PP,I, 141). But when he eventually returned to the problem in his metaphysics of radical empiricism, he still drew on the phenomenal findings he had established in *Principles* and elaborated in his other writings.

4. Concrete Beginnings: The Fundamental Facts of Knowing-Things-Together, Intentionality, Context, and Temporality

Principles was a sustained investigation into the conditions for the possibility "of that altogether unique kind of complexity in unity which mental states involve" (CER, 400). Disputes about the nature of the synthetic unity of consciousness divided not only the schools of philosophical psychology among themselves, but also distinguished them from empirical psychologists of various persuasions. James thought that if he could explain how states of consciousness are related and how it is that many distinct things can be grasped in a single mental state, then he could begin to dissolve the differences separating the contentious scientific and philosophical schools of thought. The solution should be sought by first establishing an unproblematic "datum," "phenomenon," or "experience," that is, a "fundamental fact of our experience" which no one would deny (CER, 373, 378; EPH, 72, 75).

James located this fundamental fact in the phenomenon of *"knowing things together"* (CER, 373; EPH, 72). The facts of the case are not in dispute. Everyone experiences the fact of knowing-things-together, for example, that sweetness and bitterness are tasted together as lemonade, that separate notes are heard as a single chord, and that a concept of a car includes all its parts, which are not first thought of one by one. It is obvious that the whole field of experience, whether conceptual or sensible, can grasp in a single moment many phenomena as one. Other explanations, such as that the mind brings things together or that various ideas somehow combine psychologically, prematurely incorporate theory before the facts are clearly described. The phenomenon under consideration is said to be that of knowing-things-together and not that of the mind combining things together.

James begins his explanation by defining what he means by 'things.' He situates himself in the first place within the idealistic tradition of Berkeley, especially as explained and further developed by Shadworth Hodgson (CER, 373ff; EPH, 72ff).[21] Things are of the same nature as thoughts are; they are that which is given to someone's experience. Even those who assume, with science, that things ultimately consist of molecules must mean that such vibrating particles would be what we would be acquainted with if a magnifying apparatus could be constructed that would be sufficiently powerful. Lacking this direct observational contact, recordable traces stand in for the presumed entities. All the sciences presuppose experiential evidence as a necessary condition for the reality of objects. 'Things,' then, mean what is given to my experience, or if not now available to me, what is given to other minds or what would be given if anyone were in a position to receive them.

Knowing-together is explicable only with reference to temporality and change. The smallest pulse of consciousness is a consciousness of passing time. The minimal feeling still has reference to the future; it involves an earlier and a later as a continuous procession. Hodgson is credited with showing that a non-temporal present moment is no datum of experience but a mental abstraction (CER, 380; EPH, 76-77).[22] The passing moment is the living moment of experience and elementary remembering consists in apprehending an earlier and a later as constituting experience. Either can be felt only on condition of feeling both together in a single apprehension.

Thought is not the static conceptualization it has traditionally been analyzed as being, but it rushes forward through its fringes, in transition toward anticipated fulfillments. This anticipation of an ideal presence which is absent in fact characterizes consciousness as such.[23] This succession of emptiness and fulfillment is the essence of the phenomenon and is found not only in sensation, but in efforts to recall and in the progress towards satisfying desire. This desire for what is not yet is originally a constituent of consciousness and shows that the scholastic faculty psychology of separate organs of volition and cognition fallaciously imposes a theoretical distinction of being on what is given in fact as a continuous, undifferentiated process.

The self-transcendency of knowledge is found inside the minimal pulse of consciousness. *"Here in the elementary datum of which both our physical and our mental worlds are built, we find included both the original of presence in absence and the prototype of that operation of knowing many things together which it is our business to discuss"* (CER, 382; EPH, 77). The past and future are already parts of the least experience that can be, even though most of these experiences are of objects perceived simultaneously and not successively. The musical chord and the glass of lemonade have already been given as examples of such knowing-together, which cannot be understood by separating the consciousness of one part from all the rest. The nature of the being-known-together of such complex facts cannot be further reduced because this unity in multiplicity is constitutive of all experience. Anything less either cannot be cognitively experienced at all or is an abnormal, privative state, such as when subjects in a laboratory are made to respond to flashing lights.

James does try, though, to give some of the conditions for the possibility of this fundamental fact. He confesses that his remarks are only preliminary attempts at a solution which still eludes him. The first condition by which one thing may be known together with another is that it take place as an event. Two or more objects come together in my field of consciousness. But the mere addition of objects is not sufficient to account for their unified apprehension; they must also be paid attention to.[24] This is the second condition. Many objects can come together and separate within a field of view, but unless they are attended to they are not grasped as a unity; mere association in time and place is insufficient.

The third condition is that "union in consciousness must be *made* by something, must be brought about" (CER, 386; EPH, 80). Four main types of theories about how the union is effected are reviewed and rejected: physiological, psychological, animistic, and transcendental. Curiously, he dismisses two with minimal arguments that will later be incorporated into his own explanation. These are that "not *object*, but *object-plus-me*, is the minimum knowable" and that it is "enough if the incoming object be related to the other objects already there.[25] To fail to appear related is to fail to be known at all" (CER, 391; EPH, 83). The conclusion reached through this cursory treatment of the conditions for the possibility of knowing-things-together is that no satisfactory resolution of these conditions has yet been demonstrated, either by himself or anyone else.

The next move is rather surprising. James recalls that in *Principles* he proposed treating psychology as a natural science, which meant eliminating from consideration the question of how we come to know things together or to know them at all. Determining the conditions for the possibility of knowing is the province of metaphysics and can be left in abeyance while the known facts are explored. It is a fundamental fact that we do know things both together and singly. Two other facts are that states of consciousness are vehicles of knowledge and that they depend on brain states. There is quite enough to do in functionally relating and expanding on these facts. Most states of mind, for instance, can be designated only by reference to the objects which they are "thoughts-of." James's intention is to develop a psychology which, though too limited to ultimately explain the facts, could at least avoid the mistakes which arise from a premature imposition of theory on data and from merely speculative solutions. Furthermore, it could provide that grounding in observed facts duly verified which has been lacking thus far in the various speculative psychologies philosophers have developed.

Instead of defending or explaining his bantling further, though, he simply gives it up (CER, 399; EPH, 88).

But he relinquishes it, not only because he cannot keep metaphysical and epistemological considerations out of scientific explanations simply by ignoring them, and therefore has to develop their precise relationship before proceeding further, but also because his intentions have been misunderstood or despised. What has been misunderstood is the radical nature of his new beginning in a philosophy of concrete experience. The "infinitely more complete" science of psychology which was begun in *Principles* consists in his radically empirical, concrete approach. That he did not, after all, abandon the project of explaining and justifying the fundamental fact of "knowing-things-together" is evidenced by its recurrence throughout his writings.

At the end of his life he was still working on the problem of "The One and the Many," that is, of how we organize or unify the multiplicity of experience both practically and cognitively. The issue still merited special attention as comprising the fifth chapter out of nine that he sketched out (SPP, 61-75). For James "the most central of all philosophic problems, central because so pregnant," was that of ordering the diversity of experience into a unity without slighting variety (PM, 64).[26]

The explication of the "fundamental fact" as the keystone to founding philosophy on a new basis should also overcome the neglect of this issue as evidenced, for instance, in Peter Hare's introduction to *Some Problems of Philosophy*. He says that James considered the problem of "the many and the one," that is, the problem of the organization of experience, as one of the fundamental doctrines of his metaphysics. But Hare then abruptly drops the topic, and — instead of demonstrating why it is fundamental — turns to the concept of novelty, which he sees as more central.[27] H. S. Thayer also overlooks the centrality of the problem of the one and the many, even though he notes that James at one time planned to write a book on it.[28] In his introduction to *Pragmatism* he introduces the topic only to demonstrate that "even the most detached and abstract of metaphysical speculations are imbued with a moral and psychological urgency by James" (PM, xxv). He limits his commentary to James's remark that knowing whether a person is a monist or a pluralist will help greatly in identifying what other positions are also held (64). Thayer criticizes this as an example of the philosophic analysis of ideas coming "uncomfortably close to resembling a diagnosis of the symptoms of a patient" (xxvi).

But this ignores the fact that James went on to explain *why* the attitude toward the one and the many reveals so much about what a person takes to be important. For James the issue was at the center of his project of reconstructing rationalism. For too long the understanding of philosophy as a quest for unity has gone unchallenged. James argued that unity is only one of the primordial drives of the intellect, the other one being a drive to become acquainted with facts, with detailed particularity (PM, 64ff). He revalued the privileging of the systematizing passion over the passion of close observation and description by approaching the issue pragmatically. What was then demonstrated was that neither interest is more valuable or more definitive of a concretely situated rationality (64-65). The centrality of the issue of the one and the many to his new beginning in philosophy was not yet fully worked out in the early writings, it is true, and Thayer may have been misled by this fact. Enough had been accomplished for us to recognize what this new terminology signifies, namely, the turn from philosophy as epistemological analysis to a reflection on what constitutes the characteristically human organization of experience.

Part Two

Interpretive Structures of Human Experience

Chapter Three

Concrete Experience and Selective Interest

> *"Our interests, our tendencies of attention, our motor impulses, the aesthetic, moral, and theoretic combinations we delight in, the extent of our power of apprehending schemes of relation, just like the elementary relations themselves, time, space, difference and similarity, and the elementary kinds of feeling, have all grown up in ways of which at present we can give no account"* (PP,II, 1280)

It is no accident that James ended his monumental work on psychology with the quoted reflection that what makes us distinctively human cannot itself be reduced to a physiological substrate, even though linked to it in significant ways worth investigating. The more we try to account for the psychological origins of our distinctive mental operations, the more we perceive "the slowly gathering twilight close in utter night" (PP,II, 1280). The list of the distinctive attributes mentioned on the last page of *Principles* provides a rough guide to some structures of human experience that he used as explanatory principles throughout his work: attention and selective interest, practical and aesthetic interests, and the creative synthesis of experienced relations.

These structures are fundamental because they are constitutive of our being in the world. They cannot be explained with reference to another order of being or level of explanation, such as their chemical components or spiritual origins, without losing their distinctiveness as experienced. They also initiate and serve as ultimate explanatory principles for more specific organizations of experience. This is a pragmatic "ultimate," however, because James took his account as being in principle replaceable or revisable if and when a more satisfactory explanation is offered which will better account for the phenomenal findings.

It has usually been assumed that questions of method in James refer to the pragmatic method. But the question has been reopened, primarily by those interested in his influence on the phenomenology of Edmund Husserl.[1] However, these writers presuppose a Husselrian model of phenomenology and investigate James's writings (usually restricted to *Principles*) insofar as they anticipate or fail to sufficiently develop the 'proper' phenomenological model. By contrast, I am trying to reconstruct James's methodology of concrete experience insofar as it structures the whole range of his investigations and on its own terms. Rather than looking over my shoulder to see how it measures up to later models of phenomenology, I am concerned to recover its original formulation and develop it further so that its strengths and weaknesses as an historically earlier and alternative phenomenological paradigm can become available for contemporary assessment. It is no longer possible to claim that the interpretive structures he employed are limited to what has been designated as the pragmatic method. Moreover, these structures, along with their presuppositions, must first be explained before the pragmatic method itself can be properly understood.

According to Peter H. Hare and Chandana Chakrabarti, James was an anti-phenomenalist.[2] In this chapter I argue, to the contrary, that James deliberately developed a concrete analysis of experience to overcome the nihilist paralysis of action and the skeptical dissolution of certain knowledge brought on by the challenge of scientific positivism. I will specifically show that he intentionally elaborated a description of the human being active in the world, which he characterized as concrete experience. This is best categorized as a variant of phenomenological analysis for three reasons. First, James argued that philosophical analysis should begin by identifying the facts of experience, which are taken to be the structures of our inter-active appropriation of the world. Experience is constituted, not passively received. Secondly, experience is phenomenal, that is, it deals with what perceptually appears. As has been shown in the first two chapters, he deliberately deferred the question of whether his phenomenal findings corresponded to being. Thirdly, he tied the success of his project to the possibility of describing, without any presuppositions, the pre-reflective moment of experience.

But his concrete analysis is also hermeneutical because of the priority of selective interest in his dealings with phenomenal findings. Because nothing can be described before it has been pre-selected as an object of investigation, there can be no determination of fact without identifying the subjective interests operative. Descriptions are always made from a specific point of view and incorporate values. James therefore more often talks about "interpretation" than about "disclosure." Analogously to Nietzschean genealogical analysis, he frequently investigates issues by identifying the interests which are guiding particular claims. But this is only a preliminary step. His own purpose is to determine the best course of action in any given case, and so he develops the pragmatic method. He also formalizes his methodological procedure in his metaphysics of radical empiricism. His philosophy can therefore be uniquely designated as a hermeneutical, radically empiricistic, pragmatic phenomenology!

I prefer to stick closer to James's own terminology in an effort to emphasize his historical status as one of the earliest, most creative, and suggestive rather than systematic, inventors of a new way of philosophizing. It is hoped that others will continue with the next stage of ordering it into a consistent system. In this chapter I seek only to establish his intention of doing something similar to what we now call phenomenological analysis, but for which he uses many phrases. In one section alone of *Pragmatism*, for instance, he uses "concrete phenomenal reality," "concrete processes," "concrete reasons," "jungle of concrete expediencies," and "concretes of experience," besides other phrases such as "our experience," "our world," and "experienceable reality" (PM, 95-113).[3] For the sake of simplicity and to avoid identifying his position with any particular later version of phenomenology, I will most often use the term 'concrete analysis.' In this chapter I will sketch out a few of the constituent features of his new approach, focusing on the principle of selective interest. The other distinguishing features of his concrete analysis of the human condition will be developed in subsequent chapters.

1. A Concrete Methodology

James consistently argued that philosophizing must begin in concrete experience, where every human being's practical life begins. Very early in his career he was attracted to the philosophy of Shadworth Hodgson and his insistence that in all reflection on experience "we are brought back once again to the *same practical common-sense* of our starting point, the pre-philosophic attitude with which we originally confront the visible world."[4] In *Principles* he called his own procedure a search for "a satisfactory simplification of the concrete facts" (PP,1, 16). Later, in 1908, in reflecting on the persistent misinterpretations of pragmatism by its critics, James realized that "concreteness as radical as ours is not so obvious. The whole originality of pragmatism, the whole point of it, is its use of the concrete way of seeing" (MT, 115-116).[5]

The cluster of meanings James attached to common sense overlap with those of concrete experience, and it is not always possible to disentangle the two. However, common sense is more often used to refer to the earliest and most widespread classifications of everyday experience, while this lived experience itself is referred to as concrete experience. The importance of both for James was that they are accessible to everyone, educated or not, and can therefore serve as an evidential base independently of reflectively generated metaphysical systems. To distinguish where he did not, although he called his own reflections on everyday experience simply describing experiential facts, this reflective analysis can less ambiguously be called his concrete analysis of the structures of lived experience. Common sense conceptual and linguistic formulations are closer to concrete or lived experience than are scientific concepts and categories, which can therefore be criticized from the standpoint of common sense. These common sense organizations of experience, in turn, can also be criticized from the perspective of James's own concretely derived structures of lived experience.

Unlike the appeal to concrete experience, the importance of selective interest to Jamesian philosophy has long been recognized. Commentators have followed Perry in singling out "the essentially active and interested character of the human mind" as the "one germinal idea from which his whole thought grew" (CER, ix). But the precise way it forces a radical reconstruction of our beliefs about reality, truth, metaphysics, and ethics — in short, the whole philosophical "machine shop"— has not been systematically developed. Also not recognized is the full import of the fact that this fundamental principle of selective interest is dialectically balanced by an equally fundamental principle that "the inmost nature of the reality is congenial to *powers* which you possess" (WB, 73).

This congeniality means that we will not be satisfied with any explanation of reality which denies that we have any power of influencing it. It also means that reality can be clearly and accurately described. This belief in a "pure" or neutral description, which James took to be a necessary prerequisite for refuting skepticism, is also a cornerstone of his thought. This sets up the mostly unresolved tension, evident throughout James's writings, between the disruptive, creative force of selective interest and the conserving, realist insistence on actual experiences as a new beginning which will drive post-Hegelian idealism from the scene.[6] I think that it is impossible to completely eliminate from the human condition this tension between what is and what is imposed. But the relationship between description and interpretation can be stated with less contradiction by exposing and eliminating the assumptions which prevented James from fully grasping the radical nature of his own analysis. The contextual interpretation of the texts is therefore guided by what I consider to be the most promising reconstructive strategies.

As can be gathered from James's insistence on concrete experience, the first methodological principle is to "take reality bodily and integrally" into philosophy "in exactly the perceptual shape in which it comes" (SPP, 53). The rational explanations of philosophy, which privilege the articulate, are still rooted in the pre-reflective world of experience. The full possession of reality is to be found only in the whole of immediate sensible experience. Concrete experience exhibits the deeper features of reality, including cause, continuity, self, substance, activity, time, novelty, and freedom (54). The limited world of coherent discourse can avoid sterility only by acknowledging its dependence on "the aboriginal flow of feeling" of which "there is always much-at-once" (53). Since we cannot wade through all future time nor share the perspectives of numberless perceivers, we must substitute conceptual systems in order to grasp experience beyond the passing moment.

James's repeated urgings for "the re-instatement of the vague to its proper place in our mental life" signals a new beginning in the concrete situation (PP,I, 246).[7] Philosophical reflection should begin with a careful description of aspects of our experience which have hitherto been ignored. In concentrating too narrowly on the objects of consciousness philosophers have ignored the horizon or fringe without which objects could not be identified as such. This horizon is not itself the content of experience but part of what sets it up. But what Kant, and later Heidegger, called the transcendental, James was determined to locate within an enlarged understanding of experience. He thought that otherwise he could not avoid the accusation that the horizon was merely a free-floating construction, as the idealist categories always appeared to be to empiricists.

Our "feelings of tendency" comprise one of the most important of these traditionally ignored and therefore unnamed states or qualities of states which James wanted to restore to their cognitive function (PP,I, 240-262). One example of such a feeling of tendency is the sense of direction different exhortations arouse in us, even when minimally expressed. We feel such differences between the command, "Wait!," and the command, "Look!," for instance. Other examples are the subtle differences felt when we are searching for different forgotten words and the strange difference between an experience tasted for the first time and when once it has become familiar.

Human speech is a fertile source of examples because so much of it consists in signs of direction which we can discriminate even though unaccompanied by any definite sensorial image. The intention of saying a thing before it is said is one example of these rapid, but nonetheless experienced, "premonitory perspective views of schemes of thought not yet articulate" (PP,I, 245). James wanted to restore feelings of tendency to their proper role in our mental life. They are often ignored because in their first expression they operate without being reflectively articulated. In his radical and sweeping reform of traditional psychology the priority of discrete sensations is replaced with the contextuality of the ongoing stream of consciousness. What has traditionally been designated a discrete image is in actuality a part of a horizon or scheme of relations embodying a sense of direction. This premonitory field of view of consciousness comprises a "halo of felt relations" which varies in extent depending on our mental freshness or fatigue (247).

This psychic overtone or fringe "is part of the *object cognized*, — substantive *qualities* and *things* appearing to the mind in a *fringe of relations*. Some parts — the transitive parts — of our stream of thought cognize the relations rather than the things; but both the transitive and the substantive parts form one continuous stream, with no discrete 'sensations' in it" (PP,I, 249, n19). In considering the cognitive function of different states of mind, those of mere acquaintance can be distinguished from knowledges-about according to the presence or absence of such psychic fringes or overtones. "Knowledge *about* a thing is knowledge of its relations. Acquaintance with it is limitation to the bare impression which it makes" (250). But even in bare acquaintance, there is still a vague awareness of a fringe of unarticulated affinities. When these are reflected upon, brought to consciousness, and articulated, then such unreflective awareness becomes an explicit knowledge of objects. The whole process, however, is cognitive in the broadest sense.

Voluntary thinking is bounded by some topic or subject about which it revolves. This topic can be a problem or gap we want to fill or it can be a "mood of interest." It functions both by inciting an active searching and by guiding the search by accepting or rejecting trains of thought, images, or phrases insofar as their fringe of relations contains affinities with the topic. This relation of harmony or discord to our topic of thought is constantly felt in the fringe. Any thought is acceptable as long as it satisfies this feeling of affinity. The meaning or topic of thought is its conclusion, that is, what stands out from the other aspects of the stream by the particular interest attaching to it. The most important element, therefore, of psychic fringes, is "the mere feeling of harmony or discord, of a right or wrong direction in the thought" (PP,I, 251). Thought itself is sensibly continuous and unified in contrast to the apparent discreteness of the words and images it uses. "Between all their substantive elements there is 'transitive' consciousness, and the words and images are 'fringed,' and not as discrete as to a careless view they seem" (262).

Another interpretive structure of our concrete situation in the world is that thought appears to deal with objects independent of itself. This is why we call it cognitive. We cannot simply assume, as absolute idealists do, that Absolute Thought is identical with its objects and that our knowing is guaranteed by this relationship. Our assumption that objects exist in the world and not just in relation to us must be based on the evidence available to us. The evidence we use is that others make the same judgments about objects of their thought as we do; for example, both a psychologist and her patient point to the same portion of a drawing and identify it as a kitten. "*Sameness* in a multiplicity of objective appearances is thus the basis of our belief in realities outside of thought" (PP,I, 262). Our habitual adult state of mind includes this stage of reflection by which we make repeated judgments of sameness and thus come to dissociate objects in an environment. But in the primordial state of consciousness no opposition is set up between self and objects. We simply exist out there with the objects of our thought. James distinguishes what he means by the "object of thought" from its usual meaning of referring to an individual subject of existence. By the object of thought he means "its entire content or deliverance, neither more nor less" (PP,I, 265). It is a symptom of vicious intellectualism to take out a substantive kernel from its whole context and refer to that fractured part as alone the proper object. "The object of every thought, then, is neither more nor less than all that the thought thinks, exactly as the thought thinks it," and *"however complex the object may be, the thought of it is one undivided state of consciousness"* (266). The structure of the unit of thought is analogous to that of sensation. The discreteness of sense data is constructed after the fact by discriminative analysis. Sensations are experienced as a multiplicity bounded by a totality. The unit of thought, as a unified, temporal process, is more akin to the semantic unit of the sentence than to that of a single word or idea. "The total idea may be and usually is present not only before and after the phrase has been spoken, but also whilst each separate word is uttered" (271).

2. Selective Interest as a Concrete Structure of Experience

> *"Selection is the very keel on which our mental ship is built"* *(PP,I, 640).*

James demonstrates that the focalized attention he thematizes as selective interest is a constituent aspect of the human organization of experience. The thesis of the selectivity of consciousness is an expression on the cognitive level of the active character of the organism in an environment, which manifests itself in varying degrees from the simplest organic response to incoming stimuli to the most considered, complex rearrangement of one's surroundings. On the physiological level selective interest is explained as the modification of the reflex arc theory to accommodate experimental evidence of the selective nature of responses. On the level of biological theory Spencer's thesis that humans, like other organisms, passively mirror the environment for the sole purpose of survival is refuted and replaced by the thesis that humans actively reorganize their environment to satisfy many more subjective needs than mere survival.

This anti-Spencerian position is argued by combining Darwinian evolutionary theses with idealist principles. The Darwinian theses are that (genetically) transmissible changes preceded environmental pressures and that the evident range of individual variation beyond what is needed for immediate utility increases the chances that some one or other of them will be found adaptive to changed conditions. Moreover, this immense variety within species contradicts the Aristotelian claim of conceptually distinct classes of species based on essential characteristics and supports a functional understanding of species as groupings based on family resemblances. These scientific findings are used to defend the idealist insistence on the unique value of individuals, the spontaneity of the moral sense, and freedom as the defining characteristic of humans.[8]

Psychological investigations, for instance, demonstrate that spontaneity operates on both the level of sensation and of thought. The idealist philosophical tradition already argued for the spontaneity of human cognition and volition, but still believed both in an extrinsic guiding source, for example, Hegel's *Weltgeist* or the romantic personification of the Kantian Ego, and that there is an absolutely true version of reality that it is our rational duty to recognize and articulate systematically. The empiricist tradition also recognized human spontaneity. Nonetheless, it is more insistent that an accurate — because passive — transcription of reality, beginning at the level of the individual sense datum, must precede and ground complexes of associated sense data and theoretical constructions. James's concrete demonstration of selective interest provides a coherent, philosophical explanation of human spontaneity. He incorporates laboratory experimental evidence into his concrete analysis and joins it with the philosophical arguments supporting spontaneity found in both traditions.

Given the fact that humans are characterized by a spontaneous organization of experience to suit our needs, what accounts for these needs? James argues that since their spontaneity is assumed in accounting for all other organizations of experience, they themselves cannot be the result of any previous cause. He therefore calls them the ultimate a priori factor in experience.[9] The model he has in mind is that of the Darwinian theory of spontaneous variation as providing a necessary precondition both for speciation and survival. The relevant point of comparison is that once they have occurred, such spontaneous variations can be used to account for other events, but they themselves cannot be fully accounted for by reference to earlier events (WB, 167ff). Their own genesis was still inexplicable in James's time, since they had not yet been related to genes, the modern synthesis of genetic theory being still some way off in the future. Even today, enough randomness remains at the level of cell division to prevent inerrant prediction. And certainly we are no closer to determining why such changes, even if explicable in terms of cause and effect at their own level of genetic interaction, should have occurred just when needed to permit survival (or not occurred and thus extinction of some species followed) under new conditions generated at the macro-level of the wider environment.

The pre-condition for meaning is the perceptual flux, which, as such, "*means* nothing, and is but what it immediately is" (SPP, 32). It is always a "much-at-once," since the data from the senses enter into consciousness in an unbroken unity, characterized in the often quoted words of James as a "big blooming buzzing confusion."[10] Given this profligate abundance of the sensible flux of experience, the need for selective interest is obvious: "out of this aboriginal sensible muchness attention carves out objects." This ordering of experience is not according to a single rational model, as Kant held, but "different universes of thought thus arise, with specific sorts of relation among their ingredients. The world of common sense 'things'; the world of material tasks to be done; the mathematical world of pure forms; the world of ethical propositions; the worlds of logic, of music, etc." are constructed to organize the chaos to suit our purposes (33-34). Although experience begins with, and depends on, the flux of experience, for a complete knowledge of fact both sense and intellect are necessary. They "impregnate and fertilize each other" and it is possible only schematically to disentangle the contributions of intellect from those of sense (34).[II]

Since concepts are secondary and ministerial forms of being, the particular consequences that follow from their use "are the only criterion of a concept's meaning, and the only test of its truth" (SPP, 45, 38). This functional understanding of the nature of concepts is expressed in the pragmatic method, which finds the meaning of a concept, "if not in some sensible particular which it directly designates, then in some particular difference in the course of human experience which its being true will make" (37). A careful examination of the way he arrives at this conclusion shows that the determination of "concrete fact" and of "conduct consequent upon the fact" should not be narrowly construed as an empiricist appeal to sense data or to behaviorist analyses. It requires an understanding of what James calls "the living facts of human nature." To develop in more detail the thesis of selective interest, we must turn from *Some Problems in Philosophy*, the last book James wrote, to *Principles*, the book that first established his reputation as an original thinker.

James analyzes "selective interest" into two aspects: attention and interests. Attention is defined as "the taking possession by the mind, in clear and vivid form, of one out of what seem several simultaneously possible objects or trains of thought. Focalization, concentration, of consciousness are of its essence" (PP,I, 381–382). We attend to aspects of the perceptual or conceptual flux insofar as we are interested in them: "The things to which we attend are said to *interest* us. Our interest in them is supposed to be the *cause* of our attending" (393). The two interests which James finds to be overriding and which he methodically employs to explain many other phenomena are the "aesthetic" and the "practical." These fundamental interests are both so central to James's concrete analysis and so neglected in the secondary literature, that they are taken up in a separate chapter (chapter 5).

Attention can be directed either to objects of sense or to ideal or represented objects, either immediate or derived. "The *conditio sine qua non* of sustained attention to a given topic of thought is that we should roll it over and over incessantly and consider different aspects and relations of it in turn" (PP,I, 400). Not everyone can sustain such attention to the same degree, and it is a mark of originality to be able to do so. Those who excel in this ability to bring out many varied aspects of something are often called geniuses, and this is so whether they excel in the sciences or the arts. They are attentive because of their special strengths in sustaining attention, and not the other way around. The practical and theoretical forms of life characteristic of whole species, as well as of lesser social groupings and of individuals, are evidence of the selections habitually attended to.

Individuals inhabit worlds partially of their own making because "each of us literally *chooses*, by his ways of attending to things, what sort of a universe he shall appear to himself to inhabit" (PP,I, 401). A pluralism of points of view is thus unavoidable, but its tendency towards chaos is mitigated by counterbalancing forces. For the most part we see only what we have already been taught to discover. Except for those few gifted scientific and artistic visionaries who renew the available social organizations of experience, we see only what we pre-perceive. If we lost the labels which we have picked up since infancy, we would be intellectually lost in the world. This position is remarkably similar to the one developed by Nietzsche in *The Gay Science*, who also argues that "what things *are called* is incomparably more important than what they are. The reputation, name, and appearance, the usual measure and weight of a thing, what it counts for — originally almost always wrong and arbitrary, thrown over things like a dress and altogether foreign to their nature and even to their skin — all this grows from generation unto generation, merely because people believe in it, until it gradually grows to be part of the thing and turns into its very body."[12]

3. Selective Interest as Organizing Principle of *The Principles of Psychology*

The thesis that attention represents a force that is voluntary, and not merely a response to external stimuli, is absolutely central to Jamesian philosophy. *Principles*, for instance, is largely a sustained argument, drawing on all the psychological experimental evidence available, to prove this claim: "Now the study of the phenomena of consciousness which we shall make throughout the rest of this book will show us that consciousness is at all times primarily a *selecting agency* (PP,I, 142). Furthermore, directive attention forms "the nucleus of our inner self," so much so, that "volition is nothing but attention" (PP,I, 423-424). As Kant had pointed out, an autonomy which defies the usual order of nature entails a source of origination not wholly accounted for as a mere effect of outward circumstance. Such a principle of noumenal activity which, according to James, can be argued for even on the scientific level, is a metaphysical claim worth pursuing with all the means at our disposal. "It is in fact the pivotal question of metaphysics, the very hinge on which our picture of the world shall swing from materialism, fatalism, monism, towards spiritualism, freedom, pluralism,—or else the other way" (424).

The thesis of selective interest provides the structural framework for *Principles* and is developed in detail in chapters 1-2, 9, and 11 to 14 of the first volume and chapters 17, 19, 21-22, 26, and 28 of the second volume. In regard to the chapters on the physiology, psychology, and epistemology of sensation, for instance, the demonstration of the role of selectivity provides the basis for arguing against the isolated monadic sense data theories of British empiricism and Comtian positivism and for a contextual explanation. It is impossible in the space available to give a comprehensive analysis of such a pervasive theme, so I will restrict myself to tracing the emergence of order out of chaos as it relates to the reformulation of the classic philosophical triad of sensation, perception, and conception into a concrete analysis of lived experience. No assumption is being made of a primordial chaos. It cannot be emphasized too strongly that philosophical reflection always begins in a fully constituted world of experience and then proceeds by asking for an accounting of some aspect that is found puzzling. The analysis of selective interest provides an indispensable background for understanding many other theses, including James's theories of knowledge and truth, metaphysics of pure experience, and his reconstruction of realism.

James criticizes Humean sense data epistemology throughout *Principles*, but is most explicit in chapter 9, called "The Stream of Thought." This pivotal chapter of the first volume was already largely written and published in 1884 as "On Some Omissions of Introspective Psychology," and can be seen as the core around which his psychology is organized. He cannot begin, as Hume did, with simple impressions and construct the higher levels of consciousness out of them for the simple reason that they do not exist as experiential data but as theoretical constructs. James undermines sense data theories from within the guidelines set up by the empiricists themselves. Like them, he argues that all claims must be experientially grounded. But what these experiential findings disclose is that "no one ever had a simple sensation by itself. Consciousness, from our natal day, is of a teeming multiplicity of objects and relations, and what we call simple sensations are results of discriminative attention, pushed often to a very high degree" (PP,I, 219).

The psychological science of his day had accepted the theory of ideas according to which thoughts were explainable as variations in the combination of simpler elements of consciousness. These unchangeable mental atoms were called by Locke "simple ideas" or "sensations." The permanence of these simplest units seems true phenomenally, since we usually seem to receive the same sensations from the same objects; for example, a red apple appears to have the same shade of red from moment to moment. But there is no experimental proof that we ever receive the same bodily sensation twice. What we do experience is the same object, the same quality of red or species of pain. We use the incoming sensations "as stepping-stones to pass over to the recognition for the realities whose presence they reveal" (PP,I, 225). We ignore, for instance, the many colors of grass seen through a window that an impressionist painter would carefully distinguish, and see merely green grass. "What appeals to our attention far more than the absolute quality or quantity of a given sensation is its *ratio* to whatever other sensations we may have at the same time" (226). By ignoring minute differences we can perceive the same object over and over, but not the same sensation. Simple ideas of sensation are not only not immutable, they are not even units of thought, since they do not come to us pure and single, but already combined into relational things.

It is even more obvious that states of mind are never precisely the same. Incoming stimuli are received from a somewhat different angle or in different relations from their first appearance. The new thought is "the thought of it-in-those-relations, a thought suffused with the consciousness of all that dim context" (PP,I, 227). We are aware of this in returning to places and people we formerly thought fascinating when we find that they no longer seem so. But this is as true of the imperceptible transitions from moment to moment as it is of the more obvious disjunctions. "Experience is remoulding [sic.] us every moment, and our mental reaction on every given thing is really a resultant of our experience of the whole world up to that date" (228). The atomistic view of unchanging simple ideas is shown to be mythological when once "this concrete and total manner or regarding the mind's changes" is adopted (229).

Two of the three distinctive ways James uses the notion of a "totality" are evident in the preceding paragraph. His explanations become less ambiguous when these meanings are clearly distinguished.

All three refer to a bounded multiplicity. One of the two preceding meanings is that of the "empirical totality," or "the whole world" as an interrelated system, encompassing all that exists in the entire universe. The other is that of the "phenomenal totality," or "thought suffused with the consciousness of all that dim context." This refers to all that structures and is partially available to — but only at the fringes of awareness — any one person's experience at any given time. The third meaning of totality, often also called the "Absolute," is the "ideal totality," which refers either to a comprehensive explanatory system or to the Absolute Being's knowledge of all that is.[13] The phrase, "concrete and total manner of regarding the mind's changes," refers to the phenomenal totality. Although only the phenomenal totality is experientially available to us, it can be analyzed only reflectively and not as it occurs. We can experience only part of the empirical totality, but this fact should not be construed as providing grounds for skeptically denying its existence. James seems to take the empirical totality for granted as a necessary condition of what we do experience.

Before his third crisis James held to the necessity of positing an ideal totality as an explanatory postulate or regulative idea. He was ambiguous as to the possibility of an ideal totality in the sense of an Absolute Being's omniscience. Although he granted the fact that belief in such an Absolute omniscience was a live option for certain temperaments, he consistently denied its explanatory power for finite human understanding. He explicitly rejected such omniscience as a defensible aspect of the ideal totality after the third crisis, but then anthropomorphized the kingdom of ideal ends as one of living, super-sensible consciousnesses. The notion of an empirical totality survived as an assumption of his unreconstructed realism. As always, it was accessible only in diminished form, as a mosaic constructed out of partial understandings. He retained throughout his writings and increasingly emphasized the notion of the phenomenal totality. His explanation of this horizon within which cognition takes place remains his most lasting contribution.

The "last peculiarity of consciousness to which attention is to be drawn" is that "*it is always interested more in one part of its object than in another, and welcomes and rejects, or chooses, all the while it thinks*" (PP,I, 273). The phenomenon of selective attention is well known as an example of this choosing activity, but accentuation and emphasis are also present in every perception. Thought of empirical objects depends on our experiences, and these in turn depend on our habits of attention. What is not noticed is not part of our experience. A trained entomologist can distinctly identify many insects which for the lay person is simply an undifferentiated swarm. Someone can swear to never having seen a particular beetle, even while swatting one away. "We actually *ignore* most of the things before us" (273). Since we are always more interested in some aspect of an object rather than another, thinking involves choice. Choice is broadly construed to include habitual and emotional selectivity as well as deliberate determinations. Every perception we have includes accentuation and emphasis. We cannot disperse our attention indifferently over all present impressions and will turn even the most regular repetition of sounds into a pattern by accenting and grouping them.

To start with, our senses are organs of selection. "Out of the infinite chaos of movements, of which physics teaches us that the outer world consists, each sense-organ picks out those which fall within certain limits of velocity" (PP,I, 273). Objects neither elicit their own eclipse nor coerce their own accentuation by conscious organisms. Physiological and psychological constraints on the part of the subject pick out what will be perceived as an object. The objective world for us is only that part of the world to which we respond. "Out of what is in itself an undistinguishable, swarming *continuum*, devoid of distinction or emphasis, our senses make for us, by attending to this motion and ignoring that, a world full of contrasts, of sharp accents, of abrupt changes, of picturesque light and shade" (274). James points out that Helmholtz demonstrates in his "work on Optics" that things differentially attract our attention according to our predispositions.[14] For instance, we notice a car reflecting light but not the retinal activity that accompanies it. But James carries the analysis further by questioning the ground of such objectifications. What are 'things,' as such? "Nothing, as we shall abundantly see, but special groups of sensible qualities, which happen practically or aesthetically to interest us, to which we therefore give substantive names, and which we exalt to this exclusive status of independence and dignity" (274).

Having chosen some out of many sensations to notice, the mind again selects, choosing certain ones as definitive of the object in question and relegating the rest to mere appearances, modified by the present conditions. We consider a table top to be truly rectangular and any other shape as only a distortion produced by a perspectival view. Thus perception involves a double choice. Out of all sensations encountered, we notice ones which stand in for other, absent ones, and we privilege some of these sensations as alone signifying the objective reality.

Selectivity thus operates both on the physiological and conscious level (See PP,I, 549). In chapter 14 of *Principles* on "Association," it is argued that there are "mechanical" conditions on which thought depends and which determine the order of presentation of material for comparisons, selections and decisions (521). The historic doctrine of psychological association derived from Locke and continued by later Continental psychologists erroneously assumes that thoughts compound themselves out of immutable simple ideas. These mythological entities were already discredited by James in chapters 6 and 9 and he instead argues that objects, not ideas, are associated. Association is caused in the first place by brain processes. Descartes and Locke had already explained that the psychological law of association of objects thought of is "an effect, within the mind, of the physical fact that nerve-currents propagate themselves easiest through those tracts of conduction which have been already most in use" (531). But in the ordinary spontaneous flow of thoughts every past experience does not equally determine what the next thought will be. "Just as in the original sensible experience our attention focalized itself upon a few of the impressions of the scene before us, so here in the reproduction of those impressions an equal partiality is shown, and some items are emphasized above the rest" (539). Physiologically, this "law of interest" means that some brain-processes are more powerful than others in influencing subsequent processes, while subjectively it can be said that these more powerful associations are those that appeal most to our interests.

There are no 'things,' therefore, apart from my interest. This should not be confused with the idealist claim that my interests create objects *ex nihilo*. The phenomenological character of James's concrete analysis must be insisted upon to avoid such an accusation. He redirects our reflective analysis from the units which can be abstracted from experience to the underlying experience presupposed in any such reflections; namely, to the concrete situation of the interaction of the individual within the world. He raises the question of accounting for such facts as that out of the multiplicity of all that is present to the child, she reaches out and touches a toy car. Why is this an object for her and not, say, the window? This, in turn, leads to further questions about how the totality of all that is present in any given situation becomes grasped as objects-for-us. The notion of an object-in-itself and not just for us on which realists always insist becomes, for the reflective analysis of the concrete situation, the question of how it is that such experiences of objects-for-us get reflected on and analyzed out as objects-in-themselves. This derivative level of the reflective abstraction of the notion of things-in-themselves should not be taken for the primary level of experience nor confused with the fundamental concrete experience on which it is parasitic.

Through selection the mind connects objects not only empirically, but rationally. The chapters in the first volume of *Principles* on "Attention," "Conception," "Discrimination and Comparison," "Association," and in the second volume on "Reasoning" and "Necessary Truths and the Effects of Experience" explain reasoning as the ability of the mind to break up the totality of phenomena into parts and pick out the best ones to lead to a desired conclusion. Aesthetics and ethics also demonstrate that consciousness consists in a selectivity out of many possibilities and the suppression of the others. The aim of selection differentiates these subject areas. In aesthetics the work of art envisioned guides the election and elimination of colors and shapes, while in ethics the quality of the moral act depends wholly on what course of action is chosen out of several equally possible. Acts are defined as ethical only insofar as they exhibit an ultimate choice out of various coercive interests. Decisions about what to do are bounded by this ultimate choice of which out of equally possible future characters I have determined to be mine. Therefore, ethics is not defined by codes of conduct or discrimination of acts into moral or immoral, but by the choice of the sort of person I will become.

Rational choices are thus only the most self-conscious ones out of many that precede it on various levels. Like artists, we manipulate experience to serve our needs and desires. But our choices are not simply spontaneous upwellings of unfathomable idiosyncrasy. Even choices which differ from person to person are, within each one's personal history, the result of earlier choices that form habitual patterns, and are themselves shaped by the processes of socialization. James still distinguished in *Principles* between the real world as science conceives it, which has become in the modern world the ultimate arbiter of reality, and the individual phenomenal world of everyday life: "But all the while the world *we* feel and live in will be that which our ancestors and we, by slowly cumulative strokes of choice, have extricated out of this, like sculptors, by simply rejecting certain portions of the given stuff" (PP,I, 277). Not until the final crisis will James directly, rather than by implication, confront scientific rationalism with the radical consequences of his new beginning in philosophy.

We still largely share a common world. Despite our various interests in different portions of it, we select in much the same way for accentuation and preference or subordination and dislike. Typically, why this is so does not arouse James's interest. Although he is developing a rich concrete analysis of the structures of being human and uses this analysis to construct exemplary patterns, he does not fully characterize these patterns as such or use them to solve what otherwise appear as unrelated puzzles. His interest is drawn instead to the "fundamental psychological fact" that each of us invests our own individual person with ultimate significance and can never feel or value other persons exactly as we do ourselves (PP,I, 278).

The solipsism of the stream of consciousness, that is, that my consciousness never partakes of yours, was for James a life-long obstacle to resolving the issue of how we nonetheless share a common world. Since my consciousness of the world is never yours, I can never be absolutely sure that the world you are experiencing and the one I am experiencing are one and the same. He had no doubt that we believe them to be so and act on this belief and, as we shall see, even provided carefully worked out explanations of how this comes to pass and how we can verify the fact. But until his third crisis, he still hoped for a philosophical proof that would transform this pragmatic accommodation into a certainty. Even then, he did not relinquish his drive for certainty but assuaged it by taking the "moral holiday" of believing in the pan-psychic doctrine of the confluence of minds, both human and more than human. Meanwhile, I will show that he had already provided a strong basis for proving that we share a common world without making such a leap of faith. This demonstration takes its cue from his own explanation of the demand for absolute certainty as an excessive reliance on just one drive constitutive of our ability to organize our experiences rationally.

What is 'given' at the level of sensation is 'taken' congruent with the physiology, psychology, and rationality of the human organism. The active rather than passive reception of stimuli dissolves the old philosophical dilemma of whether we receive incoming sense data as they 'really' are or whether we recreate them according to a rational schema. James defended both the veracity of our sensuous contact with reality and the creativity apparent in the many worlds we make out of that contact.[15]

4. Selective Interest Developed in Other Texts

A presupposition of the argument for selective interest is that perceptual focusing and its translation into the conceptual order is always for the sake of some subjective interest because what is presented to consciousness is not an already ordered world of objects but a chaos of incommensurable relations (WB, 95). In *Some Problems of Philosophy* James assumed that a primordial experience must be presupposed in order to account for the selectivity of consciousness

(SPP, 32). He set up a thought experiment, suggesting that if his readers could succeed in abstracting from all conceptual ordering of experience and lapse back into the flux of sensible experience, they would find a "big blooming buzzing confusion" which exhibits the characteristics of over-abundance, a "much-at-onceness." Out of this aboriginal overflow of immediate experience attention carves out objects and names and classifies them for posterity; for example, constellations, beaches, bushes, day and night.

In *The Will to Believe* he appealed to an actual simultaneity of the totality of all beings and events as literally beyond the capacity of anyone to comprehend. A cross-section of all existence at any one moment of time is the real world and no one has access to this order as simply given. The variety of organizing schemas that will take into account even some of these myriad goings-on is limited only by our imaginations. As a matter of fact no rational bond is evident among the millions of disjointed events, such as of a baby sneezing, a Canadian widow committing suicide, a religious conviction, and the price of cheese in Denmark, that would constitute for us a world. The sum of experiences available to us at any one moment is chaotic and their own order, whatever it is, is so foreign to our subjective interests that we would be hard pressed even to recognize it.

We cannot simply reflect the actual order of events, such as the exact configuration of dust particles dancing in a sunbeam through which I am looking at a plane crash. "We have to break that order altogether — and by picking out from it the items which concern us, and connecting them with others far away, which we say 'belong' with them, we are able to make out definite threads of sequence and tendency; to foresee particular liabilities and get ready for them; and to enjoy simplicity and harmony in place of what was chaos" (WB, 95). In fact, the condition for maintaining sanity is that most of what is going on be ignored. If I am attending to the sounds in my own inner ear and other peripheral sights and sounds, for instance, I will not be able to carry on a conversation.

We do not take in all that is available to us, but we break it into meaningful units and react on these groupings and ignore the rest as though they did not exist. We discover relations never given to sense at all, such as mathematical relations and law-like behaviors, and treat them as though they revealed the essence of the situation. "Essential these relations are, but only *for our purpose*, the other relations being just as real and present as they; and our purpose is to *conceive simply* and to *foresee* (WB, 96). Simplicity and foresight are subjective ends, ones definitive of science, but to which nature answers. Nature lends itself to remodeling according "to many of our aesthetic, to many of our practical purposes or ends" (96).

If nature were understood in the Kantian sense of the rational laws which order phenomenal experience, then the plasticity of nature could be accounted for, but James presupposed the empiricist understanding of nature as consisting of existent realities. Consequently, he could never satisfactorily explain the relationship of such realities to phenomena. His concrete accounts, which drew on both Berkeleyan and post-Hegelian idealism (Royce, for example, pointed out his affinities with Fichte), do not mesh well with his empiricist realism. He acknowledged the unsatisfactory state of affairs by calling the responsiveness of nature to our subjective purposes "the miracle of miracles, a miracle not yet exhaustively cleared up by any philosophy" (WB, 96).

In *The Pluralistic Universe* he appealed to process as the evidential basis in reality for the need for the selectivity of consciousness. The structures of the flux of experience were already developed in *Principles*, but he always identified them with the subjective side of experience. This kept him from arguing that the structures of (subjective) experience were also the structures of (objective) reality. But his metaphysics of radical empiricism can be interpreted as a demonstration that the traditional distinction between subjective and objective is only functional. His familiar formula that experience is as experienced, a motto taken from Berkeleyan idealism, could then be justified without denying that something always escapes interpretation.

He could then consistently assert both that experience is receptive inasmuch as it does not create the existence or resistances of the facts it encounters, but it is also spontaneous inasmuch as such data do not enter into experience 'bare,' but only according to the predispositions of the one experiencing. Like nineteenth century romantics, he differed from Kant in denying the universal character of such organizations of experience, arguing instead that each person was a unique organizing center, but unlike the romantics, he gave a concrete description of the structures of experience which have evolved over time.[16] This historicist and functionalist explanation can account for the legitimate demands of both subjectivity and objectivity by pointing out the organizing structures operative through such individual syntheses of culturally transmitted patterns.

The flux of the passing moment of experience can be called 'real' and the organizations of such experience, of which conceptualization is the prime example, would then be 'ideal,' comparable to the spontaneous variations of Darwinian evolutionary theory. One should be wary of using such terms as 'ideal' and 'real,' however, since they undergo subtle modification through James's use of genetic analysis and other transformations of evolutionary theory to suit it to philosophical problems. The genetic method, developed in *Pragmatism,* means calling into question truths that are taken for granted as self-evident by showing how they are interpretations that originated to answer a particular interest and were then passed down through the generations because they were found helpful by others until, finally, their origins were forgotten.

Evolutionary methods include, but are not limited to, the presupposition that process is fundamental to experience and stability needs to be explained. Classifications are taken as being fortuitous, not revelations of the inner nature of reality, and must be proved adept at explaining experience if they are to survive by becoming part of the tradition. The past is explained by taking processes observable in the present and extending them to previous times of which we have only scanty evidence (that is, gradualism rather than saltation). In contrast to conceptions, perceptions always occupy a privileged position in regard to experience. As a process they just are experience, but when identified individually as 'a' feeling or 'a' percept, they become problematic in the sense that their exact nature can be determined only retrospectively, as a result of discriminative analysis. As felt, they just are as felt, but as expressed, even to ourselves, they partake of the fallibility of all reflections on experience.[17]

In *The Pluralistic Universe* life is identified as continuously changing, in contrast to concepts, which are static (PU, 113ff). Consequently, the only way to fit concepts to reality is by arbitrarily arresting the flux. Such conceptual cuts are therefore not part of reality, but suppositions on our part "and you can no more dip up the substance of reality with them than you can dip up water with a net, however finely meshed." Conceptualization always isolates and distinguishes some aspect and excludes everything else and is thus at odds with reality, the concrete sensible flux in which experiences "compenetrate" each other and there are no hard and fast divisions. The division of the present moment into the tripartite division of past, present, and future are classic examples of the way in which concepts must distinguish in order to specify. This gives the false impression that past and future are held at bay by the present, and creates false dilemmas as to how to rejoin what has been rigorously separated. Experientially, past and present do not exclude each other, but to some extent are co-present. "The literally present moment is a purely verbal supposition, not a position; the only present ever realized concretely being the 'passing moment' in which the dying rearward of time and its dawning future forever mix their lights. Say 'now' and it *was* even while you say it" (113).

Traditional rationalism cannot escape this intellectualist distortion, since it presupposes a one-to-one relation between isolated sense data and their conceptual substitutes. The chimera of absolute clarity (what James calls "simplicity") keeps us "wedded to the conceptual decomposition of life" and makes process philosophy appear as a bundle of confusions (PU, 114). But its vaunted superiority leaves as unresolved puzzles what is easily performed on the level of everyday, non-reflective experience. In concrete experience there are no clear-cut divisions, but confluxes of the same with the different. "What really *exists* is not things made but things in the making" (117).

5. Radical Finitude

The methodological appeal to selective interest, which encompasses a complex set of interdependent presuppositions and principles, is central to James's reconstruction of philosophy. It undergirds the turn from speculative theorizing to concrete phenomena and from the illicit, and largely uncritical, traditional philosophical assumption of a universal point of view to the limited human dimension of mind that is all that is available to us. Despite the fact that religions have attributed omniscience only to divinity, this ability to take in the whole of time and space in a single glance has been adopted by rationalist philosophers and scientists alike as the model of thinking in the strictest sense.

It is all too often still the case that philosophical statements are only taken seriously if they are demonstrably universal and necessary and immune to disconfirmation by physical events. In ethics, for example, situational or utilitarian arguments are invariably criticized as not exhibiting a proper universality. But since our universal statements actually generalize specific interests and we are not omniscient, we must acknowledge and work within our limitations if we are to avoid self-deception. To avoid mistakes which result from reading a later stage of abstraction back into the pre-reflective process, an investigation into the conditions under which thinking takes place, along the lines developed by James in *Principles*, must precede and establish the context of philosophical reflection. One of the basic discoveries of such an investigation is that the human mind is essentially partial. When we attempt a general point of view we must rely on abstract propositions, such as that particular events display natural laws of a determinate sort. But in the vagueness of general propositions we under-utilize concrete facts and links, "and in all practical matters the concrete links are the only things of importance" (WB, 165).

Ends-in-view both restrict the data taken to be relevant and provide a framework for determining when the goal has been achieved. Without the restrictions imposed by purposes, there is nothing to discover. Calculation is only possible within pre-determined goals. The accuracy and amount of data gathered, for instance, is strictly correlative to the purpose for which it is being sought. The kind and amount of data needed to determine weather patterns, for instance, is a function of the purpose for collecting it. One level of accuracy and quantity of information is sufficient if someone wants to know whether they should bring an umbrella to work and another level and amount are appropriate if someone wants to know the time and place a hurricane is going to come ashore.

The multiplicity of our different interests also discloses the fact that there are different cycles of operations in nature. It may be true that seemingly incommensurable cycles are actually related in an over-all pattern, and that such a universal plan would become obvious if the whole universe were taken into account. But, given the way our intelligence actually operates, the belief that we actually possess such a pattern is a chimera. The recognition and acknowledgment of the concrete, practical point of view would eliminate the many tragedies caused by a blind insistence on reducing every aspect of nature to the one assumed to underlie and account for all the rest, whether this is ultimately thought to be physical, political or religious. Connections have to sought among the appearances as well as imposed on them, and we should not lose sight of what does not fit.

Chapter Four

Concrete Acts of Thinking

"To wonder why the universe should be as it is presupposes the notion of its being different, and a brute which never reduces the actual to fluidity by breaking up its literal sequences in his imagination can never form such a notion. He takes the world simply for granted, and never wonders at it at all" (EPS, 25-26).

Although William James never fully grasped the implications of his radical critique of traditional rationalism, present-day readers can recognize the fundamental reconstruction of human experience which was already worked out in great detail in his earlier works. The methodological appeal to selective interest as a constituent feature of "the full concrete act of thought," as well as of the more specialized concrete or "living acts of reasoning," incorporates a powerful critique not only of naive realism and essentialism, but of the traditional rationalism which underlies modernity.[1] He points out, for instance, that the Kantian categories of pure reason cannot account for the fact that the mind often makes quite unreasonable connections nor for the fact that knowledge changes over time (PP,I, 520-521). His own investigations, which reveal that "thought works under conditions," expose the sterility of the traditionally abstract understanding of reason.

We have seen that James rejects Hume's atomistic theory of sensation by arguing that complexity precedes and is not built up out of individuated sense data. He also denies Descartes's claim that our first ideas of things are absolutely clear and distinct. To disprove these two claims he reviews the psychological experimental data gathered since their time. One of the fundamental facts he discovers is that our sensational memory is more like a sketch than a finished portrait of perfectly distinct traits. Hippolyte Taine also reported that in getting a general idea of a previously unknown plant, after viewing many specimens, none of the sensations "completely survived in its echo," and left instead a "vague representation" (PP,II, 692-695).

99

James's own position is that "meaning is a function of the more 'transitive' parts of consciousness, the 'fringe' of relations which we feel surrounding the image, be the latter sharp or dim" (PP,II, 695). Beyond our first crude sensations consciousness is a matter of suggestion, and therefore we must look to perceptions, not sensations, as the basis of knowledge (722). Both sensational and reproductive brain processes combine in our perceptions. But we do not simply passively assimilate what strikes our senses; instead, out of "a conflux of sensible qualities" some are regarded as "more constant, interesting, or practically important" and we therefore consider them "as essential constitutents of the thing," thus distinguishing the reality of the object from its mere appearances (724).

Since selection has been shown to be operative, both "mechanically" or automatically and consciously, at the level of sense perception, how does it function also in the intellectual sphere? This question sets up the organizing schema of chapter 22 of *Principles*. In it James shows how reasoning is a process which utilizes signs to pick out the essential qualities of even novel phenomena. It extracts characters out of a phenomenal totality according to purposes, the chief of which is prediction. These essential aspects are then taken "as equivalent to the entire datum from which it comes" (966). James's new beginning in philosophy consists in just this insistence on the primordiality of "the world's concrete fulness," the reality of which overflows our purposes in organizing it (962-963, n11).

Our particular organizations of experience into real objects are thus revealed as "teleological weapons of the mind" (PP,II, 961). James's radical critique shows how we construct a world to suit our purposes and then by ignoring the fact of our participation in the outcome surreptitiously pass off as an independently given, purely objective world what is in fact a subjectively human world. Our finite world, which is abstracted out of the concrete fullness of experience, is always less than, and therefore often a "rotten or miserable substitute" for the encompassing reality (PP,II, 962, n11). But organize we must, if our human form of life is to survive. James warns us about the danger of forgetting the fortuitous character of the world we take for granted, since such forgetfulness increases the danger that we will not take responsibility for recreating it more satisfactorily. He also warns us about the added power gained by those in a position to enforce their views of reality on us while pretending to merely describe a pre-existent state of affairs. But he does not emphasize this terroristic aspect as much as Lyotard and Foucault do.[2]

Rational thinking is thus placed within a much wider continuum of the human organization of experience, of weaving chaos into order.

This continuity is emphasized when James begins the chapter by reminding us that Darwinian evolutionary biology shows that we are continuous with other animals,and not of another, immaterial, order of being as philosophers have traditionally emphasized. Furthermore, just as there are no sharp breaks between sensation and perception, there are also intermediate stages, which shade into each other, between perception and rational thinking. The Darwinian basis of the critique is even more evident in the earlier article, "Brute and Human Intellect," (1878), which is incorporated into the chapter, as well as into chapter 13, "Discrimination and Comparison."[3] In this article he explicitly introduces his analysis of human thinking as a careful investigation into precisely what distinguishes brute from human thinking, turning to the experimental record for a more exact account than that given so far in "the traditional intellectualist position."

Arguing against the mechanistic interpretation of British associationists that reasoning primarily consists in the association of sense data, James contends that it is the ability to dissociate that best characterizes human reasoning. Far from distinguishing humans from other animals, association by contiguity, that is, the coupling of two sense experiences, is an ability shared by both. Insofar as the human is characterized by reflective self-consciousness, then our distinctiveness is attributable to this ability to dissociate from "the full concrete act of thought" the object thought about and the operation of thinking it (EPS, 28-29).

In his introduction to James's *Essays in Psychology* William R. Woodward defines 'dissociation' as "the process whereby the human thinker breaks up the concretes of immediate experience and substitutes those similar essences, attributes, or abstractions in ways that solve problems and serve interests."[4] The Jamesian thesis of selective interest as a distinguishing characteristic of human reasoning is an expansion of this psychological explanation of dissociation, rather than association. Dissociation or discrimination is one of the four "foundation-pillars of the intellectual life" the others being association, retentiveness and resemblance (PP,I, 500). Each are treated separately in chapters 13, 14, 16, and 22 of *Principles*, but should be seen as interrelated, organizing principles.

1. Contemplative and Rational Thinking in "Brute and Human Intellect"

"Brute and Human Intellect," published in 1878, was the only article incorporated in *Principles* which was written before signing the contract for that book. This underscores the significance of its central theme of selective interest as providing an organizing schema for *Principles* (EPS, 393). It has recently been described as drawing on a basically Kantian analysis to elaborate "the central tenets of Darwin's theory into a theory of mental development."[5] By identifying it as his earliest attempt to describe reasoning as a concrete process arising in everyday life, we can recognize that he was developing a model that is presupposed in his subsequent writings. James frequently returns to the process of concrete reasoning to explain how we can legitimately order multiplicity into unity or, conversely, how the unity of phenomenal experience gets carved up into multiple perspectival units.

James distinguishes two kinds of human thinking: the contemplative and the rational. Their distinguishing characteristic is that "each case of reasoning involves the extraction of a particular partial aspect of the phenomena thought about" while contemplative thought "simply associates the phenomena in their entirety" (EPS, 12). Contemplative thinking is also called narrative, descriptive, or empirical thinking. It can be further subdivided into two kinds: association by contiguity and association by similarity.

Association by contiguity is characterized by a presiding interest and is defined as "a procession through the mind of groups of images of concrete things, persons, places, and events, together with the feelings which they awaken, and in an order which, if our attention is guided by some dominant interest, such as recollecting an actual set of facts, or inventing a coherent story, is in the main derived from our actual experience of the order of things in the real outward world" (EPS, 2). James remarks that in a dry, prosaic, literal sort of mind association by contiguity predominates, thus revealing his distaste for it and his estimation that the mere reduplication of associated phenomena is the least developed form of consciousness. It is the furthest removed from that distinguishing characteristic of the human which consists in the ability, based on association by similarity, to reduce "the actual to fluidity by breaking up its literal sequences in [our] imagination" (25). The second division of contemplative thinking is revery, characterized by association by similarity. No presiding interest is discernible in it. In revery thoughts bud out of one another by caprice, and thoughts will call up other, similar thoughts that may not have occurred at the same time or place as the originating episode.

The distinguishing aspect of both kinds of association is that they are "always of matters taken in their entirety" (EPS, 3). The thinker passes from one concrete, holistic, representation to another. Both kinds can be reduced to contiguity and differ only in that in contiguity proper a cluster of ideas operates together to call up a whole other cluster, while similarity is a special case in which part of a cluster calls up another cluster which also has that aspect, among many other different aspects. The two clusters are held together by their sharing, that is, having in common, and therefore "pulling along" the rest of the cluster which is different but kept together with the part selected for by their being contiguous to the selected feature. (He also calls this to 'redintegrate', that is, to recall associates (8)). However, James's categorization of similarity as a type of contiguity seems to me to be mistaken because only the associated characters are contiguous to the characters selected for, but the original cause of bringing both clusters together in the first place is not their contiguity, but their mere similarity. He is on stronger ground in emphasizing the fortuitous character of association by similarity according to which clusters of images are spontaneously related and not arrived at by any consciously ratiocinative process.

In contrast to contemplative thinking, rational thinking is divided into two spheres; namely, the theoretic, which is the power to understand things by their causes, and the practical, which consists in having an end in mind and finding the means to attain it. Both involve the same process, which is to find an intermediate representation which will link together two data.[6] In the theoretic sphere, this intermediate representation is the reason for inferring the consequent, while in the practical sphere it is the means or instrument for attaining the result. The advantage of reasoning to merely habitual, empirical, thinking is that conclusions can be inferred or consequences obtained that may never have been conjoined in actual experience. Thus, reasoning is essentially the substitution of parts and their couplings for wholes and their couplings. The utility of the process consists in the fact that having become clear about the couplings of the parts, their couplings in turn become more obvious and evident than the connections of the original wholes.

2. Extracting the Right Character from the Whole Phenomenon

For this process to work it is absolutely necessary that the partial character chosen should be the right one. Unlike purely logical analysis, where the correctness of the solution is guaranteed as long as one follows the rules, "our concrete acts of reasoning are almost always liable to error" (EPS, 7, n3). The cogency of the reasoning depends on identifying the correct ingredient out of the totality, and ignoring all the irrelevant ones, but there is no self-evident way to decide in any given case which part of a phenomenon should be considered its essence. What we are confronted with is a "phenomenal totality" (9). What we must discern is the right "partial character." Therefore, the crucial question is: How does one choose rightly?

The answer to this question is said to divide the a priori philosophers from the empiricists. The a priori school holds that the phenomenal data are bound together in a primordial synthesis. The empiricists, by contrast, hold that aspects of the original phenomena that can be identified as discrete elements are essentially distinct, and their bond is an illusion of necessity produced in us through familiarity and generalization. James then thwarts our expectations because he does not continue by affirming or denying either position, both of which are referred to as "pretty dry description(s)" (EPS, 10). But it turns out that they are 'dry' because overly technical and uninformative about what he takes to be the crucial issue of deciding how to choose rightly. He designates this crucial issue as "a matter of the deepest philosophic importance," but one to which he is going to refer only in passing, rather than developing further its philosophic implications.

James thus deliberately separates psychology and philosophy in the early writings in order to satisfy the positivist model of science as value-free and limited to phenomenal description. As a result, his reconstruction of the philosophical enterprise is covered-over and its roots are obscured. Rather than continuing the debate on the terms inherited from a priorists and empiricists, for instance, he deliberately returns to his own description of reasoning as the substitution of parts and their couplings for wholes and their couplings. He redefines the crucial philosophical issues involved by pointing out that in actual situations it is absolutely necessary that we choose the right partial character because momentous consequences can ensue if we do not. The outcome could be death if the right antidote is not chosen, for instance, because we have not picked out of the total phenomenon of an emergency room situation the fact that the unconscious patient was poisoned.

James has been leading up to a fundamental postulate of his new beginning in a philosophy of concrete experience. He insists that the particular part which is substituted for the whole in the reasoning process, and considered its equivalent, "wholly depends on our purpose, interest, or point of view at the time" (EPS, 10). There are no rules which will necessarily generate correct choices, except one, which operates after the fact. The right choice is the one that must lead to the expected result. Those who can successfully follow this rule are designated geniuses, and this aspect of the issue is followed up in 1880 in "Great Men and Their Environment" (WB, 163-189).

In *Principles* he also recalls this linkage of the determination of the real characteristics of objects with ends-in-view. Consequently, it is impossible to generate rules for identifying objects in the absence of this linkage: "In our study of reasoning we found it impossible to lay down any mark whereby to distinguish *right* conception of a concrete case from *confusion*" (PP,II, 1267). In hindsight, it can be seen that the pragmatic method, as the only sure means for determining the correctness of the "marks" abstracted from the phenomenal totality, was already being explicated and applied. It is clearer in this earlier formulation than in the later, more extensively developed writings on pragmatism, however, that pragmatism is not merely a method, but is grounded in a concrete analysis of human rationality.

Illustrative arguments are provided next for two points that James wants to emphasize. The first point is that "in every reasoning an extracted character is taken as equivalent to the entire *datum* from which it comes" (EPS, 11). Rational thinking always involves extracting a partial aspect of the whole phenomenon thought about, while empirical thinking always compares phenomena globally (12). Experience can often be successfully negotiated by repeating past performances found to be successful; for example, a child can start a clock just wound up by tipping it on its side and an adult can expect that a piece of ice will melt if placed near a fire. For these actions to be called the result of reasoning the person must consciously use an idea to mediate between the initial phenomenon and the conclusions drawn. This would be the case if the child tipped the clock because she knew that the pendulum must be set swinging in order to start the movement and if the adult knew that heat is motion and that liquefaction is identical with increased motion of the molecules. Reasoning, as such, is discursive and partial. But every phenomenon has an infinity of aspects or properties. For reasoning to be effective it must extract just that antecedent part of the phenomenon that will lead to the consequent desired. Once found, such ingredients are thought to constitute the essence of the phenomenon for that occasion and the rest can be ignored for the time being.

This leads to the second point to be illustrated, namely, why the couplings of extracts are more evident than those of the entire phenomenon. There are two reasons: first, the extracted characters are more general than their concrete manifestations. Therefore their connections are more familiar because more often met with in experience; for example, if heat is motion then what is true of motion will also be true of heat. Secondly, the properties of the parts are fewer than the characteristics of the whole and therefore their possible consequences are more readily drawn.

To see why it often takes a genius to extract the right characters for a conclusion, for example, why the law of squares was not noticed before Newton or the survival of the fittest before Darwin, we must undertake an investigation into how knowledge arises from experience.[7] It is important to emphasize that, for James, experience is global. Objects are not first discriminated and then pieced together to constitute a situation, but they are only gradually disentangled from a pervasive totality. In James's words: "All our knowledge at first is vague" (EPS, 14).[8] Not only for children, but also for adults thrust into new situations, a confused whole precedes recognition of distinctive aspects and things. A new zoology student, for instance, asked to dissect and describe a frog, simply will not see everything that her instructor sees, despite the fact that everything to be seen is present to both.

Knowledge begins with vague confusion which only gradually takes on discrete characteristics as familiarity grows.[9] Sensations do not group or associate themselves together to build up a whole experience, rather some parts must be dissociated from the whole in order to recognize distinguishable objects. It is a characteristic of the holistic constitution of experience that it can be reflectively reappropriated and will yield new insights: "Any original Whole of experience is an eternal well of ever new and more delicately differenced [sic.] ingredients, which little by little come to light" (EPS 15). Intelligence is said to increase as more aspects can be discerned.

The original question presses on us with more insistence than ever. How are the elements of the originally vague whole singled out? They have to be noticed, of course, but what causes us to attend to one aspect and not to another which is also present? "There are two immediate and obvious answers: first, our practical interests; and, second, our aesthetic interests" (EPS, 15). This appeal to practical and aesthetic interests which direct our attention is an appeal to two fundamental structures of experience which constitute the core of James's concrete analysis.

In his schema they are the ultimate appeal beyond which we cannot go and they, in turn, are the ultimate explanation for many other phenomena. Although they are most often used in explanations of human experience, particularly as it functions as the basis for knowledge and action, they designate something basic to any conscious selectivity out of a multitude and therefore have some equivalence in any animal behavior where preference is exhibited. The sense of smell is acute in most animals because it discloses aspects of their environment which are practically important for their survival, and children are attracted to flames because they are pleasing sights. Our practical and aesthetic interests make aspects of a more encompassing experience stand out. We notice what they accent, but why we have just those practical and aesthetic interests that we do we cannot say. "We must content ourselves here with simply accepting them as irreducible ultimate factors in determining the way our knowledge grows" (EPS, 16).

Since humans have immensely varied practical wants and aesthetic feelings, our ability to dissociate aspects of phenomena and thus reason about them is greater than that of other animals. But we are also able to recognize aspects that do not primarily appeal to either practical or aesthetic interests and this propensity, called by James the "law of dissociation by varying concomitants," provides a functional account of the underlying process operative in our consciously practical and aesthetic choices. He is relying on an explanation already made by Mill, Martineau, Spencer, and other empiricists, but differs in the greater emphasis he gives to the process (EPS, 16ff). This law states that when characters are dissociated from others, but not for any obviously practical or aesthetic interest they arouse, they are found to do so because they were previously associated with other characters than the ones with which they are presently associated. Thus, if one sees only red balls and then sees a blue ball, the observer may for the first time dissociate red as a color from its being always present in a spherical shape. If red and sphericalness were invariant, they would most likely never be analyzed as separate elements.

Once again, it is evident that red balls are not recognized by the convergence of separate sense data, but are first experienced within a totality of perceptions, the aspects of which must be singled out because of some interest or variance to be recognized as such. Helmholtz is credited with showing that vast numbers of unseparated sensations underlie our perceptions and we therefore think of them only as embedded in that totality.[10] In James's time there was not yet in psychology enough experimental evidence to show how or why the repetition of a character in combination with different wholes will elicit recognition, but it was enough for his purposes to recognize the empirical evidence of this operation.

James denies Spencer's claim that the mind evolved as a mere product of its environment. He appeals to both philosophical arguments and scientific experimental evidence to prove the emotional and practical reactive spontaneity of animals. He argues that, contrary to Spencer, all sentient beings exhibit peculiarities of interest and selective attention and do not merely mechanically respond to stimuli. Otherwise, the frequency of outward occurrence would be directly correlated with responsive attention. Instead, we often find that novel phenomena attract our attention more than repetitious ones. The overabundance of environing stimuli must mostly be ignored in order to operate adequately. We are not even aware of most of what is transpiring around us. Only that to which I attend enters into my experience.[11]

After stressing the continuities between humans and other animals, James draws on animal experiments to account for the perceived differences that remain. These are attributed to the greater number and strength of our practical and aesthetic interests and our ability to associate by similarity. Characters are dissociated, not only because they have occurred at some time in someone's experience, but the various instances must be brought into the consciousness simultaneously. As Mill argued in his methods of induction, scientists searching for laws embedded in phenomena deliberately accumulate all the analogous instances of phenomena in hopes of recognizing some common aspect ignored when each instance was originally experienced in isolation. Without this ability to associate by similarity, the deliberate scientific method of collecting analogous instances would be impossible.

In highly gifted minds this collecting of analogous instances does not seem to be the result of laborious deliberation but rather of a spontaneous recognition of identical aspects of phenomena widely separated in space and time in the midst of different circumstances. James then recalls the record of animal experiments to provide evidence that in other animals association by contiguity rather than by similarity predominates. Particular aspects picked out by other animals from the complex in which they are embedded, such as a dog retrieving a paper from a front porch, are invariably related to the animals' immediate interests or emotions and depend on association by contiguity, while dissociation by varying concomitants, largely based on association by similarity, hardly seems to take place.

Even language, the traditionally cited difference between humans and other animals, is analyzed by James as itself a result of the dissociation of a representation into its ingredients and association by similarity. It is argued that other animals both employ and recognize signs, such as scratching at a door to signal the urge to go outside and coming to attention in response to a particular verbal command or intonation. But in humans the linguistic impulse is generalized and systematic. We have "a deliberate intention to apply a sign to everything" (EPS, 26ff). This general purpose arises as soon as the notion of a sign *as such*, apart from its immediate utility, is recognized, that is, "it is born by dissociation from the outstanding portions of a number of concrete cases of signification" (27).

Even human children have the ability to isolate the signness of signs from their immediate entangling associations and in this rupture of contiguous associations recognize the crucial similarity of one sign to another, even though both the actual symbol used and that of which they are signs may be overwhelmingly different (EPS, 27). The thesis that the most characteristic difference between other animals and humans is the ability to associate by similarity is very provocative because it places analogy and metaphor at the core not only of language, but of reasoning, and of being human. This will be explored further in chapter 8, "Analogy and Metaphor."

3. Critique and Reconstruction of Reasoning in *Principles*

When "Brute and Human Intellect" is incorporated into the chapter on reasoning in *Principles,* James deepens and expands the reconstruction of thinking and reasoning begun in the earlier article.[12] He continues to emphasize a holism that fundamentally characterizes thinking in both humans and other animals before he develops the specific differences tied to human reasoning. He says that thinking, for the most part, consists of trains of images suggested one by the other and designated as "spontaneous revery" (PP,II, 952). In this "irresponsible" thinking the terms are empirically concrete rather than abstractions. Such thinking approaches reasoning insofar as single terms are dissociated from their settings and call forth other terms out of their settings (953). Such mostly unconscious inference of sensations forms the texture of our perceptive life. In it signified and signifier pass unobtrusively into each other; for example, a whiff of a particular odor almost instantaneously produces a recognition of 'skunk.'

Reasoning is distinguished from revery in that an end is consciously sought rather than being spontaneously produced. Moreover, the foremost end is prediction, which though theoretical, eventually leads to some kind of action. In reasoning properly so called, as distinct from the associative sequences of revery, the connections made are linked by intermediate steps "formed by *general characters* articulately denoted and expressly analyzed out" (PP,II, 956). Therefore, the inferences need not be related either by habitual association or by similarity. This "productive" rather than "reproductive" nature of reasoning is what makes it such a useful tool in dealing with unprecedented situations. It is this ability of reasoning to deal with novel data which sets it off from common associative thinking and marks for James its distinguishing characteristic (957).

Conceptualization always involves reducing the plenitude of reality to a limited number of aspects chosen for some particular purpose (PP,II, 959-963). "Every reality has an infinity of aspects or properties" and we may regard them from an endless number of perspectives (959). Furthermore, realities do not come singly, but in relation, and these relations may also be traced out along many different paths. Any of these aspects which are apparent from your particular angle of vision are as truly part of the phenomena as any other. A person, for instance, is a complex reality. For an usher taking tickets in a theater, the relevant aspect of the person is reduced to one, namely, whether she has a ticket. Whether she is also an engineer has no practical bearing and can safely be ignored.

Given the immensity of combinations of aspects and points of view that can be brought together to reveal some truth about anything, there can be *"no property ABSOLUTELY essential to any one thing"* (PP,II, 959). Essentiality is always an interplay between some phenomenal characteristic and some intentional point of view; given other ends in view, other characteristics of the object will acquire an essential status, and an aspect essential for some other purpose will cease to be so. Since to classify an object at all means to pick out some limited number of characteristics and ignore the rest, "I am always unjust, always partial, always exclusive" (960).

Although reasoning discloses real aspects of objects, it also really distorts them because it cannot grasp them in their original fullness.[13] It strings elements together serially according to the interest of the moment, which, however, may be of a long-standing pattern. The only remedy for this partiality is the partiality of subsequent acts of appropriation which, mosaic-like, can be pieced together to display a wider array of refractory surfaces and aspects of the situation. Our piecemeal appropriation of the world "to suit our little interests" is, in principle, insurmountable, since we must ignore "the solid fullness in which the elements of Nature exist" (PP,II, 960). The necessity is not a logical constraint, but one deriving from our finite and practical nature.

For common sense and the scholastic tradition built on it the denial that any quality is absolutely essential to a thing is blatant nonsense and wholly irrational. Without an essence to make a thing to be what it is, there would be nothing to understand because mere being, without formal structures, is just an undifferentiated and unnamable prime matter.[14] But to thus insist on any one characteristic of a thing as its essence is merely to insist that the one aspect which answers to our purpose at the time, for example, that coal burns, shall be the most important characteristic. That coal is also a prime pollutant may be its essential characteristic in an environmental impact study. Since the reality encompasses both,and much more besides, the property chosen often only signifies our usual relation to that particular reality. Therefore, our purposes "characterize *us* more than they characterize the thing" (PP,II, 961). We are usually so stuck in our prejudices and so partial to our own point of view that we insist that what is obviously the case for us must also be the most important aspect of the thing. We therefore denigrate other properties disclosed in different perspectives as merely accidental or subjective.

Conceptualization and valuation are thus inextricably linked. Locke and Hume had already undermined the fallacy of essentialism, but its full implications were drawn out only by James. He explicitly linked essences to purposes and thereby revealed their basis in power struggles. To label some property an essence is to mark out its importance to my interests and to ignore other properties. But importance varies with interests which, in turn, can vary from person to person and moment to moment, although there is also a conserving aspect of classification which will later be explained in the fifth chapter of *Pragmatism* as the genesis of common sense categories.[15] "Many objects of daily use...have properties of such constant, unwavering importance" because our interest in them remains constant, and we end up believing that our stereotyped names reveal the only truth about them (PP,II, 962). It can be agreed that no 'truer' way of conceiving them may be found as long as it is realized that this means that no more 'useful' way of classifying them has been found or imagined.

Only if one purpose were more true than another could its correlative conception of reality be the truer conception. But for a purpose to be absolutely rather than partially true it would have to conform "to some absolute standard of purpose in things" (PP,II, 962, n11). This shows that the whole notion of essentialism is tied to the traditional assumption of a teleologically determined universe. James develops instead a teleology of personal organizations of experience. He uses the Darwinian thesis of natural selections out of spontaneous variations to refute the doctrine of the essentialism of natural kinds.[16] Absolute teleological standards have traditionally been defended by appealing to a belief in God's purposes. To deny belief in God and yet retain a belief in essences without showing how such essences are uniquely true is tantamount to abandoning rational discourse.[17] James thus argues that traditional rationalism is itself irrational because it provides no good grounds for its essentialism beyond a traditional belief which has long since been abandoned.

4. How Facts Come to Be in "The Importance of Individuals"

In the chapter on "The Importance of Individuals" in *The Will to Believe*, James uncovers the hidden power of reasoning, which had been disguised as merely neutral description in the rationality that characterizes modernity. In so doing an issue central to his philosophical reconstruction is highlighted. Reality appears already structured, yet small differences arising from various appropriations of environments eventually produce independently existing structures of reality. An understanding of the process by which subjective preferences pass over into objective reality is vitally important to the eventual success or failure of the human project of transforming the world into a better place to live. It is the philosopher's task to make us aware that each of our interventions changes the world for better or worse. Then even our mundane choices could be made with a conscious understanding of their wider implications.

This short, polemical work was written to answer Grant Allen and John Fiske, critics of an earlier article, "Great Men and Their Environment" (WB, 163-190). In the earlier article James had argued for a parallelism between Darwinian zoological evolution and the facts of social evolution to explain why communities change from generation to generation 163-164. According to the Darwinian theory of natural selection, the environment can only select among genetically based differences which arise independently of environmental forces. James uses this principle to rebut Allen's appeal to the Spencerian evolutionary theory that historically important individuals are simply the result of the aggregate of conditions out of which they came. James's refutation of Spencer's view that consciousness passively mirrors outer relations is extended from the individual to interactions between individuals and groups of which they are members.

"The Importance of Individuals" is an existentialist argument that the differences between great individuals like Aristotle, Goethe, Napoleon, and the average person, even if it is as small as Allen suggests, nonetheless is as deserving of philosophical investigation as is what accounts for the average behavior which is usually taken as the proper subject matter of sociology. From the point of view of vast social upheavals the importance of the individual shrinks almost to nothing, while from the point of view of a suffering individual, the larger social forces which are causing it are of little immediate interest. No appeals to the reality of nature can decide which view is the true one which should be adopted in philosophical discussions, since both experiences refer to real events in nature. Selective interest must be introduced to account for the paramount importance each side attributes to environmental or individual forces: "accentuation, foreground, and background are created solely by the interested attention of the looker-on" (WB, 191). That foreground and background shift with interest is developed in more detail using the terminology of 'fringe' and 'focus' in *Principles* (PP,I, 249ff, 260). The possibility is still left open in these early writings that a complete philosophy, which could impartially account for all interests, might some day do justice to all of them.

James's defense of hero worship in this article appears anachronistic, even dangerous, today; moreover, he did not altogether escape the racial and gender prejudices of his time.[18] But his insistence that "the preferences of sentient creatures are what *create* the importance of topics" was a powerful impetus to appreciate rather than denigrate those who differed from himself, and this sympathy that went beyond mere tolerance, even serving as the cornerstone of his ethics, was not typical of his time or class (WB, 194). He criticizes even the attitudes of Jesus as being too limited and says that they must be corrected by taking into consideration the points of view of other species: "What animal, domestic or wild, will call it a matter of no moment that scarce a word of sympathy with brutes should have survived from the teachings of Jesus of Nazareth?" (194). Preferences are the only absolute lawgivers. Only those who adopt the charade of scientific neutrality could be satisfied with studying the "law of averages" without inquiry into how they came to be average. Adopting the point of view of a spectator to the human scene ignores the fact that we are participants. Sociological talk about general laws, statistical averages and predetermined tendencies undervalues the importance of individual differences. James retrieves the question with which we are all faced, one which is usually hidden under the guise of a seemingly objective inquiry into the constitution of the world, namely, "Whose preferences are going to prevail?"

Like many nineteenth century thinkers, James feared that the forces which tend towards uniformity, such as industrialization, would snuff out creative individualism. He therefore argued that differences, however slight, were to be cultivated as the source of innovation. He drew support from Darwinian theory, since what is called in aggregate a 'species' is actually a 'family' of genetically related individuals, which nonetheless still exhibit variations among themselves. In fact, the variations between what is called one bird species and another may be no larger than those found within the species itself. Without these variations no innovation is possible.

In explaining selective interest James argued that anomalies attract our attention more than the usual pattern of events does. That things behave as we expect them to calls forth no particular notice, but let someone or something fall above or below the expected standard and our interest is aroused. These slight differences are compelling because they exhibit the range of variations possible within a species and not the more fixed differences that we do not expect to see altered. A dramatic interest attaches to such a 'zone of insecurity' because "this is the formative zone, the part not yet...a typical, hereditary, and constant factor of the social community in which it occurs" (WB, 192). Just as life is found only in the growing layer of a tree, and its dead bark records past changes and not future possibilities, any change that is going to occur in human or other animal species is going to arise out of such differences.

James was always interested in the processes that brought about change because only by understanding what inclines change in one direction rather than another can we hope to gain power over our own lives and successfully bring about a better society. Individual differences and the social changes they influence provide a living laboratory of formative processes and exhibit real possibility, the line where the past and future meet. As such possibilities are acted upon and pass into the social fabric of everyday existence, they become part of the archeological record and the moment of possibility passes to another living center of activity. By focusing on differences "in the making" we can hope to catch a glimpse of the working units which produce the accumulated results of the already structured life we take for granted.

5. Conclusion

"To reason, then, we must be able to extract characters, and not *any* characters, but the right characters for our conclusion" (EPS, 14). 'Rightness' cannot be determined merely by reading off some aspect of the phenomenon, as the positivist model assumes. Careful observation alone, even when buttressed by the exactness of scientific protocol, cannot be a sufficient explanation for the correctness of the data chosen. The rightness "wholly depends on our purpose, interest, or point of view at the time" (10). James argues in this early formulation of perspectivism that only by identifying the relevant purpose can there be a determination of correctness. As Rorty puts it, "What ties Dewey and Foucault, James and Nietzsche, together — the sense that there is nothing deep down inside us except what we have put there ourselves, no criterion that we have not created in the course of creating a practice, no standard of rationality that is not an appeal to such a criterion, no rigorous argumentation that is not obedience to our own conventions."[19] But the purpose we choose, by itself, is no more a sufficient criterion than passive observation would be, because it only supplies us with the parameters within which a choice can be made. After choosing out of the phenomenal totality those aspects which we think will lead to the goal desired, it still has to be determined whether through the use of these selected elements the goal is, in fact, reached.

As with Nietzsche's experimentalism, this testing of the accuracy of the elements selected by their success or failure in leading to the goal intended is not a separate validation process in addition to the reasoning process. It is an indispensable part of reasoning itself, which is incomplete without it.[20] We can distinguish as temporally distinct processes reasoning and validation. But such a notion of unvalidated reason is more accurately described as revery or pure speculation. In actual reasoning processes the feedback from experience constitutes an essential aspect of reasoning, which is incomplete and cannot be accurately described without it. Therefore, in answer to what Rorty calls "a bedrock metaphilosophical issue;" namely, whether one can "ever appeal to nonlinguistic knowledge in philosophical argument," the answer is an unambiguous 'yes' and 'no.'[21] 'No,' if this means outside of our meaning-giving organization of experience. 'Yes,' if this means outside of talking about talking. In addition to linguistic acts, we also act. We change situations, for better or worse, and not just our thinking/talking about them. These changes can then be evaluated. The pragmatic method is thus shown to be indispensable for understanding how we reason: The 'right' choice is the one that *"must lead to the result"* (EPS, 10). This practical corollary of the thesis of selective interest is developed in the following chapter.

The insistence on designating the concrete situation in which reasoning takes place is meant to block the tendency of reasoning to go on a holiday by engaging in free-floating speculation. It is not meant, however, to denigrate revery and imagination as an indispensable aspect of human thinking. "The great, the fundamental defect" of other animal's minds seems to be an "utter absence of fancy," an inability of their thinking "to break across in unaccustomed places" (EPS, 25). We must have the creative moment of free association in order to multiply the chances that some fortuitous coupling will arise that will prove to be the very one desiderated. The selectivity characteristic of reasoning thus presupposes the free play of the concrete holism of contemplative thinking. There are no rules to generate the correct choice, if 'correctness' means letting the various aspects of the object appear as they are in themselves. It is possible to investigate how choices are generated and how better ones are distinguished from worse ones. This aesthetic basis of selectivity will also be taken up in the next chapter.

Chapter Five

Practical and Aesthetic Interests

"That theory will be most generally believed which, besides offering us objects able to account satisfactorily for our sensible experience, also offers those which are most interesting, those which appeal most urgently to our aesthetic, emotional, and active needs" (PP,II, 940).

Selective interest is William James's explanation of how we organize the phenomenal totality of experience into the familiar world of everyday life. In his concrete analysis of living acts of reasoning he argues that reasoning consists in picking out the right partial character out of a totality. The rightness of the choice can only be determined pragmatically according to what, in fact, leads to the expected result. But the discrimination of the relevant character precedes its validation. To provide an account of those interests which focus our intention on some aspects of the big blooming buzzing confusion rather than others we must turn to James's understanding of selective interest as exhibiting recognizable patterns, which he usually classifies as practical and aesthetic.

1. Postulates Given in Our Nature

Practical and aesthetic interests are most often spoken of as a pair, and although the practical is given priority, the aesthetic also functions as a fundamental explanatory principle. Any explanation of their role in James's philosophy is problematic because he does not systematically develop them with anything of the thoroughness he devotes to selective interest itself, despite the fact that they constitute an indispensable aspect of it. He does not consistently call them needs, their relative priority is not clearly explained, nor is any proof given that they must function as explanatory principles. Not even their exact number is clear. Although they are usually limited to two basic divisions, emotional and moral dispositions are also sometimes explicitly included as fundamental categories.

117

Despite this lack of systematic attention, I would like to make two claims, which can be judged by how satisfactorily they unify the texts: selective interest cannot be understood without explaining how the practical and the aesthetic function as ultimate explanatory principles, and these activating dispositions constitute an essential part of James's explanation of the human condition. This is evident from the fact that they are appealed to at crucial junctures throughout his writings. He explains both the constitution of objects and the rational determination of essences by their means. He explains, for instance, that "Helmholtz says that we notice only those sensations which are signs to us of *things*. But what are things? Nothing, as we shall abundantly see, but special groups of sensible qualities, which happen practically or aesthetically to interest us, to which we therefore give substantive names" (PP,I, 274). Likewise, "the mind chooses to suit itself" in determining essences: "It chooses certain of the sensations to represent the thing most *truly*, and considers the rest as its appearances, modified by the conditions of the moment" (PP,I, 274-5). Furthermore, we have seen that aesthetic and practical interests are designated by him as the "irreducible ultimate factors in determining the way our knowledge grows" (EPS, 16). Therefore, I would like to reconstruct James's scattered remarks into a more coherent explanatory model.

The practical and the aesthetic will be taken as the two broadest categories, under which other fundamental sources of selective attention can be grouped. The practical, for instance, includes the emotional, the moral and other active needs, while the aesthetic includes, but is not limited to, intellectual drives such as those of profusion and simplicity and their reconciliation or harmony: "After the emotional and active needs come the intellectual and aesthetic ones. The two great aesthetic principles, of richness and of ease, dominate our intellectual as well as our sensuous life" (PP,II, 943). The distinction is reminiscent of Aristotle's division of human action into the practical and the contemplative, except that the order of priority is reversed, and of Kant's separate treatment of pure and practical reason, except that they are taken to be the phenomenal ground of the human organization of experience. In *A Pluralistic Universe*, a late work, reason is being used in this broader sense: "But rationality has at least four dimensions, intellectual, aesthetical, moral, and practical; and to find a world rational to the maximal degree *in all these respects simultaneously* is no easy matter" (PU, 55).

As fundamental psychological determinants of our sense of reality, in chapter 21 of *Principles* James calls these practical and aesthetic needs "postulates...given in our nature" (PP,II, 945). This seems to be the most fruitful and defensible way of taking his appeals to the practical and aesthetic: they will be understood to be postulates, the use of which allows the fullest disclosure of the concrete grounds of our human organization of experience. But they are postulates "given in our nature" in the stronger sense that the designation, 'need,' connotes, because of the concrete evidence of their functioning.

As he says in *The Will to Believe*: "The preferences of sentient creatures are what *create* the importance of topics. They are the absolute and ultimate law-giver here" (WB, 194). In the last chapter of *Principles* he argues that the connections of things in the outward environment cannot account for our predominate tendencies of reaction and that the genesis of our aesthetic principles and feelings of personal activity, as well as the other "elementary mental categories," can be best explained as examples of the Darwinian process of spontaneous variation. Once having arisen, we can encourage or suppress the aesthetic craving for harmony, for example, but it becomes one of those dispositions of which we must take account if our explanations are to be grounded in a careful examination of human experience. There is no necessity that such cravings should have become fundamental aspects of a human organization of experience. Therefore, they cannot be accounted for or justified as an a priori, essential aspect of human nature. Instead, they are what might be called, with C.I. Lewis, a pragmatic a priori, that is, as a matter of fact, they have become part of the functioning of human consciousness and therefore will necessarily enter into our decisional processes.[1]

In addition to being felt needs, the worlds of aesthetics and ethics (as an expression of active needs) have been built out into ideal plans of action and will be an accurate reflection of the experienced world only if we remake the world according to their demands. Aesthetic principles and moral sensibilities are initially feelings of pleasure in or repugnance to sensory impressions or patterns of action. Through repetition, memory, and anticipation, they can also function as crucial aspects of self-initiated actions and selective responses to new stimuli. They can even eventuate in judgments expressing harmony or discord among objects of thought. "Where harmonies are asserted of the real world, they are obviously mere postulates of rationality, so far as they transcend experience" (PP,II, 1268).

We have seen in chapter 1, sections 3 and 4, that the practical and the aesthetic are understood as two irreducible sentiments of rationality. Although to be human is to unify the chaos of experience and order it to answer to our needs, philosophers are peculiarly driven to push unification as far as it will go. They not only privilege aesthetic ordering over the practical, but within the aesthetic the passion for simplification tends to overrule the passion for distinguishing. Although individual philosophers and schools of thought vary in the emphasis they give to either simplicity or clearness, James argues for understanding them as "sister passions" rather than as rivals (EPH, 37-38). Therefore, while not neglecting the benefits to be gained from both, he also undermines over-reliance on either aesthetic passion by pointing out their excesses.

Aesthetic rationality, for instance, often unifies the diversity of phenomena by ignoring data that do not fit, and James gives "contemporary examples of the hypertrophy of the unifying passion" (EPH, 36). On the other side, "the craving for clear representability...leads often to an unwillingness to treat any abstractions whatever as if they were intelligible" [39]. In this excessive reductionism to mere "lumps" of "tangible thinghood," an exaggerated emphasis on distinguishing the particulars of experience can lead to denying even the legitimate function of "relational terms...namely as phenomenal elements or 'laws,' cementing the mosaic of our feelings into coherent form." James argues that we need to harmonize both of "the two great aesthetic needs of our logical nature, the need of unity and the need of clearness," in order to correct the excesses of either when they subordinate the other (41). This harmony can only be achieved, however, by relating aesthetic rationality to practical rationality.

The practical is ambiguously used by James to designate both the fundamental, concretely describable and verifiable situation of humans active in the world and the sub-category of praxis definable by contrast with the aesthetic. It therefore functions both as the most fundamental explanatory principle defensible on concrete, experiential grounds and as an explanatory principle coordinate with the aesthetic. As the most fundamental principle it also functions as ultimately explanatory even of the aesthetic, but as co-equal with the aesthetic, it functions as an alternative source of action which can be contrasted with the aesthetic.

This ambiguity mirrors the central puzzle at the core of James's fundamental project of synthesizing the idealist and empiricist traditions. From the first, the priority of praxis anticipates and forms the basis for the final resolution, but while it is being worked out neither the idealist nor the empiricist dimensions of experience are reduced to the other. In James's genealogical analyses, for instance, sometimes the practical and sometimes the aesthetic are given as the predominate origin of some particular selective interest.[2] Some passages will therefore reflect the primordiality of the practical and some its equi-primordiality.

A problem still to be addressed in later chapters is what to make of the equi-primordiality when James finally denies the demands of the aesthetic in his rejection of rationality, given the fact that the tension demonstrated as obtaining between the practical and the aesthetic has served as an insightful interpretive principle.

2. The Practical as Coordinate with the Aesthetic

The practical is a protean category. Put most simply, as it was first introduced as one of the two fundamental motives for philosophical systematizing, it is "the desire for a solid outward warrant for our emotional ends" (CER, 22-23). But it provides the organizing framework for so many explanations that it can best be understood by distinguishing the following distinctive aspects. Five meanings predominate: (1) the relationship of reality to ourselves (PP,II, 919 n7), (2) that we cannot, in principle, be ultimately mistaken about our relation to reality, which includes the belief that our efforts to come to terms with the world will be realized in the long run (the practical, in this sense, means the adoption of an anti-skeptical stance), (3) acting for a purpose (PP,II, 941) and (4) the relation of a thing to its future consequences (WB, 67) or of beliefs to the consequences of acting on them (PM, 28ff). Besides these interpretive structures delineating the human dimension of experience, the practical is also developed (5) as a methodology to determine when any specific organization of experience has sufficient grounds and is worth pursuing.

Interestingly enough, as a means of determining just when our thoughts of an object are perfectly clear, practical needs over-rule aesthetic needs on the model of the Darwinian selection by nature of variations that spontaneously arise (see PM, 29). The determination of meaning by its possible difference to practice is so central to James's thought that he calls his philosophy both 'practicalism' and 'pragmatism.' But the practical is used by James so expansively that the clues to family resemblance have to be sought out. Some of these meanings include individuation, that is, that all the termini aimed at in a process are particular, even when mental (PU, 111); that perception and thinking are always for behavior's sake (WB, 92); and that mundane responses are practical in contrast to theoretical explanations.

(1) "The home of interest" (PP,I, 285)

James's concrete analysis of the human mode of being in the world is nowhere more apparent than in his development of the theme of selective interest as determined by the practical. The meaning of the practical as the relation to self is clearly *prima pares*, the first among equals. By beginning with the individual as an organizing center of action in the world, 'what is,' that which exists, is brought within our experience in a mode of interaction which undercuts reflective skepticism, since it not only predates the reflective turn, but is necessarily presupposed even when later called into question. It knits together what is as actually existing with the peculiar mode of human being which perceives the world as radiating from itself as the organizing center of experience.

This fundamental schema is referred to by James in an argument showing that existential propositions, such as that the horse, Henry, exists as an outer reality, and attributive propositions, such as that Henry is brown and bad-tempered, differ only in degree and not in kind. This is because all propositions, including existential and attributive, are believed in the very act of conception, unless they clash with other propositions already believed at the same time. The passage will be quoted in full, since it expresses so well the fundamental meaning of the practical.

> In both existential and attributive judgments a synthesis is represented. The syllable *ex* in the word Existence, *da* in the word *Dasein*, express it. 'The candle exists' is equivalent to 'The candle is *over there*'. And the 'over there' means real space, space related to other reals. The proposition amounts to saying: 'The candle is in the same space with other reals.' It affirms of the candle a very concrete predicate — namely, this relation to other particular concrete things. *Their* real existence, as we shall later see, resolves itself into their peculiar relation to *ourselves*. Existence is thus no substantive quality when we predicate it of any object; it is a relation, ultimately terminating in ourselves, and at the moment when it terminates, becoming a *practical* relation (PP,II, 919, n7).

This practical relation to the self both unifies experience and situates consciousness within the world and not apart from it. Considered abstractly, a certain portion of the stream of consciousness is more closely identified with ourselves than the rest. It is felt to be "a sort of innermost center within the circle . . . constituted by the subjective life as a whole" (PP,I, 285). As the active element of consciousness, it goes out to meet qualities and contents, which seem to come in to be received by it, and welcomes or rejects them. "It is the home of interest" and presides over the perception of sensations, and its assent or rejection influences the movements aroused. "It is the source of effort and attention," the process by which ideas or incoming sensations are inhibited or pass over into outward acts. It is "a sort of junction at which sensory ideas terminate and from which motor ideas proceed, and forming a kind of link between the two" (285).

This is how the active self is felt. But as soon as this concrete description is extended into defining more accurately the essence of this felt sense of self, then all the empiricist and rationalist controversies over the nature of the self arise and are unresolvable from a consideration of the facts available. Lacking any basis for settlement in objective phenomena, James, in *Principles*, leaves the nature of the experienced self an open question and refuses to come to a premature conclusion. Psychology, as a natural science, must stick with functional formulas. Since he holds that only philosophy can deal with real, ultimate reasons, which require an understanding of "the total sense or meaning of the world," he avoids coming to terms with these traditional philosophical problems within the parameters of his psychological work (PP,I, 379). As it turns out, even in his later, explicitly philosophical, writings James dissolves rather than solves these controversies. He deliberately stays within the limitations he already delineated as the only defensible basis for an investigation into the human condition that would avoid idle speculation. But in these early writings he lays the foundation for a philosophical analysis which he hopes could eventually legitimately transcend merely phenomenal description, perhaps even attaining comprehensive rather than merely regional understanding.

But after arguing that "this central part of the Self is *felt*," why would James characterize his analysis or concrete description of this felt sense of self of which we have direct sensible acquaintance as 'abstract,' rather than 'concrete'? (PP,I, 286). He calls it abstract, not because it develops a general notion absent from particular experience, but because it abstracts from the situating stream of consciousness of which the self is a part. Just as the feeling of the body alone is an abstraction from experience, so is the feeling of the activating self as an isolated unit. Both the body and the self are always felt "together with other things." James's concrete methodology always entails situating the object of discourse within the experienced field where it is originally found.

James follows his abstract discussion of the central active self with a concrete description of his own experience. The only active self he can discover is "a feeling of bodily activities whose exact nature is by most men overlooked" (PP,I, 288). He then treats his own discoveries as hypothetical, probably because they have not yet been corroborated by further experimentation, and speculates on what consequences would follow if they were indeed true. He identifies the nuclear self as the locus of the process elsewhere described as his correction of the reflex arc concept. The nuclear self can be identified as the collection of those physiological acts that adjust to incoming stimuli and execute action. These primary reactions "are the permanent core of turnings-toward and turnings-from, of yieldings and arrests, which naturally seem central and interior in comparison with the foreign matters, *apropos* to which they occur." We "feel them as the birthplace of conclusions and the starting point of acts" (289).

If these feelings really denoted our ultimate experienced self, then all our experiences would be objective, and this objectivity would be divided into the 'self' and the 'not-self.' The indispensable subjective condition of the experienced world being known would be the stream of thought. But James recalls that, according to the Kantian analysis, such a condition of experience would not itself be experienced. Known only in subsequent reflection, the stream of thought accompanies all acts of knowledge but would not itself be an object of knowledge. Both a thinking self which accompanies all thought and matter as that which lies behind physical phenomena are merely logical postulates and we take phenomenal appearances as revealing sometimes the one and sometimes the other. He therefore concludes that the identity of the thinking self, and even whether there is one or many selves, cannot be experientially determined and must await metaphysical inquiry.

These conclusions are then said to be contrary not only to common sense, but to the fundamental assumptions of every philosophic school, whether spiritualist, empiricist or transcendentalist, since these all agree that we have "a continual direct perception of the thinking activity in the concrete" (PP,I, 291). Nonetheless, the denial that we have such a direct experience, but only postulate it, is at this time the logical conclusion of James's own concrete inquiry. This is highly troubling to him, given the fact that belief in the direct awareness of consciousness and its contents is one of the few bulwarks to which he can appeal against skepticism. not being able to investigate this central puzzle within the stated limitations of *Principles*, he brackets the results of the investigation of his own experience by saying that he will treat them "as a parenthetical digression," and will "revert to the path of common-sense again" and assume a direct awareness of our thinking as such. In fact, the pivotal ninth chapter on "The Stream of Thought" was written utilizing this assumption.

James's "digression" in the tenth chapter on "The Consciousness of Self" draws attention to the fact that what looks like straightforward description of an object, albeit the special sort of object that is the process of thinking, is understood by him as the construction of a hypothetical model which can account for all the facts so far discovered, but which makes no claims as to the actual existence of the functional entities referred to. His insistence that the process of thinking is a more "subtle phenomenon than most of us suppose," despite the fact that he adopts a straightforward, common sensical way of talking about it, should alert us that he is still puzzling out the problem and will return to the topic in more depth in his later writings.[3]

The core of his abstract analysis of the self as the originating center of experience, the juncture between self and world, is programmatic for the development of his 'concrete' philosophy of praxis. Just as in the brief discussion in *Principles*, his new beginning is a turning away from what has proved to be a barren argument about the identity of the self and a turning toward what an investigation of this active self discloses about how we come to know the world of which we are a part. As he says later in the first volume: "The sense of a peculiar active relation in it to ourselves is what gives to an object the characteristic quality of reality, and a merely imagined past event differs from a recollected one only in the absence of this peculiar feeling relation" (PP,I, 614).

The relationship of reality to ourselves, then, does not refer to the traditional philosophical ego or soul at all, except to criticize this substantializing of an experiential process. James reconstructs the issue of the nature of the self by putting the process of the interactive construction of both self and world at the center of his new beginning. It is significant that he characterizes this practical relation to the self as: "the home of interest," "the organizing center of experience," "a sort of innermost centre within the circle," "the source of effort and attention," and "a sort of junction at which sensory ideas terminate and from which motor ideas proceed, and forming a kind of link between the two." The interactive process is emphasized in the communicative avoidance of reifying the terms of the relation into a substantial self and a passively received reality. This reaches its mature expression only in his last works, such as in *The Varieties of Religious Experience*, where what I have called his 'full fact' is given. The minimum unit is a transactive conscious field which includes its object as distinctively apprehended (VRE, 393).

(2) "The inmost nature of the reality is congenial to powers which you possess" (PP,II, 942)

The relation to the self that motivates the rest is the desire for a solid outward warrant for our emotional ends. This desire can be satisfied in the understanding of the practical as the adoption of an anti-skeptical starting point and in the confirmation that these feelings are reciprocated in nature. The first, the adoption of an anti-skeptical starting point, provides the subjective condition for the possibility of the second, which is satisfied by the adoption of the pragmatic method. This section will develop only the meaning of the practical as the desire for an outward warrant, which consists of two related theses. The first is that our dearest desires and most cherished powers will not ultimately be frustrated. The second is that they are not useless epiphenomena.

The first thesis is taken by James as a necessary presupposition for any conscious human action whatever. If the future were truly incompatible with our active tendencies, if we thought that our actions were illusory and only seemed to accomplish what they did, that is, that we were not really engaged with reality but only with a mocking substitute for it, or if we thought that whatever we accomplished in our puny lifetime would be wiped out in the next, then we would not have sufficient incentives for action. A condition for human action in the present, for instance, is the continuous transition from past into future. Without a usable past, present actions cannot have meaning and become random, as Alzheimer's Disease only too vividly illustrates. Without a future, there is also no meaningful human action because there would be nothing for present activity to change into. People who think that the end of the world is at hand do not usually engage in significant actions, that is, actions that will bring about desired changes and instead either despair or celebrate. Camus's *The Stranger* and Sartre's *The Wall* make the same point about persons facing their own imminent death.

The second aspect of this Jamesian postulate of practical reason is a consequence of the fact that our emotions are as revelatory of the nature of reality as are our senses. Like our senses, our emotions are understood as having an objective reference.[4] We fear, for instance, because there is an outward cause of fear. If the fear is merely subjective and has no object in reality, then we judge that something has gone wrong with our usual emotions. And just as this is true of particular emotions, the more fundamental feeling we have that our actions are worthwhile, that they are literally worth doing, is a necessary precondition for human action. If we knew that our purposes would be ultimately frustrated, that all the emotions that drive us to act are but hollow mockeries with no answering responses in reality, then what could motivate us to the expansive use of our powers? We demand of the universe "a *character* for which our emotions and active propensities shall be a match" (PP,II, 941).

"It is far too little recognized how entirely the intellect is built up of practical interests" (PP,II, 941). Evolutionary theory has rightly called attention to the fact that cognition is a part of a larger motor phenomenon, known as a type of reflex action. Cognition, both in other animals and in our own case, is a guide to appropriate action. "Cognition, in short, is incomplete until discharged in act" (941). In the more theoretical sort of human cognition, the demands of action are only postponed, and not ultimately denied. James says that the attractiveness of creeds like primitive Christianity and its expression by Luther and Wesley and philosophies like those of Kant and Fichte, Goethe and Schiller, lies in their assurance that we have the power to grasp the inner nature of reality (942). No philosophical system will be widely accepted which does not emphatically legitimate the more powerful of our emotional and practical tendencies.

(3) acting for a purpose

Acting for a purpose was explained in chapter 3 as selective interest and in chapter 4 as dissociation. One of James's fundamental theses, derived from his concrete investigations, is that "experience, from the very first, presents us with concreted objects, vaguely continuous with the rest of the world which envelops them in space and time, and potentially divisible into inward elements and parts" (PP,I, 461). This experiential flux makes absolutely central the question of how we divide up "our original sensible totals" into those objects which comprise for us the objective world. Thus, the investigation of discriminative attention and its corollary, association, occupies many chapters of *Principles*, from 11 to 14, in fact. After developing the largely involuntary physical and physiological conditions of discrimination, he turns to the voluntary ones in a section called "The Improvement of Discrimination by Practice" (481-487).

After showing how the effects of education can induce awareness of small differences as though they were large ones, he continues his discussion of the voluntary aspect of discrimination in the section called "Practical Interests Limit Discrimination" (PP,I, 487-494). Our conscious determination of objective reality is explained by appealing to practical interests. "A distinction in which we have a practical stake" is defined as "one which we concentrate our minds upon and which we are on the look-out for" (487). This distinction is then frequently drawn because of the benefits to be gained by doing so. Likewise, when we have no practical interest in some distinction we habitually ignore it and eventually become oblivious to it. Many pages from Helmholtz are then quoted verbatim, since he is credited with being "the first psychologist who dwelt on these facts as emphatically as they deserve."

The practicality of purposes is based on James's transformation of the reflex arc thesis into a concrete analysis of the human organization of experience. The conclusion of the chapter on emotions in *Principles* provides a good example of how James not only demonstrates but also utilizes his thesis that without a determination of purpose, there is no way to decide what is essential to any given phenomenon or to describe the organization of experiential data. "If then we should seek to break the emotions, thus enumerated, into groups, according to their affinities, it is again plain that all sorts of groupings would be possible, according as we chose this character or that as a basis, and that all groupings would be equally real and true. The only question would be, does this grouping or that suit our purpose best?" (PP,II, 1097).

(4) Relation of things to future consequences or of beliefs to consequences of acting on them.

It is a fundamental finding of James's concrete investigations that "we humans are incurably rooted in the temporal point of view" (PU, 23). For the relationship of the practical to temporality see chapter 1, section 6; chapter 2, section 4; and chapter 11, sections 3 and 4.

(5) The pragmatic methodology

James's philosophy has often been reduced to the pragmatic method. We have seen that it is much more than this, but the pragmatic method nonetheless remains central to his lifelong project of overcoming nihilism and skepticism. For the meaning and importance of the practical as a methodology, see chapters 1, 6, and 9.

3. The Practical As Primordial

We have seen how 'the practical' can refer to James's whole philosophical approach, which is pragmatic, that is, founded on praxis. This is a broader characterization than the reference to pragmatism as a validation procedure, as in sub-section 5, above. In a 1907 letter to Perry the extension of the category of the practical to mean his concrete analysis of the human condition is explicit. He begins by chiding Perry for taking the practical as a test for the meaningfulness of concepts as excluding intellectual relations and interests (TCW, II, 475). But Perry was correct in pointing out that the practical in its usual signification is defined in contrast to the intellectual. Here we have evidence that James's inability in his published works to systematically formulate the radically new concrete methodology that he was literally inventing contributed to serious misunderstandings even by some of his most astute pupils.

Shortly afterwards, in a January 1908, article reprinted in *Meaning and Truth* James tries to clear up this misunderstanding of pragmatism as a philosophy which ignores the theoretic interest, but still without sufficiently indicating its concrete context (MT, 111-114). He deplores the fact that practical workings as a criterion of truth has been taken in a narrowly useful sense, but nonetheless defends by genealogical arguments the basic premise of "subsequential unity" as the good originally sought by the affirmation of truth. He also reaffirms that by "the practical nature of truth" he means "the distinctively concrete, the individual, particular, and effective, as opposed to the abstract, general, and inert."

But he also points out that the inference of remote facts which will confirm ideas held to be true is a theoretic activity as is the re-ordering of past beliefs that the verification of new facts requires. He asserts that the whole process which constitutes truth includes many interests, not the least of which is consistency. One cannot even explain what satisfactory practical working means without including the logical operations of analysis, deduction and comparison. Once again we can recognize that the cogency of his arguments presupposes an understanding of his concrete analysis of the cognitive process as inextricably related to those practical and aesthetic interests constitutive of our human condition. But since he does not explicitly make the connection, each of his arguments appears *ad hoc* instead of the logical outcome of his concrete analyses of lived experience.

Oddly enough, in the earlier letter to Perry, James had already explicitly linked the meaning of the practical with a concrete analysis of "the *total* world" and says that for this reason it should not be taken as excluding theoretical interests as it does when understood in the everyday sense (TCW, II, 475-476). He points out that since the differences in experience that the pragmatic method uses as a criterion include possible differences, then "pure observations" and theoretical differences are also included. He also calls the cognitive intention "only one species of the genus human urgency," thus situating it within an understanding of our being in the world. As a part "of our human emotional endowment' it includes "curiosity for new fact, insistence on non-contradiction, and on simplification of form, and love of tracing applications." Since these are aesthetic needs, the practical is being used in its broadest, most inclusive sense as a synonym for his radically empiricist concrete analysis and therefore refers to his basic methodological procedure. "Sensation, relation, and funded truth" are still the primary criteria for the "degree of satisfaction" the pragmatic method demands, but the gratification of "our aesthetic or utilitarian demands" are also satisfactions that constrain beliefs. There are as many ways that our ideas fit with the primary criteria "as there are ways in which animals can fit their environment. The truest fit is the *richest* fit." Ideas are not only determined by objects; they are "*co*-determinants."

James's concrete analysis helps us to realize that particular interpretive structures take place within "the *total* world," of which we are a part. The natural, physical world minus ourselves that is self-evidently true for everyday life and for science is shown to be "an abstraction, useful for certain purposes," but actually it is "always...envelopable in wider teleological or appreciative determinations." Only within this total world can meaning and truth emerge, but the history of positivism, the impact of the Vienna school on American philosophy departments, and the persistent misinterpretation of James's new beginning in philosophy demonstrate that it can remain hidden for a long time.

4. The Aesthetic

Just as the postulate of our practical interests discloses structures which guide both our sensuous and our intellectual life, so does the postulate of our aesthetic interests. The broadest meaning of the aesthetic is found in the correlative motive for philosophical systematizing, namely, "the craving for consistency or unity in thought" (CER, 22). As such, it both essentially characterizes philosophy insofar as it is traditionally understood as the epitome of rationalism, and represents only one of the two co-ordinate aspects of the aesthetic as it informs James's reconstruction of philosophy. In this reconstruction, the aesthetic has two co-ordinate divisions, and not just the one drive towards unity. These two parts of the aesthetic are what were earlier designated as clarity and simplicity, but which are later also called richness and ease (See CER, 99).

To these are added a third, harmony, which was also given earlier as the goal of philosophic activity. Harmony can be understood as the ultimate goal of the aesthetic drive, which is realized by means of both richness and simplicity: "And, *certeris paribus*, no system which should not be rich, simple, and harmonious would have a chance of being chosen for belief, if rich, simple, and harmonious systems were also there" (PP,II, 943). As an interpretive principle, we must consistently distinguish, as James does not, between his use of the category of the aesthetic to mean the simplifying reductive drive towards absolute unity characteristic of traditional, rationalist philosophy, and to mean a balance of the simplifying drive with the drive to gather up the abundance of the rich variety of the world as it enters into our experience, which characterizes his reconstructed philosophy and which is called harmony.

In discussing the aesthetic needs James quotes from Josiah Royce's "remarkable book," *The Religious Aspect of Philosophy*. This is in keeping with his linking of the practical with empiricism, especially as earlier developed by the Scottish common sense philosophers and later by Shadworth Hodgson, and of the aesthetic with intellectual rationalism, especially post-Hegelian romantic idealism. Since he intends a better synthesis of the two traditions than has yet been developed, the phenomenal grounds for both the aesthetic and the practical are emphasized. Royce is quoted to clarify the two aspects of the aesthetic:

> All our thought is determined, in great measure, by this law of least effort, as it is found exemplified in our activity of attention . . . The aim of the whole process seems to be to reach as complete and united a conception of reality as is possible, a conception wherein the greatest fullness of data shall be combined with the greatest simplicity of conception. The effort of consciousness seems to be to combine the greatest richness of content with the greatest definiteness of organization (PP,II, 944).[5]

James's gloss on this passage provides his clearest statement of the definition and scope of the aesthetic as he reconstructs it. "The richness is got by including all the facts of sense in the scheme; the simplicity, by deducing them out of the smallest possible number of permanent and independent primordial entities: the definite organization, by assimilating these latter to ideal objects between which relations of an inwardly rational sort obtain" (PP,II, 944).

Recall that in "Brute and Human Intellect" James gave as the essential difference between ourselves and other animals our ability to associate by similarity rather than by contiguity (EPS, 20ff). What characterizes us as human, therefore, is our spontaneity rather than our receptivity, and since spontaneity is a mark of the aesthetic, the aesthetic as a defining characteristic of the human is given an explicit priority over the practical. This ability to associate by similarity is at the basis of both our reflective or methodically constrained reasoning and our intuitive or artistic activity. Scientists, for instance, deliberately accumulate all the instances which have any analogy to a phenomenon being studied, seeking to detach from them all some important characteristic which is not evident in the one at hand. What scientists do methodically, some highly gifted persons do spontaneously, namely, collect analogous instances, uniting what was never contiguous in experience. Individuals differ to a greater or lesser degree in this ability; those who are easily able to make associations through similarity and thus to extricate the relevant character which ties them together, are more prone to reasoned thinking, while others seem more at ease associating by contiguity.

In the association by similarity a single instance can call up, or redintegrate, former experiences where something similar occurred, and thus provide us with an essential clue for responding appropriately to a situation. By contrast, in association by contiguity, one total thought suggests another total thought, and if this routinized thinking predominates, then only the characters which relate to some immediate interest or emotion are extracted (EPS, 25). Thoughts then call up their habitual successors, not similar instances. Humans are metaphysical animals and can wonder why the world is as it is because we can conceive of its being different, which presupposes our ability to break up the literal sequences of phenomena by our imagination.

Less imaginative persons have a lesser ability to break up the literal sequences of their experiences and, like animals, remain "swamped in the total phenomenon which they help constitute" or else fall back on conventional analogies (EPS, 29-30). In emphasizing association by similarity James is drawing on Alexander Bain's thesis that "in the arts, in literature, in practical affairs, and in science, association by similarity is the prime condition of success" (30).[6] James refines Bain's thesis by distinguishing between two stages in reasoned thought, one in which we call up cognate thoughts because of their similarity and one in which we notice the bond. Analysts, that is, all abstract thinkers, scientists, and philosophers, are those who notice and abstract the bond of association, while intuitionists, that is, poets and critics, "judge rightly, classify cases, characterize them by the most striking analogic epithets, but go no further (30).

In this early work James does not dispute the claim, based on evolutionary theory and Comte's sociology, that analytic thinking represents a higher stage of development than the intuitive one. There is some historical evidence to support the claim, for instance, that humans reasoned by analogy before they could do so by abstract characters, and some psychological evidence that persons with little or no formal schooling are more adept at analogical than abstract thought. Reasoning by similarity and true reasoning can give identical results, but differ in that philosophers and scientists, in their abstract discourse, are able to state the point in which cases are similar. In oral tradition and in early literature persuasion is most often carried on by parables and similes, without necessarily pinpointing the relevant point of comparison. But James also deliberately rethinks the relation of analogical to abstract reasoning and in this revaluation undermines the positivist dismissal of analogical reasoning as a primitive and therefore dispensable stage of human thinking. His primary argument is that analogical thinking is not wrong, but incomplete, as when, in response to the question as to why snow is white, someone answers that it is for the same reason that a light bulb or milk is white. But this furnishing of "parallel cases is the necessary first step towards abstracting the reason embedded in them all" (EPS, 33).

James calls into question the positivist contention that analytic thinking is simply a higher intellectual stage and intuitive thinking an arrested stage by referring to Bain's suggestion that the scientific stage of abstracting the bond of association may actually depend on the absence of certain emotional sensibilities (EPS, 30). It would be easier for a mind less interested in details and lacking a fertile analogical imagination to disregard most of the details of a situation for the purpose of concentrating on one or a few aspects that it has in common with other situations. James thus suggests that rational thinking may have evolved out of an impoverishment of sensibilities and is therefore not the ultimate development of highly gifted, imaginatively creative individuals.

The poets are testimony to the fact that a richly aesthetic nature may keep one at the intuitive stage, since those who are attuned to the prolixity of analogy are less likely to be interested in the ground of the analogy. Far from being a sign of intellectual inferiority, a feeling for the splendor of the riot of experiential abundance has given us such immortal works as Shakespeare's. Would anyone say that the dry critic who points out the hidden connections running through Shakespeare's drama is more brilliant than the bard because his method is abstractive rather than analogical? Thus, even if the analytic mind represents a higher or later stage of historical development, in the sense that its evolution presupposes the holistic, contemplative stage, there is no absolute superiority of the analytic mind, as such, to the intuitive one.

According to the positivist model, primitive, analogical thinking is succeeded by a higher stage of analytic thinking in two successive historical epochs. James replaces this with the model of the embeddedness of reason in an experiential totality, in which analogical thinking is a first moment which may or may not be followed by analysis.[7] Just as parallel cases of phenomena must be first brought together in order to abstract the reason embedded in them, so the first words probably referred to entire things and actions, that is, extensive, coherent groups. New experiences can be grasped only through names given to earlier experiences, and the resemblance of one experience to another must precede the ability to abstract out of the totality some aspect which they both have in common. "The first words are thus neither particular nor general, but *vaguely concrete*" (EPS, 33). For instance, certain words, such as oval face, velvet skin, and iron will, may first have always been conjoined as an "adjective-noun" and applied together to any other thing like it, and then the entire thing, or conjunct, may have received another name and the original, in whole or in part, became a true abstract or general term. Finally, oval, for example, comes to suggest only a shape.

Much of our thinking still takes place analogically; in whole departments of our thought we mostly think in terms of similarity without ever abstracting out the relevant terms of comparison. In ethical, psychological, and aesthetic matters we are often reminded of other things, actions, or situations like the present ones and intuitively choose the correct response or course of action without being able "to justify ourselves to others" (EPS, 34). Art connoisseurs, doctors, and judges become experts insofar as their saturation with a particular class of materials enables them to intuitively classify newly-reported facts or to choose the most promising course of action or likely hypothesis, even when unable to articulate a reason to back it up. "The reason lies embedded, but not yet laid bare, in all the countless previous cases dimly suggested by the actual one."

The essential characteristic of the human, then, is the negation of all fixed modes of organizing experience. We are reminded of the psychological context of the article when James draws a final conclusion concerning the cerebral hemispheres to back up his distinction between habitual and reasoned thinking. He hypothesizes on which brain activity could account for the mental facts of interest, attention, and dissociation, and suggests that there must be some indeterminateness in the connections between the different nerve paths in the brain which results in the tendency of action to focalize itself in small localities which vary infinitely at different times.

This is based on the assumption that a necessary condition for the possibility of the generation of original relationships on the phenomenal level of intellectual activity is an unstable equilibrium in the human brain. If focalization of brain activity be the fundamental fact of reasonable thought, then it would account for why the intensity of interest or passion concentrates and distills thinking. As there was not yet enough evidence to support this hypothesis, James suggested that his thesis of the selectivity of human consciousness pointed the way to the direction further physiological research should take. He argued that instability in humans replaces instinctive behavior to a significant degree. Our whole preeminence as reasoning beings, our whole human quality, lies in "the facility with which a given mode of thought...may suddenly be broken up into elements, which re-combine anew" (EPS, 36).

5. Both Irreducibly Ultimate

James's writings exhibit a sustained intention to reinstate the aesthetic to its proper place in the specialized aspect of the human organization of experience called the cognitive. This is in direct opposition to the positivistic reductionism that was rapidly taking over both the sciences and academic philosophy. When he wants to describe what is quintessentially human, he emphasizes the spontaneous creativity of our organizations of experience. The aesthetic is then enthusiastically valued as the highest ability and celebrated in a flood of metaphors. This can be seen, for instance, in a long passage from *The Will to believe:*

> Man's chief difference from the brutes lies in the exuberant excess of his subjective propensities — his pre-eminence over them simply and solely in the number and in the fantastic and unnecessary character of his wants, physical, moral, aesthetic, and intellectual. Had his whole life not been a quest for the superfluous, he would never have established himself as inexpugnably as he has done in the necessary. And from the consciousness of this he should draw the lesson that his wants are to be trusted...The appetite for immediate consistency at any cost, or what the logicians call the 'law of parsimony'—which is nothing but the passion for conceiving the universe in the most labor-saving way — will, if made the exclusive law of the mind, end by blighting the development of the intellect itself quite as much as that of the feelings or the will" (WB, 104). [Our] moral, aesthetic, and practical wants form too dense a stubble to be mown by any scientific Occam's razor that has yet been forged. The knights of the razor will never form among us more than a sect (WB, 105).

He concludes by calling on his audience of Unitarian clergy to "avert the formation of a narrow scientific tradition, and burst the bonds of any synthesis which would pretend to leave out of account those forms of being, those relations of reality, to which at present our active and emotional tendencies are our only avenues of approach" (WB, 105).

But when he wants to justify any specific organization of experience, when he proposes to develop his own radically empiricist pragmatic philosophy, for instance, then our situatedness, our purposeful transformation of given conditions to bring about a world answerable to our deepest needs, is paramount. Aesthetic models are then denigrated as merely speculative insofar as they are free-floating and the practical is praised as the highest category. The search for harmony — an aesthetic category — guides all his own investigations, it is true, but this coalescence of knowing and being can only take place in praxis, that is, it must be won through an actual transformation of recalcitrant aspects of experience.

He sometimes uses the aesthetic as a negative valuation, moreover, in a way that he does not use the practical. A position that does not have sufficient grounds for determining whether it is true or not, for instance, will be criticized as merely expressing an aesthetic need, but as commentators have noted, he seems uncritical about any resolution as long as it has some practical bearing. James frequently criticizes the various positions adopted with regard to philosophical or scientific disputes as dogmatic stances or beliefs which reflect an aesthetic demand. In the 1879 article, "Are We Automata?," for instance, he gives as a prime example of a merely aesthetic demand the insistence that mental and physical events are such different orders of being that they can never interact. He then counters this aesthetic claim with arguments undermining the supposed incommensurability of feelings or mental facts and physical facts (EPS, 38-61).

He claims that the assertion that physical and mental events are not only different, but independent, is an uncriticized belief which is held without the effort of searching for evidence. Such uncritical beliefs can be recognized as answering to aesthetic demands, and the ones he identifies in this case are those of simplicity and absoluteness. But the opposite, common sense claim that mind and matter interlock in action and reaction and form a single dynamic whole is likewise the result of an aesthetic demand, most obviously that of a craving for unity. Such rival aesthetic claims cannot be decided either on the basis of these aesthetic motives nor by ostensible reasons and they remain dogmatic as long as evidence is not sought to corroborate one or the other demand. He subjects his own thesis of the efficacity of consciousness to the same canons of evidence.

James frequently precedes his own defense of a thesis by claiming that the existing formulations of the philosophical or scientific dispute can be traced to some aesthetic demand. It is easy to overlook the systematic implications of this procedure. The aesthetic as a category is derived from his understanding of reasoning, which, in turn, is situated within the concrete context of the human appropriation of the world. In "Are We Automata?" he succinctly sums up the position developed in "Brute and Human Intellect" by recalling that reasoning means the mind's ability to break up the totality of the phenomena in question and choose the partial factors that will lead to the proper conclusion as determined by the theoretical or practical initiating context (EPS, 50). Different predicaments will call for the selection of different aspects and this creative stage of coming up with possible factors by breaking up represented things into their elements is called association by similarity. "But this association is only the minimum of that same selection of which picking out the right reason is the maximum."

Therefore, his characterization of the various sides to an intellectual dispute as deriving from aesthetic interests is meant to situate them as the first stage of a reasoning process whose final stage is the successful outcome of an experimental procedure. As long as the dispute remains on the merely speculative level of argumentation, which for philosophy is, unfortunately, the usual procedure, then the reasoning process remains dogmatic and incomplete. In James's reconstruction of the reasoning process by grounding it in concrete experience, aesthetic spontaneity is the indispensable first stage of reasoning, but practical experimentation is its necessary culmination. Philosophers tend to overvalue the aesthetic moment and think that the reasoning process is ended when they have presented convincing arguments for or against an issue,whereas scientists tend to overvalue the experimental outcome of an investigation and neglect a thorough investigation of its aesthetic basis. James wants to reintegrate the two aspects as parts of a reasoning process which is itself "but another form of that selective activity which appears to be the true sphere of mental spontaneity" (EPS, 50).[8]

Therefore, the practical and the aesthetic function together as organizing principles for the human appropriation of experience, sometimes the one and sometimes the other predominating, and they are not ultimately independent sources of action. The aesthetic is understood both as having its origins in the practical and as raising issues which can only be solved, if at all, insofar as they are amenable to a practical test. James uses his genealogical analysis to demonstrate that the attractiveness of disinterested, pure description, and of absolute truth, beauty, and goodness is not due to their being objects of innate human appreciative 'organs,' nor does their value derive from their intrinsic goodness. Rather, "it is obvious that, altho interests strictly practical have been the original starting-point of our search for true phenomenal descriptions, yet an intrinsic interest in the bare describing function has grown up" (MT, 53). True accounts are now valued whether they bring collateral benefit or not.

In fact, a theoretical curiosity seems to be a distinguishing characteristic of being human. True ideas prepare us not only for immediate actual perceptions, but also for possible, future perceptions. Thus, it is obviously advantageous to organize into a consistent and stable shape this ensemble of perceptions, both actual and possible. The common sense notion of substance, for instance, performed this useful function until called into question. Eliminating the notion of substance, however, does not eliminate the need to find some other principle to organize present sensations consistent with future expectations. The gratification of a purely theoretic need for system and order thus turns out to have been initiated and sustained because of its practical utility, after all. We pass by means of such theoretical constructs from the immediate actual to the future possible and back again to the future become present actual again. The aesthetic and the practical thus interact not only in a hermeneutic circle of interpretation, but also in a pragmatic circle of reappropriation.

Chapter Six

Natural History Methodology and Artistic Vision

In an early work James says that art requires "inventiveness and sympathetic concrete observation" (TT, 16). In a late work he repeats the same theme when he denies that activity and change can be conceptually grasped, since they are accessible "only to sympathetic apprehension at the hands of immediate feeling" (PU, 123, n1). Throughout all his work runs a perplexity as to how to accurately translate the immediacy of experience into appropriate symbols, since experience is indefinitely pluralistic and symbols embody only a limited number of characteristics. What he calls his "natural history methodology" is a means for working out this dilemma, and it embodies his hopes for revolutionizing philosophy by returning it from barren speculation to its origins in the concrete situation. He expects by its means to avoid both the speculative nature of neo-Hegelianism and neo-Kantianism and the reductionist positivism of the natural sciences.

What James adds to the scientific assumption of the accuracy of "immediate concrete perception" is an insistence on the importance of sympathy. (PU, 123, n1). Just as his appeal to a natural history methodology refers to his own reconstruction of scientific procedure into a concrete analysis of the structures of human experience, so also his appeal to the accuracy of scientific observation refers to his reconstruction of it. This reconstruction combines the notion of careful and exact observation, which is characteristic of the natural sciences, with observation as romantic vision, the act of 'seeing into' as practiced by Emerson, Tennyson, Whitman, and his other favorite poets.

In the first chapter of *Talks to Teachers* James argues that the relationship between art and science is one of mutual support; neither one should dominate the other. "It fructifies our independence, and it reanimates our interest, to see our subject at two different angles — to get a stereoscopic view, so to speak (TT, 17). Our knowledge should ideally utilize both perspectives and thus benefit from intuitive and analytic insights. But in the same chapter he strongly concurs with Hugo Münsterberg that in the art of pedagogy "the teacher's attitude towards the child, being concrete and ethical, is positively opposed to the psychological observer's, which is abstract and analytic. Although some of us may conjoin the attitudes successfully, in most of us they must conflict" (18).

Congruency or opposition, which is it to be? James is never quite sure. This is because he refuses to allow the drive toward harmony to erode the legitimacy of particular angles of vision. His efforts all tend toward the "stereoscopic view," using both science and art and calling on both the aesthetic and the practical points of view to bring into proper focus some recalcitrant problem. But in the complementary effort to preserve the uniqueness of each without merging them he frequently points out that they are in conflict. After first showing what the scientific view has to contribute to some problem, for instance, he then often advocates adopting as a working hypothesis the often conflicting position available to an aesthetic or practical point of view. He hastens to add that this solution is only temporary, due to our finiteness, and adopted to help us to get on with the investigation until all the results of everyone's endeavors eventually converge on the total truth. We will then see that there is no conflict in ultimate truth between science and art, between the way things are and the way that we perceive them.

What this means in practice, however, is that despite James's expressed intent to rejuvenate philosophy by bringing to it both the results and the method of science, he often proceeds through "divination and perception," rather than through "theoretic strategy" (TT, 17). This procedure subverts the stereoscopic model by deliberately privileging unique angles of vision. Moreover, James himself would not see this as a conflict with his scientific commitments because he is only blocking the intrusion of science into areas of concern that do not fall within its competence and thereby recalling its inherent limitations. At most, it can only reveal the "general laws" within which particular practices and the arts operate, but cannot supply their actual configurations because there are so many actualizations which would still be in accordance with such laws. Besides, the original insight or working hypothesis which sets up an experimental procedure or an entire disciplinary paradigm best expresses the unique contributions of creative individuals, rather than the necessary, but less creative, day to day business of ordinary science in carrying it out. The absolutely guiding aim, according to his concrete analysis, is the organization of experience that serves human purposes.

Positively, then, scientific investigation can supply some fundamental methodological procedures, conceptions, and particular facts to help us in organizing experience satisfactorily. Negatively, it can reveal faulty rational or behavioral procedures and can supply the means for articulate criticism (TT, 15). But it cannot have the final say, and its methodology is only one of many ways of approaching reality. In one of the many productive paradoxes of James's thought, the very methodology he is urging on philosophy to overthrow idle speculation is also thought by him to have no monopoly on access to reality. When properly understood, however, it can provide a valuable check on the tendency endemic to the rationalism of philosophy and theology, namely, to go into business for itself and speculate irresponsibly. He argues both that science has more in common with the subjectivity and creativity usually identified with art than positivists were willing to admit, and that philosophers and artists would do well to emulate the natural history concern with objectivity and fidelity to facts.

1. Natural History Methodology Transformed

We have just seen that James appeals to natural history both as empirical science and as concrete analysis of human experience. As empirical science, it strives to determine general laws through inductive inference, which presupposes a patient collection of all the relevant facts. It signifies especially that the beginning of investigation must be some factual situation whose existence and description is assented to by everyone, regardless of their philosophical persuasions and personal beliefs. This preliminary determination of the specific facts of experience is, in fact, the defining characteristic of science for James. It is successful insofar as it identifies just those marks or characteristics out of the phenomenal totality which can be usefully extended to the maximum number of other phenomena. The great advantage of science over other methods of determining the defining characteristics of phenomenal experience is that it tests its findings through formal validation procedures and is always willing to revise its claims in response to new or recalcitrant evidence.

James never tires of extolling the modesty of this fallibilism which is a defining characteristic of science and recommending that it replace the dogmatism that is endemic to philosophy with its privileging of rationality. In this first meaning James often refers to the facts which have been experimentally determined by science as an external check on philosophical explanations. He also deliberately emulates the scientific procedure of gathering together a wide variety of relevant data before developing an explanation which will account for them. His lengthy examination of a broad range of religious experience in *The Varieties of Religious Experience* is a good example of this natural history procedure.

But James also appeals to natural history in another sense, namely, in his own transformation of it into a concrete analysis of human experience. Central to this transformation is the recognition that all human organizations of experience are constrained by purposes.[1] This fidelity to the fullness of experience, to the irreducible importance of the many and diverse interests and needs deemed important over time, provides a check on the findings of natural history in the first sense. These interests are not haphazardly jumbled together, but are organized according to James's understanding of harmony and his aesthetic and practical postulates.

This transformation is already evident in his earliest writings. In "What the Will Effects" (1888) he says that the new psychology is a result of the reawakening of the human sciences. So far, "the results of this natural-history method of studying human nature" are to add to our store of facts and have not yet settled a single issue debated by classical philosophical psychology (EPS, 216). But there is one conception developed by the new psychology which he thinks had the potential to revolutionize our thinking and that is its claim that all our activity is really a type of reflex action.[2] The importance of this finding is that it demonstrates that feeling and thinking are "little more than half-way houses towards behavior" (217).

Despite the fact that this same conclusion historically paved the way for a reductionistic theory and practice of behaviorism, James in no way endorsed this development, although there were aspects of behaviorism with which he was in agreement.[3] The reason for his divergence from the psychological school of behaviorism as it subsequently developed lies in his fundamentally different conception of the role of the sciences and of the significance of their findings. Through the experimental collection of data about human behavior, the natural sciences can provide the raw material needed for reflection by philosophers, theologians, and all those who are concerned with the ultimate questions of human destiny. But to provide this usable base of facts the sciences have first to be reconstructed to include the whole range of human experiences and to systematically incorporate the relation of the subject matter to the subject.

Philosophers should utilize the sciences in their analyses of metaphysical issues such as free will and determinism. These important human issues arise in the first place in everyday life, as do their most fundamental descriptions, and their ultimate resolutions. What the empirical sciences can contribute is twofold: an explanatory pattern establishing facts and verifying procedures. These findings can then be taken up and reconstructed in light of issues of ultimate concern. Such findings as that of the reflex arc are significant because they provide verifiable empirical evidence for the fundamental premise of James's long-range project of overcoming nihilism. He argues that progress in affirming human significance cannot be made by further speculation but only by turning to an examination of our actual experience of being in the world. Far from letting the sciences dictate the boundaries of reality, he confines their role to that of adding a few pieces to a concrete explanation developed out of a broad experiential base including the many realms of reality he discusses in *Principles* and a whole range of beliefs, intentions, feelings, and needs (PP,II, 920ff).

The two meanings of natural history, as a science and as concrete analysis, are parallel and mutually supportive, but the concrete, radically empiricist one is James's guiding structure of interpretation. For instance, both scientific laws and concrete findings are derived by induction, that is, by trying to simplify into a predictive rule all those marks gathered from the multiplicity of instances organized according to a clarifying purpose. But they are distinguished by their differing organizing purposes. Natural science is fragmentary in that each branch defines itself in relation to limited means to ends, while concrete, radically empiricist philosophy has as its goal the harmonious organization of all experience as a human project. Even when James finally despairs of being able to order the phenomenal pluralism of experience into a single, harmonious whole and rejects the aesthetic postulate as temporally realizable, he still retains the practical postulate as a central organizing principle. It still remains the task of philosophy to reconstruct the findings of the particular sciences congruent with human purposes even after philosophers recognize that they must relinquish their claims to providing a comprehensive, systematic explanation of reality.

2. Natural History Findings and Metaphysical Speculation

In his defense of "the selective pressure of consciousness" in "Are We Automata?" James concludes by reaffirming "the Common-Sense-Theory" (EPS, 59-61). In doing so he defends and explains further his natural history methodology. Its fragmentary findings, though only probable, are at least supported by the study of factual details, whereas the appeal to universal principles satisfies our need for simplicity without adding anything to our store of facts. Science has risen in contemporary estimation by its careful attention to the details of physical facts at the expense of metaphysics, which has fallen in esteem because of its disregard of them. Science, though, oversteps its bounds when it rules out the possibility of the causality of feelings on the grounds that its effects are not evident in the cause. This line of reasoning would also undermine many beliefs which science holds despite the fact that it is unable to satisfactorily account for them, such as how — in light of Hume's critique — physical objects can affect other physical objects or how knowledge is possible at all given our ignorance of the workings of the brain. This admonition to science not to overstep its bounds is said to derive from a level of argument which has itself kept "upon the plane of concrete facts."

James refers to concrete facts in two related, but distinct ways. In the first place, they refer to facts as they appear in common sense, ordinary situations. In everyday life, for instance, we operate as if our actions are under our conscious control. But this phrase can also refer to James's concrete analysis of the human appropriation of experience, which discloses, for instance, that knowledge is always guided by interests. His failure to carefully distinguish the meaning of concrete as ordinary, unreflective experience and as an explanation of such experience, is often a source of confusion.

James continues by saying that "new discoveries of detail" can "oblige us to reinterpret the facts we already know" (EPS, 60). But any reinterpretation will side with the "Common-Sense-Theory" that consciousness is efficacious because failure to do so will render the continuities of our conscious life meaningless and the world irrational. Notice that his use of the findings of experimental science is guided by his concrete analysis of the human condition. He is reminding us that the purpose of science is to support and further our creative appropriation of the world. He explains that common sense rightly supports our feeling that we actually bring about changes in the world because "all meaning, relevancy and purpose are symbolized to our present intelligence in terms of action and reaction and causal efficacy." It is possible that our feelings are not what they seem to be, and new facts and conceptions may come to light which will demonstrate that they merely sham causal efficacy. In the meantime, we have less to lose by fighting to realize our interests, than by taking ourselves to be mere spectators at the game of life. The choice is between recognizing our active participation in creating the world in which we live or denying our responsibility.

In "The Feeling of Effort" (1880) he proposes "to offer a scheme of the physiology and psychology of volition" (EPS, 83). In other words, he will be following the natural history method. He begins with the undoubted fact "that we *have* a feeling of effort." He reviews at length the scientific findings to date on the causes of muscular movement before reaching "the first philosophical conclusion properly so called into which our inquiry leads us, [which] is a confirmation of the older sensationalist view that all the mind's materials without exception are derived from passive sensibility" (115). The feeling we have of mental spontaneity is not on the same level, but dominates the incoming sensations by choosing to attend, to reinforce, to call to mind. The contents of the mind are all empirical in origin; "what is a priori is only their accentuation and emphasis" (116). Indeed, our selfhood is said to consist in this cooperation with or balking at incoming stimuli. This early understanding of sensation as passive does not cohere well with his equally strong insistence on the spontaneous ordering of such sensations, although I do not think that he ever repudiated this distinction. Despite the fact that he could not satisfactorily harmonize sensational immediacy and intentional ordering, he could not deny either phenomenal finding. This is because the passivity of sensation grounds his empiricist realism and the spontaneous ordering grounds his defense of metaphysical freedom. In *Principles* these two aspects are distinguished as sensation and perception (PP,II, 651-658). He argues for the transparent grasp of simple qualities by simple sensations (PP,II, 653), but also insists that they are simple only in the first moments of life because as soon as they are undergone they are modified and reinterpreted in relation to earlier experiences.[4]

In a section discussing another "mighty metaphysical problem" concerning the efficacy of volition, he argues that we have no conscious knowledge of how mind affects the material world (EPS, 116-123). This "curious view" is explicated as the mind's believing in the reality of its ideas unless controverted by outer forces. Except in the singular case of bodily movement, where the mind can directly exercise volition, these outer forces are not constrained by the mind's beliefs. When beliefs are backed by both the mind and outer forces, then these "ideas...are the Reality" (116). There is no intrinsic difference between belief and volition, only a difference of the behavior of outer forces. Since both belief and will are concerned only with realities for the mind, "the notion of *reality for the mind*, becomes thus the pivotal notion in the analysis of both" (117). He agrees with J. S. Mill that "we seem to have reached, as it were, the central point of our intellectual nature, presupposed and built upon in every attempt to explain the more recondite phenomena of our being."

We see here James's natural history method understood as the concrete disclosure of the structures of our interactive appropriation of the world. In this methodological procedure analysis and description are always restricted to a consideration of reality for the mind and not reality in itself. But he also always deliberately assumes that there is such a reality apart from us, despite his identification of this reality for the mind as central to our nature. However persistently James tries to get behind the veil to reality in itself, he always falls back on this central limitation of human knowing. The reality that is assumed as independently existing can only enter into our sure rational grasp as a promissory note.

As a result of this central point we are led to acknowledge that "the sense of reality" can only "be postulated as an ultimate psychic fact" (EPS, 117). According to Hume, Bain, and Taine, our everyday, pre-reflective state is one of simple credulity. Only "extrinsic ideas" can reduce this "primal state of theoretic and practical innocence." Once this simple credulity has been called into doubt, a stable state of belief can be reacquired only after reflection. Reflection is defined as "a conflict between many ideas of possibility" (118). A sense of reality is regained only when this conflict is resolved. The crucial problem as James sees it is to determine whether this sense of reality, which so often comes only with effort, corresponds to the return of "an independent entity," now affirmed, or only "a conclusion decided by the intrinsic strength of the conflicting ideas alone." This is said to be a metaphysical problem because if the latter be true then there would be "no genuine spontaneity, no ambiguous power of decision, no real freedom."

Against the school of "psychic statics and dynamics" and the "English associationist school," which deny such freedom, James upholds the existence of independent entities in order to reduce the certainty with which the determinist thesis is held. Since, according to Hume, the liveliness of the conviction carries with it the sense of reality, a reflective conflict prevents either position from being self-evidently true of reality and reveals the status of both alternatives as being hypotheses. Not wanting to dogmatically settle the issue in favor of freedom, James at this point says that "a little natural history becomes here necessary" (EPS, 119).[5]

But in turning to natural history he rejects the "mechanical language" of science, which supports determinism, and suggests that "our *spontaneous* language is by no means compatible with the law that mental action always follows lines of least resistance" (EPS, 119).

He then examines the language we use in situations where the question of effort arises. In doing so he begins developing an original concrete analysis of effort and does not turn to the physiological record as we would expect him to do if he were using natural history in its more limited scientific meaning. Since there is evidence both for and against freedom, then the question can be left open while further evidence accumulates for those for whom there is no urgent need to settle it. But for those who, like James — quoting "the French philosopher of genius," J. Lequier — awaken to the love of life which is shocked at so much discourse,then the speculative question takes second place to the practical one of "peace or power" (120). Risking error, we can make of one of the alternatives, as James does for the alternative of freedom, a reality-for-us.

James finishes the section by taking up one further point that he says is also important philosophically (EPS, 121-123). Against the contention that only muscular resistance to force "makes us aware of a reality independent of ourselves," he argues that all our sense impressions equally reveal to us the "attributes of the phenomenal world" (121). To the naive all these sensible attributes are alike objective, while to the critic all are equally subjective. Moreover, "the physicist knows nothing whatever of force in a non-phenomenal sense." James concludes that moral effort acts on the inner world alone and not between the inner and outer world. It applies to an idea and "its achievement is 'reality for the mind,' of that idea" (123). The correlation of physical event with mental ones is only a fortuitous harmony.

Since James sometimes supports the naive position and sometimes the critical one, careful attention must be paid to the context of his explanations to determine which one he is defending. We have seen that "The Feeling of Effort," for instance, is developed by him as "a scheme of the physiology and psychology of volition" (EPS, 83). It is a work in natural history, therefore, which he understands as limited to the phenomenal level alone. It is a careful investigation of reality-for-us as a preliminary to determining reality in itself, which is the proper sphere of philosophical metaphysics. The closest he comes to second order reflection on whether the phenomenal attributes he has identified are subjective or objective is in his metaphysical essays. In *Essays in Radical Empiricism* he says that the central thesis of his "pure-experience theory" is that subjectivity and objectivity are reflective determinations only, made with certain ends in view, and not properly attributable to "what an experience is aboriginally made of" (ERE, 70-71). These essays can be profitably read as cogently criticizing such distinctions as reality-for-us and reality-in-itself as category mistakes.

But a couple of years before he died James wrote in a letter to John Russell (1908) that, as a pragmatist, he is still only assuming that reality exists, and challenges anyone to demonstrate that their assertion of such a reality is anything more than a belief. His "dying word" is that "no one can show at any moment that he possesses it [reality]—only the critical verdict of the rest of experience can show retrospectively whether either you or I have possest [sic.] it" (ERE, 293). Unlike Nietzsche's more radical genealogical analysis, which demonstrates the error of presupposing that there is something behind or above the phenomena, James stops short at concrete analysis still understood as preliminary to metaphysical analysis. Oddly enough, this is despite the fact that his own metaphysics of radical empiricism seems to dissolve rather than resolve such pseudo-problems as inner/outer, subjective/objective, and appearance/reality, much as Nietzsche had. It is also despite the fact that the discovery of the ultimate truth about reality as such is never claimed to be possessed by any metaphysics, although this is given as its defining purpose, but is instead always projected into an unrealized future.[6]

This leads me to conclude that the assumptions informing the natural history method, which encompasses both concrete findings and the concrete structures of reality-for-us, continue to be held even in the metaphysical writings. This method finally displaces the traditional role of metaphysics, despite James's best efforts to preserve a space for it. As a rational endeavor metaphysics can only identify limited marks of the whole and cannot transcend the limits of its own approach. Metaphysicians therefore delude themselves insofar as they try to think being as such. But James's natural history method is actually developed and applied until the very end of his life with the understanding that he is only laying the foundation for a non-speculative metaphysics.

3. Re-defining Definitions

James's use of definition does not conform to the usual models. This is not only due to his particular style of writing, but also to his deliberate adoption of natural history methodology. Since he characteristically fails to explain his procedure, the fact that he employs an alternate model, rather than the obvious fact that he fails to provide good ones on the usual model, can easily be missed. Reference to the object is essential to his notion of definition. Preciseness of articulation is of secondary importance. But how can it be known with certainty what is being referred to if there is no precise delineation according to which it can be recognized whether the object picked out is indeed the one intended? It is recognized by other marks than those of verbalization primarily.[7] As he explains in "The Function of Cognition," context is crucial (MT, 21ff). Within an actual situation we know what someone means when we can both act towards the object referred to in such a way as to leave no doubt. Agreeing that we mean the same thing by an analysis of the linguistic formulation alone is a promissory note, which in no way guarantees that we do in fact understand the marks in the same way nor that we can correctly identify their objects of reference.

Definitions are complex signs and signs are clear when they successfully disclose the object and not for something intrinsic to verbalization. Furthermore, since the accuracy of a verbal formulation means picking out some aspect of the experiential matrix which successfully fulfills our expectations in regard to it, the essentiality is tied to both purposes and verification procedures as much as to formulation.[8] There is no way to say that a definition is precise in its formulation apart from this whole process. Preciseness in the sense of unambiguous formulation does not depend so much on using terms in carefully defined ways, built out of earlier definitions, as much as it means that some aspect of the object can be recognized for what it is. And for James, the object is clearly grasped through careful and exact observation guided by interests. Since there can be no essential definitions apart from guiding interests, both of which are multiple, there can be no preciseness apart from both identification of purpose and some feedback mechanism.

One of the reasons James was so attracted to Darwinian evolutionary biology was that it combined a careful enumeration of a multitude of factual details with an open-ended theory. Like Peirce, he was fascinated by what has since come to be called a 'logic of discovery.' In *Principles* he says that "at a certain stage in the development of every science a degree of vagueness is what best consists with fertility" (PP,I, 19). His definitions are therefore deliberately vague because preciseness is defined as the outcome of a process, not something that can be dogmatically predetermined.[9] Preciseness is a function of the accurate representation of all the results of investigations in regard to the relevant facts.

Because of James's fundamental belief that experience always overflows any conceptual grasp or linguistic formulation he undermines any claims that a given signifier exactly identifies what is signified. He insists that all we ever have is a rough equivalency and therefore identity claims are systematically misleading. A global formulation permits many variant interpretations to guide experimental verification processes. It is intellectually preferable to an exact formulation which narrows the area of research before we have gathered enough information to allow us to decide with confidence that our delimitation of the field coincides with what there is to be known. He defends his own reworking of the Meynert Scheme of the reflex arc, for instance, on the grounds that it "allows for zoological differences as we know them, and is vague and elastic enough to receive any number of future discoveries of detail. (PP,I, 85).

But this deliberate refusal to precisely predelineate the area of investigation to avoid premature closure too often prevents James from coming to any closure at all. His empiricist assumptions that percepts precede concepts and description precedes theory lead him in practice to operate with loose definitions and implicit theoretical assumptions which never become more exact or more explicit. Since concepts are taken by him to be either generalizations or crystallizations of facts, he lacks the notion of concepts or theories as framing or setting up what we take to be facts. He shows in his explanation of the genesis of common sense categories his awareness that our inherited concepts predetermine the way that we understand experiences and he is expert at getting us to see in new ways that will break the hold of our unexamined presumptions (PM, 83-94). But he does not draw the conclusion that he should carefully examine and disclose — to himself as well as to us — the particular patterns governing his own investigations.

He does recognize that such pre-delineation takes place, but his attribution of this function to purposes, rather than to concepts or theories, seems to blind him to the importance of being as careful in formulating his guiding assumptions, concepts, and experimental plans of action as he is in identifying the guiding purpose. He seems to mistake the injunction to treat our formulations and the results produced as a result of applying them to experience as being in principle subject to revision for an injunction not to be too definite in the formulations themselves. In trying to mirror the variety and indefiniteness of experience in the reflective formulations which seek to disclose experience, he too often succeeds in keeping all our options open at the cost of not being able to resolve particular issues.

If it should turn out that his subordination of theoretical issues to practical ones on the grounds that they are unsolvable on theoretical grounds alone can be attributed to this failure to be reflective enough about the theoretical issues involved, then a basic premise of his whole philosophy would be called into question. But I think that his lack of explicit reflection and criticism about the interpretive structures he employs obscures but does not ultimately undermine his larger project. He does begin identifying the limits of rationality and provides a defensible way of proceeding in view of these limitations. But in order for these insights to become available today his interpretive praxis first has to be recovered and his assumptions made explicit before his conclusions and methodology can be evaluated.

4. Re-describing Description

The descriptive or analytic level consists in classifying, identifying natures, analyzing wholes into elements, and tracing habitual successions (TT, 19). On the explanatory level origins are identified and why things are as they are is disclosed. James claimed that the science of psychology of his day was still at the descriptive stage of classifying and analyzing states or fields of consciousness and could not yet answer fundamental explanatory questions about their origin or precise inner constitution. We know they are related in some way to brain states and that they are influenced by past experiences and education, but only in general and conjecturally. For the immediate purpose of passing on to teachers what will be useful to them from psychology he therefore dismisses even promising speculation in order to "turn to mere description" (20).

What follows in *Talks to Teachers* is a brief summary of the most important facts described in *Principles*. These include "the first general fact" that we have states of consciousness and "the second general fact" that these "concrete fields are always complex," (TT, 20-21). In concrete states of consciousness the different classes of ingredients such as sensations, memories, feelings, expectations and desires, are present simultaneously but shift and vary in proportion to one another. In most of our fields of consciousness there is a pronounced core of sensation, called the center or focus, within a margin of thoughts and feelings. But the focus and margin of our mental attention can shift, with present sensations becoming marginal, displaced, for instance, by memories or expectations.[10] Changes in our fields of consciousness between focus and fringe can be abrupt alterations of the whole field but are more often gradual, and various aspects of either fringe or focus can remain, shift to the other, or disappear in any degree. Because of this variability, "there can seldom be sharp description." The exactness of description for

James, then, varies with the stability of the object within the process rather than with accuracy in regard to the process itself. We are said to know that fields have a practical unity for their possessors, and we can therefore classify fields from this practical point of view as a state of emotion or of sensation, or whatever.

What is suppressed in this last remark of James is what other unity is available to us besides the practical one, which thereby renders it only a temporary expedient until it can be obtained. It is the actual situation as it is in itself, undistorted by our participation. When we can exactly describe every permutation and combination as they are and can correctly identify the laws governing them, then our descriptions and explanations would not be practical but would bridge the gap between knowing and being in the accomplished harmony of identity. In his early writings James characterizes modern skepticism as the reduction of the relative certainties with which we operate in everyday life by the withering challenge of the rational demand for absolute certainty. His first step in reducing the reductive is to distinguish the amount of certainty appropriate for human action from that required in a complete system of explanation. But he apparently puts off rather than resolves the challenge because he still accepts as a legitimate distinction the disjunction between the practical and the ultimate levels of explanation. He even contributes to the reduction of the practical level of experience by understanding it as a temporary expedient until such time as the real situation will be disclosed.[11]

The methodological starting point for investigation and reflection is said to be careful observation and description of facts. Since what this investigation discloses in the case of consciousness is a process with no sharp boundaries, the description cannot be couched in discrete, sharply delineated conceptual terms without illicitly going beyond the evidence and positively distorting it. Spencer, Taine, and Locke are all criticized for their building block theories of elementary mental particles combining in an elegant "mental architecture" because they are based on no experimental observation whatever. In contrast to these merely conjectural theories, James claims that his own "unpretending conception of the stream of consciousness, with its total waves or fields incessantly changing," even though vaguer, is preferable because descriptively accurate (TT, 21-22).

Thus, while he recognizes the theoretical frameworks of others, which distort what should be described with limpid lucidity, he does not recognize that he employs any framework not derived from what is observed: "Vague and hazy as such an account of our stream of consciousness may be, it is at least secure from positive error and free from admixture of conjecture or hypothesis" (TT, 21). In this belief in pure description and in the accuracy to the facts of vague over exact distinctions he is following Wilhelm Wundt, the founder of the 'new' laboratory psychology. According to Wundt the experimental method has made exact observation of inner phenomena possible. And among the most important facts which have been discovered are (1) "the fact of creative mental synthesis," (2) "the indivisibility and inner homogeneity...of the mental life," which are artificially distinguished into "ideation, feeling, will," (3) that the verbalization of the deluded "notion of distinct mental 'images'" has distorted our perception of the reality of the "melting and fleeting" process of ideation, and consequently, (4) that "the older doctrine of association of 'ideas'" is "no longer tenable" (22, n1).

5. Observation: "The primal state of theoretic and practical innocence" (EPS, 117)

James's own natural history method consists in beginning with some process actually observable in nature, carefully describing it by picking out aspects or marks according to his end-in-view, and relating these aspects to others found to be similar. A general explanation of the cause and nature of the original process is then proposed as a hypothesis to be tested by his audience or readers. The method assumes that the initial set of facts can be clearly observed without any bias and accurately described. The belief in 'pure' seeing and transparent description is a tenet of positivism that became a defining characteristic of science. It is uncritically accepted by James, as it was also by many thinkers of the late nineteenth and early twentieth century, because it merely reformulates in scientific terms what he already accepts on both empiricist and poetic grounds.[12]

This belief in exact observation and pure description can be found throughout James's writings. In 1887 he writes in a letter to the psychologist, Carl Stumpf, that "of course, the experimental patience, and skill and freshness of observation of the Helmholtzes and Herings are altogether admirable, and perhaps at bottom *worth* more than philosophic ability."[13] In an 1896 speech in honor of Louis Agassiz, delivered to the American Society of Naturalists, James praises him as the paradigmatic student of nature.[14] James's earliest and most striking impressions of the method of natural history were formed in 1865 when he joined the Thayer expedition to Brazil under Agassiz's leadership. They are summed up in a maxim of Agassiz that James liked to quote: "Go to Nature; take the facts into your own hands; look, and see for yourself!" (MS, 12)[15] Agassiz is also praised for "the extreme rigor of his devotion to this concrete method of learning." But he is said to have an undeveloped "capacity for abstraction and causal reasoning and tracing chains of consequences," which are associated with reasoning and Comte's characterization of the scientific stage. He instead exhibits a "genius for acquaintance with vast volumes of detail, and for seizing upon analogies and relations of the more proximate and concrete kind," which James associates with the narrative, descriptive, and contemplative thinking, characteristic of the poetic (MS, 13; see EPS, 2ff).

In favoring the richness of empirical detail over simplification through theory construction Agassiz represented the older natural history tradition.As a student of the new, experimental sciences, James is aware of the importance of abstracting elements out of the whole and using these partial characteristics as the basis for scientific thinking. Nonetheless, he also emphasizes that he had "never been able to forget" the priority of living "in the light of the world's concrete fullness" to such abstractions (MS, 14-15). His own concrete approach represents a unique synthesis and transformation of the older and the newer traditions of science. The search for causal elements rather than totality is said to characterize contemporary science, "but the truth of things is after all their living fullness," and someday the elements being discovered will again be gathered up into a "higher and simpler way of looking at Nature."

It is obvious, then, that although James uncritically assumes the empiricist bias of the priority of gathering facts to reasoning about them or even delineating an experimental program, he critically rejects the empiricist assumption of the experienced world as built up piecemeal out of such bits and pieces. He argues that the elements are abstracted out of the "concrete fullness" of the world, which structures them, and without which they would neither 'be' nor 'be meaningful.' As his concrete description of our human interaction within the world of our experience points out, our living in the concrete fullness of the world conditions any experimental selectivity, whether or not we advert to it. James wants to make explicit this concrete world within which and according to which all particular human projects take place to demonstrate the falsity of the positivist claims of a purely disinterested observation and access to primal units of sense data on a foundationalist building block model. To the first he opposes the necessarily interested character of all human appropriations of the world and to the second he opposes a holistic view according to which we are an irreducible part of any investigative field and, therefore, the identification of discrete units of consciousness presupposes a cohesive experiential field.

James does share the empiricist bias against the necessity of an explicit conceptual framework to a recognition of facts. The concrete fullness of the world provides a sufficient setting within which facts can be experienced. It is enough if the conditions which set up and make possible the recognition of particular facts are only implicitly operative. In everyday life we need not advert to them. James has made a lasting contribution to the way we understand ourselves by replacing the traditional, speculatively generated system of categories, which emphasizes essential invariance and necessity, with his concrete analysis of our living world of experience, which emphasizes temporality and fortuitous origins. But it is difficult to see how the naturalist gathering facts partakes only of the world of everyday experience and not also of an experimental project with explicit protocols.

Agassiz never explicitly reflected on the scientific interests which guided his picking out of a phenomenon those structures which were worth reporting. Even less did he advert to the more general structures of human experience which allowed him to recognize and describe a particular phenomenon as an object of interest to a naturalist out of the phenomenal totality with which it was continuous. It is therefore understandable that he naively assumed that he was merely describing exactly what was present as it was in itself. He was infamous, for instance, for preventing students from entering into a course of studies with him if they could not intuitively observe and describe the very same features of an organism that he did (MS, 12).

But James did reflect on the shared structures and subjective interests which make it possible to disengage an object as an object out of the big blooming buzzing confusion of phenomenal continuity. He also insists that the being of a thing cannot by itself determine how we will apprehend it, which depends upon our selective interests. How can he nonetheless claim that we have direct observational access to facts which can be exactly described as they are? He never explicitly resolves this issue, but some insights will follow in the next sections as to why he never even recognized the discrepancy between his assumption of a naive direct access to things in themselves and his explanation that we cannot know objects except as they are related to us.

Some clues as to how James could hold both that we can have an unproblematic access to reality in sensational immediacy and that we construct reality by constraining it to answer to our needs can be found in passages where he talks about a primitive state of both theoretic and practical presuppositions. In the chapter on "The Perception of Space" in *Principles* it is clear that the primal state refers to the "primitive sensations" that comprise "the original data of feeling" (PP,II, 838). It is absolutely essential to James's long-range project of overcoming skepticism and nihilism by reestablishing philosophy on the secure basis of empirical evidence that all our categories be derived in the first instance directly from sensations. He argues, for instance, that no "mysterious 'mental chemistry' or power of 'synthesis'" need be invoked to explain how orderly space perceptions are built up out of "primitive incoherency."

He does grant that such ordinary intellectual operations as discrimination, association, and selective emphasis are involved in space perceptions, but these only disclose what is present, although vaguely, in our first chaotic impressions. Anything lawfully attributed to real space can be "experienced directly as a presentation or ideally suggested by another feeling which has come to serve as its sign" (PP,II, 838). We do, it is said, degrade "some sensations to the rank of signs" and exalt "others to that of realities signified," and "make a continuous order out of what was a rather incoherent multiplicity." What he says must be insisted upon, however, is that "the *content* of the order remains identical with that of the multiplicity — sensational both, through and through."

A problem immediately presents itself as soon as we try to identify such a content in its sensible, but incoherent, immediacy and also recognize it as identical to its ordered form. Of course, it cannot be identical, but for James it is enough if it shows similarity in difference. What, then, do discrimination and ordering add? Can there be a sensation that is not a sign or a reality not grasped through a horizon of meaning? If James only means to assert that both sensational immediacy and intellectual ordering operate together to give us a real, recognizable object, then no such problems arise. But he seems to have fallen into "the psychologist's fallacy" of attributing what is available only on reflection to the original experience. He wants to assert both that objects are immediately sensed and known as such and that they can be known only through the ordering of such sensations, which then are not bare sensations but interpreted perceptions. Elsewhere in *Principles* he had explained the difference between sensations and perceptions functionally, as places in a continuum from the limit concept of a 'raw feel' through gradually more clearly articulated and delineated objects to the limit concept of a pure meaning. But in this case he wants to reify the functional distinction of more or less reflectively conscious ordering into a distinction of kinds of reality that not only 'are' but 'are known' as such.

This is clear in an earlier passage in the same chapter. The primitive sensation James has in mind is that of a retinal magnitude, that is, literally the sensation of the size of an image on the retina. He thinks that a draftsman can learn "to feel directly" such a retinal magnitude (PP,II, 817). "To do this he must recover what Ruskin calls the 'innocence of the eye'—that is, a sort of childish perception of stains of color merely as such, without consciousness of what they mean." This is clearly a recovery, something that must be learned, and not the primitive state, however, since "with the rest of us this innocence is lost." But is learning to ignore certain aspects of incoming stimuli and accentuate others really a return to a lost innocence or is it a new construction?

The explanation for how it is that we pass over and ignore in the usual course of events the primitive sensation to grasp the object signified is instructive in this regard because it gives a concrete explanation for why seeing is always 'seeing-as,' that is, is always already interpreted. The selectivity which James places at the center of the human organization of experience means in this case that out of all the retinal magnitudes which impinge on us one is selected as the real one and all the rest are relegated to the status of signs. "This 'real' magnitude is determined by aesthetic and practical interests" (PP,II, 817). In the case of visual sensations, for instance, objects are observed at the distance which best brings detail into focus for our eyes. Since we know that distant objects appear smaller, we pass over their visual image as a mere sign of their real size.

Furthermore, we construct real space by ordering the incoherence of our primitive space-experiences by two operations (PP,II, 819-821). These two are that some experiences are apprehended as along side each other and some as interpenetrating. These apprehensions are guided by the fundamental act of space arrangement, that is, according to "the great intellectual law of economy, we simplify, unify, and identify as much as we possibly can" (821). We can recognize this law as a fundamental finding of his analysis of concrete rationality. He draws on these findings at crucial points in his arguments. He says, for instance, that "the selection of the several 'normal' appearances from out of the jungle of our optical experiences" is a substitution "of terms few and fixed for terms manifold and vague" (872).

Given these careful descriptions of the structures of the human appropriation of a world in which we can be at home, it seems obvious that the recovery of a bare sensation, apart from any interpretive context, is a chimera.[16] James's holding to such an intuitive indubitability can be understood as defining a pre-reflexive state of affairs which forms the necessary horizon of all knowledge claims. Since the constructive theories of knowledge which dominated the philosophical scene at the time, neo-Hegelianism and neo-Kantianism, were understood as too idealistic and speculative, too disdainful of the messy world of everyday life, he countered by holding on to an empiricist explanatory paradigm that was stubbornly realistic. Neither neo-Kantians nor neo-Hegelians, for instance, were known for such claims as those James makes throughout *Principles*: "Empirically we find this probability confirmed by many facts" (PP,II, 834); "This opinion has not lacked experimental confirmation" (845); "This subject will close our survey of the facts" (846); and "I am unfortunately prevented by the weakness of my own eyes from experimenting enough to form a decided personal opinion on the matter" (860). The realist assumptions underlying these approaches prevented him from recognizing that crucial aspects of the empiricist program were already being undermined by his own concrete explanations.

James also seems to systematically confuse the transcendentalist claim that there are conditions according to which experience operates, which can be reflectively delineated, with the claim that experience cannot take place unless we are explicitly aware of these structures while we are experiencing something. His refutation of Fichte, for instance, depends upon this confusion.[17] Why, then, does James seek to make explicit the human structures of our experience? This is not straightforwardly obvious. He usually does so in order to disprove what he takes to be the extremes of the over-conceptualized, transcendentalist position and the atomism of the empiricist and positivist positions. But he draws a sharp distinction between what is available to us on reflection and the way in which we originally experience the world. He seems to assume that if the structures become obvious only on reflection, then they cannot be assumed to be operating when we are not aware of them. In this he seems to be relying uncritically on the Berkeleyan *esse est sentire* doctrine.

6. Bare Facts in a Real World versus Interpreted Facts of Experienced Phenomena

James expresses his ideal in 1879 as: "the union of the mathematician with the poet, fervor with measure, passion with correctness" (CER, 138). In *Principles* he characterizes the philosopher, physicist, and psychologist, Gustav Theodor Fechner, as instantiating such an ideal: "Fechner himself indeed was a German *Gelehrter* of the ideal type, at once simple and shrewd, a mystic and an experimentalist, homely and daring, and as loyal to facts as to his theories" (PP,I, 518). This conjunction of science and poetry, of fact and theory, of exact description and flights of fancy, of accurateness and passion describes both the ideal which guides his own work and the reconciliation he wants to achieve as his most lasting contribution to the debate over how to resolve the challenge positivist science posed to traditional beliefs and values. Some have taken James's critiques of science and praise of art as evidence of an animosity to science as such.[18] They are rather his attempt to balance the contributions of both in our organizations of experience by detaching the genuine contributions science can make to our understanding of the world from those illegitimate positivist claims made in the name of science which would make it the sole avenue to truth and not one contributor among others.

James says that according to "the modern mechanico-physical philosophy" of positivism the only facts are motions of primordial solids and the only laws are changes of motion (PP,II, 1260). Future states are predicted from our knowledge of present states by considering only "the necessary geometrical, arithmetical, and logical implications." Nature becomes a bare world for science so construed, consisting only of atoms and ether with no properties but masses and velocities expressible by numbers and analytic formulas. He reiterates this accepted view of science as positivistic at the end of *Principles*, which is a sustained argument for including those sensible phenomena which are considered to be pure delusions for the mechanical philosophy. He is trying to tread a thin line between helping psychology to become an exact science by distinguishing in the literature between what has been determined as the result of strict laboratory procedures and is therefore 'factual' and what is merely ungrounded speculation. He then criticizes these same laboratory procedures for being unduly reductionistic and ignoring the human context of experience, as well as for taking as pure description of phenomena what is actually constrained by theoretical presuppositions.

He denies that science simply replicates reality, arguing instead that its world is as much a construct as that of sentimental philosophy, since both activities originate in the belief that nature conforms to mental relations, that is, we constrain the phenomena to make it answer to our subjective interests (PP,II, 1260-61). Scientific facts are not simply impressed on the mind from without, but are constructed according to our interests; "The craving to believe that the things of the world belong to kinds which are related by inward rationality together, is the parent of Science as well as of sentimental philosophy; and the original investigator always preserves a healthy sense of how plastic the materials are in his hands." This would seem to indicate that James, already by 1890, believed that all perception is theory-laden as well as context-dependent, and that, therefore, there can be no appeal to an irrefutable level of pure seeing and exact description.

But James is only bringing the scientific enterprise within his concrete analysis of human action, according to which all purposeful activities, whether scientific, philosophical, artistic or practical, are ways of ordering the flux of experience to answer to our needs. But once having acknowledged the world as a human context which sets up and makes possible and explicable particular acts, it does not necessarily follow that within these constraints the 'real' world may not be disclosed as it is. Since the disclosure is tied to our subjective interests, some additional moves are still required to determine whether what anyone takes to be the case is actually the case. But it does not follow that just because further acts of verification are required if we are to know that we have in a particular case accurately identified some fact, that we have not in the first place correctly identified it.[19]

This distinguishes the realism of James's position from transcendental phenomenology. According to Nietzsche, for instance, there is no world behind the world which answers to our interests to which we can compare it. For us there can be no other world than the world as it appears to us, and thus the phenomenal/noumenal distinction breaks down. What we have in the past faulted as a mistaken appearance in light of some newly discovered fact is better characterized as the replacement of one appearance/fact by another. For James, too, only further confirming instances can establish that we know some fact and even these confirmations are in principle subject to further verification procedures. As finite beings we can never know that any particular fact is grasped as it is.

But James differs from Nietzsche in claiming that we do, as a matter of fact, sometimes grasp aspects of the world as it really is, even though it may take all future time for us to know that we do so with certainty, that is, that no new facts will arise which would cause us to revise our opinion. He says, for example, that "the so-called metaphysical principles are at bottom only expressions of aesthetic feeling" and yet these subjective feelings are "of course quite compatible with Nature also turning out objectively to be of that sort, later on" (PP,II, 1265). But applying the pragmatic maxim to this aspect of James's realism leads to the conclusion that this is a distinction without a difference, since we operate in finite time and not at the end of time.[20] It seems that Nietzsche had a clearer grasp of the consequences of our radical finiteness and temporality in that he recognized that the interpretive character of all our organizations of experience cannot in principle be transcended.

By contrast, James vacillates between affirming the merely tentative character of all our organizations of experience and affirming the realist assumption of a world understood as a thing in itself. There are passages in James which seem to suggest that he also realized that we cannot get behind our interpretations to a bare, uninterpreted universe, despite the fact that this insight did not easily cohere with his realism. At the end of *A Pluralist Universe*, for instance, he says that "if such a synechistic pluralism as Peirce, Bergson, and I believe in, be what really exists, every phenomenon of development, even the simplest, would prove equally rebellious to our science should the latter pretend to give us literally accurate instead of approximate, or statistically generalized, pictures of the development of reality" (PU, 154). By understanding his natural history methodology as a concrete analysis rather than an empirical explanation, the difficulties inherent in the realist model do not arise.

7. Creativity

Without belittling the real accomplishments of science, James situates it in a wider context or more fundamental activity, that of inventiveness or creativity.[21] In section five of "The Stream of Thought" chapter of *Principles* he describes consciousness as always choosing and rejecting objects (PP,I, 273ff). Both selective attention and deliberate willing are examples of the activity of choosing, which is inseparable from life.[22] Examples are given to demonstrate that this native selectivity is operative at every level, from sensation to cognition. James incisively undercuts the naiveté of the presumption that the scientific method alone discloses the real world by situating science along a continuum of selective, creative activity. He dislodges scientific explanations as paradigmatic for all explanations by showing that such explanation itself is a subset of the creative imposition of form on an otherwise chaotic world.[23] It is only one among many such systematic structurings of the data of experience and nothing is lost in conceding that in its chosen sphere it is extraordinarily successful. Over millenniums we and our ancestors have carved out the world we live in, but with other interests other parts of the world would have been and yet may be revealed, no one of which is intrinsically truer or more real than any other.

James again subsumes scientific activity under creative activity in the last chapter of volume two. While "science thinks that she has discovered the outer realities in question," it is actually manufacturing "a world about which rational propositions may be framed" (PP,II, 1258). Sensible phenomena do not survive the imposition of the "mathematico-logical network," but this replacement of common sense data with scientifically defined entities and processes should not be viewed as progress from mistaken opinions about the world to true knowledge of it. Science is placed in an historical framework where it takes its place beside other attempts to impose order on "the chaos of nature's sequences and juxtapositions" (1259). Over thousands of years we have used many ideal prototypes of rational order to make sense of experience — teleological, aesthetic, logical, and mathematical, among others. In earliest recorded history the emotionally richer myths and world-views were more successful in ordering experiences, but very gradually scientific explanations advanced, until the verification by nature of the scientific claims that nothing really exists except as it can fit into some mathematical scheme has convinced many of the exclusive truth of scientific explanations of the world (1259ff).[24]

James faults this popular view of science as final arbiter of truth because it ignores the nature of scientific propositions as constructions for the sake of imposing a rational order on an otherwise chaotic manifold of sensations (PP,II, 1260). All interpretations, scientific and non-scientific alike, originate in the need to order our experience, which does not favor one interpretation over another except in the sense that we can demand desiderata to be fulfilled, and which would count as a real confirmation of the interpretation by the phenomena. But these teleological considerations originate in our needs and not in an independent nature. James does not at this point go into the criteria we do in fact use to choose one interpretation over another, criteria which he derives from reconstructing the Darwinian notion of survival. He does, however, insist that the activity of science, like all our organizing activities, is explainable only on the supposition of the plasticity of phenomena which must be shaped by us.

Science seems to be distinguished from other, non-scientific, interpretations in that the phenomena answer so consistently to the demands imposed on them by specific scientific disciplines. Such fittings of theory and data appear to be discoveries rather than creations. These translations of sensible experience have such great predictive value that the world seems to be just what science discloses it to be.[25] But James undercuts this assumption of the unrelativized truth of scientific propositions by pointing out that science only appears so secure if the postulates of rationality are mistaken as being themselves propositions of fact (PP,II, 1263).

James challenges the hegemony of the scientific world view by showing how aspects of our experience cannot be subsumed under scientific categories. They are therefore considered to be of no account, indeed, to lack any reality, from the scientific point of view. The illusory things of common sense, for instance, are "butchered," as merely naive interpretations of reality which can be more accurately and truly explained in mathematical-logical terms. But it would be as accurate to counter that the "vast field of irrationalized fact" has not been disproven by science, but simply ignored because it cannot be made sense of as long as one stays within the boundaries of the system. This can be seen as a limitation of the scientific world view, however, rather than as a proof of the unreality of other phenomena.

Scientific endeavor necessarily presupposes the postulate of rationality, which is in turn rooted in the desire for a harmonious universe. Every time an ideal network of relations succeeds in disclosing real potentialities, we feel confirmed in our hopes that other systems will also be applicable. But just how far the world may be made answerable to our hopes for rational order cannot be predicted. However, the desire for harmony, the source of our efforts at creating a human, understandable world, whether by scientific or non-scientific means, can be understood only through understanding the structures of creativity. These structures are more apparent, because more self-consciously elucidated, in aesthetics and ethics. An uncovering of the human project in aesthetic making and moral behavior can reveal structures which are also operative in science. Aesthetic and ethical world-views are not only prior to scientific views historically, but ontologically, as more explicit of the embeddedness of creativity in facticity.

It should be noticed that in this context, James defends the common sense world-view as one among many non-scientific views that delimit the scope and application of science. But common sense is no more paradigmatic for experience than is science. Both have to be reconstructed along Jamesian lines. If he frequently argues more strongly against scientific interpretations, it is because science is often taken as the best or the only true interpretation of reality, rather than as one valid interpretation among others. Since James consistently applies the methodological postulate that no one point of view can ever encompass the fecundity of reality and that a plurality of points of view is necessary for disclosing more real possibilities of experience, then he obviously does not intend to replace a scientific world view with a common sense one, despite his frequent appeals to ordinary, common sense experiences.

Such reconstructions as are available in common sense, the sciences, and arts, are products, and James is struggling to provide an explanation not of the product but of the process by which such productions come about. This is why his own attempts to explain or reconstruct experience are central to his discourse. This process of reconstruction can be termed 'creativity,' since it involves a rearrangement of some act of experiencing in order to bring out or bring about some aspect of interest. That this interest may be shared by others and thus have a wider applicability, can be known only through the active corroboration of such others. The pragmatic method is the formulation of such a process of extending an interest through confirmatory procedures.

8. Artistic Vision: "Mystic Sense of Hidden Meaning" (TT, 138)

When James says in his last book that "philosophers may get into as close contact as realistic novelists with the facts of life," he may have had Goethe in mind (SPP, 19). This can be gathered from a letter written over thirty years earlier (1868) in which he says that Goethe "*is* a perfect natural-born *collector*, as much as Agassiz, and he does hate to lose *anything* in creation....Through every individual fact he came in contact with the world, and he strove and fought without ceasing ever to lay his mind more and more wide open to nature's teaching — more and more to efface those subjective wrinkles in which we all force the objective matter nature gives us to lie in our minds" (TCW,I, 159-160). The task of artists as well as scientists is to disclose nature in ever greater detail. Neither has a monopoly on exact and careful observation and both are engaged in thinking, although not to the same extent. Whereas the scientist privileges the moment of the abstraction of qualities that range over many phenomena, the artist privileges their embeddedness and does not seek to go beyond analogical thinking to abstract reasoning. In the descriptive move which follows observation, the poet and novelist often surpass the scientist.

The poet and the scientist do not differ along the lines of subjectivity and objectivity, since the artist can seek to disclose reality as objectively as any scientist. As was pointed out earlier in chapter 4, they differ in that scientific rational thinking always extracts only part of a phenomena, while contemplative thinking associates entire phenomena. The creative aspect of our appropriation of the world in intellectual constructs is more evident in artistic creations, but not absent from rational ones. Both the scientist and the artist abstract partial aspects of the total phenomena, but the degree of simplification and their intentions in doing so differ significantly. Experiences are originally global and artists do less violence to the "much-at-onceness" than do scientists, so their work, like originating experiences themselves, can be returned to again and again to discover new connections. Since experiential reality has an infinity of aspects the differing ones discovered and communicated by scientists and artists are not rivals so much as complementary angles of vision. The ability to recognize unusual couplings, to discern relationships where no one has yet seen them, is the basis for both scientific and poetic genius.

The abstract reasoner and the poetic intuitionist both begin by associating by similarity, but the former attends to the ground of the analogy, while the latter does not. Artists "judge rightly, classify cases, characterize them by the most striking analogic epithets, but go no further". Far from being evidence of a failure to reach the highest levels of human reasoning, these preferences reveal "a mind fertile in the suggestions of analogies, but, at the same time keenly interested in the particulars of each suggested image" (EPS, 30). Since James's revolution in philosophy consists in a call to renounce the aesthetic pleasure to be gained in perfecting rational systems for their own sake and turn instead toward a careful examination of "the full concrete act of thought" and develop a philosophy of praxis, the artist's insistence on revealing the richness of experience through analogy and refusal to transcend it by ratiocination can be seen as a parallel effort to his own (28).

It is possible to recognize in James's encomium to Ralph Waldo Emerson on the occasion of the centenary of his birth the source of the notion of artistic vision that he joins with scientific observation to construct his own model of sympathetic concrete observation. He says that Emerson's genius consisted half in the perception of every natural revelation and half in the expression of these insights. "The day is good, he said, in which we have the most perceptions." As artistic expression it is impossible to separate the thought from the medium of communication; cladding the truth "in the right verbal garment" forms "a chemical combination" (MS, 21; ERM, 110). John Dewey also emphasized the poetic contribution of Emerson to our understanding of philosophy as creative making as well as reflecting, and of philosophers as seers as well as reasoners, and he made the same connection to the importance of fidelity to what is: "To

Emerson, perception was more potent than reasoning; the deliverances of intercourse more to be desired than the chains of discourse; the surprise of reception more demonstrative than the conclusions of intentional proof."[26]

The artist's duty is to report worthily each perception because, according to Emerson's "most characteristic note,...in a life at first hand there is something sacred" (MS, 24-25; ERM, 111). But 'to see' is 'to see into' since "each of us is an angle of [the Cosmic Intellect's] eternal vision." This task "of spiritual seeing and reporting" puts one under an obligation to observe accurately and report worthily. The world is still new and untried, and insofar as we are able to respond to it in seeing freshly the truth will be disclosed. But the cosmic vision is found in one's own private conscience and not in any sacred texts. Rather than the natural history emphasis on accuracy, the watchword is now worthiness. A perception is accurate, not to a predelineated reality, but to an eternal vision which clothes itself in physical garments. Individual facts and moments are absolutely radiant on condition that they are worthy, that is, "sincere, authentic, archetypal," that they are expressive of moral sentiment "as symbolic mouthpieces of the Universe's meaning" (MS, 32; ERM, 114).

In taking over Emerson's message of the transforming effect of the appropriation of reality, according to which even description is never merely passive, James rejects all transcendental appeals to the Absolute and to eternal visions. The poet as visionary is not one who transmits to earth a divine message, but one who divinizes life at first hand. In his later writings he directly criticizes Emerson's appeals to the absolute as derealizing the only world we know: "What boots it to tell me that the absolute way is the true way, and to exhort me, as Emerson says, to lift mine eye up to its style, and manners of the sky, if the feat is impossible by definition?" (PU, 27). It is impossible because "I am finite once for all, and all the categories of my sympathy are knit up with the finite world *as such*, and with things that have a history."

This sense of an anthropomorphized divine mission gives new importance to the smallest details of the experienced world, which can by artistic attention be saved from obscurity. "There are times when the cawing of a crow, a weed, a snow-flake, or a farmer planting in his field, become symbols to the intellect of truths equal to those which the most majestic phenomena can open" (MS, 21; ERM 110). This does not entail denying the more unpleasant aspects of this imperfect world. Far from it, "the full squalor of the individual fact" could be faced by Emerson because "he could also see the transfiguration" (MS, 32; ERM 114). Furthermore, because of his individualistic creed, neither the contours of the factual world nor the cosmic intellect overly constrain the creativity of the acts of seeing and reporting. His message of "the sovereignty of the living individual electrified and emancipated his generation" (MS 25-26; ERM, 112). "The same indefeasible right to be exactly what one is, provided one only be authentic, spreads itself, in Emerson's way of thinking, from persons to things and to times and places" (MS, 29; ERM, 113). What James admired in Agassiz applies equally to Emerson: in their anti-nihilistic self-confidence neither wasted "a moment in doubts about the commensurability of his powers with his tasks" (MS, 5).

Emerson's understanding of the artist as a sovereign individual who transfigures rather than merely reflects reality seems to have "electrified and emancipated" James as well as Nietzsche.[27] When Nietzsche quotes Emerson in an epigraph for the first edition of *The Gay Science*, for instance, he stresses this same theme: "To the poet and sage, all things are friendly and hallowed, all experiences profitable, all days holy, all men divine."[28] The authenticity of the artist's vision can be recognized in James's concrete examination of conceiving as a fact which reveals that because "every reality has an infinity of aspects or properties" I can only recognize any at all insofar as it "is *so important for my interests* that in comparison with it I may neglect the rest" (PP,II, 959-961). Thus, what is observed is really there but it is also a function of my own interests and may for that reason be unavailable to others.

This teleological conception of essence not only undermines the traditional notion of realism, but discloses the irreducible ambiguity at the heart of observation. James's practice of sympathetic concrete observation brings together as a unified process 'seeing' and 'seeing into,' that is, seeing as scientific observation whose ideal is exactness and seeing as poetic transfiguration whose ideal is worthiness. The rare ability "to seize fresh aspects in concrete things" is inextricably perceptive and inventive at the same time and characterizes the great scientist as well as the great artist, but is more likely to be found in poetic rather than scientific praxis (PP,II, 958). James quotes a long passage on observation from Mill in which the ambiguity is patent. Mill denies that there can be an art of observing, any more than there can be rules for inventing. There can only be instructions for putting ourselves into a frame of mind "in which it will be most fitted to observe, or most likely to invent" (957-958, n7).

The reclamation of feeling as cognitive is central to James's reconstruction of philosophy. He objects to some characteristic failings of abstract rationality, such as its repudiation of subjectivity. It therefore claims more certitude than it has evidence for. It also privileges logical criteria, even when they distort experience more than they clarify it. By way of contrast, he often identifies his own position simply as empiricism, but from the earliest references to it he is already transforming it. He does so by exploiting the ambiguity of the use of word 'feeling' as a synonym for 'sense data.' He expands it to include every aspect of feelings as celebrated explicitly in poetry and literature.

In an early article, for instance, he says that "the one *fundamental* quarrel Empiricism has with Absolutism is over this repudiation by Absolutism of the personal and aesthetic factor in the construction of philosophy."[29] He argues that for finite beings who are still searching for comprehensive understanding feelings "may be as prophetic and anticipatory of truth as anything else we have" and expresses his reconceptualization of the goal of philosophy as harmony rather than clarity. He says that if philosophers still under the spell of absolutistic solutions would consider the evidence they would "admit that all philosophies are hypotheses, to which all our faculties, emotional as well as logical, help us, and the truest of which will at the final integration of things be found in possession of the men whose faculties on the whole had the best divining power."[30] This provides a clue to help us recognize that James's model of 'seeing' is 'divining' or 'seeing into' and that therefore 'feeling' is a preferred mode of access to reality.

The difficulty James experiences in reconciling his scientific, empiricist realism with his emphasis on poetic imagination and concrete analysis of knowing as interested appropriation of the world is apparent in his simultaneous attraction to the humanist position of F.C.S. Schiller and Dewey and his reluctance to totally embrace it. In a 1904 article later reprinted in *The Meaning of Truth*, James contrasts his narrower pragmatism from Schiller's broader one precisely on the grounds that Schiller made the truth of any statement to consist solely in its consequences, especially in good ones (MT, 38ff). Although this sounds suspiciously like James's own pragmatic method, he understands his approach as a method merely, that is, he is still bracketing the relation of the outcome of investigation to reality.

He thinks that humanism's concrete analysis and instrumentalism cannot account "for so curious a congruence between the world and the mind" (MT, 41). Despite his unwillingness to embrace what seems to him to be a relativistic philosophy, he makes "a decided effort at sympathetic mental play with humanism" and recommends this same exegetical approach to the reader (42). But in the course of his own sympathetic appropriation he concludes that its account "of phenomenal knowledge is accurate" and that "the humanist does not ignore the character of objectivity and independence in truth" (49-51). He resolves the apparent contradiction by subscribing to the "quasi-paradox" that "in one sense you create" reality, and "in another sense you *find* it" (56). He had not yet, though, worked through what this position would entail.

The common ground on which he could come to terms with humanism is an original understanding of the method of inductive argument. An induction is defined as "a generalization working itself free from all sorts of entangling particulars" (MT, 38). He says that if what Schiller and Dewey say is true, then many traditional positions have to be re-thought. Given the revolutionary character of their humanistic program, exactness of expression cannot be expected. It should be given instead some creative leeway. He excuses his own presentation of humanism, which "has been rambling in the extreme" on the same grounds of being an inductive presentation; therefore, "sharp logic is hardly yet in order" (59). Its promising character should be given a chance to work itself out. Instead of "logic-chopping," the critic "should weigh it as a whole, and especially weigh it against its possible alternatives" (38). To criticize it only from the point of view of logical consistency, instead of judging its success as an explanatory principle, would be to miss its status as a gestalt change or paradigm.

It has also long been recognized that James's natural history methodology draws heavily on Darwinian evolutionary principles. At the same time his Darwinism differs from both the mechanistic evolutionists of his time and that of contemporary socio-biologists. As we have seen in his model of seeing as encompassing both scientific and artistic dimensions, it does so because of his transformation of some idealist presuppositions in his pragmatic evolutionism. I think it can be shown, however, that his reconstruction of Darwinian biological theory into a pragmatic philosophical evolutionism is a defensible outgrowth of Darwinism and not a relic of a pre-Darwinian romantic evolutionism.[31]

I have been developing the first two of three discernible aspects of James's model of sympathetic concrete observation: seeing as exactness, seeing as worthiness, and seeing as 'feeling with.' In James's transformation of the model of natural history observation, accuracy is a function of our interests as well as of the fullness of the concrete situation and therefore it is a mistake to understand it as a one-to-one correspondence of symbol and thing. In his transformation of the mystical vision of poetry the communication of some aspect of reality is judged by its worthiness, that is, it is accurate not despite but because of its incorporation of worthy intentions. It must embody a deliberate decision to see into the world its genuine possibilities of a better reality as a first step to bringing them about. And when this method of sympathetic concrete observation is applied to our relations to others, it becomes the basis for James's reconstruction of morality.[32] Without this injunction to sympathetically appropriate the point of view of others and thus recognize their dignity as independent centers of feeling, judgment, and action, there would be no positive content to what he argues is the only legitimate role for moral philosophers, namely that of adjudicating conflicting claims.

Part Three

Hermeneutic Methods

Chapter Seven

Interpretive Theory and Praxis

It has often been remarked that James is delightfully easy reading the first time around, but gets more difficult with each successive reading.[1] This is usually attributed to his refusal to use technical language, since he believed that "*technical* writing on *philosophical* subjects...is certainly a crime against the human race" (TCW, II, 387). It also follows from his ubiquitous use of metaphor. Both these factors certainly contribute to the difficulty experienced in developing the initial grasp of the text into a sustained understanding. This difficulty is compounded by James's habit of tailoring his speeches to fit the intended audience and his preference for striking phrases over plodding demonstration. He also delighted in exploiting the ambiguities of language. Furthermore, his hermeneutics of cooperation led him to exaggerate the commonality of his position with those of others, including adopting the terminology they have already introduced and developed. Since he also reinterpreted these terms, confusion results when the two meanings are not distinguished. He frequently does not do so himself, having an aversion to tediously minute discriminations. This is especially noticeable in his use of traditional philosophical terms, such as realism, empiricism, idealism, feeling, and concept.

James's use of methodological structures which are not identified by him as such is even more likely to lead to misunderstanding because it is not so easily recognizable as these characteristic stylistic features. One gets the impression that his essays have no particular organization. Since the force of his arguments cannot be grasped unless these structures are identified, he then seems to be merely asserting some proposition that he is actually carefully defending according to his own novel structures of argumentation. It also turns out that he does have a technical vocabulary. He uses concrete experience and selective interest, for instance, to refer to specific, interconnected sets of principles, but since the terms are neither systematically introduced nor always consistently developed, they have not usually been recognized. Furthermore, with the exception of *Principles*, his writings are first and foremost lectures, which get reworked as essays. With a few notable exceptions, the relevant organizational unit is therefore not the book but the lecture and its written equivalent, the essay.

It is no wonder that James has been slighted by those interested in interpretive theory because — when he is not being praised or chided for his supposed voluntarism — he is usually discussed from the perspective of those interested in the empirical basis for his claims. James lends himself to this appropriation because of his use of the scientific terminology of observation, hypothesis formation, and validation procedures and his urging of the experimental process as indispensable for determining truths about the world. These do comprise an essential part of his philosophic program, but I want to show that even this tough-minded empiricism is better understood from the perspective of his hermeneutics. Despite his frequent appeals to experimental testing, for instance, his own practice was one of interpretation, rather than any literal adoption of scientific method. His dislike of laboratory work is a matter of record. He even avoided it in preparing his thesis for his medical diploma: "I shall not make any experiments for my thesis but just compile what I find in the books under my hand" (TCW, I, 293).

He does report experimental results in his writings, but they comprise only part of a larger interpretive procedure. One such procedure begins by setting up a problem in terms of the logical alternatives available, subject to the limitation of formalizing them into two extremes. This is sometimes followed by a critical review of the relevant literature, with an emphasis on the latest facts supported by evidence, both experimental and anecdotal. These findings are summarized and reinterpreted according to his own problematic. In light of this critical hermeneutical reconstruction of all the evidence available, he then formulates as the most probable hypothesis the one which best harmonizes the interests informing the extreme positions. Finally, he proposes this mediating hypothesis for confirmation by the audience. He favors this particular pattern of interpretive methodology for the opening chapters of some of his books, such as *Pragmatism, A Pluralistic Universe,* and *Some Problems of Philosophy.*

His methodology, therefore, replicates neither strict scientific procedure nor philosophical analysis restricted to logical coherence. He was part of a larger effort, in Europe and America, to make philosophy less speculative and more scientific, but the precise way to do so was a matter of some debate, as we have already seen. It is closest to what today is called a phenomenology in that it tries to give an accurate account of facts, beginning with a description of the features of our specifically human interaction in the world. It also has affinities with hermeneutics, but is stylistically closer to Nietzsche than to later, more formal developments. James's original interpretive strategy is based on a refutation of the traditional theory of knowing as passive correspondence with or mirroring of being and a reconstruction of knowing as the selection and interpretation of marks or signs constrained by interests. The unique features of James's own radical empiricist interpretive methodology are worth investigating on their own terms, however, since they do not simply anticipate later developments but also surpass them in such aspects as the construction of a workable methodology for avoiding relativism.

The immediate problem to face is that James neither explicitly reflected on his own interpretive methodology nor systematized it. It has to be reconstructed from his praxis. The first objection that can be made to this project is that James did not have a hermeneutics or theory of interpretation at all but merely muddled along. That he often 'winged it,' there can be no doubt, but if I can show that he repeatedly employed various interpretive strategies, then there should be no objection to making them explicit and pointing out their limitations and accomplishments. It can also be objected that he was in principle, on the basis of his pluralism, opposed to any systematic method, and this is why he never articulated one. But throughout this book evidence is provided that the problems of unification and justification were central issues for him. The formula, 'the one and the many,' expresses a continuing theme in his writings and is a cryptic reference to his attempts to provide a satisfactory explanation for the quintessentially human efforts to unify experience. He rejected hegemonic interpretations of unity, but only in order to pluralistically reconstruct the problem of how we justify our various unifications of experience. A radically empiricist hermeneutics can be reconstructed out of his praxis that is less than completely systematic but more than the sum of scattered remarks. A preliminary sketch of such a concrete hermeneutics is given in this chapter and the next, with the understanding that it is worth developing further.

1. Hermeneutic Structures

James was not blind to questions of textual interpretation, despite the fact that he never wrote a single article defending his own approach. He nonetheless held definite views on the subject. In a letter responding to an unflattering essay written on his own philosophy by a student, for instance, he criticizes the usual style of philosophical discourse, that taught as appropriate for writing a Ph.D. thesis, and describes his own interpretive style.[2] This consists in sympathetically divining the author's "centre of vision," which cannot be grasped by any technical skill, but only "by an act of imagination." He criticizes the usual critical principles, not because they designate procedures wrong in themselves, but insofar as they are employed for their own sake or apart from what he takes to be the indispensable hermeneutic principle just given. His student's technically correct philological procedures are ironically complimented. Since they are only useful insofar as they illuminate the author's center of vision, her failure to do so renders her fidelity to these procedures irrelevant.

James was arguing that an essay can be technically correct philologically, that is, objective and dispassionate, and employing correct analytic subdivisions, and still be a failure as a sound interpretation of the text. He was seeking to rehabilitate subjectivity and passionate engagement at the very time in the history of American universities when the positivist scientific model of dispassionate objectivity was gaining ascendancy. He does so, not by arguing against the adoption of scientific methodology, but by arguing that the positivist model of science was itself seriously flawed because it ignored the irreducible subjective element constitutive of all human organizations of experience. The recognition of and systematic incorporation of this subjective element into the scientific outlook would strengthen science and not, as was feared, weaken it.

James also attributed the failure of most critics of his pragmatic account of truth to understand his position to their adoption of the same traditional philological methodology for which he had chided the student. They also tried to build up an author's meaning out of separate texts without first having imaginatively grasped his center of vision.[3] In chapter 8 of *The Meaning of Truth* he also blamed the persistent misunderstanding of pragmatism by its detractors on their failure to recognize "the concrete point of view which pragmatism assumes" (MT, 99). He contrasts this failure to identify the controlling interests of the author with an interpretive procedure that begins with mutual understanding. When author and interpreter understand the basic point of view, then mere hints suffice and everything does not have to be spelled out in precise detail. James says that his use of elliptical language presupposed a ready intelligence, that is, an ability to fill in the gaps.

He does not mention that this is absolutely crucial to the comprehension of metaphorical language and less so of the discursive style thought more appropriate to a philosophical profession that was seeking to emulate scientific methodology. He cites the fact that his critics boggled at every slip of the pen as showing that they "refused to take the spirit rather than the letter of our discourse" (MT, 99). In other words, they were lacking in that principle of benevolence which is central to his own interpretive procedure. But he attributes this lack to their "genuine unfamiliarity in the whole point of view." He does not accept the accusation that the misunderstanding is due solely to his own obscurity of speech because he has made himself understood on other issues. He concludes the paragraph on hermeneutics with a conciliatory acceptance of some of the blame, however, and apologizes for having pointed out the faults of his opponents because "recriminations are tasteless." This is because he takes mutual understanding, rather than conviction of errors, to be the goal of interpretation.

That the basic hermeneutic task is to sympathetically identify the center of vision which organizes and gives meaning to a position is frequently reiterated by James. But as usual, it is difficult to develop a procedure for doing so from his texts. That he does not identify such a center simply with a discursive proposition is evident from his sometimes equating a person's whole life as its expression: "Let me repeat once more that a man's vision is the great fact about him....A philosophy is the expression of a man's intimate character, and all definitions of the universe are but the deliberately adopted reactions of human characters upon it" (PU, 14).[4] He also said that although theories have to be developed discursively, or piecemeal, they must be grasped as a whole in order for them to be understood. But the metaphors he uses are all of persons, not texts. He says that the system then stands out "like a living thing, with that strange simple note of individuality which haunts our memory, like the wraith of a man, when a friend or enemy of ours is dead." He also quotes Walt Whitman's saying that whoever "touches this book touches a man" (PM, 24). This emphasis on the individual's purpose in constructing a theoretic system or artistic oeuvre is due to his belief that philosophic systems, like all theoretic reconstructions of reality, are not objective replications of the universe but reflect the way the universe appears to some individual person. Likewise, the ultimate arbiter of the text is the individual interpreter: "We measure the total character of the universe as we feel it, against the flavor of the philosophy proffered us, and one word is enough" (PM, 24). But he also develops it as an interpretive principle applicable to specific oral or written texts, as in chapter 9 of *Principles*, called "The Stream of Thought."

In the section on "Feelings of Tendency" in the chapter James had already provided the reasons for his fundamental hermeneutical principle. He explains what accounts for the sensible continuity and unity of thought in contrast to "the apparent discreteness of the words, images, and other means by which it seems to be carried on" (PP,I, 262). It is that "between all their substantive elements there is 'transitive' consciousness, and the words and images are 'fringed,' and not as discrete as to a careless view they seem." Furthermore, "in all our voluntary thinking there is some topic or subject about which all the members of the thought revolve...Relation, then, to our topic or interest is constantly felt in the fringe, and particularly the relation of harmony and discord, of furtherance or hindrance of the topic." Insofar as any discrete thought or part of a longer discourse is felt "to have a place in the scheme of relations in which the interesting topic also lies, that is quite sufficient to make of it a relevant and appropriate portion of our train of ideas" (PP,I, 250). The position developed in "Feelings of Tendency" provides the necessary background for understanding why James insists that only by grasping the center of vision which determines the rest of a person's discourse can we hope to understand what is being said. Without the unifying center of a topic of thought, there can be no production of any coherent discourse to begin with. And any subsequent understanding of that discourse must begin by identifying this organizing center.

Besides sympathetically identifying the center of vision, James's hermeneutics also emphasizes the context of discourse. Context includes the speaker's intention, the audience addressed, the universe of discourse, and the style of communication. His basic paradigm is oral discourse, not the written text, because of the necessity to avoid idle speculation by testing what is being presented according to how well it illuminates the listener's own experience. Interpretations are ultimately judged by their value for life. For this to take place satisfactorily, there needs to be cooperation since this has been found to be a better approach than recrimination for arriving at mutual understanding.

What is wrong with relying on technique alone is clearly stated. "You take utterances of mine written at different dates, for different audiences belonging to different universes of discourse, and string them together as the abstract elements of a total philosophy which you then show to be inwardly incoherent."[5] There are two things wrong with such an approach: it ignores context and it takes abstract coherency as the ultimate criterion, as against the coherency achieved within a single essay by relating its various aspects to its topic or purpose. Part of the context ignored is the speaker's understanding of the needs of the audience addressed and the discrimination of "universes of discourse." James, for instance, distinguishes between what is appropriate when speaking as a scientist, as a metaphysician, as an artist, as an educator, etc. Although the technical discourse thought appropriate for scholarly writings such as Ph.D. theses may be taken by some to be "splendid philology," it can only distort the meaning of an author's writings because it ignores the centrality of context without which there is no way to determine the meaning intended other than by just substituting the critic's own. Correct interpretation requires a recognition of context, which includes the occasion for the discourse, the time and place as well as the audience addressed, and the universe of discourse, for example, sub-atomic particles as the ultimate data in the realm of physics and phonemes as the assumed basis for language development in linguistics.

It also includes a sensitivity to the nuances of language and style of the author. When James recounts someone else's philosophic position, he renders their style as well as their theories. This is the hermeneutical equivalent of his philosophy of concrete experience. In seeking to reproduce the analogical style as well as substance of Gustav Fechner's writings, for instance, he says that "it is the intense concreteness of Fechner, his fertility of detail, which fills me with an admiration which I should like to make this audience share" (PU, 64). Just as we must return to experience again and again to correct and enrich what is necessarily left out of its conceptual translation, so we ought to seek to reproduce the style as well as the ideas of a position in order to lessen the possibility that we have distorted it in the act of appropriation. "Concrete life exceeds our powers of abstract formulation,...[and] what we see, feel and think in the world of reality are only approximations which the intellect uses to make fact more amenable to its powers of treatment" (EPH, 227, n166.18).

In reporting on a lecture series at Harvard by Emile Boutroux in 1910 he remarks that he can only briefly sketch out its essence, "without following the lecturer's own order, or going into any detail" (EPH, 168). He then apologizes in the last paragraph of the essay that "even less than I expected, have I followed his own order or language, but it is too late to re-write" (EPH, 171). In the first line of Lecture Five of *A Pluralistic Universe*, he also makes the point about the preceding lecture, "Concerning Fechner," that he "gave a miserably scanty outline of the way of thinking of a philosopher remarkable for the almost unexampled richness of his imagination of details" (PU, 83). In one of his last writings he tries to translate into rational philosophic discourse the "aphoristic and oracular" pronouncements of the mystic Benjamin Paul Blood.[6] He recognizes that in doing so "I have to run my own risk in making him orate *pro domo mea*, and I am not quite unprepared to hear him say, in case he ever reads these pages, that I have entirely missed his point" (EPH, 174). But he appeals to Blood's own dialectic style as providing some excuse for fragmenting his discourse, which is otherwise not an approach of which James approves: "I am using my scissors somewhat at random on my author's paragraphs, since one place is as good as another for entering a ring by, and the expert reader will discern at once the authentic dialectic circling" (EPH, 176-177).

Another time, after quoting excerpts from various sources to back up a point he is making James says that he is only going to discuss the issue in abstract terms of possible opinions because the original authors used several different points of view in their works and it is impossible to convey exactly what they meant without giving the context (ERE, 85, n8). This decision reflects his hermeneutic principle that it is impossible to separate content from its entire context without loss and distortion. Since he cannot convey the context, which includes point of view, he does not claim to be accurately rendering any particular person's position. Consequently, he calls his own reformulation in this case only "a possible position."

It is important to realize that James's paradigm was not the written text, but oral discourse, in which he excelled. Speech includes rhetorical techniques, such as exaggeration for the sake of emphasis and broad strokes to communicate an attitude or an overview, rather than sharp distinctions and minute detail more appropriate for written communication that can be pondered at leisure.[7] In the aforementioned report for the *Nation* of Emile Boutroux's 1910 lecture series at Harvard, for instance, James praises the benefits of oral over written communication.[8] Written texts excel at recording details, but a lecture is better at "tracing perspectives, defining tendencies, bringing out contrasts, and summing up results. It ought, above all, to generalize and simplify, and it ought to avoid technicality of language." James did not share the new professional denigration of popular lecturing as something less scholarly because he thought that for an excellent lecture "complete mastery of the subject is an indispensable condition." On a playful note, he wrote after sending an article to a journal for publication: "I appear to be growing into a graphomaniac. Truth boils over my organism as muddy water from a Yellowstone geyser" (ERE, 216).

It is no accident that most of James's output were originally lectures. He argues that although we only directly experience and interpret our worlds as individuals, we do so within a social context of interaction and discourse. We constantly test what we take to be the case, not only by the factual results of acting on such beliefs, but also against the reactions of others. He therefore always has an explicit audience in mind when he writes or talks. It is integral to his experimental methodology that the results reached through his critical reconstruction of a problem be understood as hypotheses to be tested by those who shared an interest in the outcome. Even in *Principles*, which was not a collection of lectures, the liveliness of the text and its departure from the standard procedure of a detached presentation of facts largely stems from the interlocutory mode of presentation. He adopts the manner of talking directly to the individual members of an audience whom he expects will respond to him.

Hanson and Kuhn have since popularized the position that comprehensive scientific theories are not discarded because they have been disproved but they are replaced by other paradigms thought to be more compelling. James also made the same point to the student already mentioned: "Not by proving their inward incoherence does one refute the philosophies — every human being is incoherent — but only by superseding them by other philosophies more satisfactory."[9] Rather than seeking to disprove him, if the student is dissatisfied with his position, she should directly study "reality in its concreteness" and develop her own alternative. Interpretations are ultimately judged by their value for life as determined by each person and therefore it makes more sense to spend time in finding such a position than in criticizing those of others. James sounded an early warning that academic philosophy was moving towards limiting its scope to merely philological criticism and abandoning any attempt to understand reality as it is experienced. What was needed was more, not less, emphasis on "constructive work."[10]

James developed a hermeneutics of cooperation. From its revival as a movement in the nineteen-sixties to current research projects feminists have drawn our attention to dominating versus cooperative styles of communication. Such heightened sensitivity allows this aspect of James's approach to be grasped with greater clarity. In publishing *Pragmatism*, for instance, he explicitly introduced a radically new approach to philosophy, using such ringing phrases as that he believed "that a kind of new dawn is breaking upon us philosophers" and that the "forerunners of pragmatism…were preluders only" (PM, 10, 30). But he nonetheless subtitled the work: "A New Name for Some Old Ways of Thinking," thus highlighting its continuity with the tradition and his activity as that of one member of a community of investigators. Since the purpose of communication is to reach a shared understanding, he criticized as profoundly disturbing and counterproductive the "polemic virulence" characteristic of many professional meetings and journals, which seeks to disparage a colleague's presentation by concentrating on its errors (EPH, 168).

Academics, "for the pure pleasure of the operation, chase [their opponent] up and down his windings, flog him into and out of his corners, stop him and cross-reference him and counter on him."[11] He says this of F.C.S. Schiller's article on Bradley, which he finds "too much like a criminal conviction in tone and temper." He tells Schiller that more is to gained from "a certain amount of positive construction...and the world will be the better for containing so much difficult polemic reading the less." He opposes to such radical stridency the "liberal and mediating" tendency to grant "cheerfully to the opposing side what it can fairly claim," thus neither harboring enmity nor creating enemies (EPH, 168, 170). Hermeneutics is sympathetic interpretation and he praises Boutroux because he has "so sympathetically...entered into the most diverse states of mind interpreting scientific men, philosophers, and religious men to each other" (227, n166.18).[12]

Because of the interactive character that James ascribed to social communication he modified what he had to say depending on the predispositions of his audience. If they were already enamored of science, he would urge them not to lose sight of the broader human dimension of experience, of which science is only a part. If the audience were predominately religious, he would point out the benefits to be gained from recognizing the strengths of the new scientific world view that was emerging. His emphasis changed with his audience because he respected their interests and wanted to convey to them only as much of his topic for which they had use. It did not therefore follow that the concomitant de-emphasis of those aspects of the topic of which they were already convinced meant that they were any less important, but only that for the moment their iteration would simply be redundant. Even in a straight lecture format, he was less an omniscient author than a partner in developing a shared world view.

While not every speaker is so considerate of the needs of their hearers, discourse is always partially shaped by the intended audience, as well as by the intentions of the speaker. Both need to be identified in order to correctly interpret what is being said. This contextualization of discourse was so congenial to James that he seldom broke out of it into supposedly neutral scientific or philosophical discourse. Consequently, he did not worry very much about holding conflicting positions. This attitude is reflected in his criticism of his student for trying to create a coherent position out of his ad hoc talks.

James did not seek clarity through theoretical consistency primarily, nor through a careful delineation of his experimental presuppositions.

He expected it to emerge out of further investigations or, in the case of his textbook procedure, to become obvious through following his explanations. Even when he tried to follow the model of strictly scientific procedure, he used a hermeneutical methodology, that is, an interpretive explanation in which understanding was the goal. He did not write *Principles* to display his own grasp of the subject matter, which, on the usual model, would have been formulated precisely before explaining it in detail, but to elicit comprehension and assent from his readers. It is organized in such a way that the reader must actively participate in the discovery of the concrete facts and structures of our being in the world. He expresses this device to carry his readers along and encourage their active collaboration by saying such things as: "if anything seems obscure about it, it will grow clearer as we advance," and "this, too, will grow clearer as we proceed" (PP,I, 229, 230). His hermeneutics, therefore, is a shared interpretive process, characterized by interactive communication and development over time.

The hermeneutic structures which have been identified are neither exhaustive nor interconnected into a strictly unified system. They are simply a first attempt to identify and begin to explore these underlying structures which inform the Jamesian texts and make them available for further analysis and development. The ones noted are (1) sympathetic identification of the author's center of vision by an act of imagination, (2) sensitivity to context, which includes the audience addressed and the universe of discourse, (3) recognition of nuances of style, to the point of seeking to replicate them, (4) the priority of oral discourse, with its rhetorical techniques, such as broad strokes to communicate an overview, tracing tendencies, a thorough-enough understanding of the subject matter to allow simplification without distortion, and the use of a non-technical vocabulary, (5) experimental approach, in the sense of presenting the reconstruction of a problem as an hypothesis to be tested by interested listeners and judged as to its value for life, and (6) cooperation or the principle of benevolence as guiding the appropriation of the work of others. The aim of interpretive appropriation is to understand, to relate the work to one's own problematic, and to develop it further rather than merely to refute it. These interpretive structures make sense in terms of his concrete presuppositions.

2. A Radically Empiricist Concrete Hermeneutics

The central thesis of James's hermeneutics which has been identified in the first place in his response to one of his students can be recognized as operative throughout his writings. The primary interpretive task is to recognize the center of vision that unifies the individual aspects of communicative discourse. In chapter 9 of *Principles* he develops a concrete analysis of thinking as a human project characterized by the organization of experience according to an end-in-view or topic. This unifying operation of a dominant interest characterizes human thinking but is obscured by its very success in allowing the objects of experience to appear as they do. James points out both its pervasiveness or constituting aspect and its aptness to be overlooked by calling it a fringe or scheme of relations that are felt as a harmony or discord in our thinking even when not consciously recognized. His hermeneutics entails just such an explicit appropriation of these "feelings of tendency" in order to identify their organizing center of interest.

The notion of a fringe which dialectically defines the center has both tantalized and eluded James's scholars. Some clarification can be found in a 1908 letter to Helen Keller. In it James accounts for the paradox that her world is "indistinguishable from ours" despite the fact of her sensory deprivation from birth on the grounds that "the great world, *the background*, in all of us, is the world of our *beliefs*. That is the world of the permanencies and the immensities, and our relations with it are mostly verbal." Sensations supply only the merest hints, which "we extend by imagination or add to by analogy." He is once again emphasizing the construction of the lived world as a synthesis of our aesthetic and practical interests, as a "marriage function" of our beliefs, imaginings and analogies with sensory experiences. The priority of the radically empiricist concrete analysis is also asserted, since the kernel of the experience is sensory and what is being grasped are the real relations that hold among physical objects. The function of the verbalization of the various sensations is said to be to symbolize "the relations existing between the things" (TCW,II, 455).

In *Talks to Teachers* we have seen that James emphasized the sensational core in our concrete states of consciousness, calling them the center or focus and thoughts and feelings the margin (TT, 20). But as one would expect, given the metaphor of focus and fringe, the focus of a field of consciousness can fade back into the periphery as something on the fringe attracts our attention. Then "some object of thought, some distant image" can become the focus and the sensations originally attended to can come to occupy "a very faint and marginal place" (20-21). Since these shiftings of fringe and focus can be gradual or sudden and more or less of the focus or margin may remain in the new rearrangement, no exact description of what must occur in any given case can be given. Whatever unity our fields of consciousness have, therefore, can only be determined from the point of view of the one who is responsible for its organization. Once again the aesthetic, theoretic need for epistemological rigor and clear separation between subjective and objective aspects of experience are shown to be dependent on our practical rationality. "All we know is that, for the most part, each field has a sort of practical unity for its possessor, and that from this practical point of view we can class a field with other fields similar to it, by calling it a state of emotion, of perplexity, of sensation, of abstract thought, of volition, and the like."

Because of James's intention to avoid skepticism and nihilism he subordinates his hermeneutics to his concrete analysis and findings. Since interpretation is an explicitly reflective, rational operation, it remains speculatively ungrounded unless related to the human dimension of experience of which it is a part. Reflection is always a later, more developed stage of an appropriative process that precedes and grounds it. In chapter 9 of *Principles*, for instance, as well as in the paragraph in *Talks* immediately following the ones examined, he explicitly rejects the empiricist presupposition of discrete sensations as the simplest unit of analysis. His own "empirical method of investigation," by contrast, begins with "the fact of thinking itself" as *"the most fundamental of all the postulates of Psychology"* (219, 185). The five characters of thought which he then develops are indispensable for understanding his concrete analysis, but only those aspects that are relevant to understanding his hermeneutics will be examined.

The first problem that confronts us is that he uses the word 'thinking' to mean both sensation or feeling and thought (PP,I, 185-186). He says that he will use these terms, as well as 'presentation' and 'representation,' as synonyms, choosing one or other merely as a convenience of context, not to distinguish them. His intent in adopting this unorthodox, wider sense of the term 'thinking' is to emphasize that he is talking about "mental states at large, irrespective of their kind." But even a cursory glance at the table of contents shows that James does often distinguish between sensation and thought, as he must if his explanations are to be meaningful and contribute towards solving the problems raised. He uses 'thinking' to stand for "every form of consciousness indiscriminately" because he is creating an original concrete analysis of human thinking as we experience it within our horizon of being in the world. This concrete grounding is presupposed in our understanding of thinking in its more restricted sense of a cognitive activity distinguishable from sensation. The failure to identify this concrete sense of thinking as weaving order out of chaos and to distinguish it from the narrower sense of thinking as conceptualization has led to many false dilemmas and will continue to block further progress unless explicitly recognized.

Unfortunately, James's project has been hampered and obscured by his decision to use non-technical, everyday words or scientific and philosophical terms already extant instead of developing a technical vocabulary appropriate to his novel methodological approach. We can recognize that he is not to be taken literally in his claim to always use 'sensation' as synonymous with 'thought' only if we know that this is to be understood as a way of signaling his concrete approach in the absence of any developed specialized vocabulary. But he does often exploit the ambiguity of the term 'feeling' to mean either thought or sensation in a deliberate effort to help us realize that the reference to objects which is taken to be a constituent feature of thinking (character number four [PP,I, 220]) presupposes an interpretive analysis and not just concrete description. The experiential fact that we take objects to be independently real does not provide sufficient grounds for any particular determination. Only an interpretation of the criteria by which we have come to accept this outward reference as self-evident can do that.

He recognized that he was developing an original starting point for psychological analysis in chapter 9 of *Principles* and that the five characters of the process of thinking did not conform to any traditional pattern of either empirical or rational psychology. As usual, he refused to begin deductively with first principles and precise definitions of terms. He describes his methodology aesthetically, in a simile: "This chapter is like a painter's first charcoal sketch upon his canvas, in which no niceties appear" (PP,I, 220). He uses rough definitions because the formulation of precise ones, which means accurate to an experienced process, such as personal consciousness, and not an a priori system of stipulative meanings, "is the most difficult of philosophic tasks" and can emerge only after the relevant evidence has been gathered. He then describes those "elementary psychic fact(s)" that "everyone will recognize" as true to their own experience (221).

He ignores the a priori structures and presuppositions that guide his organization of the material on the grounds that they are not developed systematically as necessary categorial restraints on research but are instead only roughly sketched out, preliminary, and hypothetical. He therefore does not reflect on his reconstruction of empirical analysis into a concrete analysis, even though such a concrete methodology is presupposed in his explanations. He only hints at the dependence of his explanations on his concrete findings by saying such things as that he is "sure that this concrete and total manner of regarding the mind's changes is the only true manner, difficult as it may be to carry it out in detail" (PP,I, 229).

James is careful to label as a postulate his fundamental presupposition of thinking as a holistic activity. Since it is one which best fits all the phenomenal evidence we have and are daily discovering in the laboratory, he also calls it a fact. Once again, this rather odd conflation of 'postulate' with 'fact' can be understood in light of his empiricist theory of thinking as given in "Brute and Human Intellect." He explains that characteristics imaginatively hypothesized as inhering in some object or set of objects are believed in over time only insofar as they actually do capture the qualities inherent in objects. But as to how ideas can abstract qualities or why spontaneous inventions of the imagination are required to recognize what is qualitatively immediate is never gone into with the thoroughness the issue requires. The reason is that, once again, the interpretive structures that he develops that enable him to give cogent explanations remain for him mere explanations until and unless grounded in indubitable facticity. The project of *Principles* is to uncover such facts through concrete analysis. He concludes chapter 9, for instance, by saying that he will continue in the following chapter "to trace the psychology of this fact" (PP,I, 278). He is astute and honest enough to recognize that his own hermeneutical insights, if systematically developed, would show that even the best fit of interpretation with factual evidence can never coalesce in perfect transparency, and he also realized that we can recognize as facts only our own organizations of experience, but he could not finally revise his empirical findings consistently with his humanist hermeneutics.

I am arguing that James's need to subordinate interpretative claims to concrete grounding blinded him to the interpretive structures he was using throughout his concrete analysis. Consequently, he often converted to the status of a fact what he recognized in other contexts as one interpretation among others. His hermeneutics can provide an explanation for his concrete analysis that he himself was never able to, since he was always trying to run the explanation the other way around. Time and again his realist presuppositions prevented him from recognizing that the solutions he has reached through his pragmatic or hermeneutic methodologies are not only valid until the ultimate truth about being is disclosed but are as legitimate as they can ever be. But to accept this necessarily finite character of all interpretations of experience, he would have to forego the nihilist reductive of an eventually fully confirmed grounding in experience that he was seeking.

In an odd reversal, he falls back on his hermeneutics to extricate himself from drawing this obvious conclusion. He gladly embraces such hermeneutic principles as that the discursive translation of signs can never completely capture that of which they are signs, that the finiteness of any angle of vision precludes an absolutely comprehensive understanding of anything, and that language is fundamentally metaphorical and richer than any straightforward formula. But rather than applying these hermeneutical principles to reconceptualize his concrete analysis as one among other interpretive strategies, albeit the most promising because the most demonstrably accurate to lived experience, he recalls them at such times only in order to put his concrete findings beyond criticism until some unspecified future when they can be taken up again and their realistic presuppositions confirmed.

3. Concrete Presuppositions of Hermeneutical Strategy

In the pioneering article, "The Function of Cognition," where James develops his concrete analysis of cognition as practical, he says that we cannot disprove the suspicion that our unique experiences trap us in a solipsism of mutually incomprehensible worlds as long as we remain on the theoretical level (MT, 22ff). This is contrasted with the practical effects of our embodied experiences, which leave no such doubt: if you are hitting me, neither of us wonders if we have the same body in mind. Therefore, the solution to the problem of solipsism, of whether I can transcend the limits of my own experience and know that I refer to the same realities that you do, can be found only in praxis. To intellectually grasp this solution, however, requires an explicit hermeneutics, an interpretation of interpretation itself and its relation to our active being in the world. But instead of engaging in hermeneutical analysis, James develops the concrete basis for his interpretive procedures without reflecting on the procedures themselves.

That feelings are for the sake of, and result in, actions is the concrete starting point of James's demonstration. It is a reconstruction of the reflex arc thesis that he argued had been sufficiently proven by the new science of psychology to justifiably serve as an initial hypothesis. We can conceive of worlds in which your feelings do not affect my world, but "by a most singular disposition of nature," in this world we live in they do affect mine and mine affect yours. This is so much taken for granted that the failure to do so is taken for a sign of a fundamental disorder, of a delusion or psychological breakdown. Therefore, "before I can think you to mean my world, you must affect my world; before I can think you to mean much of it, you must affect much of it; and before I can be sure you mean it *as I do*, you must affect it *just as I should* if I were in your place" (MT, 23-24).

This criterion of praxis, tied to a concrete analysis of being in the world, profoundly separates James's hermeneutics from the relativism of many contemporary versions of interpretive theory that are solipsistically locked within the textuality of texts. He credits Royce's arguments that only the appeal to a transcendent mind can guarantee that we are not dreaming the harmony of mind and reality with helping him to clarify and grasp the full import of his own "practical and psychological point of view" (MT, 23, n6). But not until later could he defend his intuition that "the practical point of view brushes such metaphysical cobwebs away" (24). He "came to see that any definitely experienceable workings would serve as intermediaries quite as well as the absolute mind's intentions would" (23, n6).

James's interpretive strategy for demonstrating that we know that we are conscious of the same world and symbolize the same realities is to develop his concrete description of our being in the world. He says that we do not practically doubt that we share a common world because we have already experienced many times the fact that someone's symbolic thoughts have developed and terminated in percepts that have practically modified our own. But this common sense view is explained and justified satisfactorily through what James calls "unravelling the fringe," that is, by making explicit those conditions which make possible the world of our experience, but which are so pervasive and taken for granted that they have been ignored in traditional philosophizing. He says that by the 'development' of our symbolic thoughts "is meant obeying their tendencies, following up the suggestions nascently present in them, working in the direction in which they seem to point, clearing up the penumbra, making distinct the halo, unravelling the fringe, which is part of their composition, and in the midst of which their more substantive kernel of subjective content seems consciously to lie" (MT, 29). We do so actively, by words, gestures and actions that demonstrate that we trace out the same concrete relations in making explicit what is included in a particular meaning complex.

Once we recognize his radically empiricist hermeneutics, based on his concrete analysis, its methodological procedures can be found throughout James's writings. Without developing an explicit model, he nonetheless consistently presupposes a knowledge of his concrete analysis of active being in the world in his interpretive strategies. His long chapter on "The Perception of Space" in *Principles*, for instance, frequently alludes to these interpretive structures of human experience. James situates his particular investigations within the context of our active being in the world. An analysis of this context reveals that we organize aspects of experience to answer to our purposes. He begins the chapter on space concretely by giving examples of everyday experiences of "varying vastness" as a way of identifying the original sensation of space. He then shows how, out of these chaotic experiences, real space is constructed or "woven by processes of discrimination, association, and selection" (PP,II, 777).[13]

In *Essays in Radical Empiricism* James is more explicit about his interpretive strategy (ERE, 81-87ff).[14] The thesis of pure experience is understood by him as an injunction to investigate experiential facts guided by the concrete structures of our active being in the world. The fundamental fact to be investigated is described concretely as "our immediately felt activity situations." He criticizes the traditional formulation of objections to the efficacy of human action as misguided because they do not adopt the standpoint of concrete analysis. He then uses his pragmatic methodology, not as an irresponsible instrumentalism, but in order to show how these formulations ignore the guiding interests without which the original experience cannot be grasped but only undermined.

These are only a few examples of the concrete interpretive strategies that can be recognized as operative in James's writings. Unless they are first identified before reconstructing his arguments in order to evaluate them, his positions will be systematically distorted. It is ironic that James, who both urged an interpretive praxis which respected context, and who deliberately contextualized his own arguments as a rejection of merely logical analysis, should so often be interpreted out of context.[15]

4. A Radically Empiricist Hermeneutics of Textual Texts

But what about situations in which nothing is going on intersubjectively, when no physical interchange is possible, as in reading poetry and fiction? In *The Meaning of Truth*, as an aside in his development of his concrete analysis of cognition as practical, James briefly considers this issue and engages in hermeneutics in the narrower sense of an interpretation of literary texts (MT, 25). He says that if we think of Sir Walter Scott's *Ivanhoe* and ignore the facts of its production, then it seems obvious that there are as many Ivanhoes as there are readers of the text. The only criterion he gives for establishing a common referent is the case of one person's version changing in such a way that it affects all the other versions. Only if this alteration "were to reverberate immediately through all the other versions" would we agree that all were thinking about the same Ivanhoe and that they thus shared "a little world common to them all" (25). Since it seems manifestly impossible that any change in my conception of Ivanhoe could immediately affect everyone else's and since the hints given are not pursued further, we are left with the conclusion that literary productions, when considered in isolation from any other shared context, cannot partake of the commonality of a genuinely shared world.

In a footnote to the paragraph James explains further this claim of the "pluralism of solipsistic worlds" when it comes to literary works. First of all, "there is no *real* Ivanhoe, not even the one in Sir Walter Scott's mind as he was writing the story" (MT, 25, n7). At most, it is the first of the "Ivanhoe-solipsisms." This conclusion seems to be based on the lack of an unambiguously singular external referent. In accordance with chapter 21, "The Perception of Reality," of *Principles*, James is reaffirming the sensible world as the fundamental meaning of reality, which de-realizes all the other ways we refer to objects, such as the object as a literary creation. As with most of us, for James "the 'things of sense' hold this prerogative position, and are the absolutely real world's nucleus." After choosing "from among the various worlds some one to be for him the world of ultimate realities," any other sub-universe of reality must fulfill this criterion of reality or be relegated to the status of non-reality (PP,II, 923). But he also holds that, strictly speaking, anything that can be thought of exists as some sort of object, that is, an object under a certain description, such as an object of myth or an object of ideal relations. In a "less real" or "relative sense," that in which *reality means simply relation to our emotional and active life,...whatever excites and stimulates our interest is real*" (PP,II, 923-924).

But as James develops this latter meaning of reality, it seems to directly contradict the priority of the earlier realist understanding based on sensational immediacy. Quoting Hume and Kant to the effect that immediate practical relations between ourselves and objects confer reality on them, he concludes that reality is subjective because its source, whether from the absolute or practical point of view, is ourselves. *"As thinkers with emotional reaction, we give what seems to us a still higher degree of reality to whatever things we select and emphasize and turn to WITH A WILL"* (PP,II, 924-925). In this understanding reality is anchored in our ego, "considered as an active and emotional term" (926). Since James takes this concrete analysis of belief as an explanation of how sensible objects come to be judged as real in the primary sense of the term, he sees no contradiction between the two explanations of reality.

By this is meant that the priority of the sensational immediacy of physical objects is itself based on the fact that they affect each of us so strongly and the dangers involved in ignoring them are so obvious and immediate, that we take them as paradigmatically real without having to reason to this conclusion. Upon reflection we can come to realize that other realms of reality also fulfil the criterion of active and emotional relation to ourselves, as the incredibly long historical struggle to separate mythical from sensible elements in our understanding of ourselves and the world demonstrates. Since James's concrete analysis of belief allows more than sensible objects to be considered real, he takes advantage of the wider latitude of the belief criterion and a certain ambiguity of explanation to demonstrate that moral and religious truths are real for those who find them to be "emotionally exciting objects" (PP,II, 935).

He makes much the same move in the footnote about the reality of Ivanhoe by saying that we can choose to take the one conceived by Scott as the real one, to which all the other references must conform. But in order to do so we must expand the referent from the isolated text to "a complex object." This means bringing in "Scott himself as the author of the real Ivanhoe," which, along with the story, "has dynamic relations with the world common to the experience of all the readers." This world includes the physical handling of the various printings of the book, comparisons of texts, and other activities "of this real world of our experience." The complex object must include the activities of at least two minds — the critic's and Scott's — because only subjects can have intentions and expectations and these are indispensable to determining meaning.

If we locate interpretation only between the reader and the isolated text, then there is no escaping the solipsism, that is, unmitigated relativism, of interpretation. If we detach the story from the conditions of its production, then there is no sufficiently discriminated object of reference that could exclude some interpretations in preference to others. The author is one necessary anchor in experience, but this means the author as can be determined from all the conditions of production and the whole world of experience, inclusive of the reader's and the physical text. Only a sort of triangulation of author, critic, and text, within a common world of interpretive praxis, can provide sufficient grounds for claiming that everyone is referring to the same, real text.

If our guiding intention is to unify all the interpretations by referring them to the same text, then such a text can be constructed through a cooperative adoption of methodology, principles, and aims, anchored in the historical and material conditions of its production and dissemination. Hints for developing such a strategy have just been given. But if our intention is to identify a pre-existing univocal text which will confirm or disprove interpretations without the prior acceptance of such a common context, methodology, and aims, then such an intention can never be realized. The primary text, like the known object, is disclosed only at the outcome of the interpretive praxis and is not a pre-existent ideal Platonic Form.

5. Metaphysical Unification and Hermeneutical Pluralism

James's radically empiricist hermeneutics exemplifies the tension experienced in trying to bridge the distance between "the actual world of finite human lives" and symbolic ways of ordering the complexity of such experiences into a harmonious unity (PM, 17). It is primarily a mediating way of thinking. There are many dualisms James tried both to preserve and to overcome. Unlike Hegel he saw no way of preserving the multiplicity in any scheme of ultimate unification so far imagined, but kept trying to do so nonetheless, since he assumed that such a harmony of all our deepest needs must be possible. He also assumed that such a postulate of practical rationality is the necessary condition for the possibility of acting, just as the postulate of aesthetic rationality is the necessary condition for the possibility of conceptual thinking.

Therefore, to admit the impossibility of an ultimate multiplicity in unity would be to accept the irrationality of the world and this he was not willing to do for most of his life. He does finally succumb to the Bergsonian temptation to affirm unmitigated plurality, although he had earlier clearly argued that even the notion of pluralism presupposes some unity, for example, of outlook. Before he surrenders, however, he develops challenging interpretive strategies that are more reflective of the unresolved tensions of life. These have so far been inescapable except by imagining either an ideal world more unified than any we live in or by a skeptical retreat into the incommensurability of all schemes of interpretation. His hermeneutics involves a sustained attempt to reconcile two equally imperative aesthetic rational demands, that of simplicity or unity, which will not tolerate "too much inconsistency and vacillation," and that of clarity, which seeks to reproduce aspects of the big blooming buzzing confusion (PM, 14).

In a letter to Friedrich Paulsen on May 26, 1895, he contrasts his own writing as consisting of "scraps and fragments" with Royce's systematic approach (EPH, 258). His evaluation of his writing as sketchy and fragmentary constitutes a claim that informs his hermeneutics. His ground-breaking chapter 9 of *Principles*, for instance, is called a "first general sketch" (PP,I, 278). This is not just misplaced modesty, but expresses a considered belief, which follows from his pluralism, that "all the ends in nature are partial," including the human interpretations of such ends, and this partiality cannot in principle be overcome (EPH, 258-259). "Radical empiricism allows that the absolute sum-total of things may never be actually experienced or realized in...[its absolute totality], and that a disseminated, distributed, or incompletely unified appearance is the only form that reality may yet have achieved" (PU, 25). James calls into question the philosophic goal of simplicity, in the traditional sense of absolute unity, and seeks to replace it with harmony. A sketch is an effort at clarity, in his reconstructed sense of a partial selection of marks out of the inexhaustible diversity of experience, which cannot be reduced to any explanatory principle of unity, but can eventually be harmoniously reconciled. He argues that there is always more in experience than can ever be captured by any merely symbolic reconstruction: "There still remains the opacity of the finite facts as merely given, with most of their peculiarities mutually unmediated and unexplained" (WB, 6).

Our "translations" of experience are systematically flawed in that the condition for any organization of experience is that some aspects of the original situation be ignored in order to identify others. There is a double partiality operative which pluralism recognizes. One is the selection of a few aspects of experience out of the abundance present and the other is the angle of vision or guiding interests operative in the selection. His hermeneutics is a will to preserve the rich complexity of experience, whether of nature, of persons, or of symbolic schemas or texts, as a bulwark against totalitarian force. All monistic schemes represent the intellectualist rationalist drive to impose more order on recalcitrant experiences than can be justified and they characterize the one who does the ordering more than what is ordered. "What [any] system pretends to be is a picture of the great universe of God. What it is — and oh so flagrantly!—is the revelation of how intensely odd the personal flavor of some fellow creature is" (PM, 24).

He resolves the conflicting demands of simplicity and clarity by subordinating both of these aesthetic, rational demands to those of practical rationality. As much unification and recognition of differences should be sought as will lead to the successful conclusion of some predetermined course of action. But such particular goals, to be justifiable courses of action, must themselves be in harmony with our situatedness in the world and fulfill the marriage or "go-between' function or criterion of "concrete satisfaction" given in chapters 2 and 6 of *Pragmatism*. In subordinating aesthetic to practical rationality, he still preserves the aesthetic moment in practical resolutions. One should strive to develop as much unity as is possible, while still bearing in mind that even the most comprehensive is necessarily limited and that therefore what is left out should neither be denied nor forcibly constrained to fit an alien pattern. Likewise, the aesthetic delight in particularity and profligate detail should inform any pattern of unification, but should not be carried to such an extent as to undermine rational action. This is a dialectic process necessitated by our finite temporality. None of the schemas, that is, the two aesthetic drives and the practical demands, ultimately can or should replace the others, making the revisability of interpretations both inevitable and desirable. Nonetheless, the practical conditions for action do and should regulate the other two.

We have seen that his concrete analysis of consciousness discloses that it is constituted by selection. The translation of the perceptual order into the conceptual one is always for the sake of some subjective interest. Since concepts are teleological instruments, this "holding fast to meanings" arises from the fact that we are creatures of distinctive purposes. "No philosophy can ever do more than interpret the whole, which is unknown, after the analogy of some particular part that we know" (EPH, 150). "We live in partial systems" and the parts are not interchangeable (VRE, 384). But we think rationally in universals and according to criteria of simplicity and transparency. The units abstracted in intellectual rational thinking are so powerful in helping us to make shortcuts through the density of experience precisely because they are interchangeable. But then how do we know that our conceptual translations, with their dual origins in our partiality and abstraction of qualities that are held to range over a greater number of phenomena than those of which we have experience, actually capture the reality they seek to articulate?

In the middle works James can handle this challenge to interpretation as translation only by bracketing its relation to reality. He could not then wholeheartedly assent to the humanism of either F. C. S. Schiller or Dewey because they could not account for "so curious a congruence between the world and the mind" (MT, 41). Likewise, his own pragmatic account of truth as "a relation, not of our ideas to non-human realities, but of conceptual parts of our experience to perceptual parts" is accurate as "phenomenal knowledge," but does not take up the metaphysical issue of the relation of such phenomenal knowledge to "non-human realities" (51). It does not seem to occur to him to question the traditional empiricist dualistic model of reality-for-me and reality-in-itself, even though in various articles later brought together as *Essays in Radical Empiricism* he seems to be suggesting a model that reconceptualizes the distinction as one of reflective analysis and not a difference in being.

In his later work he no longer takes the inherent limitations of personal vision and the concrete level of analysis as needing correction by a theory which relates the marks abstracted from a phenomenal totality to the real totality of which it is a part. He says that Boutroux's originality, for instance, consisted in "his firm grasp of the principle of interpreting the whole of nature in the light of that part of it with which we are most fully acquainted, namely, our own personal experience. The filling in of the picture will require endless research of detail, but the working direction, once given, cannot easily be forgotten" (EPH, 171). It is obvious that he is reflecting on his own position since he continues that "it seems not unlikely that at a future not remote the whole earlier efforts to substitute a logical skeleton of as few 'immutable' principles and relations as we can dissect out cleanly for the abounding richness and fertility of the reality we live in, and to call this skeleton the deeper truth, will seem an aberration." It is to adopt an outside view instead of taking the "inside view of how things really happen."

He was always suspicious of the aesthetic rational drive toward unity and its characteristic fallacy of demanding more unity than can be defended. Its danger is the violent suppression of whatever does not fit within the predefined unity. But he also recognized that the failure to even try to unify the disparate aspects of our experience would mean the end of our most characteristically human accomplishments, such as the various movements to unify phenomena philosophically, scientifically and religiously. When he finally embraces unmitigated pluralism he does so because he thinks that he can preserve a guiding force behind the scenes in a pan-psychism that is not monistic. But he did not live to work out the implications of this position. For those for whom pan-psychism is not a viable alternative, his mediating position seeking to balance the demands of both aesthetic and practical rationality offers a more promising procedure.

On the one hand, his later decision can be interpreted as a healthy recognition of the bankruptcy of metaphysics in its stubborn insistence on an absolute ground of unification which has historically contributed to totalitarian righteousness in supressing dissent. It can also be seen as an affirmation that the dialectic of the reconciliation of aesthetic and practical demands is not a temporary expedient, but a permanent condition of our being-in-the-world. This would reaffirm the value of the never-ending process of unification, its dismantling by appeal to what is not included, and the subsequent struggle towards a new synthesis.

But it can equally well be interpreted as a loss of nerve, that is, as the yearnings of a "sick soul" for a harmony of knowing and being that, since it cannot be grounded with certainty in the world of finite existence, is projected into a beyond approachable only through religious belief and mystical experience. This is accompanied by a loss of faith in the value of any aesthetic schemes of unification, but not necessarily in the value of a practical unification of ideal good and actual conditions. In an odd way this latter interpretation would mean that James finally accepts skepticism as the price of reducing or overcoming nihilism. It seems to me that the resolution he defends as sufficient for a concrete level of inquiry, if reinterpreted as in principle insurmountable, is both more defensible and preferable to the later, more extreme, pluralism, which goes far beyond his earlier, more carefully balanced thesis of plurality in unity.

This concrete hermeneutics is developed, for instance, in James's essay on Boutroux. He first gives the principle guiding his exposition, which is analogous to sketching, in that "the quickest way to get at the character of anything is to know what to contrast it with" (EPH, 168). He therefore begins by contrasting his "concrete view," which places interactive experience of self and world at the center, with both the classic and scholastic traditions, according to which rational formulas can in principle contain all there is to know of reality, and with the scientific belief that it had "stripped reality naked of disguise, revealed its intimate structure." The concrete view is diametrically opposed to reality as "abstracted, simplified, and reduced, the inalterable and self-identical" (169). Reality is instead understood as "the element we wholly live in, it is what Plutarch's and Shakespeare's pages give us, it is the superabounding, growing, ever-varying and novelty-producing. Its real shape is biography and history, and its 'categories,' far from sterilizing our world for all purposes of living reasoning, keep fertilizing it indefinitely." Not only reality, but also reason is reconstructed by James. Boutroux is said to have rescued this term "from its purely classic use of tracing identities, concealed or patent. It is for him the faculty of judgment in its widest sense, using sentiments and willingness, as well as concepts, as its premises, and abounding in power, as everything else does, the more abundantly it is exercised" (EPH, 169-170).

I think that much of the misunderstanding about what is being communicated in the texts can be cleared up once it is realized that James was developing and following an original theory of interpretation. As usual, his characteristic failing is that he did not develop it into a consistent model. It is therefore not surprising that it has been overlooked. Nonetheless, by recovering and making explicit both the interpretive procedures he was following and his scattered reflections on it, it is possible to reconstruct such a radically empiricist hermeneutics and hold it up for closer scrutiny. This theory of interpretation can then be used to illuminate his writings by allowing us to recognize methodological procedures heretofore invisible. It can therefore provide a better basis for evaluating his positions than the usual one of measuring him against exegetical standards which he was not only not following, but also often explicitly rejected. Furthermore, the radically empiricist hermeneutic position thus derived has some unique contributions to make to the field of hermeneutical studies and would repay closer examination, critical analysis, and further development. It is the key both to his successes and his failures.

6. Interpretive Structure of *The Varieties of Religious Experience*

The organization of *The Varieties of Religious Experience* exhibits James's radically empiricist hermeneutics more clearly than any of his other works.[16] This is perhaps due to his having to explicitly bring together two aspects of his life-long project that he usually handled piecemeal, that is, as either primarily philosophical or primarily scientific. But in *Varieties* he felt competent to apply his scientific expertise in psychology to religious phenomena, thus bringing together both his metaphysical interest in the ultimate values upheld by religion and his natural history method (see VRE, 5). The two viewpoints are informed by equally compelling but seemingly antithetical interests. In *Varieties* his transformation of both into a radically empiricist concrete hermeneutics is most apparent.

He frames the experimental question in terms of his psychological interest in the religious aspect of our human mental constitution (VRE, 12). Since psychology is a human science, its proper methodology is the natural history one of description and so James invites us "to a descriptive survey of those religious propensities." In keeping with his hermeneutical principle that hypotheses be tested as to whether they better explain each person's experiences, he explicitly asks for the participation of the audience at the beginning of the first lecture of the series. He also delimits the subject matter to what is appropriate for his natural history methodology, namely, "religious feelings and religious impulses."

Consistently with his concrete hermeneutics, which begins with a careful description of some fundamental aspect of phenomenal experience, he is free to disregard the superstructures of religious institutions and theological dogmas which have been built on these personal experiences. Their cogency cannot be tested until the concrete findings have become available as the basis for judgment.

Since theology, like all reflective interpretations of experience, is parasitic on the phenomena it seeks to explain, the traditional theological debates should neither define the subject matter nor should they guide the inquiry. Instead, James proposes as his subject matter religious feelings and impulses, and among these, the "more developed subjective phenomena recorded in literature produced by articulate and fully self-conscious men" and women [VRE, 12]. Since the reduction of religious claims to their material conditions is the surest way to discredit them, James must defend his methodology from this accusation. To do so he has to distinguish his reconstruction of the natural history methodology, which is nothing less than an original concrete analysis, from positivist interpretations of scientific method. He defends his "existential" approach by arguing that not only does "every religious phenomenon [have] its history and its derivation from natural antecedents," but "scientific theories are organically conditioned just as much as religious emotions are" (VRE, 13-20). Rather than shielding religious phenomena from scientific scrutiny, James argues both that science deludes itself if it thinks that the same passions which influence religion do not influence its own analyses and that more is to be gained than lost in carefully investigating religious phenomena. By first discrediting the reigning scientific positivism, which he calls "medical materialism," he is preparing the way for the recognition and acceptance of his own reconstructed natural history methodology.

In the first place, human cognition is not a free-floating reality, but is embodied: "Modern psychology, finding definite psycho-physical connexions to hold good, assumes as a convenient hypothesis that the dependence of mental states upon bodily conditions must be thorough-going and complete" (VRE, 20). Since all states of mind have organic conditions it is no refutation of spiritual states to recognize that they also do. The superiority of one mental state to another "is either because we take an immediate delight in them; or else it is because we believe them to bring us good consequential fruits for life" (21). But these two criteria "do not always hang together" and "merely 'feeling good'" is often at odds with what follows (22). Momentary satisfactions are often counter-productive in enabling us to interact successfully with our environment.

In fact, it is this very discrepancy which has historically caused much religious anguish. Inner experiences of a mystical sort do not usually illuminate other experiences, and often even contradict them outright. But if it is thought to be inappropriate to discredit scientific hypotheses based on the frenzied enthusiasm with which they are held, it is no less illegitimate in regard to religious opinions. In science and technology opinions are "tested by logic and by experiment" (VRE, 23). In religious matters the appropriate criteria are "based on our own immediate feeling primarily; and secondarily on what we can ascertain of their experiential relations to our moral needs and to the rest of what we hold as true."

The pragmatic methodology can be recognized in these criteria, especially as explained in terms of its marriage function of joining the beliefs which comprise the funded character of our experience with novel experiences. But it also emphasizes the concrete centrality of feeling as disclosive of reality. But when he paraphrases what he has just said a new emphasis emerges: "*Immediate luminousness*, in short, *philosophical reasonableness*, and *moral helpfulness* are the only available criteria." These two criteria are nothing less than the satisfaction of the demands of our aesthetic (philosophical reasonableness) and practical (moral helpfulness) rationality. His concrete principles are thus being introduced one by one, without any acknowledgement that he is doing so. His consistent use of the interconnected set of principles and rules of interpretation that guide his radically empiricist concrete analysis accounts for the persuasiveness of his position on first hearing or reading. But his failure to explicate the basis for his interpretation within the text itself also accounts for the frustration afterwards encountered when trying to reconstruct and evaluate his argument.

He disingenuously says that he is only applying "the general principles by which the empirical philosophy has always contended that we must be guided in our search for truth" (VRE, 23-24). But he then criticizes the very search for foundations that has historically characterized both empiricist and rationalist philosophies, namely the search for some "direct mark" immediately intuited in experience as the basis for further claims. He shows that both religious persons and medical materialists are dogmatic when they take such an origin in immediate intuition as the stock warrant for our truth claims. By way of contrast, his rallying cry is: "By their fruits shall you know them, not by their roots" (25). He characterizes his "own [radically] empiricist criterion" of belief as found, not in its origins, "but *the way in which it works on the whole*" (24-25). Our beliefs are warranted, not by how things appear to us, but by how well they allow us to organize our particular experiences congruently with our expectations and with the wider context of historically transmitted, funded experience.

Given this pragmatic criterion, why even bother with his "existential study of [the] conditions" of religious phenomena? (VRE, 26). To this question James gives both an aesthetic reason, namely his "irrepressible curiosity," a curiosity that for him, in fact, defines the human, and a reason based on his natural history methodology, namely, that the gathering of the whole range of a phenomenon's appearances is a necessary prerequisite for understanding its significance. In fact he sees the originality of his contribution as developing a wider range of religious phenomena than anyone else heretofore, thereby placing "religious experiences in a wider context than has been usual in university courses" (29). He sees the success of his larger project as depending on demonstrating those hitherto neglected empirical findings which will secure our beliefs from skeptical refutation. But this is to claim both less and more than he has really accomplished. 'More,' insofar as this notion of a level of facticity that will not ever be reduced by further discoveries or points of view is a chimera, a superstition exposed by James's own analysis, and 'less,' in that I think that his real contribution was the development of an original concrete hermeneutics, a methodology rather than a set of facts.

James opens his second lecture by defending his practice of not beginning with an essential definition of the subject matter (VRE, 30). He argues that such premature simplification leads to "absolutism and one-sided dogmatism." We should resist the very real satisfactions such an intellectualist approach gives us because if unchecked the drive for intellectual rationality leads to over-simplification. Unification before the whole range of phenomena has been identified can only lead to unjustifiable distortion through the neglect of relevant data. He is reaffirming his methodological principle that clarification, that is, the recognition and description of the vast richness and over-abundance of phenomena, should precede and guide the subsequent conceptual simplification. Nonetheless, the field of religion is too vast to cover exhaustively and he must predelineate his subject matter by setting up workable limits. He defends his exclusion of both institutional religion and systematic theology by arguing that personal religion is more fundamental than either in one significant sense, namely, that both are in fact superstructures extending and building out the primordial event of the original founder's "direct personal communication with the divine" (33).

But rather than strongly defending his definition of religion by explicitly relating it to his concrete methodology, he is willing to let it appear as an arbitrary choice: "We escape much controversial matter by this arbitrary definition of our field" (VRE, 34). In a certain sense he is only following his own analysis of cognition because he holds that any selection out of the experiential "much-at-onceness" must focus on a few aspects of the original totality and arbitrarily disregard the rest as though they were of no importance. Such dissociation is, in fact, a necessary condition for rational thinking. But he does not point out this connection to his concrete analysis of cognition. Once again he is being disingenuous in claiming that his choice is arbitrary and in not disclosing why he considers his orientation towards the subject matter as being more defensible than other approaches. This is despite the fact that he fully expects that his radically empiricist concrete hermeneutics will lead to a revision of both institution and creed.

This disingenuousness is a direct outcome of his hermeneutics. His expository procedure consists in gradually bringing his listeners along with him until they can spontaneously conclude from the accumulation of evidence to the judgment that has been implicitly guiding the exposition all along. He thereby seeks to replicate what his concrete analysis of cognition has revealed is the process by which we dissociate from the overabundance of data just those aspects that will lead us to make worthwhile connections. However, what he gains in persuasiveness by this technique of eliciting the cooperative assent of his listeners he loses in the comprehension of the basis of his own position and in a systematic exposition of the interconnected principles.

James then picks his way through various opinions as to what constitutes religion by relying on such phrases as: "from the experiential point of view" and "man's total reaction upon life," that is, "our individual sense of it," which is then qualified further by the common belief that it "signifies always a *serious* state of mind" (VRE, 36-38). He concludes that "there must be something solemn, serious, and tender about any attitude which we denominate religious" (39). But what is the criterion by which he rejects some concrete descriptions of the attitudes which constitute religion and decides which attitudes are necessarily religious? He says that he is again making only an arbitrary proposal and he once again loses the opportunity to relate the basis for his choice to the concrete presuppositions that are structuring his argument. He does, however hint at them by criticizing the demand for scientific exactness as a precondition for investigation. He argues that no conception can be so sharply drawn if we are to be faithful to the field of experience. In experience "boundaries are always misty, and it is everywhere a question of amount and degree" (39-40). The inherent ambiguity of ordinary religious states of mind, which are more or less definite, more or less total, can most profitably be dealt with by considering as paradigm cases those in which "the religious spirit is unmistakable and extreme."

His natural history methodology incorporates the rule of physiology that meaning is best determined functionally (VRE, 44). What, then, functionally distinguishes a religious attitude from all others? Even the strongest persons trying to lead a good moral life sooner or later are frustrated in their attempts and recognize their "irremedial impotence" to effect lasting and universal change. Everyone, therefore, has need of the religious state of mind which alone can allay our deepest fears and replace them with an "enthusiastic temper of espousal" that evil will eventually "be permanently overcome" (45-48). His ultimate concrete criterion is the value for sustaining an enhanced form of life. And since "we are in the end absolutely dependent on the universe," and the experienced universe is at best indifferent to human aims and at worst hostile to our form of life, religion alone can save us from the bitter nihilism that is the inevitable result of these realizations (49). James concludes that "the vital importance [of religion] as a human faculty stands vindicated beyond dispute...from the merely biological point of view."

This conclusion is said to have been reached "by following the purely empirical method of demonstration which I sketched to you in the first lecture" (VRE, 49) But we have seen that this "biological point of view" and "empirical method" are actually his terms for his concrete reconstruction of natural history methodology. But this method has not been sufficiently developed in the first lecture for his audience to recognize the basis for the claims he is making. Without an understanding of his analysis of nihilism and skepticism and what is required to overcome them, for instance, his claim that religion alone can provide the necessary condition for human action is just an unsubstantiated claim. His argument presupposes, furthermore, a knowledge of his critique of traditional intellectual rationalism and replacement of it by a concrete analysis of cognition as an interactive process of organizing experience according to our interests. It also presupposes his arguments supporting the necessity of an aesthetic postulate of reason as the reductive of nihilism. One can dispute with him whether only religion can provide such a practical postulate or even whether such a postulate is a necessary prerequisite for action, but first the inadequacy of his terms, "biological point of view" and "empirical method," for his radically empiricist hermeneutics must be recognized.

In the third lecture James adds some more strokes to his sketch of his concrete hermeneutics by rephrasing his analysis in terms of "fringe and focus" to explain how "the sentiment of reality" attaches itself to objects of belief (VRE, 53). He does so by pointing out the normally unrecognized horizon or fringe which is a necessary condition for objects appearing as they do: "The whole universe of concrete objects, as we know them, swims...in a wider and higher universe of abstract ideas, that lend it its significance." These ideas "form the background for all our facts," but themselves do not appear as part of the object apprehended. "This absolute determinability of our mind by abstractions is one of the cardinal facts in our human constitution" (54). But he has in mind intentions, purposes and feelings as well as "abstract ideas," as is evident later in the chapter where he argues that the intellectual rationalist criteria for beliefs are inadequate because they privilege the articulate. "If we look on man's whole mental life as it exists," it is evident that "your whole subconscious life, your impulses, your faiths, your needs, your divinations, have prepared the premises, of which your consciousness now feels the weight of the result" (66-67). He critiques the realist fallacy of taking as the primordial sense of 'the world' that totality of material objects which can only be distinguished from ourselves on reflection, by pointing out that "the practically real world for each of us, the effective world of the individual, is the compound world, the physical facts and emotional values in indistinguishable combination" (127).

True to his hermeneutical principle of beginning with concrete abundance rather than the 'thinness' of analytical concepts, the chapters are filled with "concrete accounts of experience" exhibiting the great diversity of spiritual lives (VRE, 89, 94). He says in another place that he is "not yet pretending finally to *judge* any of these attitudes. I am only describing their variety" (122). They are organized according to his hermeneutical principle of opposite types as displaying the range of human responses, temperaments, or needs. The two he uses are "healthy-mindedness," which minimizes evil, and which he aligns with pluralism, and the "radically opposite view" of the morbidness of the "sick soul," which is monistic (112-113).

Having stuck to "practical common sense and the empirical method" through fifteen lectures and described one "genuine first-hand religious experience" after another, only heterodoxy, rather than any one orthodoxy, can be the outcome (VRE, 270, 299). In responding to those for whom truth, not utility for life, is the ultimate justification for religion, James turns to some theoretical considerations, which always mean for him a unification of phenomena according to a defining purpose (300ff). He finds in mysticism the experiential paradigm for religious truth, which is characterized by reconciliation and "incommunicableness of the transport" (308, 321). In its inarticulateness it resembles more closely sensational knowledge-by-acquaintance rather than conceptual knowledge-about. Like sensible intuition such experiential mystical states are epistemologically "authoritative over those who have them," but this indubitableness does not extend to those who do not (335-336). At most, mystical experiences can offer us hypotheses about the meaning of life (339).

In chapter 18 James argues that the content of mystical revelations can never be objective sources of truth claims. Mysticism "is essentially private and individualistic; it always exceeds our powers of formulation" (VRE, 340). All its authority and conviction derives from the experience as experience, not as revelation. He wants to defend "feeling at the expense of reason, to rehabilitate the primitive and unreflective" (341). Feeling is the source of religion and not philosophical and theological expressions, which "are secondary products, like translations of a text into another tongue." But since, as thinking beings, we cannot avoid intellectualizing our experiences, he indulges in explicitly criticizing intellectual rationalism in its limited aesthetic sense because it privileges "logical reason alone" (342). He argues that intellectual or aesthetic rationalism in its drive for simplification must be checked by both the other intellectual rational drive for clarity and the practical rational drive for appropriate ends for action. All "intellectual operations, whether they be constructive or comparative or critical, presuppose immediate experiences as their subject-matter." Aesthetic rationality can only be inductive or interpretive, and both operations depend on experience.

The logical cogency of philosophical arguments cannot warrant the truth of beliefs, religious or otherwise; they can "only corroborate our pre-existent partialities" (VRE, 345, 347). What is finally needed to overcome the relativism which seems an inescapable consequence of the partiality of reason is a recognition that our "thinking is organically connected with [our] conduct" (349). James introduces the principle of pragmatism as a formulation of the empiricist principle "that every difference must *make* a difference, every theoretical difference somewhere issue in a practical difference" (350). Reflections on actual practical differences can thus provide what rational arguments alone can never supply, namely, that evidential base which allows for the possibility of mediation between conflicting, self-sustaining beliefs. Intelligible meaning therefore consists in concrete verification. "Beliefs, in short, are rules for action; and the whole function of thinking is but one step in the production of active habits" (351).

No purely intellectual process can prove that any religious claim is true. This is due to the function of intellection in human life, which is to "class facts, define them, interpret them" (VRE, 359). Since the intellect cannot produce facts, it cannot be primary. This is the function of feeling, which is productive and revelatory of individuality, of "a *plus*, a *thisness*." James then defines the function of aesthetic rationality after its enlightenment hegemony has been discarded. It remains useful to the extent that it "will abandon metaphysics and deduction for criticism and induction." Since in concrete experience the intellect spontaneously defines reality "in ways that harmonize with its temporary intellectual prepossessions," aesthetic rationality as privileged by philosophers still has the task of eliminating "the local and the accidental from these definitions," of removing "historic incrustations," and of challenging one's constructions to eliminate scientifically absurd or incongruous doctrines.

Through this sifting out philosophy can then deal with what is left as "*hypotheses*, testing them in all manners, whether negative or positive, by which hypotheses are ever tested." Through "distinguishing between what is innocent over-belief and symbolism in the expression of it, and what is to be literally taken,"…it "can offer mediation between different believers, and help to bring about a consensus of opinion." This consensus is brought about as a result of discriminating "the common and essential from the individual and local elements." Although aesthetic rationality has this legitimate critical function, it will go wrong if it does not recognize that it can "never get away from concrete life" (VRE, 360). Since it depends "for its original material on facts of personal experience" and "its formulas are but approximations," it is bound to "square itself with personal experience through all its critical reconstructions." The replacement of modern philosophy's epistemic turn by a radically empiricist concrete turn is succinctly stated: "Philosophy lives in words, but truth and fact well up into our lives in ways that exceed verbal formulation."

True to his hermeneutics, James in the concluding chapter weaves together the concrete findings of the earlier nineteen chapters into a comprehensive unity or inductive theory. He calls this being "dryer and less sympathetic in the rest of the work that lies before us" (VRE, 383). He defends his emphasis on individuality and rehabilitation of feeling by connecting it to his radically empiricist concrete analysis: only in the concrete situation of individual feeling can "we catch real fact in the making, and directly perceive how events happen, and how work is actually done" (395). Since both thought and feeling determine conduct and any particular practice may be more determined by one than by the other, inquiry should seek to ascertain and relate both subjective utility and intellectual content. James's own 'over-belief' "that the conscious person is continuous with a wider self through which saving experiences come," is defended as a hypothesis which must be finally judged by how well it fulfills his pragmatic criteria (405). In his "Postscript" he seeks to defend it as "the hypothesis by which the largest number of legitimate requirements are met" (411). Only on this ground of whether it satisfactorily accounts for "the total expression of human experience" can it be justifiably either supported or rejected (408).

In his concluding chapter James sets out his most mature formulation of his radically empiricist concrete hermeneutics. He says that all experience is both subjective and objective, and that although the objective part is "incalculably more extensive" than the subjective part, it is only an ideal picture of the reality which is the subjective experience itself. He then defines this *"full* fact," which characterizes reality as reality-for-us. In doing so he finally provides a model for his concrete approach. The goal of hermeneutics is to postulate and develop this full fact (VRE, 393).

Chapter Eight

Analogy and Metaphor

"For him the abstract lived in the concrete" (PU, 70)

William James's use of analogy and metaphor is more than a rhetorical device. It is integral to his hermeneutics and reflects his concrete analysis of human thinking, which begins with the abstraction of marks or signs out of a concrete totality of experience. These marks can be recognized only because we preperceive them according to our interests. Minds fertile with analogies, whether artistic or scientific, will be able to recognize many more aspects of experience than those whose senses are dulled by convention, who can recognize and relate under appropriate classifications only what has already been pointed out to them. Analogy, the recognition of similarity despite appearances, is the basis for the distinctively human creativity which characterizes and unifies both poetic and conceptual thinking.[1]

1. The Genial Play of Association by Similarity

James explains the deep reach of the principle of selective interest by comparing it to analogical insight, since for both the links are presumed rather than explicitly recounted: "As the art of reading...is the art of skipping, so the art of being wise is the art of knowing what to overlook" (PP,II, 992).[2] The same phenomenon is evident in any high order conversation which is characterized by "the summariness of its allusions and the rapidity of its transitions." The "genial play...make(s) these conversations seem true feasts for gods to a listener who is educated enough to follow them at all." Such abridgment and elision are true of both genius and everyday conversations when the participants know each other well. Explanations are clearer when analogies are used. James says, for instance, that he "may appear to have strayed from psychological analysis into aesthetic criticism. But the principle of selection is so important that no illustrations seem redundant which may help to show how great is its scope" (993). He often expresses the principle that concrete examples help to overcome obscurity and to reinforce specific points.[3] He also invites his hearers to join in this hermeneutical procedure: "Every reader's mind will supply abundant examples of the process here described; and to write them down would be therefore both unnecessary and tedious" (725).

Plainly, James was most comfortable using language as a poet does, to create such a compelling interpretation of life that the reader can appropriate it as her own, rather than in using language as a logician does, to elaborate a consistent system and avoid errors of technique.[4] Like Nietzsche and Wittgenstein, James found multifaceted aspects of experience more clearly communicated in terms which were themselves richly allusive. This is not an escape into ambiguity or mysticism, but a careful explication drawing on other uses of language than the strictly denotative. It is well known that his philosophy was deeply influenced by Darwin, but not sufficiently realized how much the style as well as the substance of Darwin's position was assimilated by, or at least congenial to, James's own. In commenting on Darwin's use of metaphor Edward Manier, drawing on Mary Hesse's views, makes a point that applies equally to James's use of language: "In contrast to the so-called *comparison view* of metaphor, the interaction view *denies* that metaphor can be replaced without remainder by an explicit literal statement of the similarities between the field to which the metaphor is extended...and the proper field of the metaphor itself."[5]

Multifaceted explanations disclose more of reality because of the much-at-onceness of experience, which consists of processive, temporal, interrelated events and not of isolated monads. There is no such thing as a single true statement, just as there is no such thing as an isolated object. As James says: "There is never a proposition that does not require other propositions after it, to amplify it, restrict it, or in some way save it from the falsity by defect or excess which it contains." (TCW, II, 328) A world or context must be recognized or supplied. At least one is always operative, but we too often selectively ignore it. Metaphors better reflect this contextuality and revisability of discourse than discursive language does. Art imitates life, which "stumbles over its own fact in a similar way; for its earlier moments plunge ceaselessly into later ones which reinterpret and correct them." James draws our attention to this contextualism by requiring us to make the implicit connections explicit. Nietzsche makes the same point about aphorisms: "An aphorism, properly stamped and molded, has not been 'deciphered' when it has simply been read; rather, one has then to begin its *exegesis*, for which is required an art of exegesis."⁶ By contrast, straightforward propositions conceal rather than reveal their own conditions because their meaning is immediately apparent.

James says in *The Will to Believe* that when we lack compelling evidence "we are free to trust at our own risks anything that is not impossible, and that can bring analogies to bear in its behalf" (WB, 52). This cryptic directive is less startling when understood in reference to the chapter on reasoning in *Principles,* which was written at about the same time. Association by similarity is given as the defining characteristic of rationality (PP,II, 970ff). Whether spontaneously or through the discipline of scientific investigation, hitherto unrecognized analogous instances are brought into consciousness at one time. Geniuses possess the ability to the highest degree, while animals probably lack it entirely, passing from one concrete object to its habitual successor and associating exclusively by contiguity. James cites Mill's *Logic* and his four methods of experimental inquiry as expounding the analogical method. It is significant that the analogical organization of experience applies equally to artists, who spontaneously collect analogous instances, and to scientists, who do so deliberately and methodically. James asserts that "after the few most powerful practical and aesthetic interests, our chief help towards noticing those special characters of phenomena, which, when once possessed and named, are used as reasons, class names, essences, or middle terms, *is this association by similarity*" (PP,II, 971-2).

James's concrete genealogy of the development of reasoning defends the centrality of analogy to human thinking. He argues that "furnishing parallel cases is the necessary first step towards abstracting the reason embedded in them all" (EPS, 33). According to this genealogy humans first thought holistically, in vaguely concrete terms, then abstracted some quality that came to stand for the whole. James urges us to recognize the pluralism of phenomenal experience as a necessary condition for the possibility of our particular orderings and arrangements: "Nature, more demonic than divine, is above all things *multifarious*" (PU, 15). Out of this "walpurgis-nacht procession" humans first tried to placate dangerous powers and curry favor with friendly ones. Eventually "the intellect awoke, with its passion for generalizing, simplifying and subordinating." As different parts were emphasized and filled in with imaginary supplements, including substance and cause, objective nature obligingly provided confirmatory experiences for many of these different schemas.

James refers to the new theories about linguistic development because he is concerned to account for the fact that we still follow a pattern of thinking that linguists were beginning to identify with earlier forms of thought. Positivists argued that holistic thinking was a primitive remnant which should be superseded by later, and supposedly higher, forms of analytic thinking. James argues instead that analogical thinking is actually an indispensable constituent of all thinking and not a disposable relic of a more primitive era. In everyday life we often note similarities without necessarily being aware of their grounds. This fact points to an ability, not a stage of thought which we can as well do without. In fact "the most characteristic single difference between the human mind and that of brutes lies in this deficiency on the brute's part to associate ideas by similarity"; they remain "drowned, swamped in the total phenomenon which they help constitute, and never used to reason from" (EPS, 29).

This phenomenal totality is always contrasted to the empiricist assumption of bare sensations as the building blocks of conceptual thinking. Contrary to this psychologistic fallacy of the empiricists, it takes deliberate effort to reduce what we normally apprehend "with a cloud of associates" into its "sensational nudity" (PP,II, 726-7). If we manage to do so, such bare entities stare at us "like a glass eye, with no speculation in it. Its body is indeed there, but its soul is fled." Rather than attending to individual words in a text, for instance, in the actuality of living experience we "habitually got it clad with its meaning the moment we caught sight of it, and rapidly passed from it to the other words of the phrase."

James argues that we continually use analogy in practical life and, with Bain, he takes genius as consisting in the power of perceiving analogies (PU, 71). Analogy means recognizing difference as well as similarity. James says that a common fallacy in analogical reasoning, according to Fechner, is the failure to make allowance for differences. It is just as important to recognize what features two aspects of experience do not share as to recognize what they have in common. Both airplanes and chickens have wings, for instance, but it does not therefore follow that they both fly. "Fechner's imagination, insisting on the differences as well as on the resemblances, thus tries to make our picture of the whole earth's life more concrete' (75). James praises Fechner for his profusely concrete imagination and for "the impression he gives of a man who doesn't live at second-hand, but who *sees*" (72). He methodically develops "a vast analogical series, in which the basis of the analogy consists of facts directly observable in ourselves" (73).

James does not just use metaphors and analogies as illustrations. He frequently forwards his arguments by extending and developing them. He explicitly argues by analogy, for instance, in defending

Fechner's panpsychist theory "of successively larger enveloping spheres of conscious life" (PU, 139). He begins by arguing that this theory has some direct empirical evidence in the testimony of those who claim to have had experiences of "a wider self from which saving experiences flow in." But philosophers are prone to the logician's bias which privileges abstract argumentation over the confusions of personal biography. It comes down to a preference for the thinner or the thicker method, that is, whether the particular and the personal are as legitimate factors in philosophical debate as are purely logical ones. James then defends his preference by rephrasing the issue in terms of a comparison: "We may be in the universe as dogs and cats are in our libraries, seeing the books and hearing the conversation, but having no inkling of the meaning of it all" (140). Next, he gives empirical evidence for this claim, which turns on a series of analogies based on the factual findings he has been describing in the rest of the book: "The analogies with ordinary psychology, with certain facts of pathology, with those of psychical research, so called, and with those of religious experience, establish, when taken together, a decidedly *formidable* probability in favor of a general view of the world almost identical to Fechner's." Admitting that the details of the superhuman consciousness are very vague, he nonetheless urges such "a pluralistic panpsychic view of the universe" as a workable hypothesis for those philosophers interested in religion (140-141).

The analogical method is not only appropriate for literary productions but is also constitutive of rational and scientific thinking: "Hypotheses, and deductions from these, controlled by sense-observations and analogies with what we know elsewhere, are to be thanked for all of science's results" (PU, 68). He thinks that analogy rests on what is essential because, according to his concrete analysis of thinking, it is through identifying similarity according to our interests that essentiality arose in the first place.[7]

2. Philosophy: Making Conventionalities Fluid Again

One way to look at James's radical reconstruction of philosophy is to see how he changes its metaphors. He does not deny that philosophers are persons who value objectivity, clarity of seeing, and preciseness of articulation more than most, but he urges them not to slight other values. We have seen that in "The Sentiment of Rationality," he argues that philosophers have overestimated intellectualist rationality to such an extent that they have distorted its relation to practical rationality and misunderstood its function as only one of the fundamental human drives to organize experience harmoniously. Nonetheless, the drive toward total unification is as worthy of fulfillment as any other, as long as it does not overstep its bounds. The frustrations encountered in his life-long struggle to satisfy his own philosophic drive for a perfect coalescence between what is said and what 'is' steadily mount until he finally admits defeat. In the end he gives up the traditional philosophic effort to "envelope our many with the 'one' that brings so much poison in its train" (PU, 141). The essential incompatibility of his empiricist realism and his radically empiricist concrete pragmatism became more and more manifest until he could no longer ignore it. But there remains from beginning to end an underlying unity of purpose and also perhaps a greater consistency in his use of analogy and metaphor than in the positions illustrated.

In one of his earliest writings (1876), James says that "philosophic study means the habit of always seeing an alternative, of not taking the usual for granted, of making conventionalities fluid again, of imagining foreign states of mind" (EPH, 4). And he repeats this in his last book, published posthumously (1911): "Philosophy, beginning in wonder, as Plato and Aristotle said, is able to fancy everything different from what it is. It sees the familiar as if it were strange, and the strange as if it were familiar...It rouses us from our native 'dogmatic slumber' and breaks up our caked prejudices" (SPP, 11). This best expresses his own philosophical contribution, which is inseparable from his metaphorical style. He was well aware of the explosive force of the unexpected use of language: "But if an unusual foreign word be introduced, if the grammar trip, or if a term from an incongruous vocabulary suddenly appear, such as 'rat-trap' or 'plumber's bill' in a philosophical discourse, the sentence detonates, as it were, we receive a shock from the incongruity, and the drowsy assent is gone" (PP,I, 253).

It is not an exaggeration to say that all of James's central concerns are expressed in striking metaphors and analogies. He concludes his lecture on philosophy in *Varieties* with a metaphorical outburst which both exhibits and reflects his keen sense of the inadequacy of all efforts to conceptually verbalize experience. Nonetheless, as a philosopher he is condemned to this impossible task. He says that, just as the science of optics depends for its facts on the experiences of seeing individuals, so too, the critical reconstructions of a science of religion would have to be squared with personal experiences. The formulations of science are only approximations of concrete life. Philosophy also cannot capture reality in words.

> There is in the living act of perception always something that
> glimmers and twinkles and will not be caught, and for which

reflection comes too late. No one knows this as well as the philosopher. He must fire his volley of new vocables out of his conceptual shotgun, for his profession condemns him to this industry, but he secretly knows the hollowness and irrelevancy. His formulas are like stereoscopic or kinetoscopic photographs seen outside the instrument; they lack the depth, the motion, the vitality (VRE, 360).

James's metaphors are richer, more informative and more provocative than their conceptual equivalents. A large part of the ambivalence encountered in his writings and the difficulty of deciphering his exact meaning is due to the fact that so much of what is being said is carried by metaphors. He even sometimes changes their discursive renderings, because no one explanation is adequate to the metaphor, just as no verbalization of experience can be its equivalent. He can be taken as demonstrating that the referent is more important than the sign and that metaphors reproduce the complexity and ambiguity of experience better than more straightforward discourse, which gains its exactness by losing its evocativeness. He is willing to reconsider his explanations when they are attacked, but he does not think that finding fault with some particular way of conceptualizing an aspect of experience necessarily disproves either the experience to which it refers or its metaphorical equivalent.

In his efforts to convey the finite limitations of our attempts to symbolize experience James frequently compares such semeiotic transcriptions to drawing a picture. His initial concrete description of those aspects of experience that he is going to analyze is often compared to the rough sketching which precedes a fully rendered painting. In the first chapter of *Pragmatism* he says that he is just giving a simplified picture of philosophy, but that "in point of fact the picture I have given is, however coarse and sketchy, literally true" (PM, 24). In sketching out this particular picture James recalls all four senses in one page, thus giving us a glimpse of the way he organized his thoughts metaphorically rather than deductively. The first sense is sight, in the metaphor of picturing itself. This is followed by sound imagery, recalling "that strange simple note of individuality which haunts our memory." Next comes taste: " ...the revelation of how intensely odd the personal flavor of some fellow creature is." The sense of touch leads him to quote Whitman, who says that "who touches this book touches a man." Finally, he uses the imagery of feeling and tasting: "We measure the total character of the universe as we feel it, against the flavor of the philosophy proffered us, and one word is enough."

His homely example of throwing beans on a table perfectly illustrates the central principle of his radically empiricist hermeneutics, which is that we order the world to suit our purposes, but such imposition of regularities is a necessary condition for discovering the facts of nature (VRE, 346-347, n7). Our interests in practical, aesthetic and moral organizations of experience lead us to pick patterns out of the overabundance of disorderly arrangements. The disorder and order which result are purely human inventions. This explanation is followed by an extended metaphor, which not only illustrates it, but clarifies what is meant such that it becomes part of the explanation:

> If I should throw down a thousand beans at random upon a table, I could doubtless, by eliminating a sufficient number of them, leave the rest in almost any geometrical pattern you might propose to me, and you might then say that that pattern was the thing prefigured beforehand, and that the other beans were mere irrelevance and packing material. Our dealings with Nature are just like this. She is a vast *plenum* in which our attention draws capricious lines in innumerable directions. We count and name whatever lies upon the special lines we trace, whilst the other things and the untraced lines are neither named nor counted (VRE, 346, 347, n7)[8]

We ingeniously discover and remember what we are already prepared to see.

James uses analogy and metaphor for rehabilitating the element of feeling, not only in religion, but as an irreducible aspect of all human organizations of experience. It is absurd for science to try to suppress the egoistic aspects of experience. Two similes reinforce these claims:

> The axis of reality runs solely through the egotistic places — they are strung upon it like so many beads. To describe the world with all the various feelings of the individual pinch of destiny, all the various spiritual attitudes, left out from the description — they being as describable as anything else — would be something like offering a printed bill of fare as the equivalent for a solid meal (VRE, 394).

James also rehabilitates the role of imagination in thinking. This was a direct assault on those philosophers who, in their eagerness to imitate what they took to be proper scientific methodology, denied that imagination had any role to play in rational investigation. Against such a positivistic understanding of science he argues that even simple sensible qualities, which provide the building blocks of traditional empiricism and its scientific offshoots, are "in literal mathematical strictness...but imperfectly imaginable things" (PP,I, 480). They result from the imaginative prolongation of the direct perception of differences towards an ideal terminus.

Towards the end of an extended defense of the proposition that objective standards can be derived from experience, James recalls Emerson as chiding those who imagine that following the laws imposed by experience is no special feat to try doing so for one day (PM, 112-113). Rather than continuing logically with the line of thought he has been following, James is seduced by the word, 'imagines,' to defend the role of imagination in thinking, particularly in philosophic thinking. He says that imagination was beginning to be defended as a legitimate aspect of scientific thinking, and it was time to urge its use in philosophy. He complains that his critics need more imagination in order to understand the pragmatist position. For his own part, he cannot make any sense of their rationalist position, despite the fact that he has stretched his own imagination to read the best possible meaning into it. He simply cannot imagine himself into their world. The unintelligibility of the correspondence theory of copying directly stems from the impossibility of imagining in what the copy consists and of imagining why anyone would want to reduce the myriad ways thought can be said to agree with reality to the one activity of copying. Misunderstanding is also linked in *Principles* with a failure of imagination (PP,I, 134).

Perspectivism is another aspect of his philosophy that is powerfully conveyed through metaphor. In the first lecture of *A Pluralistic Universe* James groups philosophies under the headings of rationalism and empiricism. He then points out that classification as such is distortive since individuality can never be reduced to any schema. He thinks, however, that the worst polemicizing of the previous decades was over. This had consisted largely of putting people in categories which they resented as distortive. He believed that positions could now be classified and related with less acrimony (PU, 7). He also believed that a revised empiricism was gaining momentum. This would indicate that the time was ripe for getting a sympathetic hearing for his controversial "pluralism or humanism" (PU, 7-9). Rationalistic philosophies have affinities with monism, since they begin with a coherent, interconnected system into which they try to fit various empirical parts. But as finite beings we can have no access to such an over-view of the whole universe. This is why he continually refers to his own writing as consisting of scraps and fragments in comparison to systematizing such as Royce's (EPH, 258). Even our most comprehensive systems are only theoretic fragments woven out of some strands of the overflowing abundance of experience.

Metaphors abound in James's defense of pluralism because they better replicate the abundance of experiential phenomena. They also instantiate the process by which we unify experience by subsuming it under one aspect which appeals to us. "No philosophy can ever be anything but a summary sketch, a picture of the world in abridgment, a foreshortened bird's-eye view of the perspective of events. And the first thing to notice is this, that the only material we have at our disposal for making a picture of the whole world is supplied by various portions of that world of which we have already had experience" (PU, 9). He is not only using metaphor and analogy in his explanation but he is arguing that philosophic systems themselves are best understood as following such basic principles of analogical thinking as perspectivism, rootedness in experience, and extension of the familiar to the unfamiliar. Some particular feature of the world captures a philosopher's attention, which is then by analogy extended to the whole world. "Thus, the theists take their cue from manufacture, the pantheists from growth. For one man, the world is like a thought or a grammatical sentence in which a thought is expressed. For such a philosopher, the whole must logically be prior to the parts; for letters would never have been invented without syllables to spell, or syllables without words to utter" (9).

This enumeration by analogy is congenial to James's own thinking and the analogies proliferate unchecked:

> Another will conceive the order as only a statistical appearance, and the universe will be for him like a vast grab-bag with black and white balls in it, of which we guess the quantities only probably, by the frequency with which we experience their egress.

> For another, again, there is no really inherent order, but it is we who project order into the world by selecting objects and tracing relations so as to gratify our intellectual interests. We *carve out* order by leaving the disorderly parts out; and the world is conceived thus after the analogy of a forest or a block of marble from which parks or statues may be produced by eliminating irrelevant trees or chips of stone (PU, 10).

Not only is James defining by analogy, he is also contrasting a mechanistic view of the world with his own. This dialectic by analogy continues:

> Some thinkers follow suggestions from human life, and treat the universe as if it were essentially a place in which ideals are realized. Others are more struck by its lower features, and for them, brute necessities express its character better (PU, 10).

All the various philosophical positions "follow one analogy or another; and all the analogies are with some one or other of the universe's subdivisions" (PU, 10). Because of his realist assumptions James believes that the subdivisions are really there, but because of his concrete analysis he also says that they would not be discovered without a special angle of vision to pick them out. Philosophers, however, who have traditionally been blind to their own subjectivity, are more likely to claim that their conclusions alone are logical and that they reflect universal reason. James stresses that it is important to realize the subjectivity of our philosophical claims because one person's "vision may be much more valuable than another's, and our visions are usually not only our most interesting but our most respectable contributions to the world in which we play our part" (10). James's long discussion of philosophy is both full of examples and guided by metaphorical rather than deductive reasoning. Analogical thinking is explicitly connected with concrete analysis and with anti-rationalist arguments. James ends the lecture by stressing the "radical discrepancy between the absolute and the relative points of view" and affirming that "we humans are incurably rooted in the temporal point of view" (23).

But James draws a different conclusion from the loss of objective universality and its replacement with personal visions than do recent post-structuralist nihilists such as Derrida. Organizations of experience are not only personal, they are also social constructions and incorporate sensible experiences. They therefore have consequences for life. It is this realization that different ways of picturing the world have different consequences that leads James and other radically empiricist pragmatists to develop strategies for affirming some interpretations and rejecting others. In his notes for the second series of Gifford Lectures, these criteria are explicitly linked to his metaphorical development of 'picturing.' Worldviews should more fully and easily disclose the facts as we understand them: "In which do you find represented most of the details of life which you know — represented without omission, addition, or distortion? — that is one way of comparing the pictures; and the other way is as to the harmony, beauty, impressiveness or suggestiveness for life, of their total effect" (VRE, 488-489).

Consequently, James agrees with Hegel that the aim of philosophy is to make ourselves at home in the world and that different persons find themselves at home in different fragments of it (PU, 10). Philosophic systems are interpreted as visions, modes of feeling, or best working attitudes. They are either cynical or sympathetic (14-15). From the pragmatic point of view, the difference between cynicism and sympathy is whether we relate to the universe as symbiotic parts or as alien intruders. Do we think of ourselves as participating in a "common *socius*" of self and nature or do we adopt "a general habit of wariness" toward the rest of the universe? (19).

Another extended example of a central issue being explained metaphorically occurs in *Essays in Radical Empiricism* at the end of the chapter on "A World of Pure Experience." James recalls that he had called his philosophy of radical empiricism a mosaic philosophy and he proceeds to draw out the implications of this metaphor: "In actual mosaics the pieces are held together by their bedding, for which bedding the substances, transcendental egos, or absolutes of other philosophies may be taken to stand. In radical empiricism there is no bedding; it is as if the pieces clung together by their edges, the transitions experienced between them forming their cement" (ERE, 42). James uses the metaphor of a mosaic to deny the appeal to either empirical or transcendental grounding in his philosophy of radical empiricism, but he had earlier criticized Hodgson's use of this metaphor to deny causal efficacy to feelings (PP,I, 134). How can James keep causal efficacy and reject foundationalism?

The mosaic metaphor provides a clue to interpreting what has been rejected in foundationalism and what has replaced it. It leads us back to "The Sentiment of Rationality." After having argued against the foundationalist excesses of "the passion for simplification," which illicitly ignores those facts which cannot be accommodated, he criticizes the excesses of "its rival,...the passion for distinguishing" (EPH, 37).[9] Delight in identifying the uniqueness of the particular should not extend to denying those relations that are also experienced. "So far is this reaction against the treatment of relational terms as metempirical [sic.] entities carried, that the reigning British school seems to deny their function even in their legitimate sphere, namely as phenomenal elements or 'laws' cementing the mosaic of our feelings into coherent form" (39).

But as soon as he begins explicating radical empiricism as a mosaic philosophy he finds the comparison too static and points out its limitations in expressing the dynamic sense of life. The metaphor is misleading because the various parts of experience do not need to be cemented together. They already dynamically interact without losing their singularity. Still, the metaphor symbolizes that experience grows by its edges (ERE, 42). In trying to convey the processive character of experience he ends up with the image of a firing line, which, in turn, calls up for him the image of a fire: "Life is in the transitions as much as in the terms connected; often, indeed, it seems to be there more emphatically, as if our spurts and sallies forward were the real firing-line of the battle, were like the thin line of flame advancing across the dry autumnal field which the farmer proceeds to burn."

James reconstructs empiricism by arguing that what we perceive are not isolated sense data, but concrete wholes, including relations. He substitutes a dynamic model of consciousness for the largely static one of Locke and Hume. This is expressed through metaphors of streams and rivers, as in this excerpt from a letter: "Once admit that experience is a river which made the channel that now, in part, but only in part, confines it, and it seems to me that all sorts of realities and completenesses are possible in Philosophy, hitherto stiffened & cramped by the silly littlenesses of the upper and the lower dogmatisms alternating their petty rationalistic and materialistic idols of the shop" (EPH, 261). The metaphor of a stream of consciousness is perhaps the one most associated with his name (PP,I, 219-278, 427). He characteristically elaborates the metaphor for the sheer joy of it; his delight in playing with language is palpable:

> The traditional psychology talks like one who should say a river consists of nothing but pailsful, spoonsful, quartpotsful, barrelsful, and other moulded [sic.] forms of water. Even were the pails and the pots all actually standing in the stream, still between them the free water would continue to flow. It is just this free water of consciousness that psychologists resolutely overlook. Every definite image in the mind is steeped and dyed in the free water that flows around it (PP,I, 246).

As with most of his extended metaphors, it is enveloped in and explained by means of further metaphors. He continues: "With it goes the sense of its relations, near and remote, the dying echo of whence it came to us, the dawning sense of whither it is to lead. The significance, the value, of the image is all in this halo or penumbra that surrounds and escorts it, — or rather that is fused into one with it and has become bone of its bone and flesh of its flesh.... " And he ends the sentence with a reflection that applies equally well to his metaphorical procedure itself: "...leaving it, it is true, an image of the same *thing* it was before, but making it an image of that thing newly taken and freshly understood."

James's hermeneutic method is explained through the metaphors of translation and weaving. Weaving expresses metaphorically his methodology of beginning with phenomenal abundance, taking up its multi-colored strands, and ordering them into a coherent pattern guided by our own purposes. He says, for instance, that the philosopher's "aim is to find an account of the moral relations that obtain among things, which will weave them into the unity of a stable system" (WB, 141). Putting experience into words is also often compared to translating a text. He says, for instance, that feeling is deeper than philosophical and theological formulas, which are only secondary products, "like translations of a text into another tongue" (VRE, 341). Translations are not only dependent on the text they are translating, but they cannot reproduce every aspect of it. In an early letter (1868) James said: "I have regarded the affairs of human life to be only a phantasmagoria, which had to be *interpreted* elsewhere in the kosmos into its real significance. But of late the sturdy realism of

Goethe and the obdurate beauty and charm of the Greeks have shaken my complexion more than anything else " (TCW,I, 161).

In an extended metaphor he returns to and expands this notion of an interpretation, which has more in common with Platonic Ideas informing this shadowy world, than of one text explaining another. He compares the pragmatic understanding of the relation between abstract ideas and concrete realities with the phenomenon of reflection: "Let the water represent the world of sensible facts, and let the air above it represent the world of abstract ideas. Both worlds are real, of course, and interact; but they interact only at their boundary, and the *locus* of everything that lives, and happens to us, so far as full experience goes, is the water. We are like fishes swimming in the sea of sense, bounded above by the superior element, but unable to breathe it pure or penetrate it" (PM, 63-64). He continues to develop every detail of the comparison because its vividness makes the position seem more plausible. The water surface reflects back visual rays and makes it appear to be an upper limit. This disguises the fact that there is a real world beyond it, one which is necessary for life to continue below the surface. James remarks on his procedure: "All similes are halting, but this one rather takes my fancy. It shows how something, not sufficient for life in itself, may nevertheless be an effective determinant of life elsewhere" (PM, 64). He later returns to the metaphor and follows Bergson in characterizing the relation of the two worlds as a Platonic inversion because the inner nature of things can be revealed only through diving into the flux of experience (PU, 112-113).

3. Rationalism and Empiricism

A family of metaphors clusters around the fundamental opposition of rationalism or intellectualism and empiricism or concreteness. In the first chapter of *Pragmatism* James says that a student thesis had contrasted classroom philosophy with the way we relate to the universe of the streets: "The world of concrete personal experiences to which the street belongs is multitudinous beyond imagination, tangled, muddy, painful and perplexed" (PM, 17-18). By contrast the simple, clean, and noble world of philosophers exhibits the features of classic architecture. As "a kind of marble temple shining on a hill, . . . principles of reason trace its outlines, logical necessities cement its parts." It is "a classic sanctuary" in which to take refuge and escape from "the gothic character which mere facts present." This craving for refinement reflects a powerful mental appetite which recoils from "this colossal universe of concrete facts, on their awful bewilderments, their surprises and cruelties, on the wildness which they show." To the empiricist temper of mind such refinement seems "a monument of artificiality," and therefore scientists turn away from metaphysics as "altogether cloistered and spectral," and practical persons shake "philosophy's dust off their feet" and follow "the call of the wild."

James concludes the first chapter of *Pragmatism* by developing further these architecture metaphors. He says that although philosophies by their nature are outlines, as compared with the world of experience, some outlines of buildings "are *fat*, conceived in the cube by their planner," and some are "invented flat on paper, with the aid of ruler and compass. These remain skinny and emaciated even when set up in stone and mortar" (PM, 25). But what makes one outline meager in comparison to another is not so much their own structure, but their referents. Herbert Spencer, for instance, is characterized as having a "dry, schoolmaster temperament" and "his whole system [is] wooden, as if knocked together out of cracked hemlock boards," but James, along with "half of England wants to bury him in Westminster Abbey" (26). This is because he nonetheless exhibits the quintessential empiricist trait of unflinching reference to the experienced world: "His principles may be all skin and bone, but at any rate his books try to mould themselves upon the particular shape of this particular world's carcase [sic.]."

James replaces the rational deductive model of reasoning with a genealogical model which exhibits the historical conditions of our ways of thinking. This practical turn is explained through multiple metaphors, including scientific, aesthetic, and everyday ones. Ancient ways of thinking have survived and left their traces in us. "Like our five fingers, our earbones, our rudimentary caudal appendage, or our other 'vestigial' peculiarities, they may remain as indelible tokens of events in our race-history" (PM, 83). Our ancestors might have struck on other categories, but the ones actually chosen continue to influence further choices. This explanation of the pragmatic a priori is so important that James multiplies it metaphorically: "When you begin a piece of music in a certain key, you must keep the key to the end. You may alter your house *ad libitum*, but the ground-plan of the first architect persists — you can make great changes, but you cannot change a Gothic church into a Doric temple. You may rinse and rinse the bottle, but you can't get the taste of the medicine or whiskey that first filled it wholly out."

In another passage where James contrasts rationalism and empiricism, the metaphors proliferate far beyond what is needed to explain his position. He seems to think primarily in analogies and metaphors, which call up their own connections, and only secondarily in discursive or deductive modes. He states that the choice between pragmatism and rationalism extends beyond epistemology to a determination of the structure of the universe (PM, 124). This is immediately explicated metaphorically. Pragmatists believe in an unfinished edition of the universe, which we help to construct. Rationalists believe in many editions of the universe, a deluxe edition that is eternal and real and many distorted, mutilated finite editions.

The two sides are also distinguished according to temperament and these are explicated metaphorically. The rationalist mind is doctrinaire and authoritarian. "The belly-band of its universe must be tight. A radical pragmatist on the other hand is a happy-go-lucky anarchistic sort of creature. If he had to live in a tub like Diogenes he wouldn't mind at all if the hoops were loose and the staves let in the sun" (PM, 124). James compares the way a rationalist would respond to such a loose universe to the way that the freedom of the press would affect an official in the Russian censorship bureau. But one good comparison deserves another. He then says that it would affect the rationalist "as 'simplified spelling' might affect an elderly schoolmistress. It affects him as the swarm of protestant sects affects a papist onlooker. It appears as backboneless and devoid of principle as 'opportunism' in politics appears to an old-fashioned french legitimist, or to a fanatical believer in the divine right of the people" (125). We are left with the impression that James is multiplying analogies for the sheer joy of it.

This impression is confirmed as he continues his explanation through metaphor. Truths, like experiences, are finite for the pluralistic pragmatist: "All 'homes' are in finite experience; finite experience as such is homeless" (PM, 125). We cannot appeal for confirmation to anything outside the flux itself. "To rationalists this describes a tramp and vagrant world, adrift in space, with neither elephant nor tortoise to plant the sole of its foot upon." Philosophers lag behind others in their ability to live in a state of relative insecurity. A universe in which we help to make the truth and do not simply express it "is a trunk without a tag, a dog without a collar, in the eyes of most professors of philosophy." The drive to ground change in the unchangeable leads philosophers to posit a *de jure* world behind our *de facto* one.

In chapter 8 of *Pragmatism* James returns to this theme of rationality and contrasts his living rationality with the spectral, traditional one. In doing so he creates one of the most memorable metaphors for his philosophy of praxis — "the workshop of being" — and one of his most scathing metaphors — "machine-shop" — for the typical philosophical penchant for multiplying distinctions for their own sake. He asks why not take our acts to be "the actual turning-places and growing-places which they seem to be, of the world — why not the workshop of being, where we catch fact in the making, so that nowhere may the world grow in any other kind of way than this?" (PM, 138). This position is thought to be irrational. But James invokes his concrete analysis of living reasoning to label as merely spectral the traditional appeals to material causes and logical necessities. "Talk of logic and necessity and categories and the absolute and the contents of the whole philosophical machine-shop as you will, the only *real* reason I can think of why anything should ever come is that *someone wishes it to be here.*"

James denies that Santayana's *Life of Reason* has any rational foundation. Like all philosophies, it reflects an individual perspective (TCW,II, 399). He compliments Santayana's integrity in expressing his convictions and calls him "Emerson's first rival and successor." But then Emerson is called "receptive, expansive, as if handling life through a wide funnel with a great indraught; S[antayana] as if through a pinpoint orifice that emits his cooling spray outward over the universe like a nose-disinfectant from an 'atomizer'." Such a metaphorical characterization of Santayana leaves no doubt that James finds "something profoundly alienating in his unsympathetic tone."

James consistently points out the rationalist tendency to dissociate itself from the messy particulars of everyday life and to go into business for itself, taking its own aesthetic criteria as definitive. He condemns rationalism insofar as it perverts its proper function of supporting life and instead actually undermines it. This tendency of philosophers "of opposing abstractions to the concretes from which they are abstracted" is called a "vulgar fallacy" (MT, 82). But his metaphorical expressions of the relation of reasoning to living go even further and often pit reason against life as irreconcilable aspects of being human rather than as complementary ones. When he does so, however, he is often only trying to diminish the excessive attractiveness of aesthetically pleasing rational thinking for philosophers. He insists on the overriding importance of reconstructing the actual world in which we live. Practical rationality should be reinstated as the central philosophical concern. James explores in depth both the danger and the promise of rationality. Whether the antagonism that his metaphorical excess implies or the balanced harmony that his overall project urges is the central message James wants to convey can only be judged by the impressions made on the reader and consequent reflective judgment as to which reading is more worthwhile. Both attitudes are illustrated in the following series of quotes, but I think that his harmonizing intentions offer more promise.

In responding to criticisms of his notion of an actually growing universe James finds that it is very significant that "on such minute little snags and hooks, do all the 'difficulties' of philosophy hang. Call them categories, and sacred laws, principles of reason, etc., and you have the actual state of metaphysics, calling all the analogies of phenomenal life impossibilities."[10] Note that the opposition of metaphysical rationalism to life is also expressed as the opposition of categorial reasoning and authoritarian pronouncements to the analogical thinking characteristic of concrete experience. In its hostility to life rationalism is compared to a serpent: "If you are the lovers of facts I have supposed you to be, you find the trail of the serpent of rationalism, of intellectualism, over everything that lies on that side of the line" (PM, 16). Rationalists escape empiricist materialism only by losing touch with concrete life.

The theological origins of the metaphor are more explicit in the earlier inaugural address introducing pragmatism:

> And yet even these more real and significant attributes [of God] have the trail of the serpent over them as the books on theology have actually worked them out. One feels that, in the theologians' hands, they are only a set of dictionary-adjectives, mechanically deduced; logic has stepped into the place of vision, professionalism into that of life. Instead of bread we get a stone; instead of a fish, a serpent (PM, 265 (Appendix)).

But since rational thinking, as simplifying and thereby organizing the chaotic abundance of experience for our purposes, is nonetheless a defining human characteristic, he also uses the same metaphor in a positive sense:

> Purely objective truth, truth in whose establishment the function of giving human satisfaction in marrying previous parts of experience with newer parts played no role whatever, is nowhere to be found…The trail of the human serpent is thus over everything (PM, 37).

James's metaphors leave no doubt, however, of the proper sub-ordination of reasoning to life. The really vital question for him is the destiny of the world: "The centre of gravity of philosophy must therefore alter its place. The earth of things, long thrown into shadow by the glories of the upper ether, must resume its rights (PM, 62).

4. Metaphorical Terminology

Although James is an indefatigable defender of pluralism, his thoughts are often organized dialectically into dualisms. Familiar instances are his characterization of philosophical positions as either tenderminded or toughminded (PM, 11ff), his distinction between knowledge-by-acquaintance and knowledge-about (PP,I, 249ff MT, 17-18), and his use of focus and fringe to explain experience (PP,I, 249ff and ERE, 35). What is not so well known is that, in his unacknowledged dialectics, many of his most striking metaphors also come in opposing pairs and illustrate extremes. Four of these recurring pairs will be developed: wet and dry, thick and thin, raw and cooked, and living and dead. This far from exhaustive list, taken together with the metaphors and analogies already explored, are being pointed out to draw attention to their importance and to encourage further exploration of the centrality of metaphor to James's philosophy.

(1) dry/wet

'Dry' and 'wet' and their cognates comprise a dialectic pair of images often used by James. He characterizes those who simply reproduce reality in literal thinking, for example, as "slaves of habit, doing what they have been taught without variation; dry, prosaic, and matter-of-fact in their remarks; devoid of humor," in short, "taking the world for granted" (WB, 184). They resemble the "*trockener ernst* of dogs and horses" in the "treadmill-like operations of their minds" (185). Dryness is contrasted to the creativity of the seething cauldron of metaphorical thinking. In such thinking "we have the most abrupt cross-cuts and transitions from one idea to another...the most unheard-of combinations of elements, the subtlest associations of analogy; in a word, we seem suddenly introduced into a seething caldron [sic.] of ideas,where everything is fizzling and bobbing about in a state of bewildering activity."

Dryness is also associated with rational analysis because it characteristically abstracts only one or a few aspects out of the concrete totality and then opposes these artificially derived parts to the whole. By contrast, the living moment of experience is juicy with life. It precedes selectivity and ultimately judges rational analysis, which it finds wanting. According to the triadic reflex model of human cognition, both lived experience and rational analysis are necessary aspects of our organization of experience. It is therefore unremarkable that analogies can be found in which both are positively valued. But the attractiveness of the associations of 'wet' and similar terms and the unpleasantness of the connotations of 'dry' undercut this balance and leave no doubt as to which is favored.

Although 'dryness' is usually associated with rationalism, in a passage in *Essays in Radical Empiricism* it is associated with empiricism and the appealing image of an aquarium as a crystal globe is associated with absolute idealism. He begins with explaining the mediating position of radical empiricism, which "is essentially a mosaic philosophy" (ERE, 22). It holds to the 'co-conscious transitions' of lived experience: "Within each of our personal histories, subject, object, interest and purpose *are continuous or may be continuous*" (25). This is contrasted with both the overly connected world of transparently obvious harmony assumed by idealism and the overly disconnected world assumed by empiricism.

> *Prima facie*, if you should liken the universe of absolute idealism to an aquarium, a crystal globe in which goldfish are swimming, you would have to compare the empiricist universe to something more like one of those dried human heads with which the Dyaks of Borneo deck their lodges. The skull forms a solid nucleus; but innumerable feathers, leaves, strings, beads, and loose appendices of every description float and dangle from it, and save that they terminate in it, seem to have nothing to do with one another (ERE, 24).

After using striking metaphors to emphasize how differently these two philosophical positions construct their worlds, James also points out that they nonetheless share a common world: "Even so my experiences and yours float and dangle, terminating, it is true, in a nucleus of common perception, but for the most part out of sight and irrelevant and unimaginable to one another (ERE, 24). Radical empiricism, by being fair to both the unity and the disconnectedness, tries to save what is worthwhile in the two extremes. But it is obvious in their metaphorical equivalents that the empiricist disconnection is painfully experienced while the ideal harmony promised by rationalism is seductively described as a crystal globe wet with life.

Despite the empiricist orientation of his philosophy,such attractive images of idealism are found throughout his writings. Positivist science, however, is consistently described as arid. A passage in *The Will to Believe* begins by explaining that the theoretic faculty "lives between two fires which never give her rest, and make her incessantly revise her formulations" (WB, 102). These two are the facts of nature and the demands of practical reason. "See how, in France, the mummy-cloths of the academic and official theistic philosophy are rent by the facts of evolution...See, in Great Britain, how the dryness of the strict associationist school...gives way to more generous idealisms, born of more urgent emotional needs and wrapping the same facts in far more massive intellectual harmonies...of maximum subjective as well as objective richness." Although positivist scientists claim to have worked themselves free of subjective propensities, they have chosen to construct a world out of "the leanest, lowest, aridest" material, "namely, the bare molecular world — and...sacrificed all the rest" (104).

We can realize how far professional philosophers have traveled from James's understanding of philosophy when he writes that philosophy is attractive to literary minds because of its poetry. Scientific minds can be saved by it "from too dry a technicality" (SPP, 11). He criticizes the narrowness of the scientific ideal of rationality, which recognizes only one aim of intelligence, by saying that "to the average sense of mankind, whose ideal of mental nature is best expressed by the word 'richness,' your statistical and cognitive intelligence will seem insufferably narrow, dry, tedious, and unacceptable" (EPH, 17). After explaining the law of association by contiguity with the help of diagrams, he says that "this will no doubt have been found by the reader a pretty dry description" (EPS, 10).

Although in *Varieties* James is primarily interested in "rehabilitating the element of feeling" in religion and other organizations of experience, such as science, he does not want to be misunderstood as arguing that intellectual rationality is bad in itself and should be discarded (395). He is seeking to redress the imbalance brought about by the overemphasis on abstract intellectuality and denigration of feeling. Dryness is emotionally less appealing than life-giving wetness, but we cannot be harmoniously balanced without both: "In re-reading my manuscript, I am almost appalled at the amount of emotionality which I find in it. After so much of this, we can afford to be dryer and less sympathetic in the rest of the work that lies before us" (383). But this is said only in the concluding chapter out of twenty, when it is appropriate to unify, that is, theorize or interpret, the concrete, phenomenal facts.

(2) thick/thin

Another pair of contrasting metaphors is derived from a "philosophic crank," an otherwise unidentified Mrs. Heywood, who said that "the world…is composed of only two elements, the Thick, namely, and the Thin" (PU, 64). Thickness refers to intense concreteness and fertility of detail, while thinness is defined by reference to such philosophical systems as transcendental idealism, with its strangely thin arguments, its terms "being shiveringly thin wrappings for so thick and burly a world as this." Reducing the world to some one or few extrinsic principles of relation "seems the very quintessence of thinness…The whole active material of natural fact is tried [dried?] out, and only the barest intellectualistic formalism remains" (65). After giving Haldane's summary of Hegel's position, James says that "he hardly tries at all to thicken this thin logical scheme" and that his "hegelianism carries us hardly an inch into the concrete detail of the world we actually inhabit" (65-66). He turns with relief to Fechner, "whose thickness is a refreshing contrast to the thin, abstract, indigent, and threadbare appearance, the starving, school-room aspect, which the speculations of most of our absolutist philosophers present (68).

Royce is said to be 'thick,' but not as thick as Fechner (PU, 96, 80). However, James praises Royce's treatment of absolute mind when it is taken moralistically. It is then "infinitely richer and thicker than that of any other contemporary idealistic philosopher" (80). Transcendentalism can therefore be either thick or thin. James contrasts the thin American and British versions with their thicker European cousins, namely, Scholasticism and Hegel himself. He uses thickness and thinness to make the central point that philosophy ought to be a matter of passionate vision and not of logic. Logic is only instrumental reasoning. Once the premises or visions are given, it can then find reasons for them. The thinness of some versions of transcendentalism comes "either from the vision being defective in the disciples, or from their passion, matched with Fechner's or with Hegel's own passion, being as moonlight unto sunlight or as water into wine" (81). Absolute idealism is criticized because it ignores bodies and psychophysical analogies. Such thinness reveals a poverty of demand which limits our access to what the universe has to offer: "Things reveal themselves soonest to those who most passionately want them, for our need sharpens our wit."

Abstract thought can only deal with surfaces but cannot penetrate to the inner core of reality, which, for us, is human activity. "It can name the thickness of reality, but it cannot fathom it, and its insufficiency here is essential and permanent, not temporary. The only way in which to apprehend reality's thickness is either to experience it directly by being a part of reality one's self, or to evoke it in imagination by sympathetically divining someone else's inner life" (PU, 112). After such high praise of sympathetic acquaintance James again seeks a balance by reminding us that it is of intense but limited duration compared to abstract thinking, which can encompass much more of reality. "Direct acquaintance and conceptual knowledge are thus complementary of each other; each remedies the other's defects." He also emphasizes this complementarity in *Some Problems of Philosophy:* "We have but to weigh extent against content, thickness against spread, and we see that for some purposes the one, for other purposes the other, has the higher value" (SPP, 43). Nonetheless, his preference is clear. For "synoptic treatment of phenomena," we turn to the conceptual method, "but if, as metaphysicians, we are more curious about the inner nature of reality or about what really *makes it go*, we must...bury ourselves in the thickness of those passing moments over the surface of which" concepts fly and on which "they occasionally rest and perch" (PU, 112).

(3) raw/cooked

James sometimes talks like a traditional empiricist in his appeal to the raw data of sense experience: "We are so subject to the philosophic tradition which treats *logos* or discursive thought generally as the sole avenue to truth, that to fall back on raw unverbalized life as more of a revealer, and to think of concepts as the merely practical things which Bergson calls them, comes very hard" (PU, 121). Since he was burned by the critical uproar over pragmatism, he also says that he is even willing to disagree with Bergson and follow the older tradition which holds that the intellect is primarily theoretical. The proviso is that theoretic or scientific knowledge is distinguished from speculative or philosophic knowledge. Then it must be conceded "that theoretic knowledge, which is knowledge *about* things, as distinguished from living contemplation or sympathetic acquaintance with them, touches only the outer surface of reality" (111). This is foolish from the point of view of the tradition, but "difficult as such a revolution is, there is no other way, I believe, to the possession of reality" (121-122).

But in direct refutation of the empiricist assumption of an original bare impression or 'raw feel,' such sympathetic acquaintance is already within an interpretive horizon which is expressed through the contrast of the raw and the cooked. He rephrases metaphorically the pragmatic circle of revising our beliefs to accommodate new experiences, which themselves are reinterpreted according to pre-existent beliefs. "Our minds thus grow in spots; and like grease-spots, the spots spread. But we let them spread as little as possible: we keep unaltered as much of our old knowledge, as many of our old prejudices and beliefs, as we can" (PM, 83). This is no Hegelian grand synthesis. James deflates our pretensions both by this mundane comparison to grease spots and by calling this process one of patching up and tinkering. "The novelty soaks in; it stains the ancient mass; but it is also tinged by what absorbs it." As if this were not enough of a deflation of philosophy in the grand tradition, he continues to explain apperception in terms of a hermeneutics of the kitchen: "Our past apperceives and co-operates; and in the new equilibrium in which each step forward in the process of learning terminates, it happens relatively seldom that the new fact is added *raw*. More usually it is embedded cooked, as one might say, or stewed down in the sauce of the old."

(4) living/dead

James's concrete philosophy of experience is an analysis of the pre-reflective context of self and world which emerges in practical rationality. Without it the reflective analyses of aesthetic rationality remain merely speculative and self-referential to the point of multiplying distinctions in endless attempts to arrive at absolute translucency. This insistence on recognizing concrete experience is encoded in organic metaphors of life, while theorizing severed from its roots is characterized as dead, or as the lifeless remains of once living processes. Metaphors of stasis abound: "To understand life by concepts is to arrest its movement, cutting it up into bits as if with scissors, and immobilizing these in our logical herbarium where, comparing them as dried specimens, we can ascertain which of them statically includes or excludes which other" (PU, 109). Conceptualization cannot capture the lived sense of life; at most, it can dissect it: "This treatment supposes life to have already accomplished itself, for the concepts, being so many views taken after the fact, are retrospective and post mortem." We assume that because we think conceptually that there is nothing behind or below thought: "We are so inveterately wedded to the conceptual decomposition of life that I know that this will seem to you like putting muddiest confusion in place of clearest thought, and relapsing into a molluscoid state of mind" (114).

Metaphors of growth and decay complement those of life and death: "There is partial decay and partial growth, and all the while a nucleus of relative constancy from which what decays drops off, and which takes into itself whatever is grafted on, until at length something wholly different has taken its place" (PU, 115). Existence can no more be captured by rational categories than organic life is captured in its decomposing remains: "What really *exists* is not things made but things in the making. Once made, they are dead, and an infinite number of alternative conceptual decompositions can be used in defining them" (117). Conceptualization cannot correspond to reality because it always comes too late. Having no unambiguous referent our interpretations can multiply indefinitely. It does not therefore follow that we have no basis for our claims. "But put yourself *in the making* by a stroke of intuitive sympathy with the thing and, the whole range of possible decompositions coming at once into your possession, you are no longer troubled with the question which of them is the more absolutely true." We are no longer troubled because we no longer understand truth as a pre-existent relation that can be simply found, like we find a dead carcass. We see that we determine both the signifier and the signified. "Philosophy should seek this kind of living understanding of the movement of reality, not follow science in vainly patching together fragments of its dead results" (118).

James chides "intuitional moralists" for spoiling their appeal to psychological facts "by mixing with it that dogmatic temper which, by absolute distinctions and unconditional 'thou shalt nots,' changes a growing, elastic, and continuous life into a superstitious system of relics and dead bones" (WB, 158). This contrast of a living organism with the bones that remain after it has died is frequently used to contrast lived experience with its conceptual translations: "But there exist no processes which we cannot also consider abstractly, eviscerating them down to their essential skeletons or outlines; and when we have treated the process of knowing thus, we are easily led to regard them as something altogether unparalleled in nature" (MT, 81).

Closely allied with life as process is the notion of conceptualization as cutting into an undifferentiated flux. This intentional organization of experience to suit our purposes is the basis for his reconceptualization of rationalism, including his warning that artificial cuts, though necessary for survival, also necessarily distort the living reality.[11]

> By means of concepts cut out from the sensible flux of the past, we can re-descend upon the future flux, and, making another cut, say what particular thing is likely to be found there; and that altho in this sense concepts give us knowledge, and may be said to have some theoretic value (especially when the particular thing foretold is one in which we take no present practical interest); yet in the deeper sense of giving *insight* they have no theoretic value, for they quite fail to connect us with the inner life of the flux, or with the real causes that govern its direction (PU, 110).

We interpret reality; our conceptual schemes do not. We are interactively involved in the process, not spectators observing independent causal nexus.

5. The Sculptor's Chisel

Analogy and metaphor are integral to James's intention to reinstate in scientific and philosophical reflection the centrality of concrete experience as described in his concrete analysis of our purposeful ordering of experience. "Sensible reality is too concrete to be entirely manageable — look at the narrow range of it which is all that any animal, living in it exclusively as he does, is able to compass (PU, 110). His metaphor of skipping over the surface of experience furthers his explanation of concrete rationality as the process by which we invent simple terms applicable to particular experiences. These terms are then found similar to many others because unencumbered by the original associations. We do not simply skip over the surface haphazardly, but *"harness up* reality in our conceptual systems in order to drive it the better" (111).

The strengths of rational thinking are also its weaknesses. This is demonstrated both through explicit discursive arguments and through analogy. It can encompass a wider range of reality than is actually experienced because it is necessarily partial, extracting only a few aspects out of a phenomenal totality. The universality gained by this lack of entanglement in any particular context is paid for by the distortion of the richness of both the original associations and the subsequent situations to which the 'marks' are applied. To make us aware of the hidden limitations as well as the obvious strengths of rational thinking James attacks the psychological view that "the mind must be a passive, reactionless sheet of white paper, on which reality will simply come and register its own philosophic definition" (WB, 102). He demonstrates the irreducibly subjective aspect of all thinking, rational as well as poetic: "As if conception could possibly occur except for a teleological purpose, except to show us the way from a state of things our senses cognize to another state of things our will desires!" (103).

This purposeful organization of experience is also expressed through the metaphor of sculpting: "To bid the man's subjective interests be passive till truth express itself from out the environment, is to bid the sculptor's chisel be passive till the statue express itself from out the stone. Operate we must! and the only choice left us is that between operating to poor or to rich results" (WB, 103). Although we actively participate in the construction of reality, James always insists that to be successful such organizations must get hold of real aspects of "the teeming and dramatic richness of the concrete world" (CER, 123). The statue, although not foreshadowed in the material used, must nonetheless be constructed within its limitations.

James constantly reminds us that our drive to reconstruct the world informs the power of language. Even rational thinking is not exhausted in the exactness of its communicative refinements. What is suggested is at least as important as what is explicitly said. The inexhaustible attractiveness of James's own writings to each new generation derives in large measure from the suggestiveness of his metaphorical approach. In his condemnation of rationalism divorced from its service to life he typically chooses to argue through metaphors which, in their emotional impact, convey much more than any straightforward propositions could. Although all philosophies are said to be abstract outlines comparable to architectural plans, and outlines, as such, are meager, it does not therefore follow that they can only refer to an impoverished universe: "It is the essential meagreness [sic.] of *what is suggested* by the usual rationalistic philosophies that moves empiricists to their gesture of rejection" (PM, 25).

Chapter Nine

The Scope of Pragmatism

Pragmatism, as a philosophic system, seeks to combine the strengths and avoid the weaknesses of rationalism and empiricism. Like empiricism, it exhibits "the scientific loyalty to facts and willingness to take account of them, the spirit of adaptation and accommodation, in short," and like rationalism, it holds with "the old confidence in human values and the resultant spontaneity, whether of the religious or of the romantic type" (PM, 17). Although in everyday life most people combine elements of both rationalism and empiricism in their beliefs, the contradictions thus generated are of little concern. Philosophers, distinguished by their "good intellectual conscience," cannot tolerate this inconsistency and either must adopt one or the other, or like James, try to reconcile them (14).

"The pragmatistic philosophy" is developed in *Pragmatism* as such a "mediating way of thinking" (PM, 26). But the scope of pragmatism is also explicitly limited to a method primarily and secondly to a genetic theory of the meaning of truth (PM, 37). James says in the preface to *The Meaning of Truth* that "the universes of discourse of Schiller, Dewey, and myself are panoramas of different extent" (MT, 9). Schiller's is essentially psychological, Dewey's "is the widest of the three," and his own "is more essentially epistemological. I start with two things, the objective facts and the claims, and indicate which claims, the facts being there, will work successfully as the latter's substitutes and which will not" (MT, 9-10).

1. A Method Merely or a Philosophy of Experience?

Despite such disclaimers, both the first lecture of *Pragmatism* and the earlier lecture, "Philosophical Conceptions and Practical Results," clearly depend on interconnected philosophical assumptions and are not just rules of method or epistemological analyses. I think that he did indeed begin developing a "pragmatistic philosophy," even before he explicitly developed the metaphysics of *Essays in Radical Empiricism*, but misleadingly still thought of himself as merely laying

238 William James's Radical Reconstruction

the groundwork for such a philosophy. James clearly intended to avoid metaphysical assumptions in his pragmatism. He contrasts his own position to F. C. S. Schiller's pragmatic humanism, for instance, which is characterized as "a metaphysical theory about the matter of reality, and flies far beyond pragmatism's own modest analysis of the nature of the knowing function...One of pragmatism's merits is that it is so purely epistemological. It must assume realities; but it prejudges nothing as to their constitution, and the most diverse metaphysics can use it as their foundation" (MT, 115).

By drawing on James's personal history and his long-range project an explanation can be developed for why he does not claim a unique philosophy but only a unique methodology, although he develops both simultaneously. Insofar as his personal intentions can be surmised, he apparently understood his radical empiricism as supporting a panpsychism he did not expect the academic community to take seriously, and therefore he did not want its 'idealistic' aspect to undermine the acceptance of his pragmatism.[1] On more solid programmatic evidence, we have seen that his natural history procedure consisted in first establishing an incontrovertible starting point in experience before developing a metaphysics. Until the third crisis he was still, like Bradley, "superstitiously loyal" to the traditional understanding of philosophy as grounded in "the old and obstinate intellectualist prejudice in favor of universals" and he did not consider his own radical empiricism as such a system. Only after the third crisis did he "eulogistically" use the name of philosophy for his own radical empiricism.[2]

In the preface to *Pragmatism*, in 1907, he emphatically states "that there is no logical connexion [sic.] between pragmatism, as I understand it, and a doctrine which I have recently (1904-5) set forth as 'radical empiricism.' The latter stands on its own feet. One may entirely reject it and still be a pragmatist" (PM, 6). But in the 1909 preface to *The Meaning of Truth*, in which he affirms the essentially epistemological nature of his pragmatism, he also says that "it seems to me that the establishment of the pragmatist theory of truth is a step of first-rate importance in making radical empiricism prevail" (MT, 6).[3] I think that the preponderance of the evidence supports the second position as more plausible, despite James's continued insistence that pragmatism is only a method.

The first reason James gives as to why radical empiricism presupposes his theory of truth is that the greatest obstacle to radical empiricism is "the rooted rationalist belief that experience as immediately given is all disjunction and no conjunction, and that to make one world out of this separateness, a higher unifying agency must be there" (MT, 7). Idealists believe that an absolute knower is needed to unify phenomena by imposing appropriate categories. Pragmatism holds, instead, that truth is the 'workableness' of ideas, that is, particular workings within concrete experience. With the acceptance of this pragmatic view of truth, one of the strongest rationalistic objections to radical empiricism would crumble, namely, its mistaken belief that the relationship between an object and an idea that truly knows it falls outside temporal experience, or is indifferent to it, instead of being a describable relationship within experience.

The pragmatic theory of truth, if accepted, would thus undercut the main objections of rationalistic philosophers to radical empiricism. But the three aspects said to be definitive of radical empiricism are already incorporated into James's pragmatism; namely, the postulate that all philosophical debate be restricted to experientially derived terms, the statement of fact that the relations between things are just as much matters of direct experience as are the things themselves, and the generalized conclusion that experience exhibits a continuous structure and therefore does not require any transcendental connectives (MT, 6-7). In fact, the establishment of these radically empiricist claims is constitutive of the pragmatism he has been developing all along.[4] Those who have taken James at his word and tried to understand his epistemology and theory of truth apart from his broader philosophical project have also been blind to what is most distinctive about it and have invariably viewed it either as a flawed version of the correspondence theory of truth or as an expression of an indefensible voluntaristic wish fulfillment.

James is a transitional figure, who was both circumscribed by the traditional philosophical categories of his time, and who went beyond them in his radical reconstruction of empiricism. It is known that he influenced Dewey, but it is not so well known that Dewey also crucially influenced James. The understanding of pragmatism as more than an epistemology by such younger colleagues as Dewey and F. C. S. Schiller helped James to reconsider his own restrictions on it. With the support of Bergson and Fechner, he finally let go of the last ties binding him to traditional rationalistic philosophy.[5] That he was already well on the way is evidenced by his pleased surprise in discovering on re-reading his earlier works that his later, more liberated views were already present. What allowed him to see this for himself was the recognition of the radical nature of his thought by a growing segment of the philosophical community, who drew out its consequences in their own work.

James's writings are, as he said, largely epistemological. He was interested exclusively in mental phenomena in *Principles*, particularly in accounting for the synthetic unity of consciousness. Even before that, he was examining rationalism and empiricism with a view to overcoming skepticism. His *Will to Believe, Varieties of Religious Experience*, and *Pragmatism* are concerned with redefining knowledge and extending its limits. Oddly enough, even when he turns to his metaphysics of radical empiricism, he is still developing the epistemological question as to what it is to know anything, since the category of pure experience is developed so that "knowing can easily be explained as a particular sort of relation towards one another into which portions of pure experience may enter" (ERE, 4).

In *Radical Empiricism* he says that pure experience is only a collective name for sensible natures: "It is made of *that*, of just what appears, of space, of intensity, of flatness, brownness, heaviness, or what not" (ERE, 14-15). It thus refers to the objective, sensible qualities of traditional empiricism. But this has also been his definition of sensations, as he acknowledges a little further on: "Pure experience in this state is but another name for feeling or sensation" (46). It thus also refers to the subjective reception of such qualities. Both the act of sensing, then, and what is sensed. The conjunct is the same, not yet differentiated, 'feeling' of *Principles*, which is subjective according to one set of relations, but objective if another set of relations is traced.

On this view it does not make much sense for James to say that his pragmatic epistemology can be accepted or rejected independently of his radical empiricism, since the latter is another version of the former. His radical empiricism provides an alternate model for the unity in multiplicity — the synthetic unity of consciousness — that is a central issue of his earlier writings. Superficially, pragmatism explains how we know and how we determine truth while radical empiricism explains what we know, that is, what the world is like such that it can be known this way. James so distinguished them, even going so far as to say that radical empiricism "squinted" towards idealism because experience, that is, what is real, is fundamentally monistic, while his pragmatism is a version of noetic pluralism (TCW,II, 549-50).

But as far back as *Principles* he preferred the word 'feeling' to either percept or concept because he wanted to emphasize that thoughts and things are experientially identical, although functionally distinct. In *Principles*, for instance, despite his natural history methodological adoption of "the dualism of Object and Subject and their pre-established harmony," he desired "a good vague neutral word" to "designate all states of consciousness merely as such," and which would "cover sensation and thought indifferently" (PP,I, 216, 185-186). Lacking such a term, he decided to use both 'feeling' and 'thought,' "in a wider sense than usual" (186). And he said in *Radical Empiricism* that pure experiences are always plural, that is, not a pervasive 'stuff' of which things are made, but a way of referring to the many perceptual experiences we have.

His radical empiricism thus differs from his pragmatism only in emphasis, and all terms, like 'pluralism' or 'monism,' have to be understood in context as relative to the issues being raised. As characterizations of experience, they are always explained as being functionally differentiated, depending on the operative ends in view, but until the third crisis, he also reserved judgment on whether reality was ultimately, in itself, one or many, ordered or chaotic. Insofar as his philosophy of radical empiricism came down on the side of a monism pluralistically developed, it was held as a likely metaphysical solution that would answer to the needs of pragmatism. However, as a hypothesis about the ultimate character of reality, it could hardly precede a method developed to settle metaphysical disputes that were insoluble precisely because there was as yet no firm grounds for determining what reality ultimately is.

I would emphasize that his radical empiricism is an alternate account of the same knowing process he has been exploring all along. In his pragmatic or epistemological writings he explicitly defers the metaphysical question of whether things are as they are known and in his radical empiricist writings he acknowledges the Berkeleyan idealism he has not exactly been hiding. But both accounts are mistaken. His pragmatic writings already incorporate a significant explanation of reality as reality-for-us and his radical empiricism transcends the idealist/realist dichotomy. We can recognize what James could not, namely, that his new beginning in philosophy not only renders obsolete such traditional compartmentalizations of philosophy into distinct areas such as epistemology, metaphysics, and ethics, but also undermines the self-evident distinction between knowledge and reality.

For one thing, 'what is,' the traditional subject matter of metaphysics, cannot be designated apart from how we know it, which is the traditional subject matter of epistemology. Neither can it be grasped apart from what we value. An analysis of the structures of concrete experience must precede the delineation of particular subject areas and in so doing alter them. The distinction between knowing and willing, for instance, the basis for the distinctive specializations of epistemology and ethics, breaks down already in James's earliest articles like "The Sentiment of Rationality" and "Remarks on Spencer's 'Definition of Mind as Correspondence.'" His insistence on the teleological character of knowing could not be sustained if any traditional account of knowing as distinct from willing were assumed. Recall in chapters 3 and 4 the explanation of his reconstruction of knowing as the selection of the right 'marks' to correctly identify a unity out of a plurality and that this rightness cannot be determined independently of our purposes in doing so. These purposes incorporate what we want to find and what we intend to bring about.

Although he says that in his epistemology he starts with objective facts and claims made about them, it is understood that he is talking about common sense objects.[6] He explains their constitution genealogically in *Pragmatism* in his genesis of the common sense categories and as a concrete ontology in the episode of the child and the candle and the many orders of reality in *Principles*. What he means by 'claims' is also explicated at the common sense level. As has already been argued, this fundamental level of explication should be called a concrete analysis of everyday experience, which constitutes a propaedeutic to both epistemology and metaphysics. It would then be true to say that his epistemology does not presuppose any particular extant metaphysics, but it certainly presupposes his own proto-metaphysics or concrete analysis of lived experience. Likewise, his insistence on the reality of the object known does not draw on the traditional cleavage between knowing and reality, since his account of reality as experiential would collapse if understood in these dualistic terms.

James's positions are understandable and defensible only if their radical nature is grasped more radically than he did. If he is classified as an epistemologist, then his epistemology must be understood as so inclusive as to constitute, simply, a philosophy, since he incorporates in it what would traditionally be divided among psychology, epistemology, metaphysics, ethics, and philosophy of religion. Another way to understand James's insistent distinction of his epistemology from his metaphysics is to recognize that his new beginning in experience grounds both. His elaboration of the 'life-world' is presupposed by his epistemology and metaphysics, which therefore do not exhibit the characteristics expected when they are traditionally defined.

As we have seen, this reconstruction of philosophy was inaugurated already at the very beginning of James's writings, by questioning the questioner, that is, by placing the philosophical tradition itself within a more encompassing human dimension of experience. James's characterization of the history of philosophy, for instance, as the clash of human temperaments was and is as unwelcome to professional philosophers as are Nietzsche's arguments that the disinterested search for truth is really an expression of the will to power, of the will to dominate.[7] James argues that the great philosophers, like Plato, Locke, and Hegel, far from contributing to an objective, disinterested *philosophia perennis*, stamp their radical idiosyncrasies on their philosophies (PM, 24). That temperaments are not recognized in philosophy as good reasons for holding any position obscures but does not diminish their importance. James exposes the insincerity of acknowledging only impersonal reasons in philosophical debate in order to demonstrate the radically personal character of all organizations of experience including the philosophical.

Rationalism and empiricism are thus shown to be not only historically developed philosophical positions distinguishable by their contrasting assumptions and principles, but also to satisfy different needs. The first step towards reconciling their differences, therefore, is to isolate these needs and then show that the satisfaction of one set of needs does not entail systematically suppressing the other set. The traditional academic opposition of rationalism and empiricism therefore poses a false dilemma. But the schools of thought of the time were at odds with one another, and since according to James, philosophy should give "an account of this actual world," should offer an *"explanation* of our concrete universe," he begins by describing their one-sidedness and uncovering the differing needs they satisfy (PM, 18). According to Nietzschean terminology, he is giving a genealogical analysis.

Both empiricism and rationalism are characterized by disclosing these unacknowledged needs. Empirical philosophy, which originated in the insistence on the experiential origin of reflection, had developed into a positivistic, materialistic naturalism. The progress of science led to an exaggeration of the importance of facts as properly coercing acquiescence. This, in turn, seemed to confirm the bias in favor of a passive, correspondence theory of truth and a discrediting of a moral view of the universe, since ideals are 'reduced' to their physiological substrate. On the other hand, the transcendental idealism of the Anglo-Hegelian school argued for the necessary existence of Absolute Mind, which can satisfy the need for security and the craving for a consistent completeness, but from which no single actual particular of this world could be deduced. The religious dimension of experience is retained but at the cost of ignoring concrete facts and actual joys and sorrows. Rationalism develops closed systems, that is, ones which exclude what is not explicitly included or cannot be logically derived. The lived universe, however, seems to fact-loving minds to be wide open. For actual persons perfection is still to be achieved, while for the rationalist the absolute ground of being is eternally complete perfection and our imperfections merely relative illusions. But the atrocities that fill even one day's news renders such facile optimism irrelevant, if not repulsive.

After thus characterizing the two extremes, James offers his pragmatic philosophy as a mediating way of thinking which satisfies both the need for asserting the dignity of the person, as expressed by the religious craving, and the need to preserve the richest intimacy with facts (PM, 26). Professional philosophers will be judged by their success in satisfying the ordinary person, "the sum of whose demands is greatest, the mind whose criticisms and dissatisfactions are fatal in the long run" (23). Ordinary persons are the ultimate judges, not because of some misplaced romanticism on James's part, but because they express the demand "to satisfy the fulness [sic.] of [their] nature's needs" (22).[8]

2. Using the Pragmatic Method to Reconstruct Philosophy

James claims that, as a method merely, pragmatism does not stand for any special results, but it would nonetheless eventually diminish the distinction between science and metaphysics (PM, 31). Here are juxtaposed two seemingly contradictory positions in one sentence. If it is true that no results, that is, metaphysical claims, are presupposed or privileged, then there are no grounds for assuming that the distinction between science and metaphysics would eventually diminish. According to one metaphysical position, at least, that of transcendental absolutism, they are irreducibly different approaches to reality and cannot, in principle, be subject to pragmatic methodology. Therefore, to adopt this method is by that very fact to deny transcendental absolutism's results and affirm a radically empiricist position.

But it can be countered that "not standing for any results" means instead that pragmatism is a genuinely experimental method that arrives at particular results as the outcome of an hypothesis-confirmation procedure and not through the usual philosophical method of logical deduction in which the outcome is already contained in the premises. Since the pragmatic method discloses that all theories are instrumental, the metaphysical quest for final answers that would end all inquiries is revealed as a remnant of a primitive belief in magic words that can unriddle the universe. Metaphysics and science must both find the meaning of their claims within the stream of experience, which even involves changing existing realities (PM, 31-32).

Pragmatism denies the legitimacy of metaphysics insofar as its principles of reality are not derived from experience and not subject to its veto. But insofar as metaphysical claims are understood as being hypotheses subject to eventual verification, then pragmatism neither excludes nor requires any particular set of metaphysical beliefs. Their cogency cannot be presupposed, but can only be determined insofar as they pass the "only test of probable truth," namely, "what works best in the way of leading us, what fits every part of life best and combines with the collectivity of experience's demands, nothing being omitted" (PM, 44).

Nonetheless, pragmatism, as one way of philosophizing, does reject other ways; for example, those who espouse "the ultra-rationalistic type would be frozen out" (PM, 31). It allies itself with empiricism, albeit "in a more radical and in a less objectionable form than it has ever yet assumed." These metaphysical positions are accepted or rejected insofar as they harmonize or clash with the pragmatic theory of truth. This is consistent with James's claims about his theory of truth paving the way for his radical empiricism. Traditional philosophy, insofar as it is 'ultra-rationalistic,' is thus rejected. The excesses of rationalism are its "verbal solutions, ... bad a priori reasons, ... fixed principles, closed systems, and pretended absolutes and origins...dogma, artificiality, and the pretence of finality in truth" (31). The pragmatist is no longer philosophizing in this traditional way and, having brought it to an end by turning "his back resolutely and once for all upon a lot of inveterate habits dear to professional philosophers, ... turns towards concreteness and adequacy, towards facts, towards actions, and towards power" (31). Both "positivistic empiricism" and "religious rationalism" are rejected as systems, but pragmatism is hospitable to any of their particular claims that satisfy its method (44).

But metaphysical claims taken piecemeal, as not embedded in an interrelated system of beliefs, are not equivalent to metaphysics in its usual meaning. As the list of what pragmatism accepts and rejects makes clear, its denial of the legitimacy of such systems is tantamount to the denial of philosophy as traditionally understood. What is left after the end of philosophy is a method. But this method, while not recreating philosophy as a systematic explanation of reality, grounded in necessary principles, is more than an epistemology, in the traditional sense of a theory of knowledge independent of psychological and metaphysical assumptions. It is also less than an epistemology, in the traditional sense of the way we ought to think, in ignorance of the sloppy ways we actually do think.

In beginning philosophy anew, such terms no longer apply in their accepted meaning, and misconceptions inevitably result when this new wine is poured into old bottles, as is James's habit. Pragmatic methodology incorporates some of the functions traditionally assigned to metaphysics, for example, supplying a set of assumptions about reality that allows specific questions to be raised and examined, and rejects others, such as the demand for absolute clarity and search for necessary principles to ground specific claims. Since James does not clearly distinguish between his radical criticism of traditional philosophy and his radical reconstruction of it, misconceptions arise which a stricter separation can help clear up.

His pragmatic methodology not only incorporates some of the tenets of radical empiricism, but also deliberately brackets beliefs about "the sensible core of reality" (PM, 120). Until the third crisis he cannot say what the ultimate nature of reality is because this would mean definitively deciding between rationalism and empiricism, taken in their broadest senses, and this cannot be done as long as it means giving up beliefs of either that he is trying to preserve in his mediating pragmatism. Before the third crisis, he could not decide between the two in regard to what he takes to be the fundamental task of any metaphysics, that is, whether the totality of all things is ultimately one or many, rationally unified or pluralistically chaotic. Since he also takes his radical empiricism to be only an hypothesis, not yet verified, but one which is in principle verifiable insofar as its organization of experience proves satisfactory, then its acceptance obviously could not be a precondition for accepting the pragmatism for which he has already provided many cogent arguments. Neither could its rejection retrospectively disprove the independently developed pragmatic methodology.

But this is to take his radical empiricism as a metaphysics in the traditional sense, as an attempt to definitively settle the issue, and the pertinence of metaphysics understood in this traditional sense to pragmatism has already been rejected.[9] However, until the third crisis James was still looking for such a solution. When he finally gives up the possibility, he actually embraces the position already established in *Pragmatism* that only such unity or disunity as can be demonstrated to hold of actual experiences can be claimed. Neither absolute monism nor absolute pluralism can be demonstrated, but "the world is one just so far as its parts hang together by any definite connexion" [sic.] and "it is many just so far as any definite connexion fails to obtain" (PM, 76).

If, however, it can be shown that the principles established in his radical empiricism are the same ones used in his pragmatic methodology, then, obviously, they are not independent but stand or fall together. This requires understanding radical empiricism, not as a traditional metaphysical system which establishes what reality must be, but as an attempt to identify those structures of experience that characterize our being in the world. To avoid confusion, this post-metaphysical understanding of the goal of philosophical thinking should be designated by another term than 'metaphysics,' but this James does not do. For clarity, I have been calling it concrete analysis. It can also be called a radically empiricist or pragmatic analysis to distinguish it from the similar, but historically distinct, movement of European phenomenology. This makes it continuous with all of James's writings. His radical empiricism is a reflectively explicit model for his natural history and pragmatic methods. He already appealed to pure experience in *Principles*, for instance, but did not develop it systematically as he later did in *Essays in Radical Empiricism*, since in the earlier work he was developing the stream of consciousness as a model.

3. Pragmatic Critique of Reductionist Empiricism and Intellectualist Rationalism

In showing what sort of metaphysics the pragmatic method would lead to, James is actually engaged in rejecting traditional metaphysics and substituting his own concrete analysis of lived experience. But in doing so, it becomes more and more evident that what is given as the outcome is already presupposed by the pragmatic method itself. James frames the question about the ultimate structure of the universe, which is thus no longer merely an epistemological question, as a debate between pragmatism and rationalism (PM, 124). Apparently, this is not only because he considers pragmatism to be an outgrowth of empiricism, but because in metaphysics he actually favors the rationalist, monistic position and thus struggles mightily to distinguish his own position from it without denying its strengths. As is acknowledged at the end of *Pragmatism*, the debate is actually three-sided, with pragmatism situated between "the two extremes of crude naturalism on the one hand and transcendental absolutism on the other" (144).

Pragmatism adopts a pluralistic metaphysical hypothesis because truth is a matter of finite experiences, which support one another, but nothing outside the flux supports them or guarantees their outcome. Not only is there no security that truth will prevail, but also none that our moral demands will be ultimately satisfied. This is a direct refutation of Kant's argument in *Religion Within the Limits of Reason Alone* that since our rational moral demands are legitimate, the fact that they are not fulfilled in this world provides striking evidence that they must be fulfilled elsewhere, in a transcendent realm. If we recall James's earlier aversion to an *unheimlich* universe which does not respond to our deepest needs, then it should be more apparent how uncharacteristically pessimistic is his remark that "all 'homes' are in finite experience; finite experience as such is homeless" (PM, 125). The transcendental position also continued to attract him, provided it could be pluralistically and temporally construed.

James says that transcendental rationalists argue that the flux of our experience cannot be understood apart form some underlying immutable reality, since no change is possible without stability. But from the point of view of such tough-minded empiricists as Chauncey Wright, there is nothing behind the bare phenomenal facts which can be the ground of such facts. The supposed grounds given are nothing but "names for the facts, taken from the facts, and then treated as previous and explanatory," as though to say that cyanide kills because it is a poison or that it is so cold today because it is winter were genuine explanations (PM, 126). In this passage explicating Wright James confuses two different meanings of grounding or legitimation: that of phenomena being comprehensible only if understood as mere appearances of some reality having specific attributes and that of phenomena explained by the appeal to those conditions which must be assumed if they are to be accounted for. This is because the rationalists he has in mind are not neo-Kantians, but the neo-Hegelians, who understood the rational explanation of the universe to mean that a rational being must be assumed, and who thus provide support for the religious belief in an absolute deity. It should be further noted that in this passage he is criticizing rationalism from the standpoint of a reductionist naturalism that he also denies.

But he does think that this positivist challenge cannot be met by rational absolutists and can be refuted only by reference to experience. He asserts as experientially given, for instance, that "the world we live in exists diffused and distributed, in the form of an indefinitely numerous lot of *eaches*, coherent in all sorts of ways and degrees" (PM, 126). This is yet another formulation of the fundamental fact of the "many-in-one" that also constitutes his radical empiricism. This appeal is not understood as refuting outright Wright's understanding of experience, but only of denying his claim that the distributed form of the phenomenal world must be accepted as final. He suggests instead, as equally derivable from the known facts, the possibility that the experienced disjunctions may be finally unified in such a way that nothing is lost. Not coincidentally, given James's irresolute state of mind, this re-introduces the possibility that Kant's moral argument may be right, after all, but not on Kantian terms. What is asserted is only the possibility that the outcome desired will come to pass and only insofar as we bring it about and what is denied is that it is necessitated by practical rationality.

James at this time still clung to a belief in the ultimate rationality of the universe, even though he recognized that the belief might be in vain. This is shown by his willingness to concede to the transcendental rationalists that the world might be an absolutely closed system, in which all our demands, moral as well as intellectual, will ultimately be satisfied. But although he says that this is pragmatically defensible — on different grounds if taken abstractly than if taken concretely — the defense turns on denying the actuality of the existence of such a closed system in order to retain it as a possibility. Insofar as this abstraction from experience is understood instrumentally, as a guide to action, then it can be as legitimately entertained as any other hypothesis. But even insofar as absolutism opposes a finished, perfect edition of the world to this finite, changing one, it still has a religious meaning because some guide their lives by it.

Since on pragmatic principles 'meaning' means consequences useful to life, then belief in the Absolute, attested to throughout a long religious history, is said to be at least emotionally and spiritually meaningful. If this meaning can be harmonized with the other uses of life, then it would also be true (PM, 131). There is more than one way of taking absolutism. Taken monistically, it means "the mystical way of pure cosmic emotion," which is quietist and indifferent to this world's problems (133). Pluralistic absolutism, on the other hand, means "your better possibilities phenomenally taken," asserting the hope that the inadequacies and even failures of attempts to bring perfect harmony to this world yet contribute to the sum total of a perfection that will eventually be realized. Both are pragmatically meaningful, because they enhance the dignity of the individual person, but the second agrees more with the pragmatic spirit because it acknowledges more plural, genuine possibles.

In a typical gesture of conciliation James says that those who hold that belief in the rational unity of all things conflicts with pluralism have not clearly thought the matter out. The reason is that, given the state of the real world, a belief in the rational unity of things can only mean their possible empirical unification (PM, 134). The whole clash of rationalist and empiricist religion hinges on the validity of possibility. Rationalism and religion seem natural allies because intellectually rationalism "invokes its absolute principle of unity as a ground of possibility for the many facts" and such guarantees are emotionally soothing (135). This is a state of affairs with which to reckon, since for James the pragmatic meaning and value of religion consists in the security it provides against the terror of nihilism (75). This is also called by him "taking moral holidays" (41). Against this optimistic security pragmatism's contention that the final, harmonious outcome cannot be guaranteed ahead of time, but is only a possibility which is contingent on our cooperation, seems unduly pessimistic and insufficient as a motivator of religious effort.

But the pragmatic doctrine of meliorism as the most defensible attitude to adopt in the conduct of human affairs bases itself on concrete grounds, not on some vague assertion of abstract possibility. As pragmatically defined, 'possibility' means "not only that there are no preventive conditions present, but that some of the conditions of production of the possible thing actually are here" (PM, 136). The ideals each of us has and works for are not merely abstract possibilities but are grounded on live possibilities insofar as complementary conditions are present. These consist in the particular configuration of events that, given the right intervention on our part, will bring about the outcome desired. This pragmatic meaning of possibility contrasts with the determinism of religious rationalism. Since rationalist monistic philosophers of religion claim that the Absolute alone has complete control and has predetermined the future, then our contributions are necessarily only subsidiary and ministerial. Therefore, according to religious absolutists, the claim that we, ourselves, will determine the outcome is not only irreligious but irrational.

James develops the central contention of his radically empiricist philosophy by denying the charge that a pluralistic universe would be irrational. We know our own acts as turning-places where we experience our creativity in regard to both ourselves and the world. This knowledge is no chimera, but the experiential basis for the claims we make as to how we relate to the world. The structure of this pragmatic, concrete hermeneutics is succinctly stated in the form of a challenge: Why may not our own activity, of which we have such intimate experience, "be the actual turning-places and growing-places which they seem to be, of the world — why not the workshop of being, where we catch fact in the making, so that nowhere may the world grow in any other kind of way than this?"(PM, 138)

Pluralism does not presuppose any totality of explanation or predetermined harmony of being as a necessary condition for the possibility of meaningful action. Critics charge that this presupposes that change is random and independent of the order of events in the universe, which would be meaningless and chaotic. Events are meaningful only insofar as they can be understood in relation to the total nature of the world, that is, insofar as they can be seen as an adequate physical response to a given set of material conditions or as logically constrained by the comprehensive set of logical conditions. According to these realist objections the 'real' agent of growth is considered to be the integral world itself, to which we must conform if we are not to succumb to mere wishful thinking.

In response to this charge of irrationalism James once again questions the naive realism that grounds such rationalist attacks. Growth "in spots" seems irrational because "the whole philosophical machine shop" of logic and categories and necessity goes into business for itself insofar as philosophers disregard the fact that they are not just reporting on a world which is simply found, but are themselves organizing a world which will answer to their subjective demands. The philosopher's own rational demand that the world will be comprehensible only insofar as it is can be made to answer to logical rules rationally determined unwittingly demonstrates the living acts of reason which James dissects in "The Sentiment of Rationality." It discloses a drive to create a world, if only abstractly, which satisfies the most rigorous aesthetic criterion of simplicity.

Such rationalist demands are shown to be themselves exercises in wish-fulfillment, since so much of the phenomenally experienced world must be denied in order to satisfy their conditions. Consistent rationalists deny that anything meaningful can escape their rational reconstruction since they have already, by a priori fiat, defined 'meaningful' as fulfilling the predetermined conditions. This is a willful creation of a world to exactly match their demands. James thus argues that, not he with his pragmatic views, but those who presuppose a fully rational world, are postulating a wished-for world, where every aesthetic desire is fulfilled because it is a desire.

By contrast, the pragmatist, while recognizing such wish-fulfillment as one condition for the appropriation of a meaningful world, does not make it the only one. Both the demands of others and the recalcitrance of experienced facts prevent us from reconstructing the world solely according to our own demands. We do help to bring about the world which we seek to understand and live in; we neither simply passively reflect it in our interpretive schemas nor do we simply remold it, without remainder, into patterns of our own choosing. "So Being grows under all sorts of resistances in this world of the many, and, from compromise to compromise, only gets organized gradually into what may be called secondarily rational shape" (PM, 139). In place of the comfort provided by the promise of ultimate success, which makes rationalist religion so attractive, given the fact that the everyday world we live in is so precarious and unpredictable, James can only offer to those hardy enough to function without such guarantees, a live hypothesis embodying "a social scheme of co-operative work genuinely to be done."

But not everyone can live in such a world where there are no guarantees that the work of a lifetime may be undone subsequently. As long as we are confident in our powers, then the possibility of failure can be borne because the thrill of achievement is worth the risk. But when we lose our self confidence, — and almost everyone does so at some time or other — when women and men "are reduced to their last sick extremity absolutism is the only saving scheme" (PM, 140). James thus brings back Kant's moral argument for the necessity of a kingdom of ends. However, he does not interpret it as answering to a rational, and therefore universal, human need but as answering to a rational, but nonetheless conditional, need. In some circumstances, such as when we are in danger of succumbing to nihilistic pessimism, then it can become a necessary condition for human action, but in circumstances of robust, optimistic self-confidence, it is not.

He also realizes the radical challenge to traditional religious rationalism that his pragmatism poses by introducing temporality and diminishing universal and necessary claims into particular, personally contingent ones. He has replaced the usual model of a timeless rational man by a concrete description of living women and men and the often conflicting needs and states of mind they experience over time. He says that some would reserve the name of religion only for the absolutistic scheme and call the pragmatic pluralist one only a morality, since "religion in the sense of self-surrender, and moralism in the sense of self-sufficingness, have been pitted against each other as incompatibles frequently enough in the history of human thought" (PM, 140-141).[10]

This dichotomy expresses for James the final question of philosophy. If they are as absolutely irreconcilable as they seem to be, then one could not be both healthy-minded and sick-minded. Because we do not usually inquire too deeply into our own incompatible beliefs, as individuals we can be both, and "most of us remain in this essential vagueness" (PM, 135). "But as philosophers aiming at clearness and consistency, and feeling the pragmatistic need of squaring truth with truth, the question is forced upon us of frankly adopting either the tender or the robustious type of thought" (141). But the price to be paid for adopting the religious absolutist position, the one James must prefer in such a draconian choice because it is the means of overcoming nihilism, entails denying the negativity experienced at the very heart of life. It would mean ignoring all the drastic and bitter suffering and failures that make up the world as we experience it.

But James actually sides with the more moralistic point of view, being willing to accept that the world is really dangerous and adventurous, that "there should be real losses and real losers, and no total preservation of all that is" (PM, 142). Genuine pragmatists should be able to live in a world of uncertified possibilities and stake their lives on the outcome. Absolute harmony would be acknowledged as a goal, not an origin to which we return. It turns out that although he admits that belief in an Absolute is meaningful, it is not meaningful on its own terms, that is, as a monistic totality already existent. It is only meaningful in the mitigated sense that insofar as the practical results of holding this belief are satisfactory, then it is as logically unassailable as its opposite. This sense is legitimate until other needs are felt or other circumstances force a reappraisal. The content of the belief has not been validated, but only its worth. It literally *is* no more or less than its results, since value for life is the ultimate criterion.

But James is personally acutely aware of more needs than he can consistently resolve in any neat, rational formula. Too honest in *Pragmatism* to pretend to a resolution he cannot feel, he does not hide the unsuccessful struggle to harmonize his own aesthetic and practical needs. After carefully distinguishing in what sense a belief in an Absolute is pragmatically meaningful and in what sense it is not, for instance, he rather inconsistently confesses his own firm belief in one of the rejected senses, namely that "higher powers exist and are at work to save the world on ideal lines similar to our own" (PM, 144). Although this can be partially explained by his distinction between a finite superhuman, which is pragmatically verifiable, and an Absolute superhuman, which is not, the inconsistency remains. He does recognize that the rational philosophical demand for consistency precludes asserting both absolutist optimism and empiricist pessimism. But James, being "neither tough nor tender in an extreme and radical sense, but mixed as most of us are," declares his faith in an inconsistent hybrid which is no less religious for being a pluralistic moralism.

This analysis is remarkably similar to Nietzsche's, but at the same time draws strikingly dissimilar conclusions. Nietzsche also argues that "it was suffering and incapacity that created all after-worlds — this and that brief madness of bliss which is experienced only by those who suffer most deeply."[11] Like James, he is, in the persona of Zarathustra, "gentle with the sick. Verily, he is not angry with their kinds of comfort and ingratitude." But he does not think that the practical results of holding this belief are satisfactory. They are actually pernicious when judged by the same ultimate criterion he shares with

James, that is, their value for life. He argues that by imagining that there exists a perfect world which mocks this eternally imperfect world, we are actually creating a heaven that is a "dehumanized inhuman world." This belief prevents us from recognizing and coming to terms with the necessarily human way in which we can alone encounter being. Therefore, unlike James, he does not defend the legitimacy of such sickness, but argues that it can and should be cured: "A new pride my ego taught me, and this I teach men: no longer to bury one's head in the sand of heavenly things, but to bear it freely, an earthly head, which creates a meaning for the earth."

4. A Doubled Interpretive Space

Since James clearly identifies philosophy with "aiming at clearness and consistency, and feeling the pragmatistic need of squaring the truth with truth," his declaration of being a mixed sort puts him in the company of those "monistic pluralists, or free-will determinists" he identifies as "amateur dabblers in philosophy" who do not think problems through to their conclusion (PM, 141). But he also strives mightily to resolve the dilemma, despite the fact that "most of us remain in this essential vagueness, and it is well that we should; but in the interest of clear-headedness it is well that some of us should go farther" (135). The problem, once again, is that James is already 'post-rationalist' — or at least anti-rationalist in its purely aesthetic, intellectualist sense — in his refusal to accept the logical veto of a formal contradiction over the real drama of the clash of two insistent, undeniable needs. He is surely aware that to be consistently radical he must deny the legitimacy of abstract aesthetic rationalism, but not necessarily of concrete rationality, or else he would not be raising the question as to whether "the disjunction is a final one," of whether "only one side can be true" (141). But since philosophy still meant primarily the satisfaction of rational, aesthetic demands, and he still hoped to ultimately resolve the problem both in its aesthetic and practical dimensions, the final break is postponed.

James struggled to harmonize all our deepest human needs. It is a testimony to the strength of his conviction that this is the most defensible goal of philosophy that he admitted his failure to accomplish this purpose, but nonetheless argued that it should be vigorously pursued. At the same time, he also insisted that it was better to continue demanding that none of our deepest needs be slighted, even if this results in logical inconsistencies, than to prematurely satisfy only the aesthetic demand for non-contradictory assertions. Acquiescing in such a logical veto is too high a price to pay if it entails denying the equally insistent practical demand that we have a sufficient incentive to continue meaningful action. He forcefully argues that the heuristic, aesthetic philosophic demand for absolute, simple comprehensibility should function as an incentive to work for a state of affairs not yet achieved. It becomes a liability rather than an asset when it seduces us to prematurely accept closure rather than keep searching for a more inclusive solution.

In these texts James lets us see the actual "growing-places" of the world, that is, he does not cover over the traces of his own struggle to reconstruct a world in which he can live, including his own failures as well as his success in this reconstructive project. He thereby both powerfully demonstrates by example that there is no uniquely correct, true, indisputable interpretation of the world outside of each person's on-going process of becoming and that, consequently, each of us is responsible for the world in which we choose to live. We cannot, in good faith, appeal to an independent source of validation apart from our own complicity.

But we operate within a doubled interpretive space in our reading of the Jamesian texts. We not only witness the moment of the struggle as it occurred and can, besides, recall the later positions he held, but we are also in our own present historical moment and can reconstruct the text taking into account many decades of reflection and our own level of understanding. This accounts for the disconcerting sense one often has in reading James that many of the resolutions he explicitly claims to have realized at a later stage seem already to guide his earlier discussions. We have seen for instance, that James reconstructed the doctrine of the reflex-arc loop into a concrete analysis of the person-acting-in-the-world-for-a-purpose. We can therefore recognize what he could not at the time; namely, that the central interpretive insight of his new philosophy can be found on the seventh to the last page of *Pragmatism*, where he brilliantly describes the living moment of experience as "the workshop of being where we catch fact in the making" (PM, 138).

The systematic development of this interpretive structure can dissolve the antinomies with which James is still struggling in this last chapter of *Pragmatism*. But we are in a different interpretive space than is the James we see struggling in the text. It seems that, after having seen the solution, as if in a brilliant flash of lightning, the darkness closes in again and he ends the chapter with the admission that he cannot yet see how to resolve the problems raised. But, since the memory of the bright illumination is still fresh, he also states that the dilemmas generated will be solved, if at all, along the lines he has indicated.

This would be of merely biographical and historical interest except for the radical nature of James's new philosophical beginning. His position has a better chance of being understood today than when it was first developed. The way the new position is gradually hammered out is as important as rephrasing its conclusions in clear and consistent terms. There is much to be learned about doing philosophy by tracing the Jamesian odyssey in the meandering of the textual record and also much to be gained from restructuring the material into a more coherent philosophical position. In fact, despite his inability to foresee how his analyses would turn out, James had already begun in *Pragmatism* the critical process which eventuates in demonstrating that what at the moment seems unresolvable are actually pseudo-problems that do not need to be resolved, but dissolved. The problem in the form in which it gripped James is that of whether we are alone in the universe or whether our efforts to harmoniously restructure the world are supported by more than human forces. Implicated in this one is the opposition between rationality and irrationality.

In the last pages of *Pragmatism*, James clearly sets out the concrete basis of his pragmatism. As starkly stated, it comes perilously close to reintroducing his old nemesis of nihilism. The radically empiricist principle of pragmatism is reemphasized: pragmatists should logically refuse to include in their explanations anything not verifiable by recourse to the concretely disclosed world of human experience. In such a world things are as they appear and they do not appear to be rationally ordered nor even hospitable to human needs. "This is involved in the pragmatistic willingness to treat pluralism as a serious hypothesis" (PM, 142). The universe seems "to be really dangerous and adventurous" with "real losses and real losers, and no total preservation of all that is." Some people can live with this denial of the ultimate rationality of the universe "and find its disseminated and strung-along successes sufficient for their rational needs." In fact, the "genuine pragmatist" is defined as one who sincerely accepts this "drastic kind of universe" and "is willing to live on a scheme of uncertified possibilities which he trusts; willing to pay with his own person, if need be, for the realization of the ideals which he frames" (142-143).

Surprisingly, James is by his own admission not such a genuine pragmatist because he firmly disbelieves "that our human experience is the highest form of experience extant in the universe" (PM, 143). He does not believe in the theistic God of rational religion, either, nor in the rational proofs for his existence, and therefore has no dogmatic certainty that his religious over-beliefs must be true. Having rejected both the atheism of "crude naturalism" and the theism of "transcendental absolutism," he calls his own "religious synthesis" a "pragmatistic or melioristic type of theism" (144). But although it may be a melioristic theism, it is indefensible as a pragmatism that is a methodological outgrowth of his own concrete analysis. This is because, like Absolutist rationalist religion, it tries to explain away rather than explain the character of the world as indifferent to and even hostile to human concerns. James surreptitiously reintroduces the traditional notion of a rational order behind the seemingly irrational kaleidoscope of the phenomenal world. As he well recognized, this irrationality is both aesthetic, in that the experienced world is pluralistically resistant to ultimate unification, and practical, in that it is neutral morally in regard to good and evil, which are alike rewarded, alike punished.

James does not seem to realize that he has introduced two meanings of rational. One is ultimate rationality, that is, the traditional aesthetic rationality, and the other is concretely rational, that is, the living rationality of creating order out of chaos in interactive collaboration with what is. He will ultimately deny the restrictions of aesthetic rationality by appeal to living rationality. But he will call this giving up rationality and its logical way of proceeding rather than realizing that what he has done is to deny a traditionally sanctioned but ultimately mistaken understanding of rationality by criticizing it from the perspective of his concrete rationality. He apparently understands rationality univocally and takes his reconstruction of the sentiment of rationality as an explanation of traditional rationality and not as an alternative to it or as a reconstruction of it which can withstand the objections that are fatal for the traditional meaning.

Insofar as he takes aesthetic rationality and practical rationality as totalizing demands, he can resolve their incompatible requirements only by rejecting one of them. It therefore should come as no surprise that he later finally explicitly rejects aesthetic rationality in asserting his belief in a radically pluralistic universe, in which the logical veto no longer applies. But his earlier explanations of reasoning as it exists concretely have already shown how both aesthetic and practical demands can contribute harmoniously to the actual process of reasoning, when reasoning is understood in its reconstructed sense as a distinctively human way of ordering the chaos of experience to suit our needs. Since the survival and enhancement of a human form of life is the ultimate criterion of success in this transformation of chaos into order of all sorts, from material well-being to cosmological speculations, then any particular rational schema or understanding of rationality that is life-denying can be legitimately rejected as irrational. But this concrete sense itself incorporates an interpretation of rationality that is obviously not being refuted.

According to this genealogical analysis rationality developed and thrived because of its enhancement of this process of ordering. From the perspective of this more defensible and fruitful concrete analysis it can be shown that the interpretation of the aesthetic and the practical as totalizing antinomies is an historical aberration arising from the exaggeration of some needs at the expense of others. Thus their absolute opposition, resolvable only by the hegemony of one over the other, poses a pseudo-problem, but one which has actually arisen in philosophical and theological debates and is therefore worth undoing. This is particularly obvious in the present case, since James himself was still caught in its grips. He wanted to preserve the solace given by belief in more than human powers guiding human affairs, but without retaining the traditional rational positions that such a higher power must be singular, not plural; absolute, not finite, and that the world must therefore be determined, not free. But while denying most of the beliefs of rational religion, he could not cast himself adrift without its central plank that there must be such trans-experiential support. He distorted the defining premise of practical rationality that we order the world to suit our purposes by arguing that we can order it by assuming that we are still under the protection of the gods. He therefore reinstated the ultimate triumph of aesthetic rationality. In his concrete analysis of living reasoning he provided the tools for its dismantling, but did not carry it out himself.

James's project of overcoming nihilism and skepticism by beginning philosophical reflection with a concrete analysis of the structures of human experience was intended to support his deeply held belief in higher powers with whom we can cooperate in transforming this world into an ideal harmony. It was this personal need for religious consolation that prevented him from drawing the logical conclusion of his own radical empiricist pragmatism, namely, that nihilism is overcome by accepting our own responsibility for creating a human world. He did not grasp Nietzsche's insight that nihilism arises from the despair we feel when religious or other grounds for an already ordered world are shown not to be the case.[12] Both Nietzsche and James were responding to the Darwinian overthrow of the rationally ordered world that bound together Western thinkers from Aristotle to Newton and which undergird the Christian philosophical cosmology. Nietzsche argued that having been deprived of belief in an all-encompassing external pattern of order, the initial response would be to feel lost in a world without such objective direction. In his first crisis James exemplified such despair. Nietzsche also argued that this despair could be overcome through the realization that there never was such an objective order. The scientific, religious, and social orders that we had thought were natural were actually our creations all along. Furthermore, we have survived and prospered as a species by creating many such orders. Our delight in our own creativity, following upon the realization that it is foolish to continue longing for an order we never had, can be sufficient to overcome nihilism.[13]

James knew that creativity was central to his anti-nihilist project, and he unswervingly defended this free creativity unfettered by determinist constraints, but he could not face a world emptied out of all gods. He was not comfortable with a merely human world, despite his own phenomenal findings, such as that our fellow women and men are among the forces on which we can call to realize our particular ideals for transforming experience (PM, 143). Although he sought to shore up religion, his own concrete analysis undermines rather than supports his belief in superhuman forces. There is no more evidence for the existence of such friendly presences to cooperate with our moral regeneration of experience than there is for an impassive absolute knower who unifies cognitive phenomena. He argued too well. As Nietzsche realized, the cognitive and the moral postulates of rationality stand or fall together. Despite James's best efforts, such a claim for the right to believe in non-human presences cannot, as he hoped, "combine satisfactorily with all the other working truths" that he has demonstrated.

But this very failure is due to the success of his "pragmatistic philosophy," which did offer an alternative to nihilism by first denying the independent rationality of the world and then showing how its secondarily rational character is brought about through our cooperative efforts (PM, 139). But this living rationality will never have the comprehensiveness nor surety that traditional rationalism offered us. James failed to reconcile healthy-mindedness, which could stomach a world without any meaning but what we give it, and sick-mindedness, which needs the consolations of a rationally benevolent world order. He could not reject either state, however. This makes him a tortured exemplar of that messy world of conflicting demands and uncertified possibilities with which we are left when we resolutely accept the human condition.

Part Four

Knowledge and Truth

Chapter Ten

"Knowing as it Exists Concretely"

"The dualism of Object and Subject and their pre-established harmony are what the psychologist as such must assume, whatever ulterior monistic philosophy he may, as an individual who has the right also to be a metaphysician, have in reserve" (PP,I, 216).

Special care must be taken in interpreting what James meant by such pivotal terms as 'meaning,' 'truth,' 'knowledge' and 'reality,' because of his original reconstruction of the task of philosophy. He did not simply anticipate contemporary formulations and his new beginning was not followed up outside the classical pragmatic movement.[1] If his revolutionary procedure had not been sidetracked from mainstream philosophy by such anachronistically positivist philosophies as that imported by the Vienna movement, then the inappropriateness of many of our preconceptions as to what these terms mean would be more obvious.[2] In hindsight, though, his radical critique should be more accessible to us now than when originally presented, since others such as Heidegger and Wittgenstein have also come to similar conclusions.[3] Nonetheless, James's complaint still rings true today: "The fantastic character of the current misconceptions shows how unfamiliar is the concrete point of view which pragmatism assumes" (MT, 99).

His description of "knowing as it exists concretely" is, if anything, even more provocative than when first developed, given the continuation of the same "shallow sense of the conditions under which men's thinking actually goes on" (MT, 80, 46). The same accusation of "confounding psychology with logic" is made today by philosophers in response to accounts of how truth is "arrived-at" as an answer to what truth means (85).[4] But it is they who fall into the "psychologist's fallacy," so named by James to characterize the confusion of one's own standpoint with that of the mental fact being reported (PP, I, 195-196).

James wrote Peirce in 1909, for instance, that "I am *a*-logical, if not illogical, and glad to be so when I find Bertie Russell trying to excogitate what true knowledge means, in the absence of any concrete universe surrounding the knower and the known."[5] Traditional theories of knowledge do not refer back to first order cognitive experiences and therefore ignore the horizon or context which sets up and makes possible particular knowledge claims. Until James's concrete standpoint is recognized and dealt with on its own terms, criticisms of his explanations of knowledge and truth are premature and miss the decisive turn taken. This turn is succinctly stated: "The pragmatist clings to facts and concreteness, observes truth at its work in particular cases, and generalizes" (PM, 38).

It is significant that James's earliest account of truth (1884) was called "The Function of Cognition" because it calls attention to the fact that theories of truth must be preceded by inquiries into the context and purpose of knowing (MT, 78).[6] In a late work he is still connecting his critique of rationalism with his starting point in concrete experience: "The belief in the genuineness of each particular moment in which we sensibly feel the squeeze of this world's life, as we actually do work here, or work is done upon us, is an Eden from which rationalists seek in vain to expel us, now that we have criticized their state of mind" (SPP, 60).

1. A Concrete Analysis of the Cognitive Function of Lived Experience

James's appeal to concrete experience relates knowledge to a horizon of meaning and action rather than to incorrigible sense data. He somewhat misleadingly characterizes his new beginning as "practical psychology." Metaphysical problems, such as the nature of reality, are bracketed in order to first describe "the practically recognized constitution of cognitive consciousness" (MT, 26, n8). In discussing the relation of minds to other things in *Principles* he deliberately limits himself to the psychological point of view, acknowledging that a full explanation must transcend the self-imposed limitations of natural science and include *Erkenntnistheorie* and metaphysics (PP,I, 213). But when he does develop his own epistemological account in *The Meaning of Truth* he nonetheless still stays within these limitations. Although he calls this procedure 'epistemological,' a better label would be, depending on one's own presuppositions, 'pre-epistemological,' 'proto-epistemology,' or 'concrete analysis.'

In *Principles* he begins, not with the skeptical challenge that has so exercised philosophers since Descartes, but with the usual belief of psychologists (and of all of us when not philosophizing) that we know the world before us and that others also seem to refer to the same world (PP,I, 213ff). In deciding whether the thoughts of patients should be considered true knowledge or whether they only represent a subjective state of mind which does not refer to anything outside itself, psychologists use the same tests "we all practically use." This test is whether the verbal report of such thoughts either resembles their own ideas of a certain reality or "seems to imply that reality and refer to it by operating upon it through the bodily organs," either directly or indirectly. If it passes these tests, then psychologists judge that the other person "takes cognizance, directly or remotely, distinctly or vaguely, truly or falsely, of the reality's nature and position in the world." If it does not resemble or operate on what the psychologist takes to be reality, then it is called a purely subjective state of no cognitive import or an aberration that needs remedying.

This psychologist's attitude toward cognition is so important to the development of *Principles* that James makes sure that it is not being misinterpreted: *"It is a thoroughgoing dualism"* presupposing two irreducible elements, namely, the knowing mind and that which is known (PP,I, 214). In contrast to the idealist account, neither element is or makes the other, but "they just stand face to face in a common world" as knower and known. Furthermore, the mere existence of something outside the brain is not a sufficient cause for knowing it. It must strike the brain in some way, and once being struck, knowledge is then constituted by a "new construction" in the mind, leaving the object itself unchanged. Even in sense impressions such an "inner construction" must take place. Beyond this dualism of subject and object and their pre-established harmony psychologists cannot go, although they may also have metaphysical beliefs that can account for the harmony, such as that subject and object are identical in the moment of knowing.

These restrictions, appropriate for the explicitly scientific *Principles*, would not hold for a treatise on knowledge and truth like *The Meaning of Truth*. And yet he opens the latter by defining the cognitive function of consciousness in the same psychological way that he did in *Principles*. He distinguishes between percepts, concepts and their objects and uses the same criteria of resemblance or operation (MT, 27-28). But in the second chapter, which is an extract of an earlier address/article, he distinguishes between representative knowledge and immediate or intuitive acquaintance. The former still refers to mental representations and their objects as two separate phenomenal facts joined within a connecting world in experience. In immediate acquaintance, by contrast, "the thought-stuff and the thing-stuff are here indistinguishably the same in nature" (34-35). Immediate acquaintance is an explicit development of a monistic metaphysical position. Has he abandoned in his epistemology his starting point in concrete experience by adopting the idealist postulate to complement the natural history point of view?

James claims an experiential, not a metaphysical, basis for the identity of subject and object in perception: "dotted all through our experience are states of immediate acquaintance just like this" (MT, 35). Moreover, in a footnote to the last line of the second chapter of *The Meaning of Truth* he says that "the text is written from the point of view of naif realism or common sense, and avoids raising the idealistic controversy" (36, n5). But this seems to be a deliberate attempt to confuse an issue he is unwilling or unable to defend. In the opening paragraph of the original article, "The Knowing of Things Together," which was omitted when the article was transferred to *The meaning of Truth*, he explained what is meant by 'things': "To this question I can only make the answer of the idealistic philosophy. For the philosophy that began with Berkeley, and has led up in our tongue to Shadworth Hodgson, things have no other nature than thoughts have, and we know of no things that are not given to somebody's experience" (EPH, 72; MT, 206-207). The identity of mental content and object which characterizes knowledge of acquaintance in his epistemology is the same position he had before described in the excised passage as the idealist position.

As a more satisfactory explanation than mere disingenuousness, or not knowing his own mind, there is also the fact that he was evolving a concrete method which borrowed from both empiricism and idealism but was not reducible to either. Even if his own beliefs about the nature of immediate experience were drawn from the idealist tradition, explicitly from Berkeley, but also indirectly from post-Hegelian idealism, he was struggling to reconstruct them consistently with his new beginning in concrete experience. James typically retreats to a common sense position when there is some, but not conclusive, empirical evidence and he does not want to settle an issue prematurely by appealing to an empirical or rationalist philosophical stance.[7] Such premature appeals caused the impasse which he wants to overcome by his experiential and experimental methods.

Only principles which are actually utilized in everyday experience can legitimately be introduced into this initial descriptive explanation. This clarifies James's earlier remark denying that the percept plus the self is the minimum explanatory unit.[8] He denies, for instance, Fichte's position that knowledge can only be constituted by a knowledge of the knowing mind accompanying whatever else is known. He argues that in common sense, that is, pre-reflective experience, such a principle is never used to discriminate between conscious states that are cognitive and those that are not. He obviously takes the Fichtean principle as a description of what constitutes consciousness and not as a transcendental explanation of what makes such consciousness possible. James's characteristic misunderstanding of explanatory or transcendental principles as descriptive ones contributed to his difficulty in reflectively grasping his own procedure.

James's remark, in the last chapter of *Pragmatism* that "this talk of rationality is a parenthesis and a digression" could not be further off the mark (PM, 139). It should be evident by now that his critique of rationalism is at the core of his pragmatic philosophy, particularly of his epistemology and theory of truth, even before he could assent to its full implications. He even singles out the instrumental character of theories, as not disclosing being once and for all, as evidence of its "*anti-intellectualist* tendencies" (32). Pragmatism initially and primarily stood for "a method of settling metaphysical disputes that otherwise might be interminable" (28). James agreed with Peirce that all pragmatists without exception understood pragmatism as a method, not a metaphysics.[9]

James also interpreted Peirce's pragmatic principle as meaning that "there can *be* no difference anywhere that doesn't *make* a difference elsewhere — no difference in abstract truth that doesn't express itself in a difference in concrete fact and in conduct consequent upon that fact, imposed on somebody, somehow, somewhere and somewhen" (PM, 30). Both Peirce and Dewey disagreed with this "substitution of particular consequences for the general rule or method applicable to future experience."[10] James, however, did not exclude the modality of possibility. He argued that, although particular consequences are the original goal and only sure resolution of experimental inquiry, we more often stop short, that is, allow the outcome predicted by general rules to stand in for the experiment as actually completed (See PM, 18; MT, 28).

Buy why propose a method to settle disputes? Why not settle disputes the way philosophers have always done, by determining the truth? As Nietzsche would say, because the truth, as such, is nowhere to be found, notwithstanding the fact that many truths have been claimed over the centuries. James also directly attacks "the pretence of finality in truth" (PM, 31). If truth were intuitively evident or demonstratively certain, then there would not be so many competing claims for it. Once found, truth in this sense would simply be cumulative. Instead, cumulative truth is only established after the fact, that is, only in hindsight by casting about for processes which led to present claims. With a different set of claims, a different historical process would be singled out. This is so, whether we turn to historical, scientific, religious, or even common sense truths.[11]

Only one class of truth claims remains in principle unrevisable and is 'eternally' true, namely, that of closed systems, which begin with stipulative definitions. These Humean relations of ideas include logic, mathematics, metaphysics, and even ethics and aesthetics insofar as they adopt the a priori, universalist mode of discourse. In fact the perfection of these systems has led to their serving as preeminent models of truth, from Plato's Ideas to the logical school of Frege and Russell. But what is meant by truth in this sense? Is it the fundamental model of truth, equal with some other, for example, matters of fact, or derivative?

According to H. S. Thayer, James's theory of truth has both a cognitive and a pragmatic aspect and this "cognitive truth is a necessary but not sufficient condition of pragmatic truth."[12] It is true that James calls himself a logical realist because he believes in the reality of universals. But he also calls cognitive truths secondary, and on the whole ministerial forms of being (SPP, 59). Cognitive truth has not proved adequate to settling the many conflicts over particular truths. To see why is to recognize its scope and limitations.

As usual, James begins neither with the cognitive nor the pragmatic theories of truth, but with their experiential origins. For corroboration he points out that the principle by which Dewey and F. C. S. Schiller also arrive at their conception of truth is the same one followed with such success by philologists, geologists, and biologists. They "take some simple process actually observable in operation — as denudation by weather, say, or variation from parental type, or change of dialect by incorporation of new words and pronunciations" and then generalize it (PM, 34). But this formula also encapsulates James's own new beginning in his concrete analysis of lived experience. This probably accounts for his enthusiastic response to the same procedure in Dewey and Schiller. Philosophy can avoid endless speculation only by beginning with an observable process and then reflectively identifying the structures of human thinking which are generalizable from it. James's development of such an experiential origin will be given next.

2. Intentionality in "On the Function of Cognition"

James considered the 1885 article, "On the Function of Cognition," to be "the *'fons et origo'* of all his pragmatism as a theory of truth" and thus reprinted it as the first chapter of *The Meaning of Truth* (1909).[13] He points to this article and the 1895 one, "The Knowing of Things Together," partially reprinted as chapter 2, as the earliest formulations of his conception of truth (MT, 78). It is significant that the first article was written while he was working on *Principles*, understood by him as providing a new beginning in experience for investigating how we know.

He does not address the problem of whether it is possible for feelings to transcend themselves in grasping the objects intended, but only how it is that in the everyday world we assume that such transcendence actually does take place. By what marks does "the common consent of mankind" recognize "that some feelings are cognitive?" (MT, 14). James's epistemology thus signals that he means to alter "the centre of gravity of philosophy" (PM, 62). Cartesian skepticism can only destroy the possibility of knowledge, it cannot account for it. That we do distinguish knowledge claims from merely subjective reports is incontrovertible. By investigating by what means we do so, we can learn how to deal with more problematic claims.

Although James thus begins with everyday experience, he does not merely describe it, but reconstructs it according to a philosophical interest in its cognitive function. He is trying to establish an uncontroversial starting point from which any developed system can be criticized, modified, confirmed, or refuted. "In short, our inquiry is a chapter in descriptive psychology — hardly anything more" (MT, 14). But Perry points out that by the time James reprinted "The Function of Cognition" in *The Meaning of Truth*, his reflections on Royce's insistence on the importance of the problem of the idea's objective reference had led him to recognize the nascent metaphysics in his descriptive psychology. Perry says: "In other words, it apparently took James eight years to become convinced that his 'practical and psychological' account of objective reference, in terms of human experience, would suffice also for metaphysical purposes."[14] This would apply to the essays on radical empiricism, as a second order explanation of the concrete findings of his natural history method, but as I argued earlier, James explicitly excluded a metaphysical grounding for his epistemological writings. What Perry calls metaphysics is actually the concrete description of the pre-metaphysical structures of the human appropriation of the world.

We have seen that James distinguished his epistemological investigations from F. C. S. Schiller's psychological ones (MT, 10). Nonetheless, his epistemology is derived from his "descriptive psychology," understood as "a pragmatic account...of phenomenal knowledge" (MT, 51). He says that his "view describes knowing as it exists concretely" (MT, 80), and in actual knowing interests are supreme (CER, 61). Speculative theories of truth derive their logical clarity and exactness from their deliberate break with the structural context of everyday processes and usages. Since these abstract accounts have no use for the various mundane ways we practically acquire knowledge, they denigrate as 'psychologistic' such investigations on the phenomenal level. But James's entire project of a new beginning in experience shows such objections to be spurious and misguided.

Since by 1904, James was already merging his narrower understanding of pragmatism as a method for settling disputes with Dewey and Schiller's wider worlds of discourse, his early texts give the basic theory of knowledge that gets refined in the later formulations. True to his intent not to assume anything as to the origin or nature of the knower, the vehicle of knowledge, or that which is known, James begins with the simplest unit of knowledge imaginable: a feeling. To begin otherwise would be to beg the question of the legitimacy of competing metaphysical claims which are merely speculative until grounded in some such more fundamental inquiry as he is undertaking. Since the *Principles* is a sustained argument against the existence of such isolated sense data and the illegitimacy of appealing to them as evidential, it is clear that his hypothesis is developed to refute fundamental propositions of both empiricists and idealists and thereby lay the groundwork for his own.

The first two chapters of *The Meaning of Truth* deserve a close reading because together they comprise one of the earliest criticisms (considerably predating Husserl's) of Franz Brentano's formulation of the problem of intentionality and its solution. Unfortunately, their status as significant precursors of contemporary discussions of intentionality has been neglected.[15] Following in the tradition of scholastic philosophy, Brentano had introduced the notion of intentionality to explain knowledge of things not immediately present as a mysterious presence in absence. James refers to this peculiar kind of existence as an "intentional inexistence."[16]

James uses the example of how we know that there are tigers in India to pragmatically refute the explanation of representative knowledge as a sort of presence in absence. Intentional reference to the tigers in India "is known simply and solely as a procession of mental associates and motor consequences that follow on the thought, and that would lead harmoniously, if followed out, into some ideal or real context, or even into the immediate presence, of the tigers" (MT, 34). It is known as our acceptance or rejection of a genuine tiger or as our ability to utter all sorts of appropriate propositions about tigers. It is even known as taking actions that put us in the presence of directly intuited tigers.

The presence of a connecting world in which knowledge takes place is usually ignored in epistemological theories. The importance of this starting point is insisted on by James: *"To know an object is here to lead to it through a context which the world supplies"* (MT, 35). But if we prescind from the environing world, "bracket" it, as Husserl will later say, and treat our own experience in the presence of the tigers as the whole universe, then seeing the tigers and the tigers seen are names for one indivisible fact, also called the ultimate datum, phenomenon, or experience. In immediate knowing the content and the object are identical. In reflective knowing, that is, when knowing is considered in relation to the larger world of which it forms a part, the connections are traced in different directions, some having reference to physical activities and others to mental activities. We can see that the core of his radical empiricism was already present in the 1895 article which is extracted in chapter 2.

The issue of intentionality is also discussed in chapter 1, called "The Function of Cognition." It is expressed as the problem of whether the self-transcendence attributed to those of our feelings deemed cognitive can be accounted for by anything intrinsic to the feeling itself (MT, 14ff). Suppose the existence of a "feeling of q" and leave out of account its origin, its duration, and the physical or psychical nature of its object. What would be the cognitive function of such a feeling? It could be said to be "the feeling's content 'q'" (15). But the quality 'q' is an entirely subjective fact, and common usage reserves the label of knowledge for the cognition of reality. Reality is understood as "things that exist independently of the feeling through which their cognition occurs." If the content of the feeling exists nowhere outside of it, and perishes with it, then it remains merely a subjective feeling. For a feeling to be cognitive, it must be self-transcendent, and therefore, short of introducing a god who obligingly creates a reality outside the intrinsic quality 'q' to which it corresponds, such hypothetically isolated 'q' feelings are irredeemably solipsistic.

With these arguments James shows that the isolated sense data to which philosophers in the Humean empiricist tradition appeal as the basic building blocks of knowledge cannot fulfill this function because such sense data have no intrinsic referentiality and therefore are not 'about' anything. They are epistemological surds, not building blocks. Therefore, in order for sensation to function as a basis for knowledge, a further explanation is needed beyond those given by the classical empiricists, one which can successfully incorporate a relation to reality within the sensation component.

James criticizes the naive appeal to reality as a self-evident termination of the process of knowledge. He begins by asking that if the relation to reality warrants calling a feeling cognitive, what warrants calling anything reality? The only answer is the faith of the critics or inquirers themselves. In the text under consideration James does not say why this is the 'only' possible reply, aside from the assertion that, as a matter of fact, at any given moment we must believe in some realities, even though they may not be identical to what we have earlier taken to be real. We have seen, however, that explanations of how beliefs and reflections on past experiences enter into our determination of what is real constitute a constant theme in James's writings. Furthermore, he is no longer speaking about a hypothetical situation, but has returned to the usual ground of his discourse, the situation of the individual human being in the world and the structures of being in the world which he has been developing through all his writings.

Since existence is uniquely embodied, the function of explanation is to illuminate to each one's satisfaction such individuated experiences. Thus, the applicability of the structures he has proposed as constitutive of human being in the world are to be determined "additively" and not "deductively." This means that he can never appeal to a priori structures as proving anything, and his constancy to this rule often obscures the fact that he is drawing on specific explanatory patterns. Only the consensus of all of us as individuals can either confirm or disconfirm the cogency of the patterns. This accounts for the 'concreteness,' to which Dewey referred above, and the refusal to talk in terms of laws or rules that are assumed to transcend the individual. James prefers to speak of the hypothetical nature of even the most time-honored laws to emphasize the source of their legitimacy, which is never a priori but only a posteriori.

Every science has unexamined assumptions, and so does epistemology. Such fallibilism precludes taking any individual epistemologist's authoritative claims about reality as necessarily constitutive of reality. This includes my own. That I have beliefs about reality is unarguable, that I take these beliefs to be true is irrefutable, but the claim that reality is as I take it to be cannot have the same epistemologically privileged status. But despite the fact that some of my beliefs about reality may be false, I cannot believe that they all are, nor can I hope to oppose or compare what is real to my beliefs in any straightforward sense, given that it is this very relationship that is being called into question. The appeal to reality is, then, an appeal to what I take it to be, that is, what I believe it to be, but with the proviso that these beliefs are only "relative and provisional." Therefore, the nature of reality, the determination of which is the proper subject matter of metaphysics, does not have to be decided prior to establishing the function of cognition. Despite its status as one of the unexamined assumptions of epistemologists, the appeal to reality still has an important role to play. No feeling will be called cognitive whose quality or content is not believed by us to exist outside as well as within it.

James does not want his demonstration of the inadequacy of the empiricist sense data theory to be construed as supporting the idealist denial of any epistemological significance to sensations unaccompanied by concepts. He realizes that both neo-Kantians and neo-Hegelians would object that such a 'bare' perception, with no relation to the mind or to anything else, far from being the least cognitive unit, would be both unknowable and the very negation of knowability. But James's critique of the empiricist sense data theory does not extend to denying any relevance at all to sensation, and he therefore insists that although this sensory unit is minimal, it is yet a qualified inner fact and not nothing.

If the bare "'feeling of 'q'" is such a psychical zero and cannot communicate anything about itself or anything else, why not agree with the 'relationists' that it is not cognitive at all? Why not, indeed, given that James himself is the most outspoken defendant of the priority of relations in all cognitive situations? It is precisely in elucidating this point that James's originality in mediating the empiricist and rationalist positions becomes most apparent. The key to the solution of the status of a bare feeling is indicated by the word 'about,' as developed by John Grote in *Exploratio Philosophica* (MT, 17 & 169, n17.36). He distinguishes between two types of knowing, which are also distinguished linguistically: to *know* something, that is, 'noscere, kennen, connaître," and to know *about* something, that is, "scire, wissen, savoir" (18).

> In the origin, the former may be considered more what I have called phenomenal — it is the notion of knowledge as *acquaintance* or familiarity with what is known: which notion is perhaps more akin to

the phenomenal bodily communication, and is less purely intellectual than the other: it is the kind of knowledge which we have of a thing by the presentation to the senses or the representation of it in picture or type, a 'vorstelung' [sic]. The other, which is what we express in judgments or propositions, what is embodied in 'begriffe' or concepts without any necessary imaginative representation, is in its origin the more *intellectual* notion of knowledge (MT, 18).

If it is understood that the supposed "feeling of 'q'" is of the acquaintance-type, it is no objection to say that it communicates nothing *about* anything. But if the sole function of mental states is taken to be their significance, that is, their standing as the sign of other mental states, then the lack of such a function in the feeling would disqualify it as a basic unit of knowledge and only that aspect of the knowledge of acquaintance that already includes some knowledge-about would be designated as cognitive. But how can (real, as opposed to possible) significance remain when no direct acquaintance with realities ever grounds such significations?

It may be interjected at this point that James is confusing meaning and truth, since knowledge-about means signification. Meaning can be explained apart from truth, that is, whether it is instantiated in, or refers to, existing objects, in a knowledge of acquaintance. On the contrary, he is showing why the distinction between meaning and truth is derivative and not primary. Recall that he is addressing the question of how we distinguish between cognitive and non-cognitive feelings, that is, what 'to know' means. By defining 'knowledge' as 'knowledge of reality' he is quite deliberately giving a genetic account of how meaning arose in the first place, if one takes the historical interpretation, or of how meaning is a function of a more fundamental relationship with objects, if one takes the ontological interpretation. Subordinating the 'sign' to the situation of the 'signer,' necessitating a prior accounting of what it means to be such a symbol-user, can be taken as a direct critique of contemporary epistemological understandings of meanings as fundamentally free-floating symbol systems.

The hypothetical feeling gives a *what*, and if succeeded by other feelings that can remember it, then this 'what' may become the subject or predicate of some judgment, some knowledge-about, and relations may be perceived between it and other 'whats.' The dumb 'q' will then receive a name. But every name has a denotation which refers to some reality with its internal relations unanalyzed, just like the original 'q.' No propositions expressing relations are possible without a basis in a preliminary acquaintance with such facts, whether the 'q' be a simple fragrance or a more complex feeling, "like that of the full-moon swimming in her blue abyss" (MT, 19). But the cognitive status of the supposed simple feeling depends, both for its having any significance and for expressing how it functions as a bearer of significations, on enlarging the original hypothetical situation to include the original relational matrix. "The knowledge *about* it is *it* with a context added. Undo *it*, and what is added cannot be *context*."

James does not object, after all, to the rationalist insistence on significance being necessarily relational, but only to denying that feelings can therefore be dispensed with as not being in any sense cognitive because, minimal though they are, they are still the only tie binding speculations to reality. Nor does he object to the empiricists' insistence that feelings are fundamental to the knowing process, but only to their mistaking an analytically distinguishable aspect of the process for the mimimal unit that can be experienced. He argues that this Humean and positivist explanation pattern of using the model of the most elemental parts that can be distinguished is systematically misleading and needs to be replaced by a global explanation encompassing the process as a totality.

The cognitive function of the feeling lies precisely in its acquaintance with an entity ejective to itself: "All qualities of feeling, *so long as there is anything outside of them which they resemble,* are feelings *of* qualities of existence, and perceptions of outward fact" (MT, 20). The italicized words emphasize that this cognitive function depends upon the existence of "a *q* other than the *q* in the feeling." But this is something that the feeling itself can never discover. This point would have been clearer if James had introduced the example, not as "a feeling *of* 'q,'" but as "a feeling, 'q'."[17] Starting with the reality, we can explain how it can be known by reconstructing it in the subjective fashion of a feeling, and starting with a feeling, we can reconstruct how it can know in the more public fashion of reality, but in either case the datum remains what it always is in the unmediated dualism of knower and known. "A feeling feels as a gun shoots. If there be nothing to be felt or hit, they discharge themselves *ins blaue hinein*. If, however, something starts up opposite them, they no longer simply shoot or feel, they hit and know."

But cannot we compare a real 'q' and a feeling 'q' and decide that their resemblance proves that the one knows the other? However, to determine this we must know that the feeling 'q' intends that very same 'q' that we take it to mean. By supposing more than one real 'q,' how could we determine which one the feeling stands for, since it resembles them all indifferently and does not declare its intention?

"Well, as a matter of fact, every actual feeling *does* show us, quite as flagrantly as the gun, which *q* it points to; and practically in concrete cases the matter is decided by an element we have hitherto left out" (MT, 22). What has been left out by framing the original question in terms of an isolated feeling is the actual situation in which such discernments take place. The situation was temporarily bracketed in order both to demonstrate the irreducible priority of feelings and the impossibility of explaining intentionality as wholly a function of feelings or even of feelings plus stipulated relations or meanings. Two criteria are invariably used in everyday life to decide intentionality: the falling of the feeling's practical consequences into the real world and the extent of the resemblance between the two worlds.

As was already demonstrated in *Principles*, "all feeling is for the sake of action, all feeling results in action" (MT, 23). Only if the feelings at issue act upon the world of the critic as they act upon my world can both the critic and I know to what reality the feeling refers. That the same world is cognized or some other world can only be determined by the consequences that accrue. If your feeling does not affect my world, then I am likely to call it a solipsism, a figment of a dream-world. Without such signs, there is no way to determine intentionality. "Before I can think you to mean my world, you must affect my world; before I can think you to mean much of it, you must affect much of it; and before I can be sure you mean it *as I do*, you must affect it *just as I should* if I were in your place" (23-4). Only in this way can I be sure not only that we are thinking of the same reality but that we are thinking of it in the same way.

We are so constituted as bodily beings in the world, that the object intended is actually known before curiosity can arise as to how feelings can intend just that object. Speculative reflection actually starts backwards, ignoring what has already been determined by calling it into question. Your interactions with a fire, for instance, poking it and warming yourself at it, must have already entered into my conscious awareness as actions that I recognizably also engage in, before I can even raise the question as to whether your words and gestures presuppose the same determinate thoughts as mine would in the same circumstances. As long as one remains on the practical level, no question ever arises as to whether an assailant's vision of my body resembles mine when he is attacking it. Only by severing my inferences from the body that made me infer it in the first place can such "metaphysical cobwebs" take on substantial importance. The metaphysical puzzle as to how two minds can know one thing is thus rendered practically irrelevant.

Surprisingly, that it is also speculatively vacuous was not yet recognized by James in his early and middle works, despite his strong expression of the pseudo-character of the specter of solipsism. Women and "men who see each other's bodies sharing the same space, treading the same earth, splashing the same water, making the same air resonant, and pursuing the same game and eating out of the same dish, will never practically believe in a pluralism of solipsistic worlds" (MT, 25). But what we can thus straightforwardly read as a rejection of speculative metaphysics he still understood as holding the metaphysical question in abeyance until it could be squarely faced from the firm ground of his still evolving "descriptive psychology," that is, concrete analysis of being in the world. "The main thing at present is to stick to practical psychology and ignore metaphysical difficulties" (26, n8).

3. The Horizon of Knowing in "On Some Omissions of Introspective Psychology"

Language, rather than feeling, is the vehicle referring to reality in an article written one year earlier than "On the Function of Cognition (1885)."[18] In "On Some Omissions of Introspective Psychology" (1884) James explains that words get their meaning by referring to some reality beyond the horizon of direct consciousness. This reality enters my awareness only as the terminus of my expectation in a certain direction. The subject or topic of the words, not explained in the later article, is given in the earlier one, where it is called the 'object': "The object of any thought is its entire content or deliverance, neither more nor less" (EPS, 164). He is speaking of the horizon, fringe, or "original halo of obscure relations," including a felt continuity with previous thoughts, that frames or sets up the possibility of thinking taking place. The *"continuity-with-the-complete-thought,"* which suffuses incomplete thoughts as a melody suffuses individual notes, is no more substantively contained in each part of the thought than the melody is in each note (165). But the topic does enter into the thought in progress as the sense of direction, the substantive reality "towards which the thinker merely points or looks." Our thinking is teleological and "large tracts [of it] exist only for the attainment of others" (167).

To say, then, that conceptual thought knows a reality when it actually or potentially terminates in a percept or its context means that it must be capable of ultimately leading to them, either by practical experience insofar as it terminates in a sensation, or by way

278 *William James's Radical Reconstruction*

of logical or habitual suggestion, if the thought satisfactorily concludes without terminating in a sensation (MT, 28). But most of our conscious thinking, using language as the symbolic medium, neither resembles nor affects the realities intended. How, then, do the speaker and the critic know that they both intend the same realities, that is, mean the same thing by what they say?

They know because of the experiential matrix in which thinking/speaking takes place. In countless instances such partial, merely symbolic thoughts have further developed into percepts which affect your perceptual field as they do mine. "By 'developing' themselves is meant obeying their tendencies, following up the suggestions nascently present in them, working in the direction in which they seem to point, clearing up the penumbra, making distinct the halo, unravelling the fringe, which is part of their composition, and in the midst of which their more substantive kernel of subjective content seems consciously to lie" (MT, 29). My thought must practically terminate in the other's realities, and affect them just as theirs would if they were of the same symbolic sort and their consequences were pursued. This mental persuasion is grounded in the sensible operations which both my thought and the other's lead us, or may lead us, to effect.

Our belief in a common world is thus based on the fact that "the percepts of each one of us seem to be changed in consequence of changes in the percepts of someone else" (MT, 30). That my acts not only change your percepts, but that my feelings when doing so resemble yours when you perform the same act, that is, that my percepts are identical to yours, can never be known for sure, but it is the simplest hypothesis to account for the phenomena described. We seem to be "knit into a continuous world, and not to form a pair of solipsisms" (30, n11). If everyone would take only their own percepts as real, then how could we ever be persuaded that those of others were not only real, but were real in an identical way?

There is no good evidence that not only do different persons perceive purportedly identical objects differently, but that conceptual, theoretical, and emotional accounts often differ to an even greater degree. The only basis for undermining the "chaos of mutually repellent solipsisms" that can follow from such reflections is the evidence that our perceptual feelings have the power of modifying one another [MT, 30]. Our knowledge-about must end in some knowledge-of-acquaintance because these perceptual termini, these sensible things, "are the only realities we ever directly know, and the whole history of our thought is the history of our substitution of one of them for another, and the reduction of the substitute to the status of a conceptual sign" (31).

James appeals to phenomenal bodily communication as what grounds, and is presupposed in, all formal epistemological and truth theories. Each person's embodied action in the world is not in the first place a descriptive level of discourse. The fact that my actions alter your perceptual field and vice versa is not only the strongest refutation of solipsism and surest evidence that we share a common world, but the necessary ground for the possibility of accurate description and reflective theories of knowledge. Communicative bodily actions provide the only reliable, verifiable disclosure of teleological consciousness and hence ultimately ground all real structures of meaning. We can never be sure we understand each other's meanings the same way until we can bring them to the test of appropriate response. But since this ultimate ground is bodily communication, which is not in the first place a linguistic expression nor disclosive of being in itself but only as it is for us, it can never have the status claimed for classic foundationalism. It is the basis for meaning but is not itself articulated in language. It therefore generates limits, but does not uniquely designate any one true interpretation to the exclusion of all others.

It follows from this irreducible pluralism of interpretations of bodily communication that any conclusions reached based on it are always, in principle, subject to revision by subsequent communicative acts. This basic appeal to human praxis is incompatible with absolutistic rationalistic theories of foundationalism, but is nonetheless a foundation of sorts. Theories grounded in praxis do not make the same claims as those grounded in absolutes. Scientific theories, unlike metaphysical speculation, always terminate in definite percepts, experimentally engendered. It is for this reason that all the pragmatists praise the scientific method as a salutary counter-model to the recurring philosophical temptation to prefer theoretical self-consistency (Jamesian 'simplicity') to experientially testable explanations of actual conditions (Jamesian 'clarity'). Echoing Kant, James admonished philosophers dazzled by the flight of conceptual reason to return from the upper air of truth to "the low earth of feeling from which the goddess launched herself aloft," that is, home to the knowledge-of-acquaintance (MT, 31). These feelings are the indispensable evidence that our several minds commune within a continuous world.

The pragmatic method is thus a radical reinterpretation of empiricism that undermines both empiricist and idealist versions of rationalism and speculative metaphysics. It is a method developed explicitly to attack classical foundationalism by showing that all theories are instrumental, that is, provide incentives for further investigation rather than final solutions. They are plans of action, showing how existing realities may be changed, rather than disclosing the inner nature of things. What at first had been taken by James to be only an anti-intellectualist method, which could be usefully employed by any sincere seeker after truth, had come to be taken as also a theory of truth. But in *Pragmatism* he puts off explicitly developing this theory until the sixth lecture (out of eight). The first five lectures are spent "paving the way" by explaining pragmatic methodology and "a genetic theory of what is meant by truth" (PM, 33, 37).

This postponement is not only due to James's constitutional dislike of the polemics which would be unavoidable in arguing for the pragmatic theory of truth, but also to the fact that his genetic theory of the meaning of truth destroyed the legitimacy of truth as traditionally understood. He does not just develop one more version of a philosophical theory of truth, just as Nietzsche did not. His wariness in presenting his theory under the expected rubric of a theory of truth is justified, as is amply demonstrated by the misunderstandings over the years by commentators who just concentrate on passages about truth as narrowly construed. It can be faulted for not fulfilling the criteria for a classic theory of truth because it demonstrates instead the limitations of all such models and proceeds to develop a radically empiricist alternative. When it is recognized that 'the truth as such' and 'the real being of things' express illusory goals, then the pragmatic method will come into its own as explaining what reality and truth 'for us' means.

4. "A Context Which the World Supplies" (MT, 35-36)

We have seen that James always distinguishes between two ways of knowing, that of 'knowing about' something, also called representative or conceptual knowledge, and that of 'acquaintance with' something, also called immediate or intuitive knowledge (see PP,I, 216-218 and MT 35-36). But in the first chapter of *Meaning and Truth*, called "The Function of Cognition," he argues that in order to know whether immediate knowledge has grasped something objectively as well as subjectively, it must fulfill the same conditions as representative knowledge, that is, its practical consequences must be exhibited. Whether we want to know if a token case of immediate knowing is also shared by someone else or we want to relate phenomenal knowing to some other substrate such as molecular structure, then immediate knowledge must be supplemented by representative knowledge. But if we prescind from the actual context in which events practically affect other events and limit the example to one's own singular experience of immediate acquaintance, "then the paper seen and the seeing of it are only two names for one indivisible fact which, properly named, is *the datum, the phenomenon, or the experience*" (MT, 36).

Representative knowledge is thus only an anticipatory name "for a further associative and terminative process that *may* occur" (MT, 34, n2). There is no inherent self-transcendency of any image/feeling and its object in itself. To know that anything knows something else, stands for that other object, and intends that and nothing else, one would have to show both what experiential activities would count for a completed act of knowing and the way in which those activities satisfy the intentions of the knower. Referentiality is not a check on intentionality. It makes no sense to ask whether that which is 'really' referred to is the same as what the speaker intended because there is no referentiality in itself apart from its incorporation in some intention and subsequent action on that belief. A formal account of reference can work only by assuming and surreptitiously drawing on those conditions of which James gives an explicit account.

To correctly refer to something is not a univocal relation but is essentially ambiguous, since there are many ways to satisfy such a claim. The fit of an idea or feeling and reality is not like fitting a coat to fixed form. Reference requires a common mediating environment if it is to be founded in experience and not in an *ipse dixit* presupposing a passive conformity between idea and reality. In a letter of 1907 to Charles A. Strong, James explicitly argues that the notion of external reference as a conformity of idea with reality is meaningless, that is, an unexamined formula which falls apart under scrutiny, and should be replaced by his experientially derived understanding of external reference as a satisfactory working or leading (see TCW,II, 540).

The pragmatic method demonstrates that cognitive reference is no inherent mysterious property by drawing out the full process required for its completion. "*That* the object is, *what* it is, and *which* it is of all the objects with that *what*, are things determinable only by the pragmatic method. The *which* means our pointing to a locus; the *what* means some selection on our part of an essential 'aspect' to apperceive the object by (and this is wholly relative to our 'situation,' as Dewey calls it); the *that* means the attitude aroused in us of recognizing reality, our *acknowledgement*" (TCW,II, 552). Thinking that something is the case and that which is the case intended are separate phenomenal facts, and to establish that the one 'points to' the other requires both a shared context or "connecting medium" and some operation which will bring the two facts together: "Now the experiential environment, which both separates the idea and the reality and mediates between them, affords many types of adjustment of the one to the other" (541).

There are therefore many activities that could signify the intentional object. Only within an objective context can it become apparent which "procession of mental associates and motor consequences that follow on the thought" would lead harmoniously to the object [MT, 34]. There is no self-sustaining univocal relation which uniquely satisfies these conditions. Only because of "the intermediary context that the world supplies" can our actions prove what the reality is that our minds point to, mean, and know (36). There are thus both subjective and objective aspects intrinsic to the cognitive process. The context which the world supplies is public and objective, that is, can be perceptually sensed and corroborated by anyone concerned. But to pick out the processes and consequences encompassed in a particular case of knowing is also subjective because what counts as "passing smoothly" or "leading harmoniously" depends on the tacit consent of those involved.

5. Phenomenalist Idealism and Trans-subjective Realism

James shifts responsibility to Dewey and Schiller for the more radical aspects of his position. This enables him to defer resolving some troubling conflicts. Until the third crisis, two conflicting assumptions are operative in his explanation of the human way of being in the world. The first, argued already in his earliest writings, explained in detail in *Principles*, and further developed in the opening chapters of *The Meaning of Truth*, is that there is an experiential identity of subject and object in the perceptual process which undermines skepticism and objectively grounds our claims about the world. The second assumption, held just as long and argued just as strenuously, and further developed in the opening chapters of *Pragmatism*, is that subjective interests are never absent in perceptions of reality and therefore what we take to be real is always filtered through a unique point of view. That the world is as we perceive it and that your world and my world are identical are thus never self-evident, but must be demonstrated. James avoided facing these contradictions by the simple expedient of calling pragmatism merely a method and its theory of truth a humanistic extension congenial to pragmatism. Their precise relationship can be gathered from notes he made for a 1905-6 course on metaphysics: *"Pragmatic method* asserts that what a concept *means* is its consequences. Humanism says that when these are satisfactory, the concept is *true"* (TCW,II, 444).

But since he also consistently defends the humanistic position and even incorporates its insights into his own explanation of pragmatic truth, this strategem does not lessen the need to explain how the individual percipient's reality is also anyone else's reality and how the identity of subject and object in perception is objectively true since it uniquely always incorporates particular interests. That he was aware of this failure to unambiguously relate methodological pragmatism and a humanistic pragmatic theory of truth is evident from his notes, which also show that the solution required adopting a metaphysical position he had not yet proven to his own satisfaction (TCW,II, 445ff). The resolution of the tension generated by the uneasy alliance of his phenomenalist 'idealism' and trans-subjective 'realism' is deferred as being a metaphysical issue, and his epistemology and theories of meaning and of truth were left to limp along as best they could.

James's uncertainty about how to assess his own position shows up in *Pragmatism* as a lack of clarity as to how humanism relates to pragmatism. Despite the fact that he reserves the name of 'humanism' for the broader extension of pragmatic methodology characteristic of Dewey and Schiller, he nonetheless explicitly adopts Schiller's humanistic view of truth as also the pragmatic one (PM, 37). This is clear in his summary of Lectures Five, Six, and Seven as expansions of the humanist-pragmatist genetic theory just given. It is explicitly stated that these three pivotal chapters explaining his own pragmatic theory of truth are more detailed explanations of what he had characterized in the second chapter as the broader humanistic theory of truth, which takes as its paradigm the process by which an individual settles into new opinions. Each of the main components of the humanist theory of truth, as explained in *Pragmatism* on pages 34-37, are taken up in turn as constituents of his own pragmatic theory of truth on pages 37-38. "Pragmatism and Common Sense" explains what is meant by "truths grown petrified by antiquity;" "Pragmatism's Conception of Truth" explains how "our thoughts become true in proportion as they successfully exert their go-between function;" and "Pragmatism and Humanism" shows "how hard it is to discriminate subjective from objective factors in Truth's development" (37-38).

His procedure in *The Meaning of Truth* follows the same pattern. A chapter on "Humanism and Truth" comes directly after the opening two chapters giving his earliest formulation of the pragmatic theory of truth. In it he distinguishes his own "narrower pragmatism" as the pragmatic method from the "wider pragmatism" of Dewey's and Schiller's humanism (MT, 38). What he then proceeds to defend in this humanist pragmatism is its reliance on the inductive method and its spirit of rejecting the "ideals of rigor and finality" which can only lead to that "pyrrhonistic skepticism" which James is also determined to overcome (39ff). But this insight into theory as instrumental and not disclosive of the inner nature of reality both replicates and supports James's own position. It also does go beyond James's position by affirming concrete rationality, not as a stage on the way to full disclosure, but as a permanent condition of human beings active in the world.

James says that humanism holds a subjective view of truth. Humanistic truth means what is useful or congruous with our residual beliefs. It is not a duplication of already completed reality but "the collaborating with realities so as to bring about a clearer result" (MT, 41). He finds this position vague and ambiguous primarily because he does not know how to reconcile it with his "Identitätsphilosophie" or knowledge-by-acquaintance. But as a "provisional attitude" he finds himself "playing sympathetically with humanism" because it expresses so well the subjective side of being in the world with which he heartily concurs, but wants to see joined with what he takes to be the equally important objective side (42). He thinks, though, that this objective side is properly metaphysical and therefore falls outside of epistemology altogether.

As in *Pragmatism*, what he then defends and explains in *The Meaning of Truth* about humanist pragmatism cannot be distinguished from his own pragmatic method as an ontology, epistemology, and theory of truth. The categorial problem for James becomes most acute in this discussion of humanism and pragmatism because humanism is thought by him to go beyond his pragmatic method in that it is a theory about the nature of reality, that is, a metaphysics. In a 1908 letter to John E. Russell, already mentioned, James reaffirms that his "pragmatism is purely epistemological," and therefore does not make any assertions about reality (ERE, 293). But because it does not engage in such metaphysical debates about reality, it does not follow, as Russell claims, that reality is denied. It is simply bracketed. (James, of course, does not use the word, 'bracketed'). Both assertions and denials of reality are metaphysical claims for James and his pragmatism cannot be a metaphysics because its aim is to clear the way for a metaphysics based at last on the facts of human existence. But since pragmatism also holds that the working of beliefs is what causes us to believe in the reality of which they are signs, he complains that other critics deny that pragmatism is even an epistemology, and call it instead only a 'psychology.'

But these responses to his critics are preceded by an admission that it is extremely difficult not to bring in aspects of a problem that are artifically divided into these different subject areas: "My pen is running away with me. I fear that metaphysics and epistemology and psychology are so mixed in the discussion that it will never to all eternity be straitened [sic.] out" (ERE, 293). His critics seemed to be more aware than James was of just how much his concrete starting point undermined the traditional philosophical categories. But their failure to recognize the radical nature of his new beginning underlies the contradictory criticisms being made that he is proposing a metaphysical solution, according to some, and that he is merely succumbing to psychologism, according to others.

A careful reading of the texts in *The Meaning of Truth* reveals that James's own explanation of truth includes the very same metaphysical components he attributes to humanism. Perry comes to a similar conclusion about the metaphysical contamination of the epistemology but does not recognize what is at stake. James is trying to develop a neutral grounding for his epistemology precisely so that it can arbitrate, rather than depend on, metaphysically speculative positions. In commenting on the note that James added to "The Function of Cognition" to bring it into line with his thoughts as of the 1909 publication of *The Meaning of Truth* (MT, 32), Perry says that "James's pragmatism here draws upon his peculiar radical-empiricist view of the continuity and objectivity of experience, just as in his radical-empiricism, on the other hand, he makes use of the pragmatic method. The two doctrines coalesce as they are deepened, and the independence which James occasionally attributes to them can only mean that they proceed from independent premises and *might* be held independently" (TCW,II, 454).

James's strongest criticism of the correspondence theory of truth, clearest explanation of the relationship of ordinary experience to pure experience, conscious recognition of the dilemma whether we find data or create the object, and explanation of truth as 'satisfaction,' which is both subjective and objective, all occur in the chapter supposedly explaining this metaphysical, wider pragmatism. Despite the fact that we would identify these positions with James's most creative contributions to philosophy, he himself deliberately calls attention to the fact that this humanistic program and his own are distinct. The problem is that he is fitting old wine — the traditional categories of metaphysics, epistemology, and theory of truth — into new bottles — his new beginning in experience and functional derivation of categories.

Not until after the third crisis does James finally let go of the possibility of absolutely accurate knowledge of being in itself and adopt without reservation the humanistic program. The pragmatic meaning of truth, therefore, is finally indistinguishable from the humanist one, even in these texts from the middle period, because in explaining the humanist genealogy of truth he is also explaining the pragmatist. But James cannot fully explain the humanist (and *a forteriori*, the pragmatist) account of truth without having to acknowledge assumptions about the nature of reality. In the chapter on "Pragmatism and Humanism," for instance, he says that *"the alternative between pragmatism and rationalism, in the shape in which we now have it before us, is no longer a question in the theory of knowledge, it concerns the structure of the universe itself"* (PM, 124).

Since, as we have seen, he wants his pragmatist methodology and epistemology, as outgrowths of his concrete analysis, to provide the basis for, but not be itself, a metaphysics, he must dissociate these metaphysical speculations from his own position in its present stage of development. Therefore, his pragmatism cannot be a humanism. But it is impossible to untangle the humanistic strands from a pristine pragmatism, they are so intertwined in the actual textual explanation. James is obviously ambivalent about the relation of pragmatism to humanism, but we need not be. By reading back the final post-rationalist position into these middle texts, the congruency of the pragmatist and humanist position is evident.

James's ambivalence reflects his failure to integrate his new beginning in a neutral description of the identity of subject and object in perception with his equally insistent elaboration of the selectivity of consciousness and consequent thematic development of the irreducible role that interests play in perception. His empiricist methodology of carefully describing facts provided the basis for proving that interests not only accompany consciousness, but are constitutive of it. But having shown that careful description supports claims for the inventiveness of human perception, he did revise his explanation of preceptual access to reality. His procedure was to emphasize the one aspect or the other, depending on the context, and resolve their discrepancies only indirectly by appealing to the pragmatic method.

The outcome of the pragmatic method was considered only provisional, but the unspoken assumption was that eventually an irrefutable metaphysics would resolve, and not just defer, the issue of the nature of our grasp of reality. The concluding sentence of *The Meaning of Truth* expresses this belief that the pragmatic/humanist understanding of truth as 'working' is "only one detail in the midst of much wider theories that aim eventually at determining the notion of what 'reality' at large is in its ultimate nature and constitution" (MT,

119). James had not yet rejected the possibility of a rational explanation of the relation of many partial interests to the totality which expresses the ideal limit of reality, nor had he yet developed a satisfactory explanation of his own. He was therefore willing to push the limits of the playful elaboration of realities to match prolific interests to see where this would lead only so long as this was not taken as his final word on the subject. He could even mischievously rejoice that "the trail of the human serpent is thus over everything" because he was leaving open the possibility that the serpent would be tamed at last by an encompassing reality (PM, 37).

A clearer distinction between 'totality' as the ideal limit of reality, that is, as an end-state consisting of our final understanding of all existing entities, and 'totality' as the horizon within which particular objects can be discerned can help us see a solution where James was stymied. He eventually denied that there was any rational link between 'my' cognitive appropriation of experience and the ideal limit of reality as a completed existent totality, while retaining a concrete totality as a fringe or totality of relations within which particular appropriations take place.[19] But he denied the rational link so that he would not have to deny his own strongly felt need for the possibility of a practical link to an ideal end-state: "The function of the intellect is practical rather than theoretical" (PU, 110).

This demand of practical rationality is that we ought to act so as to bring about a perfect harmony of our own actions and desires with the reality of a complete community of shared interests. Because rational logics, both transcendental and empirical, prove that there cannot be any metaphysical coalescence of our subjective knowledge with being or reality, then they, not our belief in ultimate harmony, have to be thrown overboard. If retained as ballast, they would sink our ship constructed out of practical interests. And since this ship of life must prevail, the rational veto must be denied.

As long as he was still thinking within the limits of a traditional empiricist distinction between phenomena and reality, or appearance and thing-in-itself, the problem remained logically insolvable: "But I hoped ever for a revised intellectualist way round the difficulty, and it was only after reading Bergson that I saw that to continue using the intellectualist method was itself the fault" (PU, 131). Insofar as he realized the radical consequences of his own new beginning in concrete experience, then the problem would not arise because the appearance/reality distinction as traditionally understood no longer applied: "The instant field of the present is always experience in its 'pure' state, plain unqualified actuality, a simple *that*, as yet undifferentiated into thing and thought, and only virtually classifiable as objective fact or as someone's opinion about fact" (ERE, 36). What has still to be decided is whether in the third crisis James finally denied the veto of intellectualism because he felt trapped within its restrictions, while still assenting to some crucial aspects of its world-view, or because he had finally made the paradigm shift that rendered it irrelevant. Was he finally irrational or was he beyond the modern synthesis of rationalism?

Chapter Eleven

Truth

"May there not after all be a possible ambiguity in truth?"
(PM, 94)

In a 1908 letter to Horace M. Kallen James responds to a criticism of Bertrand Russell's by proposing that the logically next step in developing his pragmatic theory of knowledge would be "to discriminate the various types of truth-making satisfactoriness" (MT, 306). But in *Pragmatism* and *The Meaning of Truth* he had already gone a long way in developing various types of satisfactoriness (MT, 80ff.). He argued that merely formal definitions of the relation between idea and object begged the question and therefore defined knowledge functionally, as providing instruments "for enabling us the better to *have to do* with the object and to act about it."

From a "practical and psychological point of view," for instance, your meanings are apparent to me because your actions in line with them affect my world in the same way they would if they were my meanings (MT, 23, also n6). You throw a rock through a window, for example, and say that the window broke. I see the glass shatter and hear it fall to the ground and it seems obvious to me that we both mean the same thing by your utterance. James criticizes merely verbal definitions of truth which deny the cogency of experiential verification on the grounds that 'real' claims about reality are simply 'true.' He argues that such statements assume that claims hold or obtain outside of any human context. But if not a human one, what context is being assumed? The hoariest expression of such a self-transcendent claim is the correspondence theory of truth itself, which James had to undermine before the radical nature of his position could be grasped.

1. Cognitive Truth and Pragmatic Truth

H.S. Thayer has suggested that making a clear distinction between 'cognitive truth' and 'pragmatic truth' will permit James's various pronouncements about truth to appear more coherent and less subjective and will help resolve the controversy over whether he ultimately held to a correspondence theory or not. According to Thayer, cognitive truth is "the agreement (or correspondence) between beliefs and statements and what these may be said to be about."[1] Pragmatic truth means (1) the assimilation of new forms of experience into the existing system of our beliefs and (2) "an instrument for enabling us the better to *have to do* with the object and to act about it."[2] Furthermore, cognitive truth is a necessary but not sufficient condition for pragmatic truth.

I would argue, instead, that the two models of truth James utilizes are based on his analysis of knowledge into 'acquaintance with' and 'knowledge about.' The first is absolute and signifies the identity of claim and object and the second is tentative and signifies the ratifying process by which beliefs come to be accepted. Since the second meaning is elaborated as an instrumentalism that satisfies our own criterion of working constrained by a context, the first sense can no longer be sustained. Nevertheless, James's empiricist realism led him to inconsistently hold on to his model of identity or 'confluence.' I will be emphasizing the radical nature of his pragmatic reconstruction of truth, but will also note the unreconstructed aspects of the traditional understanding of truth that accompany and distort it.

The classic correspondence theory of truth is one way of formalizing the relation of claim to object that James criticizes for its vagueness. He has no objection to its being retained as a formula, and in this minimal sense those critics who say that he holds to a correspondence theory of truth are right. James's conciliatory retention of this empty notion of 'corresponding' is misleading, however. The formula can be retained only if its meaning is 'cashed out' according to the pragmatic theory of truth. In this stronger sense, the same critics are wrong because the correspondence theory has actually been reduced to the pragmatic one. 'Working' has replaced 'agreeing.' Therefore, I would turn Thayer's cognitive-pragmatic schema upside down and argue that pragmatic truth, if anything, provides the foundation for cognitive truth, or it has nothing new to offer. Moore, Russell, Pratt, and Lovejoy are thus correct in seeing James's position as a repudiation of their own, but incorrect in their assessment of the nature of the attack. Their mistake lay in trying to make sense of James's assertions within their own universe of discourse, which assumes that cognitive truth must somehow undergird all empirical theories of truth, including the pragmatic.

Thayer's adoption of the Jamesian term, 'belief-assertion,' as standing for ideas, beliefs, judgments, and statements as "several kinds of token instance of truth or falsehood" is a good way of calling attention to the irrelevance of any more technical term when dealing with phenomenal experiences of the knowing process and truth claims. I will continue to use these various terms interchangeably in this sense of 'belief-assertion.' In defining cognitive truth Thayer quotes James to the effect that the objective reference of a belief or statement is "one relation of it to the reality."[3] But he also notes, under pragmatic truth, that James "is fond of saying" that "reality is what it is known *as*...and what an object is known *as* depends on a certain prior focusing of interests and needs that guide conceptualization, and partly upon similarly conditioned terminations in sense experience."[4] Thus, cognitive knowledge presupposes an ordered world. In fact, what James tries to show over and over is exactly how the otherwise chaotic world becomes ordered.[5] But then the cognitive truth model could not be fundamental and presupposed in the pragmatic model. It is precisely the forgetfulness of this ordering of experience that opens the way to claiming that the cognitive understanding of truth is fundamental instead of derivative.

The "anti-pragmatist" says in the last chapter of *Meaning and Truth*: "Doesn't common sense believe that every state of facts must in the nature of things be truly stateable in some kind of a proposition, even tho [sic.] in point of fact the proposition should never be propounded by a living soul?" (MT, 155). James agrees to this empty or cognitive notion of truth, then shows how it is parasitic on the pragmatic explanation of truth. One cannot even hold that the meaning of truth is the correspondence of proposition with reality except within a context in which these words make sense. This does not refer to the narrowly linguistic or philosophical context, but the more inclusive human context. James delineates the structures of this context and demonstrates that the traditional definition of truth as correspondence, which is useful for certain purposes, is nevertheless dependent on the suppressed context.

Traditional theories of truth assume that there is a necessary relation between any fact and its appropriate proposition, even without our knowledge of this relation. James says that this amounts to claiming that the facts that exist, exist, and that when we know them, we know them. In the absence of any actual process of completed knowing, there is a danger that one will make pseudo-entities out of these place holders. To say that there is a real relation that holds or obtains before there is any humanly constructed relation is to create "a sort of spiritual double or ghost." The problem arises because the original experience, which led to the cognitive truth formulation, has been covered over and yet is still operating implicitly. Truth as correspondence is literally meaningless outside an interpretive context.

And the interpretive context is what Thayer puts under the heading of pragmatic truth. The marrying of old opinion to new fact and the working or leading to satisfactory results according to our interests set up the epistemological world, rather than the other way around.

2. Criticizing Truth as Correspondence

We have seen that James's explanation of representative or symbolic knowledge as a 'leading' can be understood either as explaining what the correspondence theory is about or as replacing the whole notion of 'agreeing' with the more defensible notion of 'working.' Since he retains the formula that truth is some sort of agreement of claims with reality, it would be technically correct to say that he saves the correspondence theory by making sense of it. But James also argues that the humanist theory of truth will force those opposing it to analyze more critically their own "lazy tradition that truth is *adaequatio intellectus et rei*" (MT, 44). Humanism can provide explanations for the terms used in the correspondence theory that are otherwise left so vague as to be of no theoretical use.

For the humanist, 'correspondence' means a whole range of relations, depending on what is at issue; for example, for propositions agreement may mean simply non-contradiction, for things it may mean acting on the first so that it brings us to the second, for inaccessible objects it may mean substituting hypothetical objects whose manipulation will result in predictable consequences. The beings corresponded to are whatever enters into finite experience. Reality, both as the legacy of past experience and content of future experience, must be continuous with present experience in order to be a proper subject for truth claims. That our thought does not create the object means that something remains when anyone's particular thought is annihilated, but it may not remain in precisely the same shape, since its determinations for us are the result of human judgments, humanly constructed.

That reality is independent of the knower "means that there is something in every experience that escapes our arbitrary control. If it be a sensible experience it coerces our attention; if a sequence, we cannot invert it; if we compare two terms we can come to only one result. There is a push, an urgency, within our very experience, against which we are on the whole powerless, and which drives us in a direction that is the destiny of our belief" (MT, 45). The question of whether there is a 'Ding an sich' or an 'absolute' which is behind and accounts for this coercive feature of experience is in principle unanswerable as long as we remain on the phenomenal level of experience. The whole sweep of pragmatic arguments, not only by James but by Peirce and Dewey, has been to demonstrate that any other originary stance is necessarily speculative and unverifiable. But within phenomenal experience invariant relations, both of physical fact and theoretical terms, can be demonstrated. Thus, we can connect relatively less fixed parts of our experience to relatively more fixed ones without any appeal to extra-experiential beings so that the notion of truth as what is opposed to mere arbitrariness on our part can grow up inside of individual human life.

Therefore, the pragmatic position that concrete truth for us will always be that way of thinking in which our various experiences most profitably combine provides as sure a foothold for nonarbitrary truth as can be provided by any believer in an independent realm of reality. The concrete conditions under which our thinking actually takes place do not permit us to play fast and loose with the order in which experiences come to us without suffering the consequences. And those who appeal to a non-experiential basis for their truth claims, such as is implied in the correspondence formula, are making idle statements of no help in determining any actual truth. Such an empty formula becomes meaningful only insofar as its stated relation of subject to predicate can be shown to be operative within the leading of finite experiences, in which case it is no longer a mere correspondence but the actual working out of "a leading that is worthwhile." Objectivity and independence in truth, instead of being undermined by the pragmatic insistence on the irreducibly human component of truth, actually receive their first clear explanation and verifiable support.

James locates the genesis of the mistaken notion of correspondence with reality as a sort of copying, in the ordinary understanding of mental terms as images and real terms as sensations (MT, 50,ff). This disjunction entered into the philosophical tradition with Aristotle, who distinguishes between mental images and sensations.[6] While this explanation may be adequate for the recognition of simple objects, like clocks, it cannot account for more complex notions of agreement, such as that clocks function as time-keeping mechanisms, since no image adequately conveys this meaning. Knowing as copying seems plausible because it contributes to a more fundamental relationship to natural phenomena, one which is of utmost importance. This is our ability to have our expectancies in regard to phenomena fulfilled. What passes for 'copying' is actually a symbolic 'fit,' in the sense of determining expectations rightly.

The pragmatist, therefore, does not ask with what true ideas agree but what concrete difference in actual life an idea's being true will make. The practical difference true ideas make is that they can be corroborated and verified. False ideas cannot. By an idea's verification is meant that it leads us into or towards other parts of experience, and the connections thus made or transitions undergone are found to be progressive, harmonious, and satisfactory. "This function of agreeable leading is what we mean by an idea's verification" (PM, 97). Thoughts are true just insofar as they are valuable instruments of action. Rorty has picked up James's criticism of thought "as a passive mirror" but mistakenly thinks that the alternative is some sort of conversation.[7] James instead argues that "the fundamental fact about our experience is that it is a process of change" and the ascertaining of truth is one way we have of interacting with reality so as to bring about change favorable to ourselves (MT, 54). Instead of passively reflecting reality or even reflecting on it or conversing about it, we help to actively bring about the reality in the very process of knowing.

Therefore, I think that the revolutionary nature of James's pragmatic theory is easier to recognize if it is frankly acknowledged that his new wine bursts the old bottles. Pragmatic truth is not the agreement of proposition with reality, but an expression of the anticipated or actual successful completion of a worthwhile leading. It explains the mediating experience that, if successfully completed, has come to be called 'true.' In fact, the whole pivotal sixth chapter in *Pragmatism* is structured as a refutation of the correspondence theory of truth. James again begins, somewhat misleadingly, by claiming that both pragmatists and intellectualists accept as a matter of course the dictionary definition of truth as agreement with reality. But he ends the chapter by concluding that those who reject the pragmatic theory of truth and yet accept the formula of truth as agreement with reality, are holding onto "an absolutely meaningless abstraction" (PM, 113). They are falling back on unnamed forms of agreeing and denying that it means copying, leading, fitting or any process pragmatically definable. In the intervening pages he explains the pragmatic theory of truth by contrasting it to the correspondence or agreement theory of truth.

3. Truth as Satisfactory Working or Leading

On the common sense level of matters of fact potentially verifying processes serve as well as full validations (PM, 101ff). We are social beings and depend on the claims of the wider community. Furthermore, since things exist in kinds and not just singly, we expect that direct verification of specimens of one kind will likewise apply to others of the same kind. We can, of course, be mistaken in either instance. If any of the beliefs held in common have not been verified concretely by somebody, then the whole superstructure can collapse, and if I have mistakenly included some phenomenon as a member of a class when it was not, then my conclusion will also be false. But the residual margin of error is tolerated, since it is literally impossible for everyone to confirm every one of their beliefs and so manifestly advantageous to accept beliefs confirmed by others.

Relations among purely mental ideas can also be true or false, but differ from matters of fact in that they can be absolute and necessary. Propositions can be framed and operations performed which, because they are internally related, are necessarily the case. James thought that such ideal frameworks followed from the very structure of our thinking. In any case, they provide invaluably reliable patterns. When sensible facts of experience are subsumed under such systems of logical or mathematical truth, the marriage of fact and theory can prove endlessly fertile. If the sensible objects have been rightly subsumed, their truth can even be determined in advance of verification.

Thus, both abstract relations and sense experiences limit our options and range of actions. "Between the coercions of the sensible order and those of the ideal order, our mind is thus wedged tightly. Our ideas must agree with realities, be such realities concrete or abstract, be they facts or be they principles, under penalty of endless inconsistency and frustration" (PM, 101). This agreement means once again an affair of leading. "True ideas lead us into useful verbal and conceptual quarters as well as directly up to useful sensible termini. They lead to consistency, stability and flowing human intercourse" (103). This practical understanding of 'agreement' in terms of unimpeded action or termination in directly verifiable sensible experiences underlines the instrumental nature of conceptual organizations of experience. Scientific explanations are not literal disclosures of reality, but ways of handling the flux of experience satisfactorily according to our interests.

But it does not follow that scientific theories, or any other explanatory schema, can be chosen with impunity. The theory must work, that is, mediate between all previous truths and the relevant phenomenon to be explained. Thus, our theories are tightly wedged. But the fit is seldom perfect, and sometimes alternate theoretic models equally satisfy these truth conditions. In such cases we choose between them for subjective reasons, inclining to the kind of theory to which we are already partial, such as the more elegant one or the one most parsimonious, as when 'Occam's razor' is invoked.

The pragmatic account of truths in the plural, of processes that lead us successfully on our way, dipping into sensible experience as often as is necessary to confirm the beliefs at issue, utterly displaces the notion of 'the Truth' as such. Truth is a collective name for verification processes, just like health, wealth, and strength, are collective names for other processes in life. Health is nothing more than the processes that produce it; it is not something prior to or in addition to a healthily functioning system. Truth is made in the course of experience and no more precedes it than health pre-exists a functioning organism. The correspondence or agreement theory of truth, by contrast, presupposes that the truth relation absolutely obtains apart from any verification process. It assumes a pre-existent condition that the confirmatory process only ratifies. But such claims for 'the' truth turn very vague indeed as soon as one tries to say what this truth is, apart from any way of having to do with it.

The experiential origin of the fallacy of holding that all claims about reality are already true or false, apart from any determination of their truth or falsity, can be found in the fact that in our world things come in similar kinds, similarly related. Therefore, one great use of knowing a truth about something is that one verification process can stand in for many others. This more often leads us into a universe of discourse, than into direct confirmation of the claim at issue. Great advantages accrue to us in bypassing repetitive and tedious confirmation processes. Thus, whatever plausibility attaches to the rationalist belief that truth simply is, follows from forgetting the practical fact that many ideas work better by their indirect or possible verification than by direct verification. Like health and wisdom, truth denotes habitual processes that need not always be exercised in order for the classifying term to be correctly applied.

The absolutely true, like the perfectly wise person, "is that ideal vanishing-point towards which we imagine that all our temporary truths will some day converge" (PM, 106-107). As a matter of fact, whatever truths we claim are always only tentative and are subject to subsequent experiential disconfirmation. This regulative notion of a potentially better truth to be established can legislate retroactively. This can fallaciously be taken as proving that the truth always was, even if we had earlier been mistaken. Instead, this process of re-definition and re-confirmation in new circumstances constitutes the concrete process of making true. The beliefs we hold as true are so much experience funded. Because reality means reality as experienced, both reality and truth are processes, and the truths *for us* can never legitimately be reified into *the* truth.

4. The Practical Character of Our Beliefs

James's explanation of the relation of facts to beliefs in this process of determining truths anticipates what has later been called 'the hermeneutic circle.' However, his version uniquely includes praxis. Because of its neglect in the secondary literature and its central importance to the pragmatic theory of truth, it deserves to be quoted in full.

> In the realm of truth-processes facts come independently and determine our beliefs provisionally. But these beliefs make us act, and as fast as they do so, they bring into sight or into existence new facts which re-determine the beliefs accordingly. So the whole coil and ball of truth, as it rolls up, is the product of a double influence. Truths emerge from facts; but they dip forward into facts again and add to them; which facts again create or reveal new truth (the word is indifferent) and so on indefinitely. The 'facts' themselves meanwhile are not *true*. They simply *are*.. Truth is the function of the beliefs that start and terminate among them (PM, 108).

This passage makes clear the radical reconstruction of epistemology and theories of truth that James is inaugurating. The starting point in concrete experiences exposes the emptiness of the appeal to agreement in the correspondence theory of truth, since such agreement, being merely a euphemism for a unique and unanalyzable relation, is no explanation. James's concrete turn in epistemology emphasizes the practical character of our beliefs, which both respond to and anticipate facts. Such facts, through their resistance to our reconstructions, force us to take account of them, which we do both by forming new beliefs and by acting on them. This emphasis on action rather than contemplation derives from the fact that as humans we find ourselves within a world with which we have to do. We are in the world as participants and not as spectators. Thinking is therefore part of a larger action loop.

The beliefs we form in response to facts alter our interactions, producing new facts, of which we again have to take account. Only by reflection on this interaction of facts and beliefs do we discriminate what belongs to each, and different interests will result in different divisions. As James says, it does not matter whether we say that we "create or reveal new truth" (PM, 108). There is no obvious line of demarcation, and in the unreflective experience such distinctions are moot. The old rationalist controversy over whether we create reality and truth, as the idealists argue, or discover them, as the empiricists argue, results from reflectively reifying as disjunctive alternatives what is operative within experience as a unified, interactive process. This interactive character of beliefs and facts is what renders impossible any simplistic comparison of truth claims with reality and accounts for the naiveté of the correspondence theory of truth, which assumes as self-evident a relation that is inherently ambiguous.

Situations simply are, but the beliefs we hold in regard to them can subsequently be found to be true or false. Before the truth conditions have been clarified and the actions taken which demonstrate in which respect these conditions are meant, it is idle to say that some mysterious agreement between beliefs and reality already obtained. Before these truth conditions and actions set up what is at issue, it does not make any sense to say that this as-yet-to-be-determined relation already was. Exactly 'what' was? You cannot give any meaning to the word until the 'what' has come to be. Werner Heisenberg makes the same point in regard to 'gravity' and the old question of whether it existed before Newton formulated the law of gravity, and Hanson makes the point in regard to whether Einstein's famous equation could have expressed a fact a million years ago.[8] It makes no sense, therefore, to say that something that was both just formulated in a determinate way and just found to be the case in this precise sense, was always true even though no one ever held that belief before, or if a similar belief were held, had not been verified according to the terms of that belief. But through retroactive legislation we can and do decree that what we have only in the present determined to be true shall now be applied to all relevant historical references. This is part of the on-going reconstruction that typifies the process of making true and which is sometimes misconceived as constituting past situations rather than as revising our opinions about them.

Only when it is recognized that the rationalist belief in rigor and finality is a chimera can the constructive rather than destructive nature of the pragmatist hypothesis also be recognized. There is no loss in substituting tentative for absolute standards if absolute standards are impossible. James argues for breaking with absolutistic hopes and adopting his "inductive view of the conditions of belief:" "Satisfactoriness has to be measured by a multitude of standards, of which some, for aught we know, may fail in any given case; and what is more satisfactory than any alternative in sight, may to the end be a sum of *pluses* and *minuses*, concerning which we can only trust that by ulterior corrections and improvements a maximum of the one and a minimum of the other may some day be approached" (MT, 40).

5. The Concrete Point of View

As was pointed out in chapter 3 the "concrete point of view which pragmatism assumes" must be clearly understood or else the misconceptions handed on over the centuries within the philosophical tradition will inevitably distort what is being said (MT, 99). James's explanation of truth can be properly understood only against the background of those structures which characterize our active being in the world. It is a direct challenge to the neo-Kantian claim that epistemology determines what we can say about the world because it argues that our situation within the world determines what sort of epistemology and truth-theory is viable. The question that pragmatism always asks in regard to any belief thought to be true is "what concrete difference will its being true make in anyone's actual life?" (PM, 97). When we put the question experientially we find out that we call beliefs 'true' insofar as we can verify them. By following their guidance one's experiences will lead one to another in a way that is "progressive, harmonious, satisfactory." Truths are thus disclosed as being "invaluable instruments of action," but not in any narrow sense (97). Only when the features of concrete experience which James developed over the years are recognized can we refute the accusation that his theory of truth is an irresponsible instrumentalism.

The concrete point of view also means remaining on the phenomenal level of description, "taking our perceptual experience of action at its face-value, and following the analogies which it suggests" (SPP, 108). Since James brackets the question of the nature of the reality which is known, any self-evident intuitive appeals to it are by definition only provisional and tentative and subject to further revision. How such knowledge and truth claims function can be fully explored without determining whether they disclose the inner nature of reality. In other words, the ultimate truth of particular truth claims is methodologically excluded.

Particular truths are verifiable in terms of their successful accomplishment, but whether they are true *simpliciter* cannot in principle be decided. Like Nietzsche, James's explication of particular truths, truths with a small 't,' involves denying Truth with a capital 'T,' that is, the metaphysical understanding of a univocal truth which dominated the philosophical tradition.[9] Belief in the Truth, like belief in the Law, the Good, the Rational, or the Self, are all rationalistic idols of the tribe, remnants both of an impulse to substantialize processes and to inhibit anxiety by providing absolutely certain answers to the mysteries of the universe. Such attitudes refuse to recognize that truths, like laws and languages, are humanly produced. "The whole notion of *the* truth is an abstraction from the fact of truths in the plural, a mere useful summarizing phrase like *the* Latin Language or *the* Law".... Truth grafts itself on previous truth, modifying it in the process, just as idiom grafts itself on previous idiom, and law on previous law" (PM, 116).

When James does develop his own radically empiricist metaphysics, it only reinforces the instrumental character of knowledge and his reconstruction of truth. The nature of reality turns out to be only what can be grasped within experience. This is evident in passages about reality which recur so often in his last book, *Some Problems of Philosophy*, that they form a *leitmotif* or structural framework. "If the aim of philosophy were the taking full possession of all reality by the mind, then nothing short of the whole of immediate perceptual experience could be the subject-matter of philosophy, for only in such experience is reality intimately and concretely found" (SPP, 53). But as finite beings we can only partake of a few passing moments of experience and therefore must build it out by ideal symbols. Although such conceptual extensions are tremendously useful, they do not encompass the deeper features of reality. Concrete percepts are primordial and conceptual systems are "secondary and ministerial forms of being" and however little may be given in the flux of our hourly experience, "what is given is absolutely real" (58-59).

He then argues that concepts derive their meaning from their intentionality and this insistence on the priority of lived experience ties together his instrumentalism, experientialism, phenomenal descriptivism, and perspectivism. "A concept can only be *designative*; and...the concept 'reality,' which we restore to immediate perception, is no new conceptual creation, but only a kind of practical relation to our Will, *perceptively experienced*" (SPP, 60). Concepts designate various grouped sensations, which are the only verifiable aspect of knowledge claims. But they are verifiable only insofar as they are grouped according to a purpose and influence events. To know what things are we can only apply the pragmatic rule, that is, ask what difference in practical experience any claim is supposed to make. Valid conceptual claims are descriptions of the fact that "certain *specific and verifiable connexions* [sic.] are found among the parts of the experiential flux" (65-66). These connections can be concretely or actually perceived in the experiential flux, also "abstractly designated as our 'world'" (67). For each finite individual system, "the world hangs together from next to next in a variety of ways, so that when you are off of one thing you can always be on to something else, without ever dropping out of your world" (69).

One passage succinctly characterizes and defends the concrete point of view. It begins:

> A material fact may indeed be different from what we feel it to be, but what sense is there in saying that a feeling, which has no other nature than to be felt, is not *as* it is felt? Psychologically considered, our experiences resist conceptual reduction, and our fields of consciousness, taken simply *as such*, remain just what they appear, even tho facts of a molecular order should prove to be the signals of the appearance (SPP, 78).

Once it is recognized that his appeals to concrete experience refer to his own methodological procedure, then we will avoid the mistake of assuming that what he is saying applies only to a subset of discourse and praxis, namely, the psychological. The structures to which he has both appealed and developed in *Principles* are part of his concrete analysis of active being in the world. He argues for the priority of concrete experience in all explanations because, no matter how sophisticated, they are all ways of organizing experience. This human dimension of experience cannot be reduced to any other without distortion, that is, without losing sight that explanation as such is a human way of appropriating the world. Furthermore, even those physical facts which come to light in scientific explanation are understood hermeneutically, as signs, and signs cannot displace their own conditions, namely the context in which they come to be and function as signs.

The passage continues:

> Biography is the concrete form in which all that is is immediately given; the perceptual flux is the authentic stuff of each of our biographies, and yields a perfect effervescence of novelty all the time....Men of science and philosophy, the moment they forget their theoretic abstractions, live in their biographies as much as anyone else, and believe as naively that fact even now is making, and that they themselves, by doing 'original work,' help to determine what the future shall become (SPP, 78).[10]

James's frequent appeals to our perceptual experience cannot be to any empiricist sense data or to behaviorist experimental data, as is clear from his clarification of "the concrete form" in which everything is experienced as being nothing less than biography. What is experienced cannot be detached, except speculatively and theoretically, from the way we experience it, and his explorations of the structures according to which we appropriate the world are meant to fill out how we live biographically. Formal structures, whether developed in science, philosophy, politics, or religion, are often taken to be the very structures of reality. Against this mistaken realism James argues that the facts so identified are novel constructions resulting from the interaction of self and world and not replications of reality. Despite the fact that science must presuppose causal determination in its explanations, for instance, scientists make choices which they expect will change future events with the same impunity as the rest of us, and do not refer their own actions to some previously determinate state of affairs. That they bracket their own complicity in their discoveries of fact in order to follow their disciplinary paradigms should not blind us to the concrete structures nonetheless operative.

It should by now be obvious that James is developing a theory of knowledge and truth congruous with the phenomenal level of experience. To do so he implicitly relies on a concrete analysis of human interaction. He frequently takes refuge, for instance, in appeals to commonsense, which allows him to presuppose an everyday world of experience, but without having to systematically develop its structures or provide sufficient grounds for its acceptance. He consistently argues that our apprehension of a "much-at-onceness" is the originating experience which commonsense both presupposes and displaces. Commonsense is the first and longest-lived successful organization of experience and as such paradigmatic for the organizing impulse which defines the human response to the encountered much-at-onceness.

This experiential unity of consciousness or much-at-onceness is one of the structures of concrete experience. Recall that it is characterized, not as a mere chaotic overabundance of undifferentiated sensations, but as process with a temporal directionality of those objects brought into focus through awareness. In *Principles* this much-at-onceness is called the 'stream of thought,' while in the *Briefer Course* it is called the 'stream of consciousness.' "And the *occurrence*, in the steam, of objects which, *when they occur, occur with specific noetic fringes developable into termini*, is the initial peculiarity of experience to which all I write about may be traced. . . ." This is further characterized as *"psychological analysis,"* which also has to be explained logically (TCW,II, 369). The explanation turns out to be even more comprehensive. This primordial experience first explained in his concrete psychology is then developed in his epistemology as a worthwhile leading and, finally, in his metaphysics as pure experience. Only with his metaphysics do the concrete structures he has been using all along begin to receive a sustained, systematic development.

This is why James's pragmatic theory of truth cannot be reduced without distortion to some formalized validation procedure. Nicholas Rescher's attempts to do so, tearing pragmatic methodology out of its vital connections with being in the world, only highlights the losses that are sustained in shifting the focus of interest to ungrounded theoretic structures.[11] In chapter 6 of *Pragmatism* James italicizes the following definition of truth: *"True ideas are those that we can assimilate, validate, corroborate and verify. False ideas are those that we cannot"* (PM, 97). But he also says that this is what truth means because it expresses"the practical difference it makes to us to have true ideas." In the five preceding chapters, as well as in the sixth, he has carefully prepared the context in which this cryptic formula of truth can be understood by grounding his theory of truth in human praxis. He had earlier explained what he meant by such validation: the "only test of probable truth is what works best in the way of leading us, what fits every part of life best and combines with the collectivity of experience's demands, nothing being omitted" (44). The reference to probable truth and interchangeableness of 'pragmatic truth' with 'pragmatic method' are indicators that his entire epistemology and truth theory, as well as the concrete psychology on which it is based, are expressions of the limitations of the human coalescence with reality.

His paradigm of absolutely adequate knowledge is always that of a "conflux or identification, such as common sense assumes in sense perception where the sensation *is* the object" (TCW,II, 538). All other models of knowledge are inadequate, since they are more or less symbolic or representative, despite the fact that they are projections towards that reality and that as finite beings we rest in these symbols as if we had adequate knowledge. They express the necessarily tentative nature of all expressions of reality until humanity and reality are one analogously with the identification of sensation and object. The possibility is left open that such a unity of being and knowing might some day be accomplished, but since there is as yet no way of knowing that it has actually transpired, James develops theories of knowledge and truth that can still operate successfully in such a world lacking ultimate certainty.

After his third crisis he finally gives up the hope that such certainty can ever be rationally grounded, and therefore his theories of knowledge and truth that were in principle discardable when the truth about reality as such was finally known, can never be superceded. It would also follow that the ideal of absolute truth, as experienced on the level of one's own unreflective identification of sensation and object, must fulfill the same conditions as representative truth if it is to pass from the domain of private feeling to that of public discourse. Therefore, appeals to intuition,while not ruled out as a preliminary injunction, can never function as the court of last resort in epistemologies and theories of truth, even though they might be sufficient for personal satisfaction and appropriate in mystical discourse.

In hindsight, this gives added importance to his procedure of beginning experientially. Although it took James personally some time to give up hope for an eventual rational absolute certainty, he had already provided good arguments for the impossibility of such grounding in his early recognition of the irreducibly subjective character of all human organizations of experience and, more explicitly, in his criticism of the correspondence theory of truth. While he continued to recognize the personal feeling of certainty in private experiences, both ordinary and mystical, and to hope for an ultimate consummatory experience, he also argued that since, in principle, rational groundings of these experiences and hopes are not themselves susceptible to experiential corroboration, the radical finitude and provisional character of the pragmatic outlook could not be overcome by any rational move.

James calls the 'rationalist fallacy' the habit of abstracting ideas like 'truth' and 'reality' from "the concretes of experience" and then opposing them to that same experience (PM, 109). All the claims of goods like wealth, health, and truth are conditional on "the concrete benefits we gain" (110). Because of the strength of the benefits and the calamity of their absence, we can come to call some goods absolute and even consider them unconditional, but we cannot take these characterizations literally without running into absurdities. To claim, as both idealist and empiricist rationalists do, that truth is indifferent to the experiential flux and that its obligations "have nothing to do with our practical interests or personal reasons" is to render it purely speculative, innocuous, and of effete interest only [109]. But the "admission that there are conditions that limit the application of the abstract imperative" is to return us to the pragmatic treatment of truth (111). It is pernicious to oppose epistemology and truth theories to "psychological facts...relative to each thinker, and to the accidents of his life" (109).

This appeal to the concrete situation in which the meaning, relevance, obligation, and outcome of truth are determined does not "destroy all objective standards," and lead to unbridled relativism as its critics, past and present, claim. Rorty, for instance, approvingly characterizes James as engaging in "floating, ungrounded conversations," while Myers and Suckiel disapprovingly call him "subjectivistic to an unacceptable degree.[12] The concrete situation, despite James's tendency to conflate it with any actual experience going on, is indeed an appeal to the actual configuration of such individualized events, but only as understood within his characterization of the structures of such experiences. The criteria for the determination of truth includes mediating "between the whole body of funded truths squeezed from the past and the coercions of the world of sense" (PM, 111-112). Our minds operate under this "immense pressure of objective control," and the penalty for not being perspicuous enough about how we relate our beliefs about relevant past experiences, the actual configuration of our present perceptions, and the satisfactions we seek, will be experientially brought home to us. If we misjudge, consequences follow, as surely as they do when we perform the marriage of all the elements congruently with their actual interrelationship.

We do not always tap wisely into the funded character of experience, which is bequeathed to us through society and to which we add our mite. Not all of us interpret correctly the actual situation we perceive through our senses, nor do we always bring realizable expectations to bear on the situation. However, all of us are subject to the sanctions experience exacts. As James puts it: "Woe to him whose beliefs play fast and loose with the order which realities follow in his experience: they will lead him nowhere or else make false connexions [sic.]" (PM, 99). Not everyone who has beliefs which have arisen in their concrete situation reflectively evaluates those beliefs by taking into consideration the structures of the concrete situation which James delineates. But because he does not sufficiently distinguish between the concrete situation as subjectively experienced and as objectively structured it is possible to read the texts and miss the constraints he is placing on the legitimacy of individual organizations of experience.

However, he does frequently criticize the claim that some particular belief is true merely because someone, in an actual situation, thinks it so because it is satisfactory to them. He can criticize such claims, not because he has access to some uncontroversial set of standards which are universal and apply equally to everyone, but because he has identified the conditions according to which judgments are made that have been thought over time to be the best instances of useful and beneficial beliefs. Having identified the process according to which those beliefs have been generated which we have then called 'true,' he can judge whether this same process has been followed in any particular case or, more to the point, he can himself apply the criteria derived from this process.

As it turns out, part of the structure of those processes found to be successful in our organization of experience is this very confirmation by all those interested in the outcome. It is absolutely necessary to explicitly develop these structures of concrete experience, to which James appeals but does not identify as such, if we are to avoid the relativism that follows from conflating them with every particular concrete experience. They are obviously related, but not identical, and the objectivity that James claims in his appeal to concrete experience can be obtained only by specifying their precise relationship and clarifying the structures that he has creatively derived through his concrete analysis. The recovery and explication of these structures has been undertaken throughout this book.

6. Truth as Value for Life

It is a central tenet of pragmatism that "truth is *one species of good,* and not, as is usually supposed, a category distinct from good, and co-ordinate with it. *The true is the name of whatever proves itself to be good in the way of belief, and good, too, for definite, assignable reasons*" (PM, 42). Some of these reasons were given in the second chapter of *Pragmatism* as part of the explanation of how we settle into new opinions and others are given later in the same chapter in clarifying why truth is a species of good. In a letter written in 1904 James said: "But this opens the whole subject of what the word 'truth' means, and I cannot enter that except to say that if inferences from 'good for life' to 'true' were on principle forbidden, not religion but the whole notion of truth would probably have to be the thing overhauled and revised" (TCW,II, 350).

If there were no good for life in possessing true ideas, or if they were positively harmful, we would shun rather than pursue them. They could, of course, be neutral in relation to life, but then some other motivation would have to be uncovered for the high esteem in which they are held. In his genealogy of intellectual drives in the two "The Sentiment of Rationality" articles James explores the various motivations and shows how even the search for truth 'for its own sake' is part of a necessary ordering of experience if human life is to be developed, preserved, and enhanced. It has been found, through trial and error, that some of our beliefs are not only agreeable to hold, or consistent with our other beliefs,but also help in life's practical struggles. If there were other beliefs that helped in the struggle better, then those are the ones we should pursue.

The only caveat is that such beliefs, even if practically helpful, should be dropped if they "*incidentally clashed with other greater vital benefits*" (PM, 42). Taken abstractly, as a rule for beliefs, the objection immediately arises that choosing as true what is better for us to believe provides no reasons for not believing in whatever strikes our fancy. But to understand the force of the injunction that such beliefs not clash with other vital beliefs one must adopt the pragmatic method of thinking in terms of concrete situations. In real life the vital benefits of beliefs with which any newly considered belief is most likely to clash are other beliefs we also hold. Whether we like it or not, our beliefs "carry supernumerary features" (43). The "marriage function" of reconciling new beliefs with old while accommodating the experiences which engendered the new beliefs is integral to the process of establishing beliefs as true. The formula which expresses this best has already been given: pragmatism's "only test of probable truth is what works best in the way of leading us, what fits every part of life best and combines with the collectivity of experience's demands, nothing being omitted" (44).

The importance of this methodological shift from constructing and criticizing abstract theories of truth to investigating how truth functions in actual situations is explicitly recognized by H. S. Thayer.[13] He points out that for pragmatists, truth and falsity are not properties of ideas, nor even the relation of ideas to facts, but instead are characteristics of the performance of ideas in situations. The traits of a situation do not inhere in its parts, whether of ideas, beliefs, statements or single facts, taken on their own. In James's functional method of analysis the sizing up of situations "is subject to those critical canons of evidence and inference that govern our talk generally about the world." Thus, "describing a *situation* is an empirical affair of recording and interpreting observed data, even making predictions....The value and accuracy of such judgments depends in part upon the description. But descriptive appraisals of situations are themselves subject to similar critical considerations of effectiveness and relative usefulness according to a further order of purposes and interests."[14]

In an unpublished fragment James criticizes rational explanations that render ordinary phenomenal experience nonsensical and thus destroy rather than reconstruct it. In doing so he asks, "If the intellect can only prey on life destructively how came life to engender it?"[15] The assertion that truths are those beliefs which have proven good for life follows from reflections on the Darwinian evolutionary model of the origin of species as it applies to the origin of consciousness.[16]

Already in the 1878 article, "Remarks on 'Spencer's Definition of Mind as Correspondence'," James argued for the irreducibility of "the teleological factor of interest" in determining when we have successfully cognized reality, that is, when our beliefs have contributed to the survival and development of a human form of life.

In "The Sentiment of Rationality" he argues that the philosophic drive for a comprehensive explanation of reality will always be stymied because no *necessary* connection with existence can ever be made. Since "the intellect is really built up of practical interests," a practical stability must suffice.[17] In *Principles* he argues that the cerebral hemispheres developed in addition to the lower nerve centers with their automatic reflexes because the flexibility thus gained more than compensated for the loss of the obviously advantageous quick reflexes in the battle for survival (PP,I, 25-87). And it is the evolution of the cerebral hemispheres which made possible the whole superstructure of cognitive thinking.

Cognitive thinking would not have evolved in tandem with the emergence and development of the cerebral hemispheres in a complicated process of spontaneous variation or, if developed, would not have survived, if its functioning were not contributory to the life process. The bridge from the claim that cognitive thinking practically contributes to survival to the claim that the purpose of thinking is to contribute to the continuance and enhancement of life is made by linking the arguments for the impossibility of the intellect passively receiving and mirroring reality with the arguments for the necessarily purposeful character of all conceptual organizations of experience. Although the purposes are many, they all share this characteristic of being spontaneous organizations of experience. Why organize experience? Because it is impossible to survive otherwise. But why organize it in one way rather than another? Because any particular organizing of experience answers both to subjective needs and objective constraints. Such organizations of experience are thus irreducibly pluralistic and both partially historically conditioned and partially idiosyncratic.

In the chapter on "Pragmatism's Conception of Truth," which is the logical culmination of the earlier chapters of *Pragmatism*, James once again argues for the inseparability of analyses of truth from their value for life. He begins his explanation of truths as what can be verified by reminding us "of the fact that the possession of true thoughts means everywhere the possession of invaluable instruments of action" (PM, 97). The importance to human life of true beliefs about matters of fact is undeniable given our experience in the world of both extremely harmful and extremely useful realities. The contention that the possession of truth in such a world is an end in itself appears ludicrous when contrasted with its obvious role as a means towards other vital satisfactions.

If I am lost in the woods, it is of vital interest to know whether the path I choose to follow will lead me out or not. True ideas are true because they lead us to act in ways that are practically important. Much of what we hold as true is not immediately useful and forms part of our collective memories, both in persons and in physical storage. The usefulness, in the long run, of such stores of extra truths is obvious. We label as true whatever can or has come through the verification process. We bother to engage in the process because such a habitual way of acting has been, and continues to be, useful. We would never have engaged in such actions in the first place, nor placed great value in ascertaining what we then labeled 'true,' unless they were useful in this broad sense of the enhancement of human life.

Thus is explained in the context of theories of truth what James has already developed in his concrete descriptions as the structure of conscious experience whereby some moments may lead us to other moments that satisfactorily complete the earlier ones. He calls this on the phenomenal or common sense level *"a leading that is worth while"* (PM, 98). True thoughts are those that allow us to make advantageous connection with the particulars of experience. It is worth repeating again what C. I. Lewis later summarized as the radical import of the pragmatists' reconstruction of truth as a species of 'good': "For the pragmatist, there can be no final division between 'normative' and 'descriptive.' The validity of any standard of correctness has reference to some order of 'descriptive facts'; and every determination of fact reflects some judgment of values and constitutes an imperative for conduct. The validity of cognition itself is inseparable from that final test of it which consists in some valuable result of the action which it serves to guide. Knowledge — so the pragmatist conceives — is for the sake of action; and action is directed to realization of what is valuable."[18] In the eighth chapter of *Pragmatism* James emphasizes the practical origins of truth: "On pragmatic principles we cannot reject any hypothesis if consequences useful to life flow from it" (131). To be designated as true, immediate usefulness must additionally square well with life's other uses.

According to the pragmatic method differences of meaning are differences of practice, and this implies that truths have practical consequences. The wider humanistic pragmatism goes beyond such a restrictive method in claiming that "the truth of any statement *consists in the consequences*" (MT, 38). To accept Dewey's and Schiller's method of inductive generalization requires a paradigm shift. Thus it is not subject to refutation piecemeal, by showing that isolated statements are contradictory, for instance, but stands or falls as a whole outlook and should properly be weighed against its alternatives. Its main alternative is rationalism, with its belief in an eternal and unchangeable reason which can exactly understand reality as it exists in itself. The humanists deny that any such literal 'objectivity' is possible, and substitute for it the 'subjective' qualities of usefulness, elegance, and congruity with other beliefs.

Both hold that reality is independent of our beliefs. For the humanist this means that something within experience escapes our arbitrary control, whether this is the coerciveness of sensible experience over our attention or the order of sequences or the various logical relationships. No matter how strong the belief in extra-experiential realities, they can enter into our calculations as revealing themselves and being correctly grasped by us only insofar as they enter into finite experiences. Therefore, even for believers in extra-experiential reality, the only way that we can know that we have in fact recognized such a reality in our truth claims is to apply the pragmatic methodology within the fabric of our experiences. "Absolute or no absolute, the concrete truth *for us* will always be that way of thinking in which our various experiences most profitably combine" (MT, 47).

By sharply distinguishing between what truth means and how truth is arrived at, critics accuse the concrete account of confusing psychology with logic. But both accounts require a psychological vehicle, if by 'psychological' we mean the complex functions of our knowing in its full, concrete particulars. Meanings do not descend from the heavens but are reflectively determined in the course of experience. "The *full* facts of cognition, whatever be the way in which we talk about them, even when we talk most abstractly, stand inalterably given in the actualities and possibilities of the experience-continuum" (MT, 85).

Satisfactoriness and truth can be opposed only when the satisfactoriness is narrowly construed as what is felt here and now, and truth is taken abstractly, as what is verified in the long run. We know from past experience that presently satisfactory beliefs sometimes turn out to be false. But in the present, concrete moment of experience each person's true beliefs, that is, those which provide the maximum amount of satisfaction, and abstract truth, that is, long-run satisfactoriness, necessarily coincide. Temporality is a fundamental fact of experience and the long range satisfactoriness that characterizes abstract truth is the sum of day by day satisfactory confirmations. It is not something additional to them. Each such retroactive judgment from a later point of view compares the earlier with the later and confirms or disconfirms the beliefs held.

The popular and traditional position holds that the humanist claim that present beliefs are held to be true because they are satisfactory can easily be refuted by comparing such beliefs to an extrinsic standard, namely whether they, besides being momentarily satisfactory, also correspond to independent realities. The humanistic counter-argument is that what is called 'correspondence to independent realities' must be interpreted in terms of some actual procedure such as that of concrete satisfactoriness if it is to be meaningful at all, rather than a merely empty formula. It is further alleged by rationalist critics that experience itself needs such an absolute support or foundation. But what is the basis for this belief in absolute foundations? Each such foundation must itself be founded until ultimately some foundation just is self supporting, like the uncaused cause of the old Aristotelian metaphysics ("the elephant and the tortoise over again"). Why, then, not let finite experience itself be self-supporting, since "somewhere being must immediately breast nonentity"? (MT, 56).

7. Objective Truth

Already in James's time, his account, like Schiller's and Dewey's, was criticized for emphasizing the subjective side of truth to the exclusion of the objective. His response is just as cogent today as then. The charge of subjectivism can be sustained only by clinging to the dogmatic view of reality characteristic of rationalism, which was already refuted by him. Not James, but Descartes, Hume, and Kant had relegated reality to the sidelines, making it wait upon experiential evidence to usher it back into the court of philosophic discourse. Any claims appealing to or designating 'reality' as the object or source of experience had either to be strictly derived from such experience or openly postulated as a belief. In his critical reconstruction of the flux of experience James drew out the radical consequences of such an experiential starting point.

James still holds, with Pierce, that "the 'absolutely' true, meaning what no farther experience will ever alter, is that ideal vanishing-point towards which we imagine that all our temporary truths will some day converge" (PM, 106-107). But what is the use of retaining this remnant of belief in an ultimate correspondence of knowledge and reality if it is in principle unrealizable? It is homologous with the perfectly wise person or the "absolutely complete experience," and will be realized only when they are, that is, when the world is perfect and complete, which is to say, not in our lifetime. We have seen that James has already given a pragmatic equivalent of such an ideal convergence in his explanation of the revelations of later moments of experience correcting earlier ones. We have to live with as much truth as we can get, knowing it will likely be overturned tomorrow, if past history is any indication. Human experience is not static, and as it changes, so do the limits within which we recognize something as being the case. An absolute truth to be ascertained someday is a regulative notion, which can be made sense of only within our world of concrete fact, one of the salient characteristics of which is expectations about the future. What we take to be truth is largely the result of previous truths, since our beliefs "are so much experience *funded*....So far as reality means experienceable reality," then truths are changeable.

This is not to say that truths are arbitrary. One has only to recall the interactive model, also called the pragmatically hermeneutic circle earlier: facts determine our beliefs provisionally, so we act on them, which brings into existence new facts, which then re-determine beliefs (PM, 108). Truths emerge from facts but also add to facts, and these facts, in turn, create or reveal new truth. On one way of interpreting the interactive process we can claim to be merely naming what is factually given, but on an equally valid interpretation of the same process, we can claim to be participants in the creation of new truth.

The fallacy of the criticism that satisfactoriness is only a sign or mark of truth, which should more properly be characterized as the objective relation between an idea and its object, consists in the assumption that a state of being true precedes its emergence in the course of experience. After centuries of taking for granted the structures that make truth claims possible, the pragmatists have helped us realize that these very structures, for too long covered over by the unexamined belief in objectivity, embody presuppositions that cannot survive close scrutiny. The unrecognized distortions have to be made apparent as a prelude to developing a more defensible explanation. For instance, it makes no more sense to distinguish, let alone oppose, signs of truth with the objective relation of idea and object than it makes sense to oppose truth claims to truth itself, as if truth had an independent, Platonic existence.

In the actual texts, however, James argues for two inconsistent standards of objectivity. The more radical pragmatic one is the instrumental view of truth explained in terms of satisfaction (see PM, 4). As "*a leading that is worth while*," objective truth cannot be determined apart from values (98). But this is incongruently combined with the traditional notion of truth as the correspondence of thought and thing. It is sometimes characterized as a confluence of thought and thing in sense perception or as the convergence of knowledge and reality in an ideal end-time. According to instrumental truth, the "immense pressure of objective control" stems from the interactive process of mediating "between the whole body of funded truths squeezed from the past and the coercions of the world of sense," where 'sense' refers to its holistic, interpretive function that is found in our biography (111-112). According to the correspondence view the objectivity is an ideal limit of the "conflux or identification" of idea and the reality in which it terminates, "such as common sense assumes in sense perception where the sensation *is* the object"(TCW,II, 538). But even this unreconstructed remnant of the correspondence theory of truth is explained pragmatically and finally collapses into the concrete one of a harmonious leading that is worthwhile.

As soon as upholders of objective truth as correspondence begin to explain in what it consists, they must enter the Jamesian field of analysis. We can conceive of a series of ideas being successively more and more true of the same object and ask ourselves what relation, being exact, would finally end such approximations. The identity of idea and object would. Moreover, this ultimate confluence of idea and object is thought to take place in sense perception. For common sense, percepts and physical realities are held to be experientially identical. The computer keyboard which is felt and my feeling the keyboard on my desk are two aspects of the same perceptual experience. But critical reflections on common sense experience have distinguished between the keyboard 'in itself' and the keyboard 'for me' as two objects. Nonetheless, the common sense experience yields as "the absolute limit of truth" such a *"total conflux of the mind with the reality"* (MT, 87-88). Thus, for those who argue that the ideal limit is never reached, the pragmatic understanding of truth as a satisfactory working or leading provides an explanation of the only truth objectively obtainable. Likewise, for those who equate objective truth with the identity of subject and object, then James's theory of truth as confluence provides such an explanation.

But both reality in itself or as it is and absolute or incorrigible truth are ideal limits of human experience and discourse. James recognizes that the appeal to a reality independent of our experiential knowing of it is just that, an appeal. As a insistent realist, he leaves no doubts that it is a postulate to which he subscribes. He also postulates that our satisfactions grow as our approximations to this supposed reality narrow the gap between our ideas and their objects. As is suggested by the use of the word 'approximation,' the ways that ideas lead us into the neighborhood of objects is deliberately left unspecified, not because of the intrinsic vagueness of the formula, but because so many different ways of truthfully relating ideas to objects have been, and continue to be, precisely specified, for instance, in the various sciences and arts.

'Truth' and 'reality' are thus reciprocally related. "Our whole notion of a standing reality grows up in the form of an ideal limit to the series of successive termini to which our thoughts have led us and still are leading us" (MT, 88-9). Insofar as each terminus proves only provisional, it leaves us dissatisfied, and the truer idea is the one that pushes us further. This pattern leads us to anticipate an ideal limit to our searches, which would be an absolutely satisfactory terminus. The ideally perfect truth would thus be an absolute identification of idea and the reality in which it terminates. But such an ideal would never have arisen in the first place, nor would ideas have been sorted into 'true' and 'false,' "save for the greater sum of satisfactions, intellectual or practical, which the truer ones brought with them" (MT, 89). It makes no sense to argue that ideas found to be totally satisfactory, both with all other ideas and with sensory experiences, would or should not also be thought to be true accounts of reality.

Thus, to say that something is true is to say that it is satisfactory, even on the correspondence model of truth, as long as the scope of such satisfaction is kept in mind and not confused with just any satisfaction anyone happens to have at the time. Given this analysis of the relationship of objective truth to subjective satisfaction, to continue to claim that truth consists in a static relation of idea to object, leaving out the whole notion of a possible or actual satisfactory working or leading which constitutes the pragmatic account, is to prefer a truth theory based on unexamined assumptions to an account grounded in experience. Absolutely objective truth can be claimed only by abandoning any attempt at relating it to concrete experience. No appeal to an independent reality can substantiate claims to absolute truth once it is realized that "truth is only our subjective relation to realities" (MT, 89). Not objective truth, but imperialist claims to absolute truth, are refuted by the pragmatic account.

Part Five

Overcoming the Tradition

Chapter Twelve

Why Metaphysics?

James used the occasion of his presidential address before the American Psychological Association in December of 1904, to announce that he was "growing more and more interested in a certain systematic way of handling questions" and to urge others to adopt it (ERE, 79-80). He was referring to what was variously called the pragmatic method, humanism, Deweyism or Bergsonian "Philosophie nouvelle." He called his own version 'radical empiricism.' In the lecture he intended to demonstrate the efficacy of the method by applying it to the vexing problem of the experience of activity.

1. Concrete Analysis of Lived Experience

James begins by distinguishing three questions about activity that are usually confused: the psychological, the metaphysical, and the logical (ERE, 80-81). The psychological asks whether we have perceptions of activity, what they are like if we do, and seeks to identify their place and time. The metaphysical question seeks to establish whether there is in fact such a thing as activity and to determine its meaning. It asks 'what is it like?' and 'what does it do?' The logical question is better characterized as the epistemological one of how we know activity, whether by our feelings alone or by some other way. But James does not begin by clarifying each in turn. Instead he opposes to a "mere description of the surface-show of experience" his radical empiricism and approaches the issue so differently that the distinctions between the three types of questions collapse.

Radical empiricism includes both the pragmatic method and the principle of pure experience.[1] The pragmatic method begins with the postulate that differences of truth issue in differences of fact. It therefore seeks out the practical or particular issues that follow from different perspectives. James demonstrates the pragmatic consequences of his own position and that of his adversaries in terms of "assignable particular differences in anyone's experience." There has been much scholarly debate over the status of pure experience, but James says clearly in this lecture that it "is also a methodical postulate. Nothing shall be admitted as fact, it says, except what can be experienced at some definite time by some experient; and for every feature of fact ever so experienced, a definite place must be found somewhere in the final system" (ERE, 81). In response to a 1906 article criticizing radical empiricism James makes it clear that, as a methodological postulate, it does not necessarily exclude "transempirical objects," but only requires that any such noumenal beings or events have a demonstrated pragmatic value (123).[2] In a later response he makes it even clearer that radical empiricism is a strategy or methodological directive, namely, "to restrict our universe of philosophic discourse to what is experienced or, at least, experienceable," without making any judgment about the possibility or activity of non-experienced objects (125). He also clarifies the point that just because it is held that things are as we experience them it does not follow that we do not sometimes experience things distortedly or even incorrectly. He does not even bother to defend this claim, since he has always held in his writings that later events can correct or force us to reassess earlier beliefs and has always distinguished between the having of an experience and the correct explanation of it in light of other experiences and beliefs.

The two methodological postulates of radical empiricism overlap in meaning and are chiefly distinguished by the fact that the pragmatic method includes directives for validating a belief, whereas the principle of pure experience includes directives for formulating the belief in experiential terms. For the first time James has a self-consciously technical term, namely, "principle of pure experience," for what he has been characterizing as concrete experience and for that aspect of the pragmatic method as developed in *Pragmatism* that I distinguished as his 'genealogy,' but to which at the time he gave no separate name. He calls on the principle of pure experience, for instance, to demonstrate that if activity is to have any meaning at all, it must be derived from "some concrete kind of experience that can be definitely pointed out" (ERE, 81). The first step of the investigation must be to seek "the original type and model of what it means" in the stream of experience. This method of turning to an experienced fact as the first step in settling a complex question can also be recognized as a more carefully worked out formulation of his natural history method.

Radical empiricism seeks to rehabilitate and preserve "change taking place" as "a unique content of experience" (ERE, 82). Since activity means in the broadest sense "any apprehension of something *doing*" or "the bare fact of event or change," it is "in the broadest and vaguest way synonymous with the sense of 'life.'" Besides being only a methodology, therefore, radical empiricism also includes some assumptions. In explaining that life is characterized by activity, it is clear that human life is meant since it is said that we would feel it in our own subjective life, at least, even if nowhere else in the world. James then develops his concrete description of human activity: "But in this actual world of ours, as it is given, a part at least of activity comes with definite direction; it comes with desire and sense of goal; it comes complicated with resistances which it overcomes or succumbs to, and with the efforts which the feeling of resistance so often provokes; and it is in complex experiences like these that the notions of distinct agents, and of passivity as opposed to activity arise. Here also the notion of causal activity comes to birth" (82- 83). James culls from experience original models for understanding not only action, but causality and freedom.

On which concrete experience is he drawing, and how does it become available for further analysis? He refers principally to our feeling of life, our experience of "this actual world of ours, as it is given," and secondarily to the analysis of complex activity situations as found in "descriptive psychology." The meaning of activity situations can be found in psychological descriptions, but these are superficial when compared to our felt activity. "We knew the facts already," and this knowledge predates verbalization and is indispensable to it (ERE, 82-83). Felt knowing is "less spread out and separated" than verbalized description, but its inchoate experiencing is the original of which the careful descriptive enumeration merely "elaborates the obvious so as to be little more than an exercise in synonymic speech." James's unreconstructed realism is most obvious in such explanations of the transparent grasp of pre-reflective experience in exact descriptions. Later versions of phenomenology also share this naiveté.

The experience of activity is then described as it is "lived through or authentically known" (ERE 84-85). What activity is "known-as" is taken from this "complete activity in its original and first intention." He goes into detail about the "ultimate *qualia*" of "these experiences of process, obstruction, striving, strain, or release" and concludes that we cannot conceive of it as lived through except "in this dramatic shape of something sustaining a felt purpose against felt obstacles, and overcoming or being overcome.... The *percipi* in these originals of experience is the *esse*."

But this "phenomenal activity" has been questioned from a metaphysical perspective (ERE, 87ff). A distinction is made between our feeling of activity and the reality of activity. How do we know that it is in reality as it appears to us? Furthermore, what brings the whole activity chain into being? Before dealing with the metaphysical question James shows how the distinction between activity as it really is and as it only appears to us can arise and be distinguished without ever leaving "the purely phenomenal plane."

Each activity situation is part of an historically wider chain of experience, which is composed of partial processes definable by participants in terms of experienced origins and particular goals. But to an observer not living through that activity, it is judged to take place within another chain of events. We have gotten in the habit of judging activities as they appear from such wider angles of vision. The person subjectively participating in the activity has a narrower view and may miss or mistake a previous source of the activity or a later outcome. The "most real agent in the field" is, for the onlooker, the earliest ascertainable agent rather than the most immediate, just as the 'real' outcome is the widest or furthest that can still be linked to the partial activity. The agent in the immediate activity is reduced to being a transmitter of forces beyond her ken; for example, a person who thinks they are engaging in a sexual act of love may 'really' be a transmitter of AIDS, the origin of which is a virus passed from monkeys to humans many decades before, and the outcome of which is a widespread epidemic some decades hence. For the observer, the participant's subjective understanding of the activity is totally irrelevant to the objective activity span.

But which of the many causative agents are 'real,' which merely transmitters? Which description is therefore accurate, which distorted? James introduces the mind/body problem at this juncture to show the complexity of the issue. Is what I am about to say really determined by the neurochemical activity of the brain or by my intentions? If the brain ceases to function, I cease to talk. Since I have no knowledge of my own brain activities, I have no knowledge of the real facts of my own speaking situation. Do I therefore not really know what I am about to say? James gives the three principle types of answers that have been made to this question of identifying the real agent and the real action: a temporally-extended consciousness, with its will as agent and its purpose the action, ideas and their combinations, or nerve cells and resultant motor discharges. To determine which of these explanations, all of which seek to "de-realize our immediately felt activity-situations," is the correct one, James applies the pragmatic method by asking what practical difference it makes which one of them is adopted.

The structure of James's interpretive strategy should be made explicit before continuing. He first defines pure experience as a methodological directive to investigate the facts of experience guided by the concrete characteristics of being in the world. He takes activity as the fact to be investigated and gives a concrete description of it as our immediately felt activity situations. He next shows that some problems which have been raised in regard to activity are a consequence of the adoption of a non-phenomenalist viewpoint. He then applies the pragmatic methodology to dissolve these interpretations on the grounds that they de-realize the original phenomenon by not relating it to those guiding interests through which alone it can be realized. In other words, concrete analysis displaces metaphysics. By relating descriptions to the interests which guide them James also undermines his own empirical realism.

James then argues that assuming a wider thinker does not de-realize my activities, since I can cooperate with such a being, who in turn, can corroborate their reality. Incredibly — given his wide reading — he thus cavalierly ignores all the arguments showing that belief in a a god effectively precludes genuine human agency. These include criticism of Descartes's deus ex machina, Feuerbach's and Nietzsche's devastating critiques, and even his own arguments against the neo-Hegelian omniscient Absolute. He apparently does so because of his view that 'the gods' are finite, but this is not obvious in the immediate context, which is therefore misleading.

He next tackles the associationist position that individual ideas, smaller than my total conscious field, are the real causative agents, in which case, not I, but ideas of lesser span than my own are somehow in control. Likewise, if nerve impulses are the real activity, then my sense that I am directing my activities is also an illusion. Since on some interpretations I am a real causative agent and on others not, the dispute is shown to be more than merely verbal. There is a real drama involved in which practical outcome is correct. If resolved according to the materialist position, then elementary, short term events blindly guide more comprehensive ones, but if resolved teleologically, then goals can call acts into being.

He returns to the phenomenal level of concrete experience to claim that we believe that both short term and long term events are real and that the activities of wider span direct and make use of those of lesser span. He also acknowledges that we have no clear idea of how this actually works, as metaphysical thinkers have long pointed out. He does not then rehearse all the philosophical arguments that deny that mind can ever affect matter, but instead effectively renders them moot, on the grounds that no discussion of general natures and possibilities can predict which tendencies will actually prevail. We have experiential evidence of long range plans directing short term events, such as war plans determining which jets will depart today, and also of short term events defeating wide range ones, as when a coronary thrombosis removes a general from operation.

Two conclusions follow from applying the pragmatic method as an aspect of his radical empiricism. The first is that the answers sought will come from investigations of empirical details of fact and not from epistemology. What we now call the philosophy of mind, including the findings of brain physiology, can eventually explain the operations of longer term and shorter term processes, that is, the mind or consciousness and the brain. The second is that the facts, nevertheless, do not define the problem. It is we who do, because of our interests, and these have to be explicitly recognized in any accurate delineation of the problem to be investigated. Our interest in the mind/body problem is not an idle one of merely gathering facts for their own sake, as the positivist attitude of disinterested scientific neutrality would have it. We want to know whether we are responsible for our activities or are determined by events outside of our knowledge and control. The phenomenal level cannot be superseded if we are even to ask the right questions or frame the experiments correctly. The issue is precisely whether events which we experience as ours are in fact so, or whether they should be reductively attributed to brain cells.

In returning to the metaphysical question James defends the position that the nature, meaning and location of causality can be determined only at the phenomenal level of concrete experience (ERE, 91ff). It is thus not a metaphysical question at all, but a concrete one, or one answerable within the parameters of radical empiricism. Not only does he show that the metaphysical question must be dropped as unanswerable on its own terms, but taking activity at its face-value, or as we experience it, we also discover "the very power that makes facts come and be." In arguing that facts are interactively constituted by us, he has finally explicitly drawn the consequences of his break with the empiricist assumption that our percepts passively mirror reality as it is in itself. This aligns him with the constructivist tradition of Kant and Hegel, although not with their transcendental analyses. "Real activities are those that really make things be, without which things are not" (91). And all the evidence of our own experience discloses that we really make things be.

To the objection that our felt activity is only an impression and the facts are to be found elsewhere he responds with the principle of the radically empiricist philosophy according to which anything, to be considered real, must be located within experience. If creative activities are to be found anywhere, "they must be immediately lived" (ERE, 92). Just as cold really exists in our feeling of it, even if the thermometer objectively registers that the temperature is in the warm range, so real causation has no other nature than that which "even in our most erroneous experiences appears to be at work," even if it should turn out to be caused by nerve-processes. These nerve processes can be identified as causal only by analogy with "our feelings of activity." What we mean by causing, even if we mislocate it, are activities of "sustaining, persevering, striving, paying with effort as we go, hanging on, and finally achieving our intention." For anything to be called a cause, it must be of the sort of activity that resembles this "creation in its first intention," this "causality at work." To call this phenomenal experience of activity a mere illusion is to prefer a hidden ontological principle, that can never be experienced and thus never verified, to an experimentally verifiable level of investigation. James, therefore, concludes that "real effectual causation as an ultimate nature, as a 'category,' if you like, of reality is *just what we feel it to be*, just that kind of conjunction which our own activity-series reveal" (93-94).

Psychology properly deals with the concrete questions of the location of effectuation, of its true agents and of its closer and remoter outcomes. The only use of transcendental inquiries would be to recognize actual cases and intelligently plot their future operations. Therefore, the nature of causality is not to be found in searching for such a transcendental cause of causes, if this means a non-experiential source of what is experienced or some 'more' real, "unimaginable ontological principle" mysteriously hidden from any of our investigations. Furthermore, the worth or interest of our investigations of activity does not even consist in discerning the elements or conjunctions of things empirically but "in the dramatic outcome of the whole process" (ERE, 94). The only reason for investigating activity and causality is to help us understand the course and meaning of life. The pragmatic stance is that we seek to know, not for its own sake, but to enable us to live better.

James admonishes philosophers that since such psychological questions as that of the mind-brain problem have hardly begun to be answered, any definite or more comprehensive conclusions must await the outcome of further investigations. After this careful defense and elaboration of a concrete analysis of activity, James then explodes a bombshell by casually mentioning that he does think, however, that the evidence so far points in the direction of the "pan-psychic and ontologic speculation" of Henri Bergson and Charles Augustus Strong (ERE, 95).

Therefore, we once again run up against the problem of James holding two incompatible positions. He has argued against the need for a trans-experiential metaphysical explanation of a reality behind the phenomenal level of felt activity. The reason is that everything to be gained by relating a subjective experience to objective reality can be gained by showing how we can phenomenally correct shorter span subjective apprehensions of activity by longer span but still subjective ones. He argues carefully and convincingly against the need for any appeal to metaphysical realities to explain experiential ones. But then he negates his own conclusion by revealing that he still believes that eventually a pan-psychic reality will be found as the real explanation of our phenomenal activities. Unlike the alternative position, this belief is not supported by convincing evidence, and serves only to obscure the very real gains he has made by developing a radically empiricist concrete methodology to replace metaphysical speculation.

2. Is Radical Empiricism a Metaphysics?

We have just explored additional evidence of James's methodological procedure of beginning with a concrete investigation, that is, a careful description of a particular experience guided by a pragmatically defined purpose. The goal is to gather results which will eventually serve as the basis, the funded experiences, for developing properly philosophical answers to our metaphysical questions. What is striking in the 1904-05 essays of his middle period is that the method he uses in regard to the investigations of the discipline of psychology is explicitly called his radical empiricist method. He vigorously denies that he is asserting any "metaphysical principle of activity" and aligns himself with Renouvier as "an out and out phenomenist" (ERE, 93, n10). But his program of beginning on the phenomenal level of experience means just that — a beginning merely. He fully intends to end up in metaphysics. Apparently his own radical empiricism both formalizes the methodology he has been using operationally and offers some hypotheses as to the eventual nature of a metaphysics based on the results so far attained through concrete investigations.

His critique of metaphysics, therefore, is not so radical as it at first appears inasmuch he does not reject it outright as de-realizing the only world we know, as Nietzsche does, and as his own words sometimes seem to assert. Rather, he rejects all metaphysical explanations *insofar as* they de-realize the concrete world of experience. He obviously thinks some do not. Besides his own metaphysics of radical empiricism, he also holds that some versions of a belief in a wider consciousness than the human are also compatible with the facts as we know them. Despite the fact that he criticizes the move to a 'more real' cause of cause as a metaphysical extravagance, he still believes in one. In criticising three hypotheses which assert that "the *real* facts of activity" are not phenomenal, he spares one of them. He thinks that when the appeal to a "wider thinker" is properly understood, it corroborates rather than undermines our own concrete activities.

Some metaphysics, therefore, are acceptable insofar as they follow from or explain further the concrete world of human experience. But does it make any sense to call this enterprise 'metaphysics'? This subordination of metaphysics to his radical empiricist concrete analysis deprives it of one of its primary characteristics in the history of philosophy. Its role as 'first philosophy,' entails setting up the categories of being which all subsequent investigations must take into account or else be out of touch with reality, or be nonsensical, or both. But James's radically empiricist concrete analyses supercede this function, and any metaphysical system must be validated in regard to their findings.

He indicates an awareness of this distinctive break with the tradition by claiming that the empiricists were the first to employ the critical method in philosophy (PM, 269, EPH, 138). They replaced our aesthetic drive for intellectual harmony with our practical drive seeking a warrant for our actions as the ultimate arbiter of rationality. He usurped the Kantian claim of having replaced speculative metaphysics, although by other means than by a transcendental deduction of categories. For James, philosophy became critical with the empiricists' move to interpret the meaning of conceptions by asking what difference they make for life.[3] Only an "appreciable difference to us in action" can distinguish valid meanings from mere speculations (PM, 269; EPH, 138). He has already denied another defining characteristic of metaphysics as traditionally understood; namely, that its categories are necessary. Since the categories that we apply a priori to experience are themselves the result of both biological evolution and historical processes, whatever invariance they demonstrate are in principle subject to further revision and thus are called 'pragmatically a priori' or 'hypothetical' rather than 'necessary,' even if we cannot now imagine any other way of organizing experience. Many other traditional metaphysical positions such as the analytic/synthetic distinction are also called into question.

James does not distinguish, except indirectly, between traditional metaphysics and the metaphysics that will be possible after making the radically empiricist natural history turn. Despite superficial resemblances, they are not the same. We need two different terms to keep these distinctions separate and to avoid the confusion arising from James's use of the same term for both. Some would call them today 'metaphysics' and 'post-modern philosophy' or that philosophy which is salvageable after having rejected the assumptions which lie at the basis of modernity. In keeping with James's own terminology, we could call his post-metaphysical analysis a radically empiricist hermeneutics, since it replaces a systematic investigation of being with interpretive strategies which both structure and reflect his concrete findings. The pragmatists themselves distinguished between the older tradition of speculative metaphysics and their own, post-Darwinian evolutionary philosophy.[4] We must ask why, given James's rejection of traditional metaphysics, he nonetheless continues to reconstruct a metaphysics rather than rejecting its possibility and desirability as Kant and Nietzsche did.

He does so because of two traditional features that he carries over from metaphysics to his post-Darwinian metaphysics. One is that our curiosity about the world will not be satisfied until our partial beliefs are coordinated into a comprehensive totality, and this driving force for absolute unification is part of our aesthetic rationality. The other is that our striving to overcome evil and create a better world is always thwarted by the partiality of our conquests. Our practical rationality demands for its complete satisfaction the fulfillment of all our drives, and one of the strongest drives is the continuation of our conscious being. However, this is not realizable except in a different realm of being than that of which we are presently aware. In James's radically empiricist natural history of rationality all the particular satisfactions sought by both aesthetic and practical rationality have as their ultimate aim total satisfaction.

But do these reasons for developing a metaphysics outweigh others in which he criticizes metaphysical pursuits? At most he adduces evidence that total satisfaction, both aesthetic and practical, are regulative principles which guide our particular actions. Since our desires are never totally satisfied, these regulative principles lead us to understand the world as incomplete until it has been exhaustively explained. As many psychological findings have corroborated, and as existentialism made a cornerstone of its position, it is characteristically human to be insatiable in our desires.

But even if it is established that the drive for intellectual comprehensiveness and complete emotional satisfaction regulates human rationality, what justifies our belief that the specification of such an end-state — which is by definition outside of all human experience — is anything more than idle wish fulfillment? James has himself provided evidence that the premature development of a metaphysical system before all the facts are in can be positively harmful. He has not shown how his own quest for metaphysics escapes these harms. It seems that he has confused the benefits to be gained from upholding the ideal of a more perfect human situation as a spur to action, with the desirability of claiming that such a better world already exists alongside of ours.

He calls the unseen or mystical world real, for instance, and "not merely ideal, for it produces effects in this world. When we commune with it, work is actually done upon our finite personality…and consequences in the way of conduct follow in the natural world upon our regenerative change" (VRE, 406). In arguing for this personal over-belief he goes beyond his earlier position that we cannot articulately account for the spontaneity of ideal impulses and makes a positive claim that "most of them do originate" in the mystical or supernatural region because "we find them possessing us in a way for which we cannot articulately account." He thus illicitly converts a lack of evidence into grounds for a positive claim, rather than suspending judgment.[5]

Therefore, despite all his acute criticisms of traditional metaphysics, James nonetheless retains the one feature of it that Nietzsche rejects as de-realizing the only world we know, namely its characterization of a real world as opposed to the world of appearance. Moreover, James retains not one, but two real worlds behind the appearances: that of a reality in itself and that of supernatural, though finite, consciousnesses. Nietzsche argues that the very distinction between the world as it appears to us and the world as it is in itself perpetuates the fiction of a reality that is not human reality, of a Platonic world of Ideas by any other name that alone is real, so that our world, as we experience it, must be false. That James maintains this distinction is not immediately obvious because he also insists on the phenomenal world of our experience as irreducible and as the dramatically human plane which can never be superceded. But he also thinks that our world may well be enveloped in another that we can as little comprehend as a cat in a study can comprehend the books on the shelves along the wall (PU, 140). He thinks that the concrete world of our experience is not false but incomplete and when understood in the more inclusive reality of which it is only a part, its meaning will not be rejected but enriched.

3. Incomplete Transformation of the Realist/Metaphysical Perspective into the Concrete/Hermeneutic

The conflicting assumptions operative in James's understanding of the philosophical enterprise and metaphysics can be usefully grouped under two headings according to family resemblance: the realist/metaphysical and the concrete/hermeneutic. He often argues for the "more objective tradition" of realist metaphysics. Against the neo-Kantians and logical positivists, for instance, he upholds examination of the "actual constitution of reality" in order to systematize it into a "single body of wisdom." He is ambivalent about the traditional method of doing so, namely, seeking the widest assumptions, the most general questions, the conditions of human knowing and acting in general. While retaining this angle of vision or attitude toward the subject matter as a regulative idea, he recasts its methodological procedure. In thus remaining both realist and a metaphysician he advocates a method based on his concrete model of thinking, namely, observation, discrimination, generalization, classificiation, looking for causes, tracing analogies, hypothesis formation, and validation procedures. This method has been best formalized in natural history, which has changed the traditional method of philosophizing by emphasizing the hypothetical or tentative attitude and the habit of seeking verification.

Scientific procedure has gone wrong, though, insofar as it has reduced the proper scope of investigation to measurable phenomena and has sought to eliminate reference to the subjective element of the investigator. These aspects of scientific methodology must be opposed by philosophic arguments for the extreme diversity of the ways in which reality is taken and for the importance of relating investigative procedures to their origin in the subjective interests of human beings. But in opposition to its own tradition of constructing "a system of 'completely unified' knowledge" in ignorance of the actual constitution of facts, James identifies the day to day work of philosophy as the gathering and testing of the facts of experience. It differs from standard scientific procedure only in its intentions, as given in the regulative ideas, and its constant reference to the human dimension of experience as developed in his concrete analysis.

But there is another dimension of James's thought that is just as pervasive as the one just given, but which is at odds with it. This is centered in his new beginning in concrete analysis and his substitution of a hermeneutic vocabulary of interpretation for the 'abstraction' vocabulary of his empiricist realism. In his own praxis he has deliberately limited himself to the phenomenal level, for which he has many synonyms, the most prominent of which are 'common sense level' and 'concrete experience,' and which he formalizes as 'the principle of pure experience.' This is an insistence that each person's living experience is the original which verbalization and interpretation seek to make explicit.

Our experience of "this actual world of ours, as it is given," as "lived through or authentically known," can be illuminated or distorted by interpretations, but can never be replaced by them or captured without remainder in any verbalization or rational formula whatever (ERE, 82, 85). The naive, phenomenal level of concrete experience not only is a pre-condition of formalizations but it cannot be finally superseded, and ought to have the final veto on theoretical explanations both to keep them from going into business for themselves and to prevent them from being life-denying. In explaining how to develop a science of religion based on his concrete principles, for instance, he says that not only should investigation begin by gathering facts of personal experience, it would also have "to square itself with personal experience through all its critical reconstructions. It could never get away from concrete life, or work in a conceptual vacuum" (VRE, 360). His concrete analysis of this lived experience attempts to make explicit its structures in order to guide our other explanatory hypotheses.

His interpretive method is based on his concrete analysis of "the structural form of the mind," namely, starting from some experience in the actual world, forming a hypothesis and then constructing a practical maxim or resolve. When this is acted on, we get feedback on which we can then reflect, thus contributing to the funded character of experience. The criterion is not representational accuracy to the original experience but long-range success in ordering our experience to better answer to our needs, that is, the construction of a human form of life. In the short run it is a successful leading that is worthwhile, which means that our expectations about the likely outcome of acting on our beliefs have been confirmed. His interpretive method is not in the first place a way of organizing or explicating language but a praxis of which verbalization is only one of the tools. "In point of fact, the *use* of most of our thinking is to help us to *change* the world."[6]

As part of his reconstruction of the methodology of philosophical theorizing he emphasized those aspects of his model of human thinking that were being increasingly neglected as newly professionalized philosophers sought to distinguish themselves from their less scientifically oriented humanist colleagues. This included a return to the origins of thinking in the specialized ability to dissociate aspects from the flux of experience and to create analogies, thus restoring the importance of the poetic to philosophizing. He favored the metaphors of interpretation and translation for the verbalization of immediately felt phenomena. Two among many examples are: "Rigorous truth and human nature's intricacies are always in need of a mutual interpreter" (VRE, 364). "I do believe that feeling is the deeper source of religion, and that philosophic and theological formulas are secondary products, like translations of a text into another tongue" (341). The appeal to translatability includes the recognition that no translation can ever do justice to the original. This theme of the poverty of verbalization and formalization in comparison with the richness of lived experience is always present in his work but grows stronger and more emphatic over the years. In *Varieties*, for instance, he praises the scientific attitude of taking its formulas as approximations, to remind his audience that "philosophy lives in words, but truth and fact well up into our lives in ways that exceed verbal formulation. There is in the living act of perception always something that glimmers and twinkles and will not be caught and for which reflection comes too late" (360).

James's appeal to concrete experience is vaguely enough conceived to straddle both the realist and the hermeneutic alternatives. He would undoubtedly take this as its strength as a mediating position. But for philosophers still responding to the aesthetics of consistency, some way must be found to reconcile these two conflicting accounts, or eliminate one of them, even though James himself was unable to do so. Even according to his own reconstruction of rationality as the harmonizing of all our interests, this is still the proper task of philosophers. If his realist/metaphysical assertions are taken as expressing his intention to begin philosophy anew by turning from mere speculation to verifiable experience, then this experiential turn can be satisfied within the second position. Its terms, however, must be reconstructed in light of his own concrete development of the structures which characterize the human situation as the active appropriation of the world according to our interests.

The missing piece in the puzzle is the lack of any explicit development of a hermeneutics or theory of interpretation and any explicit attempt to distinguish it from, or relate it to, his concrete analysis. Many hints of such a hermeneutics are given in the texts, and I reconstructed one in chapter 7, basing it on the interpretive strategies actually operative in his writings. But James did not reflect on his own practice or organize its structures into an interpretive model. This prevented him from utilizing it to eliminate the residue of his naive realism and metaphysical assumptions and develop the robust pragmatic humanism of his concrete analysis. Pragmatic humanism rejects appeals to a fixed ideal of human nature and thus is not subject to such criticisms as Heidegger makes in *The Letter on Humanism* and which are later taken up by Derrida and other post-structuralists.

Chapter Thirteen

Unexamined Empiricist Assumptions

In the last chapter we saw that James's various formulations of a philosophy of concrete experience were not developed thoroughly enough to enable him to consistently draw the radical consequences of his own radically empiricist concrete analysis. This chapter continues to probe the reasons why he could not himself break loose from the very controlling assumptions that his own original critiques undermined. Unfortunately, some of these same assumptions have become enshrined in traditional interpretations of his philosophy and have prevented the recognition and discussion of some of his more challenging positions that break with the tradition.

1. The Tangle of Science and Metaphysics

We have seen that James deliberately tried to keep scientific and metaphysical explanations distinct in *Principles*, even though he could not consistently do so. Despite the fact that soon afterwards he rejected the possibility of excluding metaphysics from the science of psychology, he never reflected on how this was to be done in practice. He continued to restrict science to its positivist definition while constantly reminding its practitioners that their understanding of the facts available for investigation was too narrow and that their investigations must explicitly include the human contribution. He argued that the positivist claim to investigate facts as they are in themselves was patently false because of what we learn through investigating human knowing in the concrete. James's concrete epistemology located knowing within the more inclusive context of our transactions in the world. He argued that we are interactive with nature and so situated that our interests in knowing about the world of which we are a part is always guided by our primary interest in having to do with the world in a way satisfactory to ourselves.

But James somehow thought that this concrete understanding of our situatedness in the world could just be added to our store of knowledge as one more set of facts. If scientists would only acknowledge these facts, they would not exclude phenomena like feelings and intentions from investigation. Incredibly, he did not distinguish conceptually between structures of interpretation and facts to be interpreted. Furthermore, he did not see that his acceptance of the principle that 'seeing' is always 'seeing-as,' which he demonstrated in many different ways, must lead to a reconceptualization of the nature of facticity and of science.

At the end of his life he was still describing science in the same positivist terms he had used in his student days. In recounting the history of the human intellect in *Some Problems of Philosophy*, for instance, James explains the development of modern science as the progressive replacement of the animistic or "'sympathetic' theorizing" that singles out those elements in phenomena that are "more dramatic or humanly interesting" by "the more insipid kinds of regularity," namely, the mathematical, or those properties of phenomena susceptible to mathematical treatment (SPP, 15-18). This leaves to philosophy the residue of unanswered questions, which are those not susceptible to mathematical or mechanical treatment. Since reality is so diverse, diverse investigations are warranted. There must be some avenue to spiritual questions as well as to material ones, for instance.

Even in his last work James is still succinctly defining positivistic science as demanding "measurable facts only, phenomena, without the mind's additions, without entities or principles that pretend to explain" (SPP, 17). Although this claim is in direct conflict with the major thesis of his writings, which systematically demonstrates or presupposes the teleological conception of human cognition, he does not criticize this definition of science as positivistic, but only its criticism of philosophy as making no progress. He is concerned to defend the legitimacy of philosophy asking questions unrestricted by the criterion of mathematical measurement and providing explanations of a greater degree of generality than is proper for science. On a close reading of his many writings, it can be verified that James's many criticisms of science as positivistic are criticisms of the illegitimate extension of the restrictions which are proper to the scientific endeavor as though they were regulative for all thinking whatever. He does argue in many places that feelings and intentions be included along with other facts that science must investigate, but this is always an argument to include them on the level of facts, not on the level of interpretation.

This is underscored by his understanding of what the turn to critical philosophy entails. He says that philosophy turned critical with Locke, in that it became more exclusively limited to the problem of knowledge, and with Hume and Kant, in that philosophy became concerned with mental and moral speculations to the exclusion of physical theories (SPP, 13-14). He is using 'critical' in both an ordinary and a reconstructed sense. He criticizes the usual sense which refers to the modern subjective turn to epistemology, which he thinks has erred in straying from the older tradition of objective realism. As was pointed out in the last chapter, he also uses 'critical' as a positive term to characterize the pragmatic turn.[1] Like others, such as Husserl, who rebelled against the neo-Kantian turn to subjectivism, James placed himself within the more 'recent' objective tradition that sought to "take some notice of the actual constitution of reality." But this determination to avoid subjectivism, abetted by his empiricist realism, led him to categorize the interpretive structures he developed as 'facts' rather than as 'interpretive structures' and blinded him to what was really critical in Kant, namely, his rejection of metaphysics because it was merely speculative, and his insistence that the categories of human thinking be subjected to as strict a verification procedure as those the sciences were developing. It was critical also in the recognition that reality was not available to us as it was in itself but only according to our means of understanding.

In his rejection of the later neo-Kantian subjective turn James was in basic agreement with these elements of Kant's own critical philosophy, but in his defense of the objectivity of our knowledge of reality he fell back on a naive empiricist theory of the abstraction of elements. This was incommensurable with his recognition of the synthetic or constructed character of our knowledge, which he called 'weaving chaos into order.' The interpretive structures of human knowing established through his novel concrete analyses were taken to be facts, not fundamentally distinct from the facts disclosed through the application of these same structures. He was therefore blind to the issues raised in categorial analysis concerning the need for justifying the categories as well as the facts gathered through the application of these categories and for specifying the precise nature of their interaction. It is ironic that he developed all the pieces of the puzzle — a genealogy of the common sense categories, a concrete analysis of human knowledge, a critique of essentialist and foundationalist rationalism, an explanation of the interpretive character of our apprehension of facts — without recognizing which puzzle he was working on. He never developed a meta-theory of his own interpretive structures and therefore never satisfactorily grasped the truly radical issues he was raising.

James excels at identifying the assumptions underlying scientific positions that he rejects and correctly labels them as 'metaphysical,' that is, as imposed on and structuring the phenomenal investigation without any justification. The identification of the materialist bias of the automaton theorists in chapter 5 of the first volume of *Principles* is one such example. But he seldom, if ever, admits to having any metaphysical presuppositions of his own. What he does claim as guiding his own investigations are variously classified as hypotheses, facts, what is "very generally admitted," the findings of his concrete analyses, common sense beliefs, personal experience, and theories such as the Darwinian. These are not metaphysical in the traditional sense of being necessary, speculative, and incapable of empirical proof, nor a priori in the usual sense of non-historical and unevolved. Since the only metaphysics he recognizes as legitimate is a reconstructed one subsequent to a collection of phenomenal facts, what does he call those presuppositions and organizing categories that structure both everyday and scientific experience and make it possible to identify facts as facts in the first place?

He does not name them at all or reflect on or theorize about such implicit and explicit structures as organizing categories. He does develop a unique concrete analysis of our interactive being in the world and refers to it in his analyses of particular problems, but he does not identify it as such nor give it any priority over other assumptions and beliefs he also uncritically assumes. Moreover, his empiricist assumption of the availability of facts to our introspection unaccountably survives his own critique demonstrating that they are never apprehended as bare facts or as they are in themselves, but only as interpreted through our interests. Thus, he often claims to be merely describing an array of facts that, to us, are obviously only available as he describes them given his particular angle of vision.

2. Inability to Formalize Structures of Explanation

We have seen how James's naive realism prevented him from critically reflecting on his interpretive structures as interpretive. How does this affect the metaphysical reconstruction to which his concrete findings have been leading? In the first chapter of *Some Problems of Philosophy*, his proposed introductory book on philosophy, he clearly states his preference for philosophy as a system of completely unified knowledge of reality which, by bringing the results of all the sciences into harmony, can show how science, metaphysics, and religion support one another. He then says that the aim of the book will nonetheless be to develop the more 'modern,' subjective sense of philosophy as complementing the sciences by investigating only mind and morals. His book will therefore "take philosophy in the narrow sense of metaphysics" (rather than in the broader sense just mentioned) (SPP, 20). This immediately poses several problems for us. Why does not James present philosophy from his own point of view as a systematic unification of all experience? In his own previous work he had undertaken the preliminary task of discovering facts and organizing them such that their results would be available for eventual philosophical co-ordination. Why does he not finally take the opportunity to systematically relate all his findings into a reconstructed philosophy?

His aim is especially puzzling because in correspondence about the manuscript posthumously published as *Some Problems of Philosophy* he claims, in fact, to be finally attempting such a systematic unification. He writes to F. C. S. Schiller that his next book "will be philosophical and constructive" and will present a *"systematic* and radical metaphysics" with as much completion as the uncompleted universe admits of (SPP, 198). In writing instructions to Horace Kallen on editing the book that by July 26, 1910, he knows would never be finished, he notes: "Say that I hoped by it to round out my system, which now is too much like an arch built only on one side" (203). And to Theodore Flournoy he writes in 1908 that he wishes to write that winter "something ultra dry in form, impersonal and exact."

An answer can be formulated using the clues the book provides. It should be kept in mind that James never finished the book and therefore did not put it into final form. Nonetheless, he had been thinking about it for a long time and had already begun sketching it out in his classes.[2] Since he left instructions for it to be published, thereby indicating that he wished it to be considered as part of his *oeuvre*, it can be taken as representing his considered position in a way that unpublished writings and notes cannot. It is therefore with heightened expectation that one turns to James's final explanation of metaphysics. The logical place to expect such clarification is in the second chapter, which is about metaphysics, especially given its position following the first chapter in which he affirms his own definition of philosophy out of the many meanings given to it over time.

He follows his usual procedure of not dogmatically starting with a definition, but of generating one out of the relevant facts. In the case of metaphysics this means beginning with some of the problems it examines. As indicated in the genealogy of philosophy given in his previous chapter, these were obscure questions about "the whole of things" which are suggested by life in general and by science, and which have not yet been solved (SPP, 21). He then randomly cites questions which, as it turns out, are the ones he takes up in subsequent chapters. Next, he dismisses as possible definitions two formulations which he had just affirmed as his own in the previous chapter, namely, "metaphysics inquires into the cause, the substance, the meaning and the outcome, of all things" and "the science of the most universal principles of reality...in their connexion with one another and with our powers of knowledge" (22). What he rejects is the assumption that metaphysics begins in possession of such understanding, that it can begin inquiring into ultimate meanings or can show how the universal principles of reality are related to each other. This is manifestly impossible because no such ultimate meanings or principles are yet available to us.

"Metaphysics as a unified science" cannot perform its role until it has the results of all there is to know, and for this it must wait until science has discovered them and handed them over. In the meantime philosophers can contribute to the results by investigating those particular problems which the other sciences do not. But they are to do so using the same natural history procedure that James has developed and practiced because it is so well suited to producing true results. James, however, does not in the text exhort the reader to adopt his methodology, as I have just done, nor does he define it or defend its relevance. Instead, as usual, he merely exemplifies it. This leaves it up to the reader to puzzle out what he is doing and to make the connections he does not. As a consequence, it often looks as if James is not employing any special methodology, much less that he consistently uses one that he has developed.

But despite the fact that he deliberately refuses to begin with exact definitions, he nonetheless develops his essays, chapters, or larger units of discourse according to guiding principles. He can examine topics like metaphysics and religion without first delimiting the subject area by a precise definition because of his natural-history methodology according to which the beginning of all non-speculative investigation is careful observation and description of, and abstraction from, the experiential continuum. On this empiricist model, then, careful description of the available evidence necessarily precedes the exact definition, which is a resultant, not an a priori imposition on the facts.

But according to his radically empiricist revision of empiricism, the experiential continuum is too diffuse to provide any one organizational concept or category as exclusively necessary and inevitable. Selective interest must cull from the totality of experience a lesser grouping which then can be interrogated. Thus, although the precise concept abstracted from the available evidence is drawn from that evidence, both the initial grouping and the concept eventually selected are guided by a priori interests. The investigator does not examine facts at random but chooses some and not others insofar as they seem to be relevant for some guiding purpose she brings to the endeavor. James thus claims that his investigations are grounded in reality, and therefore are non-speculative, and yet incorporate a significantly human dimension of guiding interests, including moral ones, and therefore are not limited to sense data, as narrowly construed by the empiricists.

It seems that because James never relates this notion of subjective interest to conceptualization, he could dismiss the idealist argument that no ordering of experience is possible without the imposition of a priori concepts. His original contribution to the question is a critique of a priori concepts of the Platonic model and an invitation to re-imagine concepts as the activity of ordering experience congruent to our needs and desires. For such ordering hazy intentions can serve as well as clear concepts, which in any case are argued as being a later development, both historically and in individual psychological development. Both in everyday life and in the particular sciences, exact definitions of phenomena are arrived at only after much effort and are part of a continuing process of transforming a looser web of experiential evidence into precise formulas. To impose exact formulas before examining the evidence is to prefer systematic simplification arrived at dogmatically to the more modest scientific procedure of announcing results only after operational definitions have been experimentally validated. There would be no way of knowing whether our beliefs are true or not if we deferred investigations of experience until the demands of intellectual rationality, aesthetic harmony, or simplicity were met. The demands of practical rationality and clarity as abstraction must take precedence.

But although it can be granted that James has given good reasons why traditional a priori exact definitions, and even more so, completely worked out systems, are not necessary prerequisites to phenomenal investigation, he has not proved that no preliminary plan of ordering is necessary. On the contrary, his thesis of selective interest argues that an intentional purpose must guide investigations to select relevant parts out of the phenomenal totality. The difference between the idealist position and James's appears to be one of degree and emphasis. Surely, the purpose must be as exact as possible, and James never argues otherwise. But he typically specifies purposes for his own investigations in the form of a question or a set of alternatives, what would be called today a 'working hypothesis.' In answering the question or explaining the alternatives, he does fill in the meaning of the terms, but loosely rather than precisely. A lot is taken for granted, not only in terms of what the audience already knows, but in drawing on the methodology and findings of his own previous investigations, to which he frequently alludes without going into great detail. This style of presentation explains why James is so difficult to interpret in the context of the single essay or even book, and why a knowledge of his other works is so necessary for understanding just what he means by crucial terms and what emphasis to give to the various parts of his text.

Peter Hare agrees with A. D. Lindsay, for example, that James's discussion of philosophy in *Some Problems of Philosophy* is "singularly indefinite" and not altogether coherent (SPP, xxxvi). The interpretive problem becomes less acute once it is recognized that James is exemplifying his concrete description of thinking. He begins with vague definitions as a preliminary step to formulating precise answers, which are then offered as hypotheses to be verified insofar as they also successfully organize the experiences of the members of the audience. This philosophical technique imitates natural history investigations which begin with inchoate facts and end in explanatory systems. There still remains the problem, though, that the notion of a guiding intention is vaguely enough expressed to obscure the bone of contention between idealists and empiricists over whether categories which organize experience are a priori or a posteriori. In insisting that selective intention is imposed on and not derived from experience and is necessary to having an experience at all, James should have no quarrel with the idealist tradition insofar as it insists on the a priori contribution of organizing structures. Even in their first appearance at the level of concept formation, as explained in his early articles on thinking, what is abstracted from the experiential continuum are those aspects of it to which attention is paid because of an independently originating interest. But he does radically differ from most idealists in insisting that such organizing structures arise in the first place in the course of experience. Furthermore, he substitutes a genealogy of interests for a logical deduction of categories.

The vagueness of James's explanation at this fundamental level of the nature of thinking systematically distorts all the explanations based on it. 'Real' aspects of phenomena are said to be abstracted, but they would not be without a controlling or 'ideal' interest. Is this the idealists' imposition of ideal categories or the empiricists' theory of general ideas as vague impressions, which contain nothing that was not originally in the sensory impressions? We would have the most to gain by interpreting James's explanation as demonstrating that such neat distinctions cannot be maintained in practice. His model of living acts of thinking provides a better explanation than either of the traditional ones of how our knowledge of the world both originates in experience and yet requires individually created intentions and reflectively generated conceptual categories. It is because we find and impose at the same time that pragmatic validation is a necessary part of the knowing process which is incomplete without it. It becomes irrelevant to the truthfulness of a belief whether it is claimed that it was strictly derived from observation of experience or came as an unsolicited intuition or inspiration, since all our knowledge consists of both found and created aspects. No matter how individual beliefs originate, they must be tested experientially if we are going to intelligently include them as part of a wider system of beliefs.

3. Reconstructing the Reconstruction

Although James struggles to harmonize his concrete findings and empirically realist assumptions, as a matter of fact, he does not expect his pragmatic criterion of a successful leading to conflict with his assumption that he is having to do with the real world because of the first and last steps of the process of living acts of reasoning. The first is that the original belief or hypothesis be in some sense creatively derived from experience. The last is the reflective determination of whether acting on the belief has led to the anticipated outcome. But this position is not traditional essentialist realism. James explicitly says that according to his radically empiricist philosophy 'real' means 'located within experience.' There is no way to prove that any particular belief uniquely captures the essential characteristics of any state of affairs. One can have good reasons for assuming that some characteristic has been effectively distinguished from an experiential process insofar as it successfully fulfills our expectations. But this model assumes that other interests will locate other characteristics and that there are no intrinsic limits either to our interests or the responsiveness of experience, although there can be many practical limits.

Do we really grasp the world as it is or do we create a world in our own image, answering to our expectations? This distinction is also no longer tenable. Nonetheless, we can still either believe that the world we create in answer to our expectations is the world that is there for our grasping, even though our limitations prevent us from ever knowing all there is to know about it, or we can believe that our interests forever distort the world as it is apart form us, and we therefore live in a world created in our own image. The classical American pragmatists optimistically believed the former, while today's poststructuralists pessimistically emphasize the latter. But as long as we remain on the level of concrete experience there is no way to decide between these two beliefs. And despite his arguments that we cannot disprove the possibility of realities not accessible to us, James nowhere argues that they are proved or self-evident. Since it is tautological that we have no access to any world that is not accessible to us, how can we meaningfully, that is, non-speculatively, say anything about inaccessible worlds? That we hold onto the belief either that we grasp or that we distort reality with such tenacity despite the inherent undecidability of the issue means that it is satisfying some deeply felt need. Therefore, we cannot get further clarification of the impasse without examining such needs.

James himself does not seem to have made this move, though, due to his lack of preciseness and failure to reflect critically enough on some of his fundamental assumptions, with the consequence that he often seems to be inconsistent or, at least, unclear. However, it is often difficult to see where in his reasoning process he goes wrong because so much of the meaning depends on context and allusion to his other works. By the time a particular concept is tracked down and made more precise certain idiosyncrasies become more apparent. These tend to undermine the force of some of his arguments. He has a systematic blindness to questions of structure, as we have seen, and does not distinguish between explanatory principles and what is explained, except when criticizing the reification of explanatory structures as though they were an original part of the data themselves. In his gloss on the definition of metaphysics as "the science of the most universal principles of reality," for instance, he conflates principles with their referential objects, saying that principles may mean 'entities,' 'logical laws,' or 'generalized facts' (SPP, 22). He then says that, in the present state of affairs, these principles are too numerous and incomplete, and are therefore merely decorative. His solution is not to winnow them down, but to complete them, not by making them comprehensive and systematically inter-related, but by answering *"separate single questions."*

He thus seems to be conflating principles with the results that the particular sciences offer to metaphysics for ultimate unification. This odd understanding of principles as being factual and informational rather than structural and explanatory does not distinguish them from facts, except in their level of generality; for example, 'this tree fell in a particular direction when struck at a given angle,' is a fact, while 'any tree struck at that angle will fall in the same direction in relation to the angle' is a principle. Since they are themselves generalized facts, principles will be complete when the facts which they generalize are complete. The notion of a complete explanation of facts is thereby confused by James with the notion of a complete enumeration of facts.

Apparently this accounts for James's inability to formalize the principles he uses in his own explanations. He does not distinguish in his examination of thinking, for instance, between, on the one hand, the assumptions which guide his choices, the over-all framework of investigation, and the principles he uses to include or exclude data and, on the other hand, from the facts which are disclosed given these parameters. Everything is therefore subsumed under descriptive categories. Only the personal point of view, including selective interest, is distinguished as organizing the phenomena rather than being a part of the phenomena organized. But interests are treated globally and not distinguished into the actual principles defining the particular experiential or experimental situation. Thus, although James gradually develops what he means by the concrete level of explanation, and constantly draws on his paradigm of thinking, of the reconstructed reflex-arc doctrine, and on various structures of human nature, he never critically examines them as interpretive structures, nor relates them systematically. In sum, he uses them operationally but not reflectively.

4. Reconstructing Subjectivity and Objectivity

Because of the intertwining of facts and interests, neither being identifiable without the other, the concepts abstracted are still subjective and must be validated by returning to experience to see if they fulfill their intended function. But this only legitimates them as far as the individual investigator is concerned, that is, whether she has good (practical) rational grounds for holding such verified beliefs and continuing to act on them. They are still subjective, though, because the very same selective interest that allows some geniuses to brilliantly discover facts which have escaped everyone else, is also operative in the personally experientially verified worlds of the insane. True enough, we can only distinguish the one from the other by also validating them in regard to the facts, but this requires not only that we recognize the selective interest which is operative, but also that we agree on what counts as validation. From subjective validation, which is good enough for everyday life, or for the specialist investigator to continue, we pass to inter-subjective validation, which provides a stronger warrant for belief in the accuracy and truthfulness of the conceptual organization of experience in question.

Interestingly, James never uses the phrase, 'inter-subjective' confirmation, although the concept is essential to his explanation of how we arrive at a world in common and of how two persons can know they are making true claims about the same object. Perhaps he does not, because for him, such inter-subjective confirmation does not differ from subjective confirmation in the one aspect in which he is most interested — its objectivity. Both are still subjective because they are based on personal interests which can always be mistaken, even if very many people hold the same interests. One need only recall shared prejudices and the scientific beliefs of earlier generations. Inter-subjective confirmation differs from subjective confirmation only statistically. With each new confirmation the likelihood that the belief is true has a higher degree of probability. James appreciates this difference as separating the scientist and anyone who is concerned with rational thinking from the non-specialist or any of us in the rest of our life outside our research fields. He even argues for this higher degree of warrant when we can get it and when the effort is worth it.

But he also argues that we cannot always get it, and this is particularly true for the initial formulation. Einstein, for example, was not obliged to wait for his theory to be confirmed by others before acting as though it were true, since acting on such beliefs before they have been confirmed by others is a necessary prerequisite for eventual inter-subjective confirmation. Nor is the effort always worth it; most of our beliefs are held until they are called into question. We learn them initially socially and continue holding them until they run into difficulties. Again, given the fact that learning entails assimilating a culture, such preliminary subjective beliefs are a necessary pre-condition for their eventual inter-subjective confirmation and dissemination. Thus, while James holds up inter-subjective confirmation as an ideal for which to strive, he also wants to emphasize its limitations in order to encourage creativity and to legitimize the practical rationality of human action, which often requires that we act on less than certain knowledge.

Only after much interrogation of the texts does it become apparent that by objectivity James means the absolute coalescence of belief with reality. Although this may be the case with some of our beliefs — James thinks that many of our concepts have already attained this eternal truth status and is even willing to point out to his students which ones — he also argues that we have no way of knowing with certitude that this is so in any given instance (SPP, 207). He agrees with Peirce that we will only know objects as they are and know that we do so when all the evidence is in and all investigators will have had their say, that is, at the end of time. But this means that his preferred definition of philosophy as the completion of the sciences can be actuated only in the indefinitely distant future, if at all. Both his notions of objectivity and of philosophy, therefore, are regulative ideas. They provide goals which guide actions but are not themselves instantiated in the process.

We do not know, in actual fact, whether any belief is objective, according to James, nor can we do philosophy proper until all the facts are in. In the meantime — and this means in all the time we have as finite, temporal beings — we can pragmatically warrant our beliefs, and we can employ the natural-history method of inquiry. This will allow us both to have sufficient grounds for action and to contribute to the store of funded beliefs in the process of objectification. According to James, among the tasks of such a radically empiricist philosophy is that of adding facts from the areas that the other sciences do not cover to the final 'pile' of results and also, somehow, to begin to bring the results of all the facts gathered so far into relation with one another. We should also continually remind ourselves that the goal of harmony should already regulate our conduct and scientific praxis.

We therefore have to explicitly distinguish, as James does not, between philosophy as a regulative idea, which he calls philosophy in the original or traditional sense, total, systematic, etc., and concrete philosophizing, which he calls an unusual effort to think clearly, pragmatism as a method merely, the natural-history approach, etc. A further distinction must be made between objectivity as a regulative idea and both subjectivity as constitutive of the given, concrete situation, and warranted subjectivity or reflectively generated objectivity as the outcome of a process of validation. Both humanism and his own radical empiricism are special cases, since James seems to believe that they operate like regulative philosophy in that they provide the requisite systematic interconnection, without falling under his criticism of the idealists, namely, that they have developed a comprehensive system before all the facts have been gathered. Since he does not realize that his understanding of traditional philosophy places it in the category of regulative ideas, he seems to think that it can already be constitutive of some particular philosophical system's disclosure of reality, without saying how it can be so, given our finite temporality.

5. James's Inability to Produce a Systematic Philosophy

Since in *Some Problems* James wants to draw on his genealogy of rationality, he presents in summary form what he had developed in detail and also placed at the beginning of his analyses in *The Will to Believe, Pragmatism*, and *A Pluralistic Universe* (SPP, 25, n2). As usual, his failure to point out that this is a methodological procedure deliberately leaves the impression that he is merely objectively surveying the history of philosophy. He is actually setting up rationalism and empiricism as types, loosely based on actual historical positions. They are defined dialectically, with rationalism representing mostly what is wrong with contemporary philosophizing and empiricism representing the core of his own assumptions and method (25). As exemplars of the two relevant extreme positions, they represent different, often incompatible but nonetheless genuine, needs. Therefore, in any harmonious resolution, what is valuable in both positions must be preserved, although not necessarily in the exact way it was originally expressed.

James explicitly admits that his book will be biased in favor of empiricism and that the clash of the two positions will be emphasized throughout (SPP, 24-25). In fact he systematically employs his usual methodology of attacking rationalism by opposing to it his reconstructed empiricism, but he does not explain this procedure. His casual mention, for example, that *"within experience,* phenomena come and go" and that "the world seems, on the concrete and proximate level, at least, really to grow" belies the fact that he is referring not just to one view among many, but to a whole complex of interconnected beliefs and methods that constitute his own concrete analysis of experience (29).

James's foray into a systematic presentation of philosophy was foredoomed to failure for reasons of which he did not seem to be explicitly aware. He certainly had forebodings, but he did not examine them too closely. His method of exaggerating the differences between rationalism and empiricism to create two ideal types linked system so closely with dogmatic absolutism and gratuitous subjectivism and its opposite — fragmentary, piecemeal accretion — with robust realism and experimental validation, that they stand or fall along with their satellite meanings. Thus, James could not imagine a systematic approach which was not thereby dogmatic and absolutistic. Empirical validation was tied by him to finite units. Therefore to present a system of beliefs as in principle subject to verification was self-contradictory because in such a comprehensive form all its units would stand or fall together. He believes that we can assent to or reject total systems, but there is no way that we can test them (see SPP, 18-19).

Therefore, the only system compatible with James's commitment to reject dogmatism in philosophy by subjecting beliefs to indefinite self-correction through experiment and observation is that of a collection. This accounts for the fragmentary and unsystematic character of *Some Problems*, rather than the fact that it was never put into final form. In the second chapter James can simply randomly list the problems of metaphysics because his intention is not to order them but to test them, and on his empiricist model, this can only be done one by one. In the remaining chapters he also takes up individual metaphysical problems as isolated units and not as forming an interrelated system.

Perhaps this restriction of the meaning of a legitimate system to a collection also accounts for James's inability to formalize the organizational structures he employs. His intention to concentrate on the object of investigation rather than the means of investigation leads to a blindness in regard to the structures of interpretation that he nonetheless uses. A system in the sense of an inter-related set of principles of *interpretation* never seems to have occurred to him. That he recognizes no organizational structure between that of a total system and individual units is also odd in light of his thesis of selective interest.

6. Beyond Metaphysics

Two recent books deliberately engage in developing a pragmatic metaphysics. In *Speculative Pragmatism*, Sandra Rosenthal defends the claim that the classical American pragmatists were engaged in metaphysical speculation because they were concerned with developing "a metaphysics that reaches the richness of the independently real in its foundational concreteness."[3] In *Self, God, and Immortality*, Eugene Fontinell develops a metaphysics based on Jamesian texts.[4] While acknowledging that he is not constructing "a fully developed and systematic metaphysics," he nevertheless claims to be engaged in metaphysical speculation in "a less formal sense...as an 'angle of vision' or perspective from which we view the world and by means of which we interact with and perhaps constitute the world."[5] He acknowledges that "pragmatism is antimetaphysical if metaphysics is understood in its classical sense as knowledge of the ultimate and unchanging character of being- or reality-in-itself...unrelated to human experience" or of the "ultimate origin or end of the world process." But pragmatism also "does not hesitate to venture some metaphysical guesses or construct some metaphysical myths by way of extrapolation from concrete experience as to what characterizes reality or the world."[6] He then gives and explains the meaning of four characteristics of reality on which pragmatists agree.

Although I am largely sympathetic to Rosenthal's and Fontinell's approaches, I think that it would be a great aid to clarifying crucial aspects of pragmatism to restrict the designation of metaphysics to its classical sense and then examine its relevance to pragmatism as understood by its various practitioners. A careful consideration of the reasons given for rejecting metaphysics and identification of what takes its place is indispensable for recognizing and evaluating the significance of the pragmatic movement. The unexamined assumptions and beliefs about the world that everyone holds do not constitute a metaphysics because they are not systematized, formally related, and do not include rules of inference or formalized methodological principles. In a word, they are not formal systems. And among systems only those are metaphysical which seek to disclose the ultimate principles of being as such. The beliefs we all hold are analogous to metaphysical systems insofar as we take them as disclosing reality as it is in itself. But to call such beliefs 'metaphysical' and to conclude that everyone, including the pragmatists, therefore has a metaphysics in this sense, is not only to confuse colloquial usage with terms whose meanings derive from centuries of philosophical debate but also to lose the precision necessary to determine when a belief has been confirmed or denied.

Furthermore, modern philosophy since Descartes is characterized by its explicit recognition of the unbreakable link of being with knowing, of an identification of 'what is' only in relation to how we know. This reflexive turn takes different forms in the various philosophies. It is not accidental that Hume turned to skepticism as the only rational response to the loss of metaphysics, that Kant, in rejecting metaphysics, substituted for it transcendental analysis or that Hegel dissolved the traditional metaphysical distinctions in dialectics. To hold that the pragmatists rejected classical metaphysics but then kept doing metaphysics of some sort anyway is to unhistorically remove them from the central debate of modern philosophy, which became more acute with the Darwinian revolution and re-emphasized with quantum physics. How can we legitimate any claims about the world now that we know that we can never grasp it as it is in itself but only in relation to us? If metaphysical claims about reality are no longer possible, what will replace them? Derridean deconstructionists say the endless play of unverifiable word games and Richard Rorty says conversations. Against such nihilism and relativism pragmatists argue for warranted assertions, understood within a hermeneutical, concrete angle of vision, not new metaphysical assumptions.

Their defense of objectivity within a subjective apprehension of the world is unrecognizable if couched as some sort of unsystematic metaphysics. To say that the pragmatists insisted that "metaphysical generalizations must be grounded in immediate experience" is to miss the force of their arguments against metaphysical speculation, against metaphysical grounding, against metaphysical experience. All these terms have specific meanings if understood metaphysically and radically different meanings if understood in post-metaphysical terms. These meanings are hopelessly muddled by retaining the word, 'metaphysics,' for metaphysical and post-metaphysical discourse. The pragmatists themselves were not always consistent in their usage and this has contributed to disagreement among commentators.[7] But given a better awareness of the nuances and implications of a metaphysical world view engendered by current debates over rationalism, we are now in a better position to be appreciative of what the pragmatists were trying to accomplish in their criticism of metaphysical thinking.

This does not make the assumptions that can be identified in the writings of the various pragmatists disappear. If not metaphysical assumptions, what are we to call them, especially when they function as principles from which to derive other claims? They should be called interpretive structures of experience. In Dewey's terms they are assertions which have been found to be warranted by applying his logic of inquiry. In James's terms they are beliefs which have been funded by experience, that is, someone's novel 'markings' which have been found by others over a long time to be successful in organizing experience to meet their expectations. They are Peirce's categories when understood as a semeiotic, as a theory of signs susceptible to pragmatic confirmation, rather than as revelations of reality. They function within a concrete analysis which seeks to identify the structures of human interaction within our experienced world. On the level of everyday experience the origins of this process of weaving order into chaos are diffuse and lost in time, making possible the debates over whether common sense beliefs, for example, are innate or acquired. The process is explicit in the sciences, where we can reconstruct historically when explanatory structures were introduced and by whom and when they became an accepted part of the practice of the discipline.

It is possible to develop from the Jamesian texts a systematic method of interpretation, a concrete hermeneutics, but not a systematic explanation of reality from a privileged or ontologically objective standpoint. This recognition that there is no archimedean point outside experience that could objectively grasp reality as a total system means that he does not have a metaphysics. The "structural form of the mind," as expressed in the reconstructed reflex arc doctrine, determines the place of philosophy, whether this is expressed systematically or as *Weltanschauung*. There are three stages. First, "the thinker starts from some experience of the practical world, and asks its meaning" (WB, 112). Next, comes speculation, theory building, or — James's preferred term — hypothesis formation, in the attempt to develop a limited, systematic, or cogent explanation which will disclose the meaning of the original experience. But no matter how attractive or logically compelling such theories are in themselves, "the utmost result they can issue in is some new practical maxim or resolve, or the denial of some old one," that applies to "the *terra firma* of concrete life again."

In saying that "whatever thought takes this voyage is a philosophy," James not only refuses to limit philosophizing to those professionals who have earned academic credentials, but he also implies that any intellectualizing that does not fulfill all three criteria should be called philosophy. These three philosophical stages replicate the three aspects of rational thinking: namely, beginning in a careful examination of an experiential situation (sensory clarification); relating these findings with others in an original, ordered system or theory (simplifying); and then applying the results to transform the original situation into the expected order. This last criterion means acting on our reasonable beliefs to bring about a better situation than the one with which we started. Although any one of these functions of the mind can be brought to a satisfactory conclusion on its own terms, philosophizing is precisely that activity which has as its explicit goal the harmonizing of all three. Philosophers not only employ such on-going interpretive strategies, but they are also uniquely determined by their primary interest in coherence or harmony. Such a pragmatic understanding of philosophy does not warrant claiming any metaphysical disclosure of reality.

Chapter Fourteen

Radical Empiricism as Concrete Alternative to Realism

"If empiricism is to be radical it must indeed admit the concrete data of experience in their full completeness" (CER, 443).

In the critical apparatus for the text Fredson Bowers says that "one of the mysterious features of *Essays in Radical Empiricism* is that its completed plan of May 1907, as exemplified by the table of contents, was not followed by publication" (ERE, 207). It is his educated guess that this was because James wanted to systematically develop "his parallel philosophy to pragmatism" rather than just printing another collection of articles. Bowers does not speculate on the reasons for the apparent failure of the project. We explored in the last chapter the unexamined assumptions that contributed to preventing James from being able to carry out such a systematic project in regard to any metaphysics. A related issue can be raised about his distribution of the articles for the projected book into other books. The same psychological article, "The Function of Cognition," that James reprinted as the first chapter of *The Meaning of Truth* and singled out as the original foundation of his theory of truth was earlier listed by him as the opening chapter of his projected book on the metaphysics of radical empiricism.[1] The absence of clear demarcations between descriptive psychology, epistemology, theory of truth, and metaphysics is puzzling.

The puzzle can be deciphered by recognizing James's exegetical practice. The same original material is returned to again and again, but each time in answer to a different question and with a richer sense of its significance. It is first grasped as descriptive psychology or concrete analysis, then as an epistemology and theory of truth, then as a metaphysics. To develop an uncontroversial description of the cognitive process, for instance, metaphysical and epistemological questions are deliberately bracketed and a natural history, psychological perspective followed. Later, his epistemology is developed to make explicit what had already been investigated within a natural history framework. It formalizes the descriptive findings from the point of view of a theory of knowledge.

When James finally unbrackets the metaphysical interests, the greatest surprise emerges. The metaphysical totality has simply vanished. This systematic inter-relatedness of reality had provided the imagined horizon for all the partial explanations developed by adhering strictly to the scientific method. At the end of his career he reaffirms even more strongly the tentativeness that characterized the opening of his intellectual odyssey. He finally has to abandon his lifelong defense of objectivity, in the sense of an ultimate coalescence of human understanding and 'the world' as the totality of what is real. Such a hoped-for consummation is attainable, if at all, through ecstasy, both religious and otherwise, but it is not possible to pass from the universe of rational discourse to such ultimate experiences. The rational goals of ultimate clarity, simplicity, and harmony can never be more than heuristic goals. He thus returns full circle to "The Sentiment of Rationality," both versions, and its earlier arguments why such a harmony is necessarily sought after but has not yet taken place, but from the later vantage point of the realization that it never can take place in time.

This would further explain why he dismantles his projected book on metaphysics. Such a book could not be written after realizing that no metaphysics in the sense he originally envisioned it is possible. There can be no disclosure that can objectively and unambiguously designate the reality that we cognitively seek to grasp. Disclosure or clarity is a mistaken formulation of the function of cognition. But objectivity does not thereby disappear. It is instead reinterpreted as that subjective transformation of experience to bring about desired ends insofar as this outcome is in turn reflectively 'squared' with the funded character of experience. Metaphysics is thus replaced by an analysis of the structures of human interaction in the world, but only insofar as these are in principle subject to revision when they are acted upon and found unsatisfactory. Despite the motivating force of his long-range project, his metaphysics finally becomes an anti-metaphysics, a philosophy of the process of appropriating the world, of weaving chaos into order, and not a disclosure of being as being.

1. Dismantling Metaphysics

Hugo Münsterberg and other neo-Fichteans pointed out the affinities of James's philosophy with their movement, which was represented in Germany by Wilhelm Windelband and Heinrich Rickert (TCW,II, 469). James, for his part, emphatically denied that his position had anything in common with "either the original or the revived Kantism [*sic*]."² In fact pragmatism expressly aimed to overthrow the rationalism that holds that human laws legislate a priori for all possible experience and replace it with an understanding of "human ways of thinking that grow up piecemeal among the details of experience because on the whole they work best" (469). He explicitly faulted Rickert's postulation of a transcendental ego for being a mere abstraction set up against the particulars of experience which are "their real source and ground" (470).

Münsterberg sharply distinguished between experience, which is describable, and the deeper reality of will, "whose four 'postulates' of 'identity,' 'harmony,' 'fulfillment,' and 'unity,' define the realms of science, aesthetics, ethics, and religion." Since James characterizes these realms in similar ways, the precise nature of his objections can be more clearly stated. The fundamental difference is between James's functionalism arising out of his concrete analysis of being human and the romantic hypostatization of functions into substances, which is monistic and dogmatic. He writes to Münsterberg in 1906 that the material for such distinctions can be found in nature, but "they are only centres of emphasis in a flux." Likewise, the attitude of will and its postulations "are also really there, but resultantly and tentatively, along with rival tendencies" (TCW,II, 471). The will as a timeless self, necessarily supporting reality a priori, is a "*pure* fiction." Moreover, this mythological construct is useless as an explanation. James can defend both our irreducibly subjective contribution to the world of experience and the objectivity of our findings without going beyond phenomenal evidence to dogmatic assertion. In James's poetic formulation he says that he agrees with Münsterberg that "emphases and tempers are only the colors the world is painted in" but he also denies that there is only one way to rationally organize the world: "If the same content is there in every color it would seem all right to let us choose our colors as we please."

But has James escaped dogmatism only by falling into the relativism of unbounded choice? What is the basis for his assertion that "the same content" is to be found in existentially distinct angles of vision? Each person's phenomenal experience is as real as any other, subject only to the veto of future experiences. Since the world is too rich and various to be completely translated into any schema, then many perspectives have the potential for contributing more pieces to the mosaic of our understanding of reality. For James there is still a distinction between the experience I am really having and the reality that I am experiencing. Our understanding of experiential reality always includes more than passive sensory perception. We must build out the hints we receive by the background of our beliefs. In a 1906 letter to Mrs. Glendower Evans, James says that we supplement our lived experience "by a *more*" (TCW,II, 473). As long as we simply experience life, rather than rationally reflect on it, these additions to our sensory life remain only vaguely apprehended. It is only when we try to become clear about them that intellectual difficulties arise.

James schematizes these explanations as the absolutist and the pragmatist. In the absolutist explanation we supplement our experience by relating it to a totality and this totalization of the finite alters the form of experience, which becomes subject to necessary laws and certain pronouncements. Since even evil, as a part, must be logically related to a totalizing explanation, then the optimism of a final resolution to all finite difficulties is guaranteed. The pragmatist, on the other hand, supplements experiences by mere "quantitative addition, indefinite in amount,and merely prolonging the finite." Since we have not yet experienced any completely comprehensive rational explanation nor any complete transformation of evil into good, then we can only believe in the possibility of such final consummations and work to bring them about by the integrity of our rational explanations and the goodness of our choices and actions. But we construct meanings and bring into existence particular goods at our peril, with no guarantees either that we have understood correctly or chosen beneficently. James once again asserts the twin postulates of pure and practical reason *as* postulates that are part of the horizon by which experience becomes meaningful and actions morally good. They are not *necessary* conditions for meaning and action for the simple reason that some persons, at least, as a matter of fact, conceptualize experiences meaningfully and choose to act to alleviate evils without presupposing that a completely rational or moral universe necessarily exists as a model, incentive, or guarantee of our finite ones.

But if James consistently rejected rationalistic assertions of absolute totalities in both senses of comprehensive, completely transparent explanations and determinations of the absolute good, he also consistently argued that the experiences we have can only be understood within a wider horizon. He was not as clear in defining this horizon or systematically relating what was included in it, although it is a constant feature of his explanations. We have seen in chapter 5 that he explained what he means by 'world.' I take 'world' to be synonymous with 'horizon,' since it refers to the holistic situation which precedes such reflective distinctions as that of the outer and the inner worlds. "The constitution of the world of naturalistic truth itself can only be understood by bringing it into line with the appreciative truth. Subjective needs have played a part in both" (TCW,II, 476). Although James himself could not consistently reconcile his "natural realism" with his concrete analyses, he has already provided the means for dissolving, rather than resolving, the problem, as is evident from the last quote. Natural realism stands for belief "in extramental facts," in "real things, 'objective' both in the epistemological and in the physical sense" (TCW,II, 392). His radically empiricist concrete analysis stands for the belief "that it is impossible to strip the human element out from even our most abstract theorizing. All our mental categories without exception have been evolved because of their fruitfulness for life, and owe their being to historic circumstances, just as much as do the nouns and verbs and adjectives in which our languages clothe them" (CER, 450-451). His radical empiricism "must indeed admit the concrete data of experience in their full completeness. The only fully complete concrete data are, however, the successive moments of our own several histories, taken with their subjective personal aspect, as well as with their 'objective' deliverance or 'content'" (CER, 443-444). Despite the fact that James seemed to realize that "after the analogy of these moments of experiences must all complete reality be conceived," he thought that some reality must be conceived differently; namely, the extra-experiential reality that his natural realism defended.

He rejected humanism, for instance, despite his acceptance of most of its positions, because he could not reconcile the independence of being with an irreducibly subjective perspective. Since his own radical empiricism shares the same insistence on perspectivism, he struggled to explain it such that it is not subject to the same objection. However, he could not see his way clear. His objection is as follows:

> Grant, for example, that our human subjectivity determines *what* we shall say things are; grant that it gives the 'predicates' to all the 'subjects' of our conversation. Still the fact remains that some subjects are there for us to talk about, and others not there; and the farther fact that, in spite of so many different ways in which we may perform the talking, there still is a grain in the subjects which we can't well go against, a cleavage-structure which resists certain of our predicates and makes others slide in more easily. Does not this stubborn *that* of some things and not of others; does not this imperfect plasticity of them to our conceptual manipulation, oppose a positive limit to the sphere of influence of humanistic explanations? (CER, 451).

Like Kant, he thinks that he has to maintain the independence of the thing-in-itself, a thing which, according to his own concrete findings and radically empiricist perspectivism is only known as objectified into an object-for-us. He does so in order to prevent his world of experience from being indistinguishable from a merely wishing world, that is, from being relativistically subjectivist.

But his fears are groundless. What the reality of the world of experience means is precisely that there are resistances to our appropriations, but these limits arise and are recognizable within experience. Any particular explanation of phenomena, of the world as it appears to us, is limited by its workableness. As Nietzsche clearly foresaw, and James dimly understood, the distinction between phenomena and noumena ultimately collapses into a single world of experience. The resistances of its cleavage-structures are themselves within and not behind experience. They are what it means to experience, which is always already interpreted. It is because experience is interactively constituted that some interpretations work and others do not. But this does not "oppose a positive limit to the sphere of influence of humanistic explanations," in the sense James means, that is, it does not show that there are some areas where the humanistic or radically empiricistic perspectivism does not apply. It shows, instead, just where the limitations are; they are neither 'out there' in things-in-themselves, nor are they 'in here' in our interpretations, but they are within experience, which can only have the shape we give it. "There's the rub! for we have no non-humanistic categories to think in" (CER, 452). It has been the traditional interpretive distinction between a world of subjective experience and the world of objective reality that has generated contemporary attacks on objectivity and verifiability. Such reified distinctions can be dissolved by drawing out the implications of the perspective that "*The* world is surely the *total* world, including our mental reaction" [TCW, II, 476].

2. Pure Experience as Concrete Analysis

James's model of pure experience in his radically empiricist philosophy is yet another formulation of his concrete analysis of lived experience. Already in "Brute and Human Intellect," 1878, he had argued that knowledge begins, not with clear and distinct ideas, but with vagueness. "When we say that a thing is vague, we mean that it has no subdivisions *ab intra*, nor precise limitations *ab extra*, but, still, all the forms of thought may apply to it. It may have unity, reality, externality, extent, and what not — *thinghood*, in a word, but thinghood only as a whole" (EPS, 14). He says that infants in their first experiences and adults in entirely new ones experience "confused wholes" and that learning and further experiences give the ability to discriminate out particular details. He also begins to develop the role of our practical and aesthetic interests in dissociating "ever new and more delicately differenced ingredients" from out "the originally vague syncretism of consciousness" (15).

James begins "Does Consciousness Exist," the first chapter of Perry's *Radical Empiricism*, by pointing out that in everyday life we unproblematically divide the world of experience into thoughts and things, but that philosophers have sought for firmer grounds for this distinction (ERE, 3). His own explanation involves his model of pure experience, which is proposed to explain how experiences, originally undifferentiated, appear as discriminated objects. He takes his cue from Locke's having the word 'idea' stand indifferently for both thought and thing to argue that all our distinctions are functional, ways of organizing experience so that it will better serve our needs (7). Pure experience signifies that experience "has no such inner duplicity; and the separation of it into consciousness and content comes, not by way of subtraction, but by way of addition" (6-7). We must understand that he is proposing a model, a "supposition," so that when he later calls pure experience also "the instant field of the present," this should not be taken to mean that unreflective experience is an undifferentiated chaos, but that those distinctions that loom so large in reflective analysis do not play the same role in lived experience (4, 13). When we act, we utilize familiar distinctions without necessarily adverting to them or having more than a vague sense of them. It is only when we retrospectively try to clarify what we have done that we try to substantialize the process by sharply distinguishing just what aspects belong to thought and which to things.

This is even clearer in "The Function of Cognition," the article James intended to be the first chapter of his proposed book on radical empiricism. He there uses 'feeling' to stand for his intention to designate states of consciousness functionally. Whether a feeling is to be taken as part of our knowledge of objects or part of the objects cannot be decided by anything intrinsic to the feeling itself. This distinction can be made only retrospectively, according to whether it is a shared activity with those of others in a common world of interactions. The fact that his proposed second chapter, "The Knowing of Things Together," was written as an explanation of what he had hoped to accomplish in *Principles* further links his concrete program with his radical empiricism. What he later called 'pure experience' is another way of formalizing "the nature of the synthetic unity of consciousness" (CER, 371; EPH, 71). Experience, as experienced, is "one indivisible fact;" only when "taken in a larger world of which it forms a part," does the phenomenal experience get its connections "traced in different directions," and designated as either mental content or physical object (CER, 378-379; EPH, 75).

"Humanism and Truth," published as a chapter in *The Meaning of Truth*, was also originally intended for *Radical Empiricism*, (ERE, 204). In it he says that "experience is a process that continually gives us new material to digest" (MT, 42). In "Brute and Human Intellect" he had put it this way: "Any original Whole of experience is an eternal well of ever new and more delicately balanced ingredients, which little by little come to light" (EPS, 15). The earlier 'dissociation' and 'discrimination' is later called 'apperceiving,' and its function is the same: "We handle this intellectually by the mass of beliefs of which we find ourselves already possessed, assimilating, rejecting, or rearranging in different degrees" (MT, 42). Some of these apperceptions are original with ourselves, as all of them were at one time individual creations, but now most of them, such as common sense assumptions, are passed on from generation to generation "to get the chaos of [our] crude individual experiences into a more shareable and manageable shape." These *"denkmittel"* have now become "a part of the very structure of our mind; ...they apperceive every experience and assign it to its place." James appeals to pure experience to prevent us from reifying these categories: "We may, indeed, speculatively imagine a state of 'pure' experience before the hypothesis of permanent objects behind its flux had been framed; and we can play with the idea that some primeval genius might have struck into a different hypothesis" (MT, 43).

Imagining a state of pure experience reminds us that the way the world appears to us, the self-evident objectivity of objects, is actually the result of inventive categories by our ancestors that have been found to be useful and therefore preserved and passed on to us through our culture and language. However, we cannot remake the world at our will. As a result of past choices, some possibilities cannot be realized any more; for instance, "we cannot positively imagine to-day what the different hypothesis could have been, for the category of trans-perceptual reality is now one of the foundations of our life" (MT, 43). The necessity of objects appearing as they do is not one of physical or metaphysical necessity; people can and have lived in alternate worlds out of touch with the everyday world of their contemporaries. The reason that we must now employ such useful *denkmittel* as that objects exist even when we do not directly experience them is that "our thoughts must still employ it if they are to possess reasonableness and truth."

But this explanation for James exposed what to him was the Achilles' heel of humanism and of his own radical empiricism. Suppose the ultimate criterion of workableness meant working a rational structure into experience because this was a necessary condition for the possibility of an ordered world. Suppose such an order is necessary if we are to distinguish and pragmatically choose among practical judgments in regard to their value for life. Then the question of whether such judgments also reveal what reality is in itself can no longer be raised. James is having a hard time going around Kant (see PM, 269). Like it or not, the humanist position expresses the most original part of his own. In fact, in summarizing it he formulates more clearly his own concrete methodology:

> This notion of a *first* in the shape of a most chaotic pure experience which sets us questions, of a *second* in the way of fundamental categories, long ago wrought into the structure of our consciousness and practically irreversible, which define the general frame within which answers must fall, and of a *third* which gives the detail of the answers in the shapes most congruous with all our present needs, is, as I take it, the essence of the humanistic conception" (MT, 43).

James points out that "humanism leaves untouched" the question of whether these structures we have worked into the fabric of experience replicate its inner structure in itself. He repeats this in "The Essence of Humanism" in *Essays in Radical Empiricism,* where he says that it refuses "to entertain the hypothesis of trans-empirical reality at all" (ERE, 99). He wants to express this as though humanism simply does not decide one way or another on the issue and so leave open the possibility that James himself will find a way beyond reality-for-us. "For us, at any rate, it insists, reality is an accumulation of our own intellectual inventions, and the struggle for 'truth' in our progressive dealings with it is always a struggle to work in new nouns and adjectives while altering as little as possible the old" (MT, 43). This sounds suspiciously like his own explanation of the pragmatic method, and not just of humanism. He is willing to accept that reality "for us" is best described in humanistic terms, including his own concrete analysis and pragmatism, but one part of him is still a "believer in an independent realm of reality" (MT, 47).

But this vain hope is self-defeating because when he explains "the character of objectivity and independence in truth," he returns to the realm of "the concrete truth *for us*" (MT, 49, 47). He as much as anyone has convincingly shown that there is no other, even if he is unwilling to admit that the reason that trans-experienceable reality is not undermined by humanism is because it is merely a speculative idea. As long as James stays within "the practical and the philosophical stages of thought," and insists that "reality, howsoever remote, is always defined as a terminus within the general possibilities of experience," then his position remains a radical challenge right up to and including the present (ERE, 102).[3] When he slips back into natural realism and religious speculation that cannot be incorporated into his own methodology, he generates unprofitable contradictions.

3. A Reconstruction of Realism and Truth from the Perspective of the Full Fact/Full Self

Did James shift from Berkeleyan idealism to Renouvierian phenomenalism to radical empiricist realism? Or was he always an epistemological realist? Perry and Max H. Fisch argue for the former, Peter H. Hare and Chandana Chakrabarti for the latter.[4] If the argument can be settled by appeal to the authority of the author, then there is little doubt that from his earliest to his latest writings James consistently called himself a realist. But when attention is paid to the context of his assertions and what he means by realism, then a choice must be made as to whether more is to be gained in terms of present interests to call his a reconstructed realism and force present day realists to take account of his undermining of their traditional realist assumptions or whether his thoroughgoing reconstruction of it should be recognized by a new term. His criticism of traditional dualistic realism is so radical, however, as is his reconstruction of the task of philosophy, that I would argue that more can be gotten from his work by trying to develop his most promising insights further rather than by trying to rehabilitate old ways of conceptualizing truth, reality, rationalism, and philosophy.

It is surely significant that the more James struggles to defend and explain his realism, the less it resembles the traditional and still widespread empiricist model. He says in *Radical Empiricism*, for example, that natural realism would be refuted by empirical facts if "our minds have no object in common." But he holds that space, "the receptacle of certain of our experiences," can be had in common, and that we know that this is so by applying the pragmatic principle that "we are obliged to predicate sameness wherever we can predicate no assignable point of difference." He then argues that the spatial placement of physical objects fulfills this condition of having no discernible differences in its qualities and functions. But this same criterion is also said not to apply to the experiences of objects other than space (ERE, 41-42).

To defend his belief in natural realism James returns to this criterion again in "How Two Minds Can Know One Thing" (ERE, 61-67). But the proof given depends on the explanation of a pure experience as neither physical or mental in its immediacy and being classed as either only retrospectively, depending on the context of relations into which it enters. In a 1905 letter to Peirce he writes that "my starting point is, of course, the doctrine of immediate perception; but the further elaboration, I [haven't] met elsewhere, except recently in two Germans, Petzoldt & Heymans, where the non-dualistic view explaining 'mental state' and 'physical thing' by different relations to context is made much as I make it" (221). And in a 1908 letter he says that no one can show at any moment whether they are in possession of reality, "only the critical verdict of the rest of experience can show retrospectively" whether it is so (293). Subject and object are retrospective distinctions and not unproblematic starting points in experience. Moreover, the intuitive grasp of reality cannot be appealed to in order to prove anything, since it needs to be verified through further acts. Therefore, he is not so much elaborating natural realism further as he is replacing it with something else.

What he is replacing it with is explained in *A Pluralistic Universe*, where he says that "the simplest bits of immediate experience," of feeling, "comes with an earlier and a later part and with a sense of their continuous procession" (PU, 127-128). In this primitive flux of sensational life before conceptualization in which everything is pooled and mutual there is a fulness of content. Naming, conceptualizing, ordering of every sort cut into and distinguish parts and relations, "but no cuts existed in the continuum in which they originally came" (129). His method is to reconstruct the structures of "life *in concreto*," which is explained in the paradigm of the full fact, that is, the minimum unit of experience is not a unit at all in the usual sense of the term, and it is certainly not a sense datum (126-129). This full fact is another term for what he had earlier designated a much-at-onceness: "In the pulse of inner life immediately present now in each of us is a little past, a little future, a little awareness of our own body, of each other's persons, of these sublimities we are trying to talk about...and of who knows how much more?"

How, then, do we distinguish the parts within the flux that we have named, that have entered into our discourse and everyday life and expectations as the individuated objects of experience? To answer: "by way of concepts," is to concentrate on the function of static logical entities and ignore the fact that, as tools, they must be wielded by someone. *They* do not; *we* do, sometimes by our use of concepts, but also by actions. But this 'we,' or 'I' is not Cartesian; it is not an isolated ego. It is a field of consciousness, a center which is fringed by subtle extension into as yet unrealized subconscious possibilities (PU, 130). Instead of the transcendental ego James creates the paradigm of the full self: "What we conceptually identify ourselves with and say we are thinking of at any time is the centre; but our *full self* is the whole field, with all those indefinitely radiating subconscious possibilities of increase that we can only feel without conceiving, and can hardly begin to analyze."

James argues that his "concrete point of view in philosophy" is vindicated by the latest findings of science, which cannot be explained on the mechanistic principles which positivists presuppose in trying to eliminate the subjective factor from scientific investigation.[5] Terms like 'force,' 'inertia' and 'atom' can best be understood as symbolic instruments which help us simplify nature and guide our investigations rather than as revealing the inner structure of nature. He is not using scientific findings to prove his philosophical claims in any straightforward sense, but as part of a refutation of the positivist position which was becoming identified with a strictly scientific approach and which, if true, would disprove his own. In fact one of the greatest obstacles to understanding his position is the belief that the triumph of science consists in its 'deanthropomorphization' of the facts of nature. But no scientific findings have shown that we can live or think apart from our human way of interacting in the world. We should therefore take account of the human dimension of experience in any theoretic explanation of how we relate to the world. Our theories help us to map the jungle of the experienced world so that we can get about in it satisfactorily, but they do not displace it. "The whole undivided jungle, with our personal life and all, is the reality immediately given; and though it is given only in small bits at a time to any one, yet the whole content and quality of it is more completely real than that of any of those conceptual substitutes" (EPH, 169).

As we have seen, from his earliest writings James sought to delineate the characteristics of the living acts of reasoning, that is, the ways we seek to appropriate the world, rather than to abstractly define reason. His is an original formulation of the characteristics "of our immediately felt life," which are different from, and will only be distorted by subsuming them under, "the units that intellectualist logic holds to and makes its calculations with" (PU, 129-130). Spontaneity is the chief characteristic of concrete human life, "where the consciousness of the present is ever of *many* future possibilities, and contains always enough causality for either of them, when realized, to be regarded as its natural effect" (EPH, 170). The realities which are confirmed experientially or more rigorously in science do not throw themselves at us, but are the outcome of choices we make all along the way. To admit this irreducible subjective aspect does not deny the reality of the objects and principles discovered, but it does demonstrate the folly of trying to strictly demarcate what is real from what only appears real to humans. We need "the creative touch of human reason" to extricate the facts of nature, which explains why just "those particular creations resulted rather than a hundred others just as possible."

This model will be distorted if reason and reality are conceived as independent entities with the essential characteristics traditionally attributed to them. By reconceptualizing these terms as "selective interactions between living minds and their environment" we can explain why we can identify the causal conditions that link one fact necessarily with preceding ones only after "it has occurred, but which no acquaintance with the previous conditions can show to an outsider that it was the sole thing possible" (EPH, 170). This is because we are part of the process and not outside it. Our theories "change the world-situation and are changed by the world-situation; but the resultant new situation is always a unique one, and none but the agents of its production are in a position vitally to understand why or how it comes into being" (171). This does not imply comprehensive understanding, but only the initial vital understanding. This must be extended through a concrete analysis of being human, which reveals that we actively organize the world according to purposes and that to try to understand the world abstractly apart from this organizing center can only result in misunderstanding.

Now James calls this his philosophy of radical empiricism, to be sure, and distinguishes it from pragmatism, but what he has actually done is to provide an explanatory model to make sense of his earlier writings, which must be reinterpreted in view of the explicit paradigm, even though he did not follow through himself. His unexamined empiricist beliefs were so strong that, although he was aware that he had a radically new explanation for how we order our experience, he did not undergo a paradigm shift. He either could not or would not accept the fact that his new position undermines the old realist abstractionist paradigm and necessarily replaces it. We can see both this compartmentalization at work and also how it cannot be sustained by turning back to two contiguous chapters in *The Meaning of Truth*, namely, chapter 9, "The Meaning of the Word Truth" and chapter 10, "The Existence of Julius Caesar." The issue can be more succinctly developed from the abstracts of earlier versions of each, which are found in Appendixes II and III of the Harvard edition of *The Meaning of Truth*. In the summary of chapter 9, James clearly says that his "account of truth is realistic, and follows the epistemological dualism of common sense" (MT, 291). He illustrates it by the example of recognizing which desk is referred to when someone says that the desk exists and then picks one up and shakes it. "This notion of a reality independent of either one of us, taken from ordinary social experience, lies at the base of the pragmatist definition of truth." But does it? This sentence is immediately followed by the claim that statements are said to be true when they agree with reality in some such way as the one illustrated. But by this agreement is meant the pragmatic one of a successful leading, of "certain actual or potential 'workings.'" Agreement cannot be determined without reference, but this is explained in pragmatic, not realist or common sense dualistic terms: "A determinate *reference* and some sort of satisfactory *adaptation* are thus constituent elements in the definition of any statement as 'true'" (291). Both reference and adaptation depend on the pragmatic understanding of working and not on an intuition of agreement.

The usual analysis of truth as a relationship of three logical terms — a proposition, an object, and their agreement or failure to agree — is an abstraction which makes sense only in virtue of the suppressed total situation. James's contribution to the theory of truth is to call our attention to this concrete situation, the ignoring of which has led to unsolvable epistemological impasses. 'Which' thing is referred to "means our pointing to a locus; the *what* means choice on our part of an essential aspect to apperceive the thing by (and this is always relative to what Dewey calls our 'situation'); and the *that* means our assumption of the attitude of belief, the reality-recognizing attitude" (MT, 291). The usual definition of truth as 'agreement' is said to be not so much false as "insufficient." In fact, it has been superseded. What is left of the prior dualism of subject and object? Outside of a situation of reference, of apperception, of choice, and of attitudes of belief, what does it mean to say that the subject and object stand face to face with each other waiting to be brought into agreement? The paradigm shift to a radically empiricist model of concrete experience is even clearer in Dewey's explanation of 'situation,' which James appropriates.[6]

In Appendix III, James develops in more detail the new paradigm of 'true' meaning 'working' and explicitly criticizes the old model of the naive and uncritical assertion that 'true' means that a statement agrees with reality, as though this were an explanation rather than an enigmatic claim. "In the ultra-simple universe imagined, reference is left indeterminate; the conditions of truth thus seem incomplete: that universe must be enlarged" (MT, 293). He uses as an example the claim that for the proposition, "Caesar really existed" to be true, it is enough for the proposition to be held and for Caesar to have existed. But the existence of prior events and facts, of which there are too many to enumerate, and most of which we will never now be able to know, do not, merely by having been, confer truth on present statements. Caesar's having existed may be irrelevant to my current proposition as well as having something to do with its truth or falsity. We who make the statement do not, like an all-knowing being, stand outside of time and place and simply look and see if a present statement matches a past event. Therefore, when we make such truth assertions, what are we doing, assuming we are not simply making wild, unsupported claims?

James argues that we cannot *"adequately define"* what more is required, in addition to some fact having occurred, if we leave out of our account the notion of 'working' (MT, 295). The usual way of calling something true outside of any actual determination of truth, as when someone says that it was already true that anthrax caused rabies even before Pasteur proved by experiment that it did, is based on our everyday experience of anticipating eventual outcomes. It is like everyone saying that they hold the winning lottery number after the winning number has been drawn but before it has been announced. Suppose further that both the announcer and the number are destroyed by a bolt of lightning. What does it mean to say that one of them has made a true statement? What is true about it now? Which is the 'it' that is true? How can we know which 'who' has won? On the supposition that all of the entrants say before the fact that they have won, in what does the winning consist? Or suppose the winning ticket and some of the other tickets were lost before the announcement and the person holding the winning number does not remember the number and so no one ever comes to know who truly said, "I am the winner" before the fact. What does 'win' then mean in that case?

In practical life it makes sense to say that one of the earlier statements was already true when it was uttered because the worth of such a claim can be literally 'cashed in' after the fact of the announcement. It is only because we can anticipate that one of the earlier statements is going to be shown to be the case that we bother to take appropriate actions like holding on to our tickets and listening for the results. As a shorthand way of talking about this anticipation of the eventual outcome, we say that we *were* right, that we spoke the truth.

"People, mixing history with the purely logical inquiry, & falling back upon inveterate habits of speech, will still say: 'The statement is true anyhow, true in advance, born true, true apart from any of its workings'" (MT, 295). But reflective thinkers have no such justification for taking only part of the conditions for truth for an adequate explanation.

If philosophers are going to continue to call 'true' what fulfills "only a part of the constituents of its full definition," then James suggests designating "the fuller concept" by another term, perhaps, 'truthfulness.' In this rare recognition by James that he should use new terms for his new explanations so as to avoid confusion with the terms as usually understood, he might have only been trying to get his critics to take his explanation on its own terms rather than attacking it because it did not reproduce theirs. But his critics were right. If his explanation finally proved more persuasive, then it would not merely expand on theirs but would replace it. James concludes by putting this in a more conciliatory way, one which indicates both that he saw his own explanation as more continuous with the traditional one than it was and that he saw that it went far beyond it: "The friends of 'truth' would still have to admit, however, that our more concrete notion of 'truthfulness' envelopes the whole of their own more abstract notion, & defines in the only adequate fashion what perfect knowledge is" (MT, 296).

Likewise, as late as 1907 he is still calling himself a "natural realist" in a letter to Dickinson S. Miller.[7] But he then gives an explanation of reality that is perfectly consistent with his full fact or full self, and no longer merely an expansion or correction of traditional philosophic realism. Realism in the empiricist tradition is strongly value-laden, since it designates the only defensible philosophical attitude in a tradition that denies solipsistic subjectivism by asserting that we have direct knowledge of the real world, which we do not construct, but find ready-made. Since James's long-range project involved demonstrating that our true beliefs are justified because they are grounded in experience, he understood his explanations as bounded within the empiricist horizon of 'realism.' But as his critics kept pointing out, this designation was no longer apt.

Nonetheless, the realist strand persisted to the end and was never reconciled with his concrete/hermeneutic alternative explanations. He says in 1909, for instance, that he is "quite willing to part company with Professor Bergson, and to ascribe a primarily theoretical function to our intellect, provided you on your part then agree to discriminate 'theoretic' or scientific knowledge from deeper 'speculative' knowledge aspired to by most philosophers, and concede that theoretic knowledge, which is knowledge *about* things, as distinguished from living contemplation or sympathetic acquaintance with them, touches only the outer surface of reality" (PU, 111). This is foolish from the point of view of traditional reasoning, but "difficult as such a revolution is, there is no other way, I believe, to the possession of reality" (121-122). It turns out that his critique of aesthetic intellectualism, which is consistent from his earliest to his latest writings, is restricted to denying that the aesthetically pleasing formal structures it sets up to account for reality can ever succeed in disclosing that reality. Instead, these intellectual constructs are best characterized instrumentally, as useful tools for handling reality to fulfill the purposes we impose on it.

Rather than continuing the philosophic tradition that, beginning with Plato, values pure reason primarily for its own sake and secondarily as a guide to action, he argues that our practical interests in carving out a human space guide our intellectual constructs, although they do not produce them in the first place. Neither are true conceptions interchangeable with reality, since he has also consistently held that conceptual abstractions from the flux of experience are necessarily partial and distortive. The fact that the reasoning process works by isolating aspects from the totality of experience gives us our power to transcend the particularities of immediate experience and extends tremendously our range of action. Such irremediable partiality does not hinder action, but is a poor guide to the fullness of reality.

What is less clear from the texts, but seems to be the case on repeated readings, is that he exempts from this restriction other avenues of access to reality. James does not make the hermeneutic move that argues that since we cannot grasp reality as it is in itself but only as it is for us, our search for a reality beyond the phenomena is a misguided understanding of the finite and temporal character of our being in the world. Neither does he take the logically next step that Nietzsche did and collapse the distinction as a category mistake. Instead, he makes the rather odd move — given his sustained defense of our finitude and temporality — of arguing that since we cannot intellectually encompass the reality behind appearances, we must have access to it some other way. Instead of understanding his own analysis as undermining the distinction between phenomenal appearances and reality, he takes it as demonstrating the bankruptcy of intellectual reasoning. Since he steadfastly refuses to examine his realist presuppositions, all the critique is aimed at those rational assumptions to which he is less committed. He does not see that aesthetic rationalism and empiricist realism stand or fall together.

It seems that the specter of the noumenal standing ready to mock the phenomenal, which he called the reductive of being and the basis for skepticism in his earliest writings, never ceased to haunt him. We have seen that in his last book "the question of Being" still remained for him "the darkest in all philosophy" (SPP, 30). According to a letter he wrote to Schiller in 1909, despite his earlier trenchant criticisms of explanations which explained by merely reduplicating what we understood on the phenomenal level by inventing a spiritual or intellectual double, he still understood his universe as being divided three ways, namely, into "mind knowing," and "thing known," connected by "phenomenal intermediaries."[8] He does not seem to grasp that the 'thing known' is as much an invented double as Kant's 'ding-an-sich,' and as little accessible. What makes this unreconstructed realism so odd is that in the paragraph preceding the one on the darkness of being he recognized that the puzzling aspects of being vanish as long as we stay "*within experience*," that is, on the phenomenal level of explanation (29). And in a second letter written to Schiller a few weeks after the one where he reaffirms his belief in the thing in itself, he gives an anti-realist explanation of truth: "Of course to work with the system is the mark of truth, but the system itself has central pins, points of anchorage, to which the rest is coordinated and *on the whole* the sensational order is the least moveable of these, but for pragmatism sensations must work with concepts and with other sensations to be accounted real and many of them fail thus to accredit themselves."[9]

The alternative model he advocates is that of "living contemplation or sympathetic acquaintance." By thus grasping only one aspect of an interactive process he relinquishes the gains made in a lifetime spent relating what aesthetic intellectualism carried to an extreme can only distinguish, namely, theoretic knowledge, or knowledge *about* things and its correlative, knowledge by acquaintance; contemplative or holistic thinking and abstractive reasoning or aesthetic discrimination; the scientific and the poetic; aesthetic and practical; subjective and objective; logical consistency and the perception of individual facts. He has abandoned his goal of harmony and his rejection of fanatical adherence to any one principle to the exclusion of other demands and forgotten his own insight that "sometimes the abstract conceiver's way is better, sometimes that of the man of instinct" (PP,II, 1266-1267). In a final effort to avoid "the Mephistophelian point of view" which submerges the absolute uniqueness of every person and every event by subsuming them rigorously under abstract classes, he instead falls into the opposite fallacy of affirming only unreconstructed concrete experience and denying any value to aesthetic rational ordering.

As with the pragmatic explanation of truth, the pragmatic explanation of reality, eventually reflectively grasped in radical empiricism, does not only account for our sense of reality. It also provides an explanation of how we have come to think of it in the passive realist ways that we do and how it is better understood as the outcome of an interactive process. Myers argues that James was never able to reconcile his common sense position with his radical empiricist metaphysics of pure experience.[10] He also thinks that it cannot be reconciled because the theory of pure experience is flawed since one cannot point to the bit of pure experience that precedes its differentiation into an objective physical object or subjective mental process. Consequently, he says that James's view of reality, as embodied in the theory of pure experience, "cannot be used for explaining the world we experience."

Myers misses the radical nature of James's reconstruction of philosophy because he situates James in the empiricist tradition rather than in his radically empiricist reconstruction of that tradition. He also fails to distinguish between James's concrete analysis of experience and his unreconstructed realism, nor does he recognize his reconstructed and unreconstructed metaphysical views. He does not sufficiently recognize James's break with the tradition nor the idiosyncratically 'transcendental' character of radical empiricism. James's rejection of transcendental philosophy is explained in detail in a little remarked section of *Principles*, called "The Transcendentalist Theory" (PP,I, 341-352), which deserves a closer analysis than it has yet received. He explicitly disagrees with the "Fichtean and Hegelian successors" of Kant, who understand the transcendental as the unifying activity of an immaterial, non-temporal agent, and he even doubts whether Kant himself ever held this position (345). He has already systematically argued against turning functions into substances and entities and understands thinking as "a cognitive phenomenal event in time" (349). He also objects to Kant's assertion of the impossibility of knowing reality as it is in itself and the characterization of "the 'Manifold' which the intellectual functions combine" as standing "*between* the Ego of Apperception and the outer Reality." Agreeing with Kant that "in the function of knowing there is a multiplicity to be connected," James places "the Multiplicity with the Reality outside" (343). But as we have seen, he had as much trouble as Kant did in attributing anything to a reality untouched by thought. This fundamental agreement that "wherever it is lodged it must be 'synthesized' when it comes to be thought" makes of him as much of a renegade transcendentalist as he was a renegade empiricist (343-344).

James's reconstruction of realism began in his earliest works and continued through his last ones, despite the fact that he apparently thought that he was only criticizing rationalism. We have seen that he was reconstructing realism already in 1878 in his exposition of rational thinking as the dissociation from a sensible manifold of some characteristics that interest us and that afterwards are taken to be obvious aspects of the object so constituted (EPS, 1-37). Throughout *Principles* he criticized the empiricist sense data theory that is at the basis of traditional realism. Chapter 19 on the perception of things and 21 on the perception of reality laid the groundwork for this reconstruction of reality. His derivation of the common sense categories in *Pragmatism* shows how what we now take to be irreducibly separate entities are in fact the result of apperceptions that had to be invented, that we have learned to apply to experience, that have become part of our language, and that we can no longer separate from the experiential object. His radically empiricist theory of pure experience formalizes the explanations that he has been giving all along.

Pure experience is not pure as experienced.[11] James would not be surprised that we cannot locate a pure experience that is not already a mental or physical experience, as Myers thinks is required by his position. As he already said in *Principles*: "A pure sensation we saw above, p. 657, to be an abstraction never realized in adult life" (PP,II, 722). Later, in *Radical Empiricism*, he puts it this way: "Its purity is only a relative term, meaning the proportional amount of unverbalized sensation which it still embodies" (ERE, 46). It is best understood as a limit concept, referring to the relatively unverbalized aspect of our experiences as reflected back on from the vantage point of a later, more articulate grasp of similar phenomena. As botanists, for instance, we can come to 'see' that the lush blur of vegetation glimpsed as tourists on the banks of the Amazon were 'really' mango and banana trees and creeper vines, but no amount of staring at them at the time could have ever disclosed this reality.

In thinking James disproved because he could not produce an undifferentiated bit of pure experience, Myers misses the point of the recourse to pure experience. Rather than a refutation, the fact that "we can never find an *it* that is sometimes a stable pen and at other times an unstable awareness of a pen" is consistent with James's explanation.[12] He is pointing out that these are distinctions we may choose to apply retrospectively to an experience that is simply had. In picking up a pen we do not wonder whether the blueness is 'in' the material object or 'in' the physiology of the eye and brain. These distinctions may be made by philosophers or psychologists because they have other intentions to which the picking up of the pen is now subsidiary and not the primary act. It is the "rationalist" or "psychologist's fallacy" to read back into an original experience distinctions made from a different perspective. James's explanation does not require that we do so. The notion of pure experience *can* explain "the world we experience," but it requires that we reject the naive understanding of a reality passively impressed on our sensibility and recognize the reconstruction of the way we both find and invent the world that is found throughout James's writings.

In the 1907 letter already mentioned James gives a succinct defense of his reconstructed pragmatic realism, and in its originality and clarity it deserves to be quoted in full.[13]

> The world *per se* may be likened to a cast of beans on a table. By themselves they spell nothing. An onlooker may group them as he likes. He may simply count them all and map them. He may select groups and name these capriciously, or name them to suit certain extrinsic purposes of his. Whatever he does, so long as he *takes account* of them, his account, is neither false nor irrelevant. If neither, why not call it true? It *fits* the beans-*minus*-him, and *expresses* the *total* fact, of beans-*plus*-him.[14]

To assert that the world can be grasped only through the interests we bring to it does not deny that it exists independently of us. We do not create the world, but we do participate in creating the world as known. Objectivity is not a given, but the result of certain subjective activities. Even what might be called the objective act of accurately counting or mapping the beans still expresses as subjective an interest as tracing figures. James distinguishes between counting or mapping and imaginative figure tracing, not as objective versus subjective ways of understanding reality, but as expressing intellectual as opposed to non-intellectual interests.

He is drawing on his model of the full fact or full self, which undermines the usual way of distinguishing subjective and objective and reconstructs these distinctions as variations among aesthetic and practical interests. For those who assess this from the traditional realistic perspective of an absolute, primordial distinction between subject and object, the results may be seen as a denial of objectivity and of reality. But those who have followed James's critical and reconstructive strategies might conclude instead that both objectivity and reality have been saved from the skepticism and nihilism that have dogged the unreconstructed position. In James's words: "All that Schiller and I contend for is that there is *no* 'truth' without *some* interest, and that non-intellectual interests play a part as well as intellectual ones. Whereupon we are accused of denying the beans, or denying being in anyway constrained by them! It's too silly!"[15] After having reconstructed James's problematic from its earliest formulations to its final expression, we are in a better position than his contemporaries were to understand just how silly the misunderstanding is.

Chapter Fifteen

Critique and Reconstruction of Rationalism

> *"Pragmatism represents a perfectly familiar attitude in philosophy, the empiricist attitude, but it represents it, as it seems to me, both in a more radical and in a less objectionable form than it has ever yet assumed. A pragmatist turns his back resolutely and once for all upon a lot of inveterate habits dear to professional philosophers. He turns away from abstraction and insufficiency, from verbal solutions, bad a priori reasons, from fixed principals, closed systems, and pretended absolutes and origins. He turns towards concreteness and adequacy, towards facts, towards actions, and towards power. That means the empiricist temper regnant, and the rationalist temper sincerely given up. It means the open air and possibilities of nature, as against dogma, artificiality and the pretence of finality in truth" (PM, 31).*

Since James's time, postmodernism has been developed as a philosophical position which criticizes the modern ideals of reason and the rational subject. Some of its emphases are strikingly similar to his. For postmodernism, according to Jean-François Lyotard, "it is above all the 'project of the enlightenment' that has to be deconstructed, the autonomous epistemological and moral subject that has to be decentered; the nostalgia for unity, totality, and foundations that has to be overcome; and the tyranny of representational thought and universal truth has to be defeated."[1] I regard James as playing the same radicalizing role in classical American philosophy as Nietzsche does for French poststructuralism. However, because of the independent development of his radically empiricist, concrete analysis of rationalism, he is not a postmodernist as this term is presently used. The postmodernist debate has to be credited, though, with bringing back into current discussions the thoroughgoing critique of rationality that was also central to James's philosophy.

In this chapter traditional rationality is criticized from the point of view of James's concrete analysis of living acts of reasoning. This is followed by a reconstruction of rationality in its fullest sense. It is this replacement of traditional rationality by a pragmatic rationality that has the most to offer contemporary discussions arising out of poststructuralism. James was an astute critic of positivism in all its forms but he did not despair of providing for legitimation after having recognized the impossibility of any universal metalanguage. With Rorty I think that the radically empiricist pragmatic model points the way to joining Foucault's and Lyotard's "postmodernist 'incredulity towards metanarratives'" with Jürgen Habermas's insistence that philosophy serves social needs by harmonizing interests.[2]

1. Critique of Rationalism

There is no doubt that from beginning to end James was a profound critic of rationalism. In the first chapter on "The Types of Philosophic Thinking" in *A Pluralistic Universe,* the last book published in his lifetime (1909), he returned to the anti-rationalist theme of his earliest essays on "The Sentiment of Rationality" (1879, 1882, 1897). His sustained critique of the insupportable claims that comprise the appeal to rational thinking led him to reflect on the structures of everyday experience as a guide to developing an alternative account. But the lateness of his explicit break with rationalism, despite his consistent criticisms of it, should alert us to the complexity of his response.

Shortly after publishing *Principles* he began analyzing the complex multiplicity-in-unity of consciousness from the point of view of philosophical reconstruction. For most of his writings he identified philosophy with rationalism, so that I think it is plausible to say that his own criticisms of rationalism, until the very end, were to be taken as calling for a profound reconstruction of philosophy rather than as a simple rejection of it. It was not until he could come to terms with the consequences of thinking beyond philosophy as traditionally understood that he could staunchly opt for a postmodernist world view. The tendency to interpret the whole Jamesian corpus as a footnote to the supposed voluntarism of *The Will to Believe* profoundly underestimates the magnitude of James's struggle to overcome rationalism and misconstrues the subtlety, originality, and cogency of his accomplishment.

In one sense, the end was already in the beginning, and critics are right to stress the continuity of James's thought inasmuch as his earliest writings already clearly identified the failings of rationalism. But it is one thing to demonstrate that the emperor has no clothes and a different accomplishment entirely to demonstrate that he has no need of them. James's negative critique of rationalism laid the groundwork for the positive contribution of a postmodernist world view that was not relativistic. It is this accomplishment that profoundly separates James and other classical American pragmatists from the nihilism and relativism of many contemporary versions of postmodernism. Such postmodernists assume that the breakdown of one world order, namely the rationalist, means that all order is suspect and that the only alternative available is a pastiche of fragmentary, ad hoc expedients.

Such writers as Derrida and Sarah Kofman ignore Nietzsche's warning against taking the breakdown of an encompassing metaphysical, religious, or moral interpretation of reality for proof that no organization of experience whatever is justifiable.[3] When the gods fall the religious horizon is also obliterated, and disciples too well indoctrinated with the belief that only religious and moral interpretations can legitimately ground experience can despairingly give up the attempt to find or even recognize alternative horizons. Likewise, the long indoctrination in the belief that rationalism equals order has led some anti-rationalists not to a post- but to a pre-rationalist abandonment to and fascination with chaos and consequent denial of other kinds of order. With the advantage of hind-sight, then, I would like to retrace the steps that led to the final, revolutionary break with rationalism and to begin to construct a model of a radically empiricist pragmatic rationalism.

"The widest postulate of rationality is that the world *is* rationally intelligible throughout, after the pattern of *some* ideal system (PP,II, 1269)." James was undecided for most of his life about whether rationalism in this broadest sense was true or false. At the end of *Principles* he summarizes the various positions that have been taken in regard to this issue (1269–1270). But he maintains an agnostic silence about his own position at the time and does not argue for or against rationalism but instead turns from this theoretical issue to more practical aspects of our organic mental structure. He thereby hints that the issue can be resolved, if at all, only on some practical grounds.

James's reticence in *Principles* can be partially accounted for by the fact that he thought that such theoretical questions were the proper subject matter of philosophy. We have seen that it was part of his long-range program to keep the findings of the natural sciences separate from philosophical reconstruction in order to establish an experiential foundation for philosophy. But elsewhere in *Principles* he did not hesitate to argue for the side of a theoretical issue in which he believed. His refusal to take sides in this particular case can also be attributed to his genuine puzzlement over the rationality of the world. We know that in his youth his realization of the nihilism of an irrational universe plunged him into a suicidal despair which was only overcome by the force of his will to live and postulate a meaning that could not be theoretically grounded. In his earliest published works he admits that skepticism can never be overcome as long as one begins by doubting because no affirmation is in principle free from further questioning. Furthermore, the contingency of being presents an insurmountable barrier to anyone who would argue for the absolute rationality of being. The two early articles called "The Sentiment of Rationality" account for the drive to prove that the world is rational, give reasons why rationality can never be demonstrated theoretically, and argue that on practical grounds the belief in rationality is nevertheless indispensable to the human intellectual appropriation of the world.

   This practical belief in rationality is held by James at the same time that he consistently attacks any supposed theoretical grounding and while he works to provide a phenomenal grounding in ordinary experience and praxis. It needs to be emphasized that he did not explicitly renounce rationalism until the end of his career. This is no belated recognition of a position he held all his life, as some would argue who value consistency over historical development, but marks the end of a struggle he had been waging since his first battle with nihilism. James was never a theoretical or intellectualist rationalist untempered by practical rationality. His early struggle with nihilism successfully inoculated him against this naive optimistic credulity. He had the strongest possible experiential evidence that no amount of intellectual reasoning could convince someone experiencing the bottomless abyss of the nothingness at the center of human existence that such existence is rationally comprehensible.

   But this same plunge into the depths of despair paradoxically also convinced him of the necessity of the belief in rationality for the sanity and well-being of the human person. He therefore vigorously attacked rational justifications of rationalism and thus can be called a consistent anti-rationalist. But he also developed many stratagems to ground the rationalist drive experientially and practically. While he was doing so, he felt himself bound by many principles of traditional rationalism. These conflicts generate many inconsistencies in his writings.

   Like others of the Scottish and British empiricist tradition, James was an experiential and not a theoretical rationalist. He was both a rationalist and an anti-rationalist, then, for most of his life. My thesis is that when he finally declares himself an anti-rationalist, he simply gives up the struggle to harmonize the illegitimate demands of rationalism with the experienced facticity of the everyday world which always overflows any conceptual organizing scheme. But he had already reconciled the legitimate demands of rationalism with his radical empiricist concrete analysis. As long as the alternatives are rationalism or irrationalism, then his claim to being an irrationalist is accurate and reflects his determination not to be put off any longer by all the negative connotations that his philosophical and scientific colleagues attached to this term. We can see in hindsight what he was too close to realize; namely, that he had already overcome the sterile dichotomy that sharply distinguished rational from irrational. A more accurate term than 'anti-rationalism' for his position would be the postmodernism of his 'reconstructed rationalism.' This reconstructed rationalism can already be found throughout much of his work, but was not explicitly recognized by James as a full-blown alternative to rationalist philosophy until after his third crisis, when he explicitly gives up aesthetic rationalism.

2. James's Genealogy of Rationality

Although what distinguishes philosophy as a discipline is its insistence on rigorous proof, that is, its intellectual rationalism, what interests us as persons is the outcome of the investigations. Without this practical rationality characteristic of persons, there would be no motivation for the more specialized interest in providing evidence for such findings. Rationalism is first of all a constituent of the human way of being in the world before it is a definable philosophic tradition. Insofar as professional philosophy divorces itself from this human-centered perspective and pursues abstract rationalism for its own sake, its specialized forms and methods can frustrate rather than fulfill their original and sustaining purpose. James terms this aberration an "abuse of technicality," since it involves treating metaphysical questions as merely technical problems rather than investigating them insofar as they represent issues that are meaningful in one's own life.

All spontaneity of thought and value for life gets destroyed when issues are determined only in relation to canonically sanctioned philosophers. The irrelevancy of merely professionalized activities can be avoided only by developing a deeper understanding of our interactive appropriation of the world. Philosophy, as methodical thought about the most consequential issues of our life, is too important to be left to professional philosophers alone or to merely technical interests. Because the "rules of the professorial game" dictate that philosophers "think and write from each other and for each other and at each other exclusively," there is a constant danger that the true perspective of the importance to human life of such thinking gets lost (PU, 13). This over-professionalism leads to the development of ever more technical vocabularies and the denigration of communication with non-philosophers as shallowness. It is a vicious aberration to overemphasize to students the technical aspects of philosophy and to lose sight of its origin and purpose in its relation to "universal human interest" (14).

James criticizes both intellectualist and empiricist versions of rationalism from the perspective of his own revolutionary new beginning in a concrete description of our purposeful ordering of experience. Intellectual rationalism presupposes a "block universe" in which particular facts can be understood only insofar as they are explainable as aspects of a closed system. It aims at total comprehensibility. Empirical rationalism, on the other hand, presupposes a world of mechanistic atomism about which we seek absolute clarity. James's critical strategy largely consists of demonstrating to the intellectualists that the universe is less systematically related, and to the empiricists that it is more closely related, than they variously suppose. But even this critique still presupposes that the rationalistic approach can legitimately disclose the nature of the world and this is what he comes to deny in his anti-rationalism.

Up until the third crisis James sought to reconcile his new beginning in a concrete analysis of the human organization of experience with a revised, but still traditional rationalism. But he failed to convince sufficient numbers of philosophers of the preferability of his revisions. Few outside the humanists recognized his new beginning in concrete experience. James gave up rationalism when even his revised pragmatic rationalism failed to dissolve the dilemmas that resulted from trying to reconcile his radically empiricist approach with rationalist principles. But in dropping rationalism as usually understood, there was no need for repudiating his own, reconstructed rationalism. Pragmatic rationalism is an expression of our interest in organizing experience congruently with our purposes. It differs radically from the rationalism which was restricted in the philosophic tradition to a specific set of beliefs.

Intellectual rationalism has its source in what differentiates us from other animals, namely the ability to translate the crude flow of experience into conceptual substitutes. Immediate experience is a dumb 'that' until named and classified as a definite 'what.' When once named and classified, such designated parts of our experience seem to exist as conceptually categorized (PU, 98). The strategic advantages of such classification are enormous. As instruments for handling the concrete flux they increase both our power and our vision. In its origins and purpose intellectualism is thus disclosed as a benign development of the human condition.

But it became vicious already with Socrates and Plato, who deified conceptualization and denigrated the ever-changing flow of experience, thus forgetting and falsifying the origin of concepts as humanly constructed extracts from the temporal flux. This dualistic distinction of the reality of essences and the mere appearance of our "feeling-experience" led to the impoverishment of the full range of experiential possibilities (PU, 98). The misuse of concepts begins with using concepts privatively as well as positively, that is, not just to assign properties to things, but to deny that the concrete object to which the name applies consists of anything else but what is contained in the definition. "Vicious intellectualism" is James's term for this exclusion from consideration of anything not specifically included in a name or definition (32). Such intellectualism unreflectively assumes that things are in reality just what and as we conceptualize them.

Thus, an originally useful ability to organize the flux of experience conceptually gradually became methodical and habitual and ended up defeating its original purpose. Since the concept 'one,' for example, cannot have the same meaning as the concept 'many,' then something referred to as entitatively singular cannot simultaneously have the property of multiplicity. This fallacy of applying to referential objects characteristics that are true only of their conceptual counterparts led historically to the denial of process as relevant to thinking (PU, 99). James responded by denying intellectual rationalism's "ancient Platonizing role of claiming to be the most authentic, intimate, and exhaustive definer of the nature of reality" (98). Since the traditional intellectual method cannot give an adequate account of human experience in its finiteness, its arrogation of the right to decide what reality can and cannot be is illegitimate.

James rejected intellectualist rationalism by denying that the logic of identity applies to the experiential world. He argued that the "conceptual decomposition of life" cannot reconstruct life again in its wholeness, since "out of no amount of discreteness can you manufacture the concrete" (PU, 114; 116). The intellectual "passion for generalizing, simplifying and subordination" is useful instrumentally in the human appropriation of the world, but becomes counter-productive when used to formulate the only legitimate substitutes for the fullness of life (15). Rationalism as James reconstructs it has "at least four dimensions, intellectual, aesthetical, moral, and practical" (55). The logic of identity itself is only part of intellectualist rationality. Aspects of all four should be delicately and recurrently balanced, rather than maximizing one at the expense of the others.

James genealogically identifies two sources of the drive to simplify, fix, and identify the same, to construct a "logical herbarium" to constrain the continuously changing character of life. One is the aesthetic and teleological sense of rationality as the feeling that whatever fits, is beautiful or good, is purposive or satisfies desires, is rational to that extent (PU, 144). The other is that whatever lets loose any action we are fond of exerting seems rational. These aesthetic, moral, and practical rationalities are expressions of our situatedness within the universe of which we are a part. They constitute for James that rationality which is found in our interactive being in the world. He proposes calling this sense of rationality 'intimacy' (145). It expresses the concrete aspect of his "new wave:" "We are, ourselves, parts of the universe and share the same deep concern in its destinies. We crave alike to feel more truly at home with it, and to contribute our mite to its amelioration" (11).

This understanding of philosophical thinking as an aspect of making ourselves at home in the world is presupposed in James's insistence on the great importance of each person's unique vision and philosophy as the expression of each one's intimate character. What are passed off as objective definitions of the universe actually exhibit our various reactions to it. Given our unique configurations of character and experience, we will prefer some way of organizing the complexity of the world to other ways more congenial to those of differing interests. Since nature lends itself to many different organizations, divergences of conceptions will continue to multiply, largely without experiential check, despite our concomitant intellectual drive to simplify and generalize.

Philosophizing that begins with the recognition of our situatedness within the world will be characterized by a feeling of intimacy with, rather than estrangement form, the totality of all that is: "the common *socius* of us all is the great universe whose children we are" (PU, 19). This intimacy of view is also characterized as a "sympathetic" as opposed to a "cynical" temper. James thinks that the majority of persons seek to be sympathetic, that is, feel themselves to be in intimate socius with the environing universe, both because this answers deeply felt needs and because the alternative is disastrous. This sympathetic intimacy is not a soft-headed romanticism but an attitude acquired and sustained at great cost and against often overwhelming odds. He thus rejects as too meager an explanation the rationalist contention that "we must translate experience from a more concrete or pure into a more intellectualized form" simply because it is our rational duty (ERE, 47).

His own "naturalist" reason is that "the environment kills as well as sustains us, and that the tendency of raw experience to extinguish the experient himself is lessened just in the degree in which the elements in it that have a practical bearing upon life are analyzed out of the continuum and verbally fixed and coupled together, so that we may know what is in the wind for us and get ready to react in time" (ERE, 47). In fact, not to want to be intimate with, or to demand a satisfactory relationship with, the world is usually taken as a sign that something has gone amiss with a person. This sympathetic socius ought to be a motivating force for philosophizing. The order of the universe in which we seek to share is one that we ourselves are helping to bring about. We help determine whether it will be beneficial or inimical to our interests (PU, 20).

James's criticism of traditional rationalism, therefore, stems from his concrete analysis of our situatedness in the world. Pragmatic rationalism as intimacy is an expression of those interests we share as fellow travelers on planet earth. These three are loyalty to the world that bears us, denial of the incoherence of the world, and the desire to grasp the world as a universe of some kind (PU, 11). Behind the internecine disputes of academic philosophers is a "deep agreement" which discloses this fundamental starting point of James's new wave. Given this agreement, philosophical disputes as to the best way to characterize our attempts to make ourselves at home in the world can be seen in their proper perspective as "small aesthetic discords" — matters of taste, dependent on our interests and psychological needs that cause us to be more comfortable with some root metaphors rather than others. The practical consequences of these disputes are not trivial, however, which is why so much emotion is invested in them.

James consistently argues that we are situated within and not apart from the world and that our philosophic interpretations should reflect this fact. The dilemma of solipsism, for instance, results from falsifying the connectedness that is prior to any reflective positing of a separation between self and world. This being active in the world finds rational expression in our care and concern towards the whole universe as the home of our being. We both always are at home in the world and we ought to make ourselves more at home, that is, to create those conditions most conducive to our further growth and development. Human activity is fundamentally the organization of experience to realize what are taken to be its better possibilities. But this is an ideal not always or even mostly realized. Not only are many human acts motivated by irrational urges to destruction rather than by care, but even with good intentions we often leave the world worse rather than better off.

3. Rationality "Taken in its Fullest Sense" (WB, 106)

In "Reflex Action and Theism" James summarized "the mind's criteria of rationality" that he had developed in "The Sentiment of Rationality" (WB, 91ff). As usual, the odd way of attributing the criteria to "the mind," as though any natural history investigation would lead to the discovery of these very facts obscures his designation of those structures which are basic to his concrete analysis. His interpretation of rationality in its fullest sense is based on his reconstruction of "the reflex-action theory of mind" (98). He says that "if the human mind be constructed after the triadic-reflex pattern we have discussed at such length" (106), then every universal formula and system of philosophy must satisfy "all three departments of the mind." These are (1) our impressions of sense or facts of nature, (2) the theoretic or defining department and (3) our fundamental active or emotional powers (which require "an object outside of themselves to react-on or to live for") (100).

The third department is called 'practical rationality' in the narrow sense, but in the broad sense, the other two stages also "subserve and pass into" this third stage of action (WB, 99). We delude ourselves about the second or middle department of definitions and general essences, of totalizing worldhood, when we take it as final rather than as a transitional stage. Its function is to transform the first department, that is, "the world of our impressions, into a totally different world — the world of our conception; and the transformation is effected in the interests of our volitional nature, and for no other purpose whatsoever." (95) We must remodel "the brute order of our experience" because it is so foreign to our subjective interests that we must break that order by picking out items that concern us in order to "make out definite threads of sequence and tendency; to foresee particular liabilities and get ready for them; and to enjoy simplicity and harmony in place of what was chaos". As finite beings we cannot think the sum of the empirical detail we encounter, much less perceive it. Only by exclusion can we rationally order our experience. Such a rational train of thought is defined as one leading to a conclusion that we can appreciate.

Although anyone may propose a philosophy which violates some one or more of these criteria, this failure will be fatal to its complete success. Privileging the second or theoretic stage of mental functioning is said to be responsible for such systems as materialism or agnosticism, since they define the essential nature of things and elaborate ultimate formulas without regard to their value for life. James thinks that such systems will never finally succeed, even if they are logically coherent, because they do not provide sufficient reasons for acting. The cycle breaks down before it reaches its conclusion because of the failure of the middle section to provide sufficient incentives for all our active forces.

Overbeliefs are necessary preconditions for rational action. They are subjective in that the particular configuration thought necessary for satisfying each person's needs can vary indefinitely. James both argues passionately for his own overbeliefs, including theism, and insists that they should not be taken as grounds for suppressing those fundamental beliefs expressive of other persons' being-in-the-world. Overbeliefs are also sufficient for rational action, and they fulfill this function from the strength of the conviction and not from intellectual clarity or independent verification. But for the full satisfaction of all our concrete rational demands, our intellectual curiosity as to whether our subjective beliefs also encompass the experienced world (the first department) and fulfill logical criteria (the second department) must also be satisfied.

James criticizes intellectual rationalism from the perspective of his own reconstruction of rationality. He accuses it of overstepping its bounds insofar as it is taken as the sole determinant of rationality and insofar as its demands have been met at the cost of inhibiting warranted action. But although the second department of intellectual rationalism should be neither the sole nor the ultimate arbiter of rationality, it nonetheless has a fundamental role to play. This role is its demand for objectivity, which James takes as an injunction to harmonize all three rational demands.

In the *Will to Believe* text James is still expressing this demand for intellectual rational probity as the metaphysical demand for a congruency between what we believe and what exists in reality. In the pragmatic rationalist model I am reconstructing out of the texts, the objective aspect of the intellectual rational demand is satisfied through the pragmatic method in the full sense explained earlier of conjoining the funded character of experience and leadings that are worthwhile. In James's earlier recognition of "how hard it is to discriminate subjective from objective factors in Truth's development" (PM, 37-38) lies the potential for rethinking the demand for objectivity as a demand for the development and application of a methodology appropriate to the full fact of our interactive being in the world. However, for most of his career James could neither reconcile the conflicting humanist and the empirical realist interpretations of reality, nor deny their cogency. He did not understand that his sympathetic attraction to the humanist explanation of the meaning of truth, when followed through to its logical conclusion, must eventuate in a revaluation of this pragmatic methodology as more than a merely temporary expedient until such time as reality and truth coincide.

The only aspect of the theistic explanation with which James finds fault is the refusal to speculate further about the "*character* of Being" (WB, 111). Feeling is much for James, but not yet everything. It does not exhaust the range of human demands. His argument proceeds as follows (108ff). For systems to be accepted in the long run, they must satisfy rationalism in its fullest sense, that is, the criteria of all three departments of sense, theory, and practice must be fulfilled. But in everyday life satisfying the practical demands is often enough. Practical rationality means that we feel at home in the universe and that our powers are a match for its demands, even though we have no clear idea as to how all this is brought about. But this practical rational equilibrium of our third department slights the demands of our second department of speculative rationality. For any belief to be considered fully rational it must satisfy our understanding as well as our volitional and emotional demands.

We are often satisfied in everyday life when our practical demands are met and think that we have no further rational obligation, since we have reached an equilibrium between our emotional and practical demands and life as we understand it. Similarly, persons for whom the intellectual demands are paramount will not be satisfied with less than absolute comprehension and will discount the need for satisfying the third department on its own terms. Rationalist equilibrium entails meeting all one's intellectual demands. Short of having done so, rationalists will not consider the attainment of a practical rational equilibrium to be a rational achievement at all, or even a desideratum, since the eventual achievement of total rational comprehensibility will also supposedly automatically satisfy our practical demands. However, this veto of the demands of our practical rationality by those of our intellectual rationality is just as repugnant as the reverse. But before providing reasons for this contention, James first shows how these excessive rational intellectual demands arose in the first place.

This methodology of tracing the genealogy of how they arose enables James to distinguish legitimate from illegitimate rational demands by making explicit the assumptions we usually take for granted. The method is genealogical insofar as it assumes that the present configuration of what we take to be rational is the result of our whole past history as beings who have gradually evolved, not only physically but mentally. This includes all the false starts, dead ends, and accidental branchings in one direction rather than another. Therefore, our present beliefs contain errors as well as truths and one way of distinguishing between them is to evaluate the desirability of the outcome of acting on them. All our understanding takes place over time. Acknowledging our temporality means recognizing that we can only correct errors from the standpoint of the understanding we have achieved up to now, and therefore all our beliefs are in principle revisable, even if such revisions are practically very difficult.

Thus, James's understanding of our interactions in the world underlies all his other critiques, despite the fact that he never organized this model beyond some veiled attempts in his essays on radical empiricism. He does, however, constantly remind us of the basis of his critiques by referring to his phenomenal findings. Once we become aware of such references, their ubiquity in the Jamesian texts becomes apparent. We can then recognize that these are not merely isolated positions, as his practice of drawing on whichever of them better fits the current issue makes them appear to be. They actually refer to an interconnected set of explanatory structures to which he returns again and again.

4. Inconclusive Conclusions

Nonetheless, the fact remains that he himself never systematized his concrete findings, and this has heightened the usual tension present in any interpretation of a text between philological probity and reconstructive license. Commentators are strongly divided over James's intentions. Some say that he was not only unsystematic but that he also advocated a pluralistic, non-systematic methodology on principle as best reflecting our chaotic, evolving "multiverse." Others interpret his metaphorical style as part of an implicitly systematic approach which needs only to be made explicit. They believe that he tried throughout his career to bring about a universe both of discourse and of fact. There is abundant evidence for both approaches.

More rationalistically minded philosophers have criticized James for subordinating our ability to know to our ability to act because this reverses the proper order of theoretic and practical reason. Knowledge for its own sake has traditionally been held to be a more worthy pursuit than merely finding reasons for action. It has also been considered the very defining characteristic which distinguishes humans from other animals. According to this line of reasoning, not only does the sphere of activity exist to provide material for our cognitive consciousness, but also sense information and the emotions are considered to be rather vague and muddled until clarified by intelligent cognition. But James points out that the logical outcome of the demand of the second department for absolute clarity and simplicity, which would entail total comprehensibility, would be to subordinate the other two departments to "an absolute unity of knowledge with its object," nothing being omitted (WB, 109). For our knowing to be absolutely adequate to all that is would require that our finite understanding become infinite, which is manifestly impossible.

This demand of theoretic rationality for total comprehensiveness, for absolute clarity and simplicity, is nonetheless considered legitimate "so long as it is held only as a postulate, as a mere vanishing point to give perspective to our intellectual aim" (WB, 110). Furthermore, this belief that it is possible to "continue indefinitely to approach it" is the chief reductive of skepticism. Skepticism takes away any incentive to discover the true character of the universe, since it argues that such an enterprise is illusory. Thus, James defends the belief that the intellect is potentially infinite, although actually finite, on the grounds that such a belief is a necessary precondition for action. But these necessary grounds are not sufficient; the belief which is so warranted first has to be legitimate, that is, there can be no empirical grounds which would invalidate it. The harmony appropriate to the second department is therefore affirmed, but only as a postulate, unlike the practical harmony of the third department, which many people have claimed to have experienced. Theoretic rationality functions as a regulative idea.

The empirical evidence which James brings to bear on his analysis of theoretical rationality is said to be drawn from physiology and psychology. But his formulation cannot be literally found in either of these sciences. He refers, instead, to his own reconstruction of their findings into an interpretation of experience which is persuasive just because it can be independently verified through empirical investigations in the narrower sense, but only on condition that an end-in-view is agreed upon. This framework, which is always presupposed in all his particular arguments, is succinctly stated: "From its first dawn to its highest actual attainment, we find that the cognitive faculty, where it appears to exist at all, appears but as one element in an organic mental whole, and as a minister to higher mental powers—the powers of will" (WB, 110). This does not refer to the isolated will of traditional philosophizing. Human cognition always takes place within a larger mental and objective world and analyzing it apart form these relations can only distort it.

James shows us how the factual evidence given to us by the physiological view of mentality does not have to be construed as proving that mind is really nothing but brain cells. On the contrary, he develops a powerful model of cognition as part of an organic mental whole in which choice about how to act emerges as the height of human dignity. This dignity has been upheld by religion and by both enlightenment and romantic philosophy, but he gives it a more secure warrant in scientific procedure. His method of reinterpreting both science and human values by re-evaluating the strongest arguments and findings of each in response to the other provides a strategy for combatting the excesses of scientism, unbridled speculation, and religious sentimentalism which still plague us. Furthermore, his unequivocal assertion that "behavior is the aim and end of every sound philosophy" challenges the prevailing academic view of philosophy as a purely theoretic procedure (WB, 111).

But he also argues that the speculative function still has plenty of scope and dignity in the task of ascertaining "the *character* of Being" (WB, 111). Despite the fact that his own unreconstructed realism allows him to slip into language like this which assumes that the aim of thinking is to understand being in itself, his actual methodological procedure operates on the assumption that the only being we can comprehend is being-for-us. Being does not stand over against the subject as the independently given surd of realist empiricists, but is our interactive being-in-the-world. By understanding how we come to distinguish self and world in an interactive process the hermeneutic or interpretive, rather than the revelatory, character of all such appropriations become apparent.

The radically empiricist concrete hermeneutics as developed in section 6 of chapter 7 has already utilized this model of reconstructed rationalism. The world appears the way it does because "we are interested in certain types of arrangement, useful, aesthetic, or moral — so interested that whenever we find them realized, the fact emphatically rivets our attention" (VRE, 346, n7). We fix these regularities in memory and record them for posterity and the order comes to seem normal and the residual disorder is ignored. Selectivity is constitutive of all our conscious appropriations of the world.

Without this ability to focus on some aspects rather than others the chaotic abundance of things and relations could be vaguely felt but not expressed. Nature is "a vast *plenum* in which our attention draws capricious lines in innumerable directions," and what is not traced sinks into oblivion, at least for the time being. But with other interests other objects and relations are appropriated out of the "infinite anonymous chaos of objects that no one ever thought of together, of relations that never yet attracted our attention" (346-347, n7).

The task of philosophy remains that of finding "an escape from obscure and wayward personal persuasion to truth objectively valid for all thinking" persons (VRE, 341). But this cherished ideal of intellectual rationality can no longer be construed as direct access to ideal truth or being in itself, which can then legitimately dictate particular organizations of experience. Intellectual rationality takes its place along with our other means of organizing experience, but this role is not hegemonic. Its constructive operations "presuppose immediate experiences as their subject-matter" (342). To warrant a system does not mean to subject it to the aesthetic criteria of being "all-inclusive, yet simple; noble, clean, luminous, stable, rigorous" as an "ideal refuge" enabling us to escape from "the muddiness and accidentality of the world of sensible things" (343). This view of philosophy as rational arbiter deducing its conclusions from some unimpeachable system is discredited, not by abstract arguments, but by the repeated testimony of history that no such system has ever been found to be objectively convincing (344).

James's reconstructed view of philosophical efforts to rationally organize experience, is that such organizations make sense only when understood as part of our interactive appropriation of our environment to bring about a better form of life. Reality is not 'out there' apart from us; "realities in the completest sense of the term" are found only in "personal phenomena" (VRE, 393). This means according to the full fact of a conscious field and its object. Objectivity is therefore interactively constituted through our activities. This is neither relativism nor subjectivism, which are criticisms from the unwarranted perspective of "the rigorously impersonal view of science" that James has shown to be "a temporarily useful eccentricity rather than the definitively triumphant position" that positivism claims (395, n8).

What are the criteria a reconstructed rationalism employs? First of all, it "would depend for its original material on facts of personal experience, and would have to square itself with personal experience through all its critical reconstructions" (VRE, 360). This insight has been powerfully returned to our attention through feminist philosophy, which resists the distortion of individual experience through false generalizations. Both James and feminists deny the authority of rational systems to tyrannize over an individual person's own living experience. But such experience can be grasped ever more effectively, as James has tried to do with his concrete analysis of the living act of reasoning as a selectivity according to aesthetic and practical needs. The ultimate criterion is that of the harmony of all our needs, not in the selfish sense of anthropocentrism, but through making ourselves at home in the world. We cannot know beforehand what will satisfy this demand, although we can search through the historical records of particular organizations of society and utilize imaginative and ideal constructions for clues. The goal of harmony cannot be accomplished merely abstractly, through aesthetic satisfaction alone, but requires the cooperative efforts of all our powers. Inclusiveness, not exclusiveness, is necessarily a goal in such an egalitarian account and, as James points out in his concrete ethics, the cries of the wounded will remind us when we have failed (WB, 141-159). We have no superior vantage point from which to denigrate as false consciousness the sufferings which others claim to be experiencing.

Rationalism as James reconstructs it still has a useful role to play in our efforts to weave chaos into order once it "abandon(s) metaphysics and deduction for criticism and induction" (VRE, 359). The primary means such a chastened rationalism has at its disposal is that of eliminating "the local and the accidental" from spontaneous constructions by which individuals harmonize their experience. The point of such siftings to eliminate what is "scientifically absurd or incongruous" — insofar as this can be ascertained from our present understanding of ourselves and the world — is to "leave a residuum of conceptions that at least are possible." Whether they should in addition become widely actual can be determined only by treating these residues as "*hypotheses,* testing them in all the manners, whether negative or positive, by which hypotheses are ever tested." In so doing some possibilities will be eliminated and others that seem more promising will be championed. The goal of such a radically empiricist pragmatic methodology is not to establish 'the truth,' which can therefore with good conscience be imposed on the rest of us. It is to "offer mediation between different believers, and help to bring about a consensus of opinion" (359). In democratic systems consensual action replaces hegemonic imposition by power elites, whether these mask their use of force by appeal to a universal rationality or to an entrenched economic or political order.

Conclusion:
The End of Philosophy and the Beginning

"The centre of gravity of philosophy must therefore alter its place. The earth of things, long thrown into shadow by the glories of the upper ether, must resume its rights" (PM, 62).

The task of metaphysics has traditionally been understood as the search for ultimate principles, sure foundations, and final answers. James argues instead that reflective attention should be shifted to the facts that seemed puzzling enough in the first place to call for abstract entities to justify or explain them. All too often rational thinking has succeeded in calling into question our most cherished beliefs and sense of self in the world without replacing them with anything of equal strength to determine action. We think that we act on the basis of our beliefs to bring about real change in the world, for instance, and are given arguments why mind cannot affect bodily changes; we think that we discover the connections of things and are told that we impose our expectations on sense data that are discrete; and we rebel against the suffering and evil all around us and are told that in God's providence everything works for the total good.

On the other hand, in the wake of positivism and in response to the encroachment of other disciplines on traditional areas of philosophic reflection, there has been a retrenchment to critical and logical analysis. Real-life situations enter into philosophic discourse only as examples. When some problematic aspect is taken up for sustained examination, it is said to reduce the level of discussion from exact analysis to inexact application. In an unpublished fragment James already labeled as "absolutely preposterous" the besetting fault of philosophers, which consists in favoring abstract reasoning over human interests: "If the intellect can only prey on life destructively how came life to engender it? It came from life, to life it must return. There must be a way of criticizing common sense intellectually, without landing in such desperate results. There must be an intellect that is reconstructive, not destructive."¹ There is no doubt that the project of reconstructing the task of rational thinking was central to his life work.

"The really vital question" for all of us, not just philosophers, concerns the future of the world. What are we to make of life? James realized that to shift the goal of philosophy from ideal descriptions and exact theories to the nitty gritty of everyday life and the problems of the mundane world would be to introduce a change as striking as the Protestant Reformation, and as unwelcome to rationalist minded philosophers as Protestantism was to papal minds. The call to pay attention to the factual world, including other disciplines, threatens the expertise earned by thoroughly grasping ever smaller subject areas. Instead, we get only the tentative gropings characteristic of strategic proposals for dealing with actual problems. The pragmatic approach is more scientific than traditional philosophy because it acknowledges relevant findings in other areas of research. But it is also more individualistic because it appeals to one's own sense of the situation rather than hiding behind abstract principles. However, such a situation will seem confusing, even anarchistic, to connoisseurs of abstract thinking, the very people most attracted to philosophy. "It will seem so much sheer trash, philosophically. But life wags on, all the same, and compasses its ends, in protestant countries" (62).

This book was not conceived as a final, coherent, systematic explanation of all of James's philosophy. This is because I am in basic sympathy with his refusal to join the sect of "the knights of the razor." An absolutely coherent explanation can be had only at the price of disregarding those aspects of his writings that do not fit. But what attracted me to James in the first place, besides a sympathetic resonance with the issues raised, was the multileveled complexity and evocative beauty of his writing and the refusal to theoretically solve an issue if it was unresolvable on the practical level of everyday life.

With each reading newly intriguing puzzles catch my attention, eliciting a desire to pursue them further and, if possible, to solve them, but they also make me wary of losing the metaphorical richness of the original. More would be lost than gained by taking up only one strand and disregarding all the rest. Sometimes when I return to the Jamesian texts with an explanatory model, I am pleasantly surprised to see how it clarifies many more texts than those from which it was originally derived. But other times some parts of the puzzle filled in one way by me are contradicted by passages in which a very different point of view is expressed. It has not always been possible to sufficiently revise the model to accommodate different discoveries made on different days and I have allowed these discrepancies to remain in the hopes that someone else can make more sense of them or, failing this, can gain some insight into the finally irreducible complexity of human experience.

Despite the realization that there are an infinite number of ways to reconstruct James's writings, not all ways are equally helpful, illuminative, or suggestive of further research. For myself, the attempt to develop yet another critical synthesis was motivated both by the desire to pursue further and possibly resolve what seemed to be intriguing but contradictory assertions by James and by the conviction that his writings still had much to offer that could be made available by rethinking his project. In the course of organizing the material to try and capture its structuring center of vision some aspects of the writings have been brought into relief that were either neglected or not noticed before. If the approach also opens up a particular angle of vision into his writings that helps others understand James better or develop their own interpretations more satisfactorily, then both motivations will be satisfied.

In any case, I have no delusions as to having finally gotten James 'right.' This is not only due to the intrinsic lack of closure of writing itself, but to James's own particular genius. His interests were simply too wide ranging and he was too honestly alert to contradictory evidence and desires to fit his texts neatly into any one systematic explanation. His own work certainly succeeds in bursting "the bonds of any synthesis" and forms "too dense a stubble to be mown by any scientific [or philosophical] Occam's razor that has yet been forged" (WB, 105). But since I also share in his passion, when in the philosophizing mood, to weave chaos into order, to intellectually unify the phenomenal multiplicity, I have tried to sympathetically reconstruct a coherent pragmatist position. Only by succeeding trials of organization can progress be made toward the ever elusive center of truth, toward a more harmonious ordering of experience, even though I never expect that we will ever arrive. In life, the journey is the end as well as the means.

Postmodernism has been succinctly defined as "diverse, contradictory, evading closure."[2] This definition fits James's writings to a certain extent, although it certainly does not exhaust them. He never sought to evade closure because it is the task of thinking to enclose the chaos of experience through conceptual translation so that we can "*revalue* life" and "drive it better to our ends" (SPP, 42, 39). But he never ceased pointing out that what evades closure is experience, which always overflows any attempts at final capture: "The world is full of partial purposes, of partial stories. That they all form chapters of one supreme purpose and inclusive story is the monistic conjecture. They *seem*, meanwhile, simply to run alongside of each other — either irrelevantly, or, where they interfere, leading to mutual frustrations — so the appearance of things is invincibly pluralistic from this purposive point of view" (SPP, 69).

In one of the last pieces written for publication before he died James took as his own final words those of the eccentric mystic, Benjamin Paul Blood: "There is no conclusion. What has concluded, that we might conclude in regard to it?" (MS, 411). James said this "speaking in the name of intellectual philosophy," which attempts to simplify the riotous abundance of experience. In concrete, everyday experience there are many practical conclusions, as James well knew, since he was anticipating his own death. It is only on the level of the reflective conceptualization of experience that there is no closure in the sense of a final, transparent, unrevisable explanation of being.

James's life and writings will continue to be rediscovered in each generation because they so strongly elicit a sense of the unresolvable tensions at the center of being human. We want both to reflect upon life and to live it spontaneously, but these two interests undermine each other as often they support one another. We crave the security of a comprehensive explanation of reality but also the exhilarating sense of the freedom of living in a multiverse that is wide open, and we therefore explore anomalies and multiply inconsistencies until they finally disintegrate the prevailing synthesis. Thus, some of us, at least, should continue to construct as coherent an interpretation as we can of our interactive being in the world because the attractiveness of simplicity is one of those "fantastic and unnecessary . . . wants" that has helped to establish us "as inexpugnably as [we have] done in the necessary" (WB, 104). But we can escape entrapment only by acknowledging the contrary but dialectically symbiotic craving for clarity, that is, for the overflowing abundance of what cannot be made to fit and which therefore keeps open the door to possibility.

It is profoundly fitting that James's last work is a fragment, prematurely cut off by his death. This is especially so in view of the fact that, according to the editors of the 1979 Harvard edition of *Some Problems of Philosophy*, it was conceived as his "metaphysic, the systematic general treatise on philosophy" (SPP, 200). According to James, it was to "round out" his "system, which now is too much like an arch built only on one side" (203). His failure to carry this ambition to completion is not his alone, but is the fate of every project of absolute unification, even those that seemed comprehensive at the time, and can thus serve as a fitting reminder of the impossibility of ever attaining an absolutely transparent understanding of reality. His legacy was not to be that of theory construction but the more radical task of uncovering the pre-theoretical context of reflection.

His own most lasting contribution is his concrete, radically empiricist method of proposing a compelling though "vague vision" of the living moment of experience by taking our perceptual experiences at face-value, and "following the analogies" suggested (SPP, 108). But "biography is the concrete form in which all that is is immediately given; the perceptual flux is the authentic stuff of each of our biographies, and yields a perfect effervescence of novelty all the time" (78). This live point of view is contrasted with the dead remains of its "conceptual translations [which] always maltreat fact" (100). The feeling "of the inner oneness of reality" is not accessible to theoretical unification. The "harmonious compenetration of manyness-in-oneness" can be attained only experientially, since it must be grasped, if at all, only holistically, and ratiocination is necessarily discursive and partial (52). With James's death, his particular sense of the unity of experience also dies, and we are left trying to patch back together its written fragments into a unified whole, a manifestly impossible task. But this Sisyphean task is one which we must ever take up anew in our human need to weave chaos into order, just as James did in his lifetime, and to which he invites us by the very shape of the fragment he bequeathed us.

In it he was following his usual hermeneutical practice of developing the strengths and weaknesses of two extreme positions when interrogated as to their value for life and then offering a mediating position which would incorporate the strengths and avoid the weaknesses of both. In *Some Problems* these extreme positions are the widest ones of rationalism and empiricism, as mediated by a pragmatic radical empiricism. This dialectic configuration is developed from many angles; for example, as symbolized in the language of percepts and concepts, of pluralism and monism, of necessity and chance, and of discontinuity and continuity. In taking up successively these traditional philosophical problems he eventually comes to the problem of causality and in chapter 8 examines the rationalist view of causality and in chapter 9 the perceptual view. This would logically be followed by the radically empiricist pragmatic resolution in chapter 10. But there is no tenth chapter.

At the end of the ninth chapter James is still struggling to overcome a "sweeping skepticism" (SPP, 106) by elucidating the relation of "the concrete perceptual flux" (109) to "the real *facts*" (108). He says that the complications raised "lead us to interrupt the subject here provisionally" (109). But before he does so, he appends a long footnote in which he reveals that Hodgson had many years before set the terms of the problem which he is still struggling to resolve (110, n3). Through a few bibliographical references he also sketches out the contours of the resolution, thus providing hints which I have tried to expand. This provisional stopping point was a final one for him, however. If the missing chapter mediating the two extremes is to be written, it must be done by those who are following the path marked out by James, through deciphering the marks blazed in passing, but then continuing on to leave behind their own unresolved puzzles. In his final, but unfinished, recapitulation of his philosophical project, he thus circles back to his inaugural address:

> So I feel that there is a center in truth's forest where I have never been: to track it out and get there is the secret spring of all my poor life's philosophic efforts; at moments I almost strike into the final valley, there is a gleam of the end, a sense of certainty, but always there comes still another ridge, so my blazes merely circle towards the true direction; and although now, if ever, would be the fit occasion, yet I cannot take you to the wondrous hidden spot to-day. To-morrow it must be, or to-morrow, or to-morrow; and pretty surely death will overtake me ere the promise is fulfilled" (PM, 258).

Notes

Introduction

1. For abbreviations used in text see Abbreviations of the Works of William James.

2. It is ironic that James came to view Josiah Royce in this way, in light of the fact that Henry Samuel Levinson blames Royce's Phi Beta Kappa lecture at Harvard in 1911 for helping to set such "enduring patterns of scholarship" as those of interpreting James from the point of view of *The Will to Believe* and for emphasizing "his temper, outlook, and spirit at the expense of his methods, arguments and conclusions." *The Religious Investigations of William James* (Chapel Hill: University of North Carolina Press, 1981), 273.

3. Before deciding that this falls into the fallacy promulgated by the new criticism regarding the author's intention, see chapter 7, "Interpretive Theory and Praxis," for the undecidability of texts when this link to the author is ignored.

4. William James, *The Letters of William James*, Henry James, ed., vol. I, (Boston: Atlantic Monthly Press, 1920), 199-200.

5. Daniel W. Bjork's book, *William James* (New York: Columbia University Press, 1988), has as a subtitle, "The Center of His Vision." Bork defends the legitimacy of trying to identify this center in the preface, xiii-xvii. He continues the current trend of drawing more heavily on unpublished material. The differing conclusions we reach largely stem from Bjork's interest in centering James's life, while mine is in developing an interpretive center that explains and organizes his writings. He quotes from James's "Notes on Cognition, folder 8," for instance, to conclude that "here was not only a psychological principle, but a biographical truth... This was a language that mirrored his own genius, the inner biography that was his own mind — consciousness charting consciousness" (161).

6. Richard Rorty points this out in regard to Wittgenstein, Heidegger, and Dewey in *Philosophy and the Mirror of Nature* (Princeton: Princeton University Press, 1979), 5-7. The change from foundational to contextual thinking is explored in William J. Gavin, ed., *Context Over Foundation*: Dewey and Marx (Dordrecht: D. Reidel Publishing Company, 1988).

7. Bjork, 266. The quotes in the paragraph are taken from the "Epilogue," 263-268.

8. Gerald E. Myers, *William James: His Life and Thought* (New Haven: Yale University Press, 1986), 298.

9. Ralph Barton Perry, *The Thought and Character of William James*, vol. 2, (Boston: Little, Brown, 1935). Edward H. Madden, "Introduction," WB, xxxviii. Peter H. Hare and Chandana Chakrabarti, "The Development of William James's Epistemological Realism," Maurice Wohlgelernter, ed., *History, Religion, and Spiritual Democracy* (New York: Columbia, 1980), 232.

10. Richard Rorty, *Consequences of Pragmatism* (Minneapolis: University of Minnesota Press, 1982), 174. For second quote see Ellen Kappy Suckiel, *The Pragmatic Philosophy of William James* (Notre Dame, IN, University of Notre Dame Press, 1982), 12. See also Myers, 96-97.

11. Myers, xi.

12. Levinson, vii.

13. Quoted in Myers, 508-509, n14.

14. James says, for instance, that indeterminism "admits that possibilities may be in excess of actualities, and that things not yet revealed to our knowledge may really in themselves be ambiguous" (WB, 118ff).

15. Richard Rorty, "Pragmatism and Philosophy," Kenneth Baynes, James Bohman, and Thomas McCarthy, eds., *After Philosophy* (Cambridge: The MIT Press, 1987), 27.

16. *Transactions of the Charles S. Peirce Society*, 20(Spring 1984), 199. Giuffrida also says that "one is left with the feeling that Levinson is seeking more unity than he is finding in James' work over these years" (195).

17. Elizabeth F. Flower, "The Unity of Knowledge and Purpose in James' View of Action," in Walter Robert Corti, ed., *The Philosophy of William James* (Hamburg: Felix Meiner, 1976), 184, and "William James, the Toughminded: An Appraisal," in Elizabeth Flower and Murray G. Murphey, eds., *A History of Philosophy in America* (New York: G. P. Putnam's Sons, 1977), vol. II, 639. Perry says that the "one germinal idea from which his whole thought grew...is the idea of the essentially active and interested character of the human mind" (CER, ix and 43, n1).

18. John J. McDermott, ed., *The Writings of William James* (New York: The Modern Library, 1968), xxi-xxvi and 7.

19. McDermott, *Writings*, xxi.

20. See Patrick L. Gardiner, ed., *Nineteenth Century Philosophy* (New York: The Free Press, 1969), 158-236.

21. *Letters*, I, 250.

22. For the crisis of confidence in philosophy brought on by the increasing success of science see, for Europe, Edmund Husserl, *Phenomenology and the Crisis of Philosophy* (New York: Harper and Row, 1965)

and Gerard Radnitzky, *Contemporary Schools of Metascience* (New York: Humanities Press, 1970); for America see Daniel J. Wilson, "Science and the Crisis of Confidence in American Philosophy, 1870-1930" *Transactions of the Charles S. Peirce Society*, 23(Spring 1987), 235-262.

23. James, *Letters*, I, 250.

24. James often comes close, but does not actually succumb, to the temptation to denigrate all unifications of experience because of the very real danger of oppression in every actualized expression of manyness-in-one. But his ideal of harmony avoids a poststructuralist version of nihilism. David Ingram points out, for instance, that "as Rorty has eloquently argued, where the Nietzschean enthusiasts of postmodernity go astray — in what is otherwise a commendable debunking of transcendental metanarratives — and where they succumb to the neoconservatism for which Habermas reproaches them, is in their sublime disregard for communication and social consensus." *Habermas and the Dialectic of Reason* (New Haven: Yale, 1987), 187.

25. See "'Experience': from Baldwin's *Dictionary*," EPH, 95.

Chapter One

1. Gary Brodsky also makes this point in "Rorty's Interpretation of Pragmatism:" "James and Dewey were not philosophers' philosophers and had serious qualms about the discipline of philosophy." *Transactions of the Charles S. Peirce Society*, 18(Fall 1982), 311.

2. Peter Hare, for instance, adopts Ralph Barton Perry's divisions: "In rough outline, James's central interests in the last decades of his life developed from psychology in the 1880s, to ethics and religion in the 1890s, finally to systematic philosophy between 1900 and 1910" (SPP, xiv).

3. Myers, *William James*, 299. When James republished the lecture as an article in 1904 he omitted the opening "2 or 3 pp. of California palaver" and began with the same reference to Charles S. Peirce that Myers does (EPH, 266). This may have contributed to Myers missing the significance of the lecture, since it is in these omitted pages that James gives his own view of philosophy as encompassing both a perfectly ideal discourse and trail-blazing.

4. "Clifford's *Lectures and Essays*," (CER, 140).

5. Peirce's well-known criticism of James as a nominalist rather than a realist could not be further from the textual record, and yet it is uncritically repeated to this day.

6. "The Sentiment of Rationality," *Mind*, 4(July 1879), 317-346. Reprinted posthumously in CER, 83-136 and EPH, 32-64.

7. "Lewes's *Problems of Life and Mind*" (CER, 4-11).

8. TCW,I, 322ff. and John J. McDermott, ed., *The Writings of William James*, (New York: The Modern Library, 1968), xxi,ff.

9. See chapter 4 for an explanation of these terms.

10. But this guide to the coherency of his life-long project was obscured by the fact that he never republished "The Sentiment of Rationality" as such in any of his books, although parts of it found their way into the chapter of the same name in *The Will to Believe*. This chapter was, instead, intended as its complement, rather than its replacement, but this connection was lost (see CER, 136, note, EPH, 64, note and EPH, 208, n64.23). Even Dewey referred to the later, truncated version: "I hope I do not do him [Ralph Barton Perry] injustice in saying that he would recommend James' *Essay on the Sentiment of Rationality* in the form in which it included the *Essay on Rationality, Activity, and Faith* (together with James' own notes now made available) as the natural introduction to James' own philosophy." John Dewey, *The Problems of Men* (New York: Philosophical Library, 1946), 389. Its importance has only recently been recognized once again. See McDermott, "Introduction," EPH, xvi.

11. Some commentators even talk as though there were an eternal essence of realism which can be automatically appealed to in determining a person's allegiance. It is no defense to point out that this is what realism currently means unless the arguments made by James and other pragmatists against just such an understanding of realism have been answered. See Peter Smith's review of Joseph Margolis, *Pragmatism Without Foundations: Reconciling Realism and Relativism,* in *The Times Literary Supplement* (September 4-11, 1987), 963.

12. "Living on the perilous edge" appears in a passage in "What the Will Effects," (1888), EPS, 234, and is repeated in *Principles*, II, 1181.

13. WB, 57-89. "This essay as far as page 65 consists of extracts from an article printed in *Mind* for July 1879. Thereafter it is a reprint of an address to the Harvard Philosophical Club, delivered in 1880, and published in the *Princeton Review*, July 1882" (WB, 57, n1).

14. "The popular mind conceives of all these sub-worlds more or less disconnectedly; and when dealing with one of them, forgets for the time being its relations to the rest. The complete philosopher is he who seeks not only to assign to every given object of his thought its right place in one or other of these sub-worlds, but he also seeks to determine the relation of each sub-world to the others in the total world which *is*" (PP,II, 921). This same contrast of the ordinary person's just "inheriting their beliefs" and the philosopher's insistence on providing reasons comes up again in *A Pluralistic Universe* (PU, 11-12).

15. It did so by demonstrating to James's satisfaction the plausibility of a supersensible world of an ideal kingdom of individual consciousnesses as the guiding forces for our never quite successful attempts to reconstruct this world harmoniously. In my own reconstruction of the basis of James's overcoming of nihilism I try to show that it remains plausible even without making this pan-psychic assumption.

16. TCW,I, 620. The reference to 'heterogeneities' was to placate Hodgson, who advocated a strict and unbridgeable separation between

psychology and philosophy. This was re-emphasized in a later letter of Hodgson to James in which he criticized Renouvier since "his system is a French *Erkenntnisstheorie*; neither psychology nor philosophy, but a *Mittelding* — half science, half philosophy. The *philosophical* problem is to find the means of philosophizing *without making assumptions...*" (TCW,I, 623). James agreed with Hodgson on the primary desiderata of a philosophy without [metaphysical] assumptions, but this meant for him precisely using the results being established experimentally in the science of psychology as a way of ascertaining those facts of experience which would be impervious to skeptical refutation and which could serve as a secure foundation for philosophy. James sided with Renouvier against Hodgson's attack, partially because he never recognized his own concrete methodology as a 'middle thing' between science and philosophy, since he understood the findings he appropriated as "living facts of human nature" as being strictly scientific and their use by philosophers as strictly philosophic (WB, 77).

17. See Peirce's theory of abduction for an extended defense of the initiating role of original hypotheses, which precede inductive proof.

Chapter Two

1. My use of 'foundation' and its variants should not be taken as asserting either that James fell into the old trap of traditional foundationalism or that he altogether escaped it. It simply represents a decision to follow his own terminology in order to explicitly raise the issue of just what sort of justification he was seeking and to explore its feasibility. The phrase, "founding level of meaning," can be found in Bruce Wilshire's *William James and Phenomenology: a Study of 'The Principles of Psychology'* (Bloomington: Indiana University Press, 1979), 19.

2. See, for instance, Andrew Reck's review of Sandra B. Rosenthal's *Speculative Pragmatism* in *Transactions of the Charles S. Peirce Society* 23(Summer 1987), 341-350. In it he calls himself a "substantialist realist."

3. Daniel J. Wilson, "Science and the Crisis of Confidence in American Philosophy, 1870-1930," *Transactions of the Charles S. Peirce Society*, 23(Spring 1987), 236.

4. See my "James's Reconstruction of Ordinary Experience," *The Southern Journal of Philosophy*, 19:4(1981), 499.

5. The material through section 3 is a revision of an earlier article: "On the Metaphysical Foundations of Scientific Psychology," Michael H. DeArmey and Stephen Skousgaard, eds., *The Philosophical Psychology of William James* (Washington, D.C.: University Press of America, 1986), 57-72.

6. Andrew J. Reck, "The Place of William James's 'Principles of Psychology' in American Philosophy," *Philosophical Psychology*, 5.

7. James, "The Religious Aspect of Philosophy," (1885), CER, 284.

8. George Trumbull Ladd rejects the entire project of a psychology uninformed by metaphysics in his review of *Principles*: "Psychology as So-Called 'Natural Science," *The Philosophical Review*, 1(1892), 24-53. Moreover, he says that despite the fact that "Professor James makes a gallant attempt to defend psychology as a purely natural science by excluding from it all metaphysical assumption whatsoever,...the entire first half of the first volume seems to me far too metaphysical for the preliminaries of a scientific treatise; while a vast amount of conjectural metaphysics of physics is woven into the very texture of both volumes" (28-29).

9. This is its strength, not a lapse, according to Josiah Royce: "He does not try, as many nowadays do, to hide the fact that every psychologist who is more than an elementary student or a Philistine must really formulate philosophical hypotheses, whether or no one is man enough to confess the fact and to take the responsibility for it." "A New study of Psychology," *International Journal of Ethics*, 1(1890-1891), 148.

10. See also James's 1897 letter to H. W. Rankin: "As Kant says I have swept away knowledge in order to make room for Faith; and that seems to me the absolutely sound and healthy position" (WB, 252, n. 7.15).

11. James even argued that religion has nothing to fear in submitting its claims to the bar of scientific evidence. See WB, 8.

12. *The Philosophical Review*, 1(1892), 146-153). Reprinted in CER, 316-327; EPS, 270-277.

13. See note 8.

14. See James, "Clifford's 'Lectures and Essays,'" (1879), CER, 140-141. "Now our science tells our Faith that she is shameful...in short, if we wish to keep in action, we have no resource but to clutch some one thing out of the chaos to serve as our hobby, and trust to our native blindness and mere animal spirits to make us indifferent to the loss of all the rest. Can the synthesis and reconciliation ever come? It would be as rash to despair of it as to swear to it in advance. But when it does come, whatever its specific character may be, it will necessarily have to be of the theoretic order, a result of deeper philosophic analysis and discrimination than has yet been made."

15. See, for instance, the remarks "To The Editor" by Manual Davenport, who argues that James's position "is pretty darn traditional," in *APA Newsletter on Philosophy and Medicine* (Summer 1987), 1.

16. "Since the heart can thus wall out the ultimate irrationality which the head ascertains, the erection of its procedure into a systematized method would be a philosophic achievement of first-rate importance" (CER, 134; EPH, 63).

17. James, "A Pluralistic Mystic," (1910), EPH, 172-190.

18. James, "The Essence of Humanism," (1905), published in both MT, 73, and ERE, 100. For an analysis of common sense in *Principles*, see my "James's Reconstruction of Ordinary Experience," *Southern Journal of Philosophy*, 19(Winter 1981), 499-515, and for his later works, see my "The

Philosopher's 'License': William James and Common Sense," *Transactions of the Charles S. Peirce Society*, 19(Summer 1983), 273-290.

19. This and the following paragraph are taken from "The Positivist Foundation in William James's *Principles*," *Review of Metaphysics*, 37:3(March 1984), 589-590.

20. PU, 94ff. See also Richard J. Bernstein's introduction to PU, xi-xxix.

21. In a footnote to this passage in CER Perry says that James later modified his view. He quotes a passage in *Essays in Radical Empiricism* in which James identified his position as "natural realism" and distances himself from both Berkeley and Mill (CER, 373, n1). But in the ERE passage James is objecting to taking ideas as discontinuous monads, and this is his constant criticism against the empiricists. He emphasizes instead that pure experience is characterized by transition and prospect (ERE, 37). Both transition, that is, the continuity found in process, and prospect, as an aspect of temporality, are positions that James arrives at and defends through his concrete analysis. In chapter 6, part 6, I argue that the long dispute over whether James is an idealist or a realist is counterproductive and has obscured rather than contributed to recognizing his new beginning in philosophy.

22. Shadworth H. Hodgson, *The Philosophy of Reflection*, (London: Longmans, Green, 1878), vol. I, 248,ff.

23. But see James's criticism of Franz Brentano's understanding of intentionality as "presence in absence" which is discussed in chapter 10, section 2.

24. The latest research seems to bear out at the level of brain activity what James explains on the level of consciousness, that is, that paying attention to objects is a separate act in addition to their presence to consciousness. "Dr. Antonio Damasio at the University of Iowa has been studying people with prosopagnosia — the inability to recognize familiar faces. Damasia has discovered that prosopagnosics actually do recognize the faces they claim never to have seen; they show no fluctuations in a test of skin responses, and skin is known to react to the unfamiliar. But the victims don't know that they know the people they see. Their problem involves a disruption of the connection between the parts of the brain that are engaged in recognition and those involved in awareness." Richard Hutton, "The Brain," *Dial* (New York: Public Broadcasting Communications), 6(October 1985), 35.

25. For his defense of the full fact of object-plus-me, see chapter 14, section 3. But to clarify what might be behind these earlier reservations, see chapter 10, "Knowing as it Exists Concretely," section 2.

26. In his "Introduction" to James's *Manuscript Essays and Notes*, Ignas K. Skrupskelis has reminded us of the importance of the issue of what James sometimes preferred to call "the many and the one" in order to emphasize the priority of pluralism (MEN, xviii-xxix).

27. Peter Hare, "Introduction," SPP, xxvii, ff.

28. H. S. Thayer, "Introduction," PM, xxv, n43.

Chapter Three

1. See Hans Linschoten, *On the Way Toward a Phenomenological Psychology, The Psychology of William James*, tr. Amedeo Girogi (Pittsburgh: Duquesne University Press, 1968); Wilshire, *William James and Phenomenology: A Study of the Principles of Psychology*; John Wild, *The Radical Empiricism of William James* (New York: Doubleday, 1969); and James M. Edie, *William James and Phenomenology* (Bloomington: Indiana University Press, 1987).

2. Hare and Chakrabarti argue that James was an "epistemological realist" and did not develop from an idealist to a "phenomenalist" (231-232). They do say that this is not the same as phenomenology but their characterization of epistemological realism does put it at odds with their definition of phenomenology as "a method of descriptive analysis of subjective processes without any claim as to what does or does not exist" (232-233, n4). Wohlgelernter, ed., *History, Religion, and Spiritual Democracy* , 231-245.

3. This jumbles together, as James also does, the different linguistic expressions that are comparable to phenomenology, phenomena, phenomenal, phenomenal findings, etc.

4. In his privately bound collection of Hodgson's essays James marked this sentence from Hodgson, "Common-Sense Philosophies," *Proceedings of the Aristotelian Society*, vol. I, no. 2, (1888), 25. This is now in the Houghton Library, Harvard University, no. WJ 539.19, p. 21. See also my "Hodgson's Influence on James's Organization of Experience," *Pragmatism Considers Phenomenology*, Robert Corrington, Carl Hausman, and Thomas M. Seebohm, eds., (Washington, D.C.: University Press of America, 1987), 187-202.

5. This is elaborated further in chapter 11, section 5: "The Concrete Point of View."

6. This clash of the contradictory assumptions of direct access to reality and of predisposing selective interests is discussed again in chapter 6, "Natural History Methodology and Artistic Vision," and developed in greater detail in Part Five, "Overcoming the Tradition."

7. See my "In Defense of William James's Picturesque Style: Vagueness and the Adequacy of Concepts," *Philosophy Today* (Winter 1982), 357-367.

8. See my "Extending the Darwinian Model: James's Struggle with Royce and Spencer," *Idealistic Studies*, 14(September 1984), 259-272.

9. He does so, for instance in EPH, 11, n1 and EPS, 16. H. S. Thayer also notes this characterization of interests: "In assigning the primary role to 'subjective interests' in our cognitive activity, James makes the interesting suggestion that these interests are the a priori element in cognition." *Meaning and Action*, (Indianapolis: Hackett, 1981), 142.

10. SPP, 32. This is originally said in *Principles* as "one great blooming, buzzing confusion" (PP,I, 462). The whole chapter is being recalled by James; cf., PP,I, 457-518.

11. Edward H. Madden, in his introduction to *The Will to Believe*, cannot make sense of James's claim in the Preface that his concept of radical empiricism is the thread that binds the essays together and thinks that "the detailed analyses of pure experience in *Essays in Radical Empiricism* are simply irrelevant to the claims made in *The Will to Believe*" (xi-xii). The explanation just given ties the two together and makes it difficult, in turn, to understand how the empiricists whom Madden says accept" the general thesis of radical empiricism, that relations are as epistemically irreducible as the elements of classic British empiricism," can "nevertheless totally reject James's fideism." James insists that such relations can only become cognitively available through the focalized attention of selective interest. And it is this same operation that he argues in *Principles* is the very definition of the freedom that grounds morality (PP,II, 1166). For James's arguments that it is impossible to say what the world is apart from our beliefs and values, see WB, 54, 165ff, 224.

12. Friedrich Nietzsche, *The Gay Science* (New York: Vintage Books, 1974), Bk. 2, no. 58, pp. 121-122.

13. A reconstruction of these three distinct meanings of totality can also be derived from "Reflex Action and Theism" (WB, 91-99). The empirical totality is called a "collateral contemporaneity," which is taken as meaning that "the real world as it is given objectively at this moment is the sum total of all its beings and events now" (95-96). James refers to the ideal totality in pp. 96-97, especially in footnote 3: "No amount of failure in the attempt to subject the world of sensible experience to a thorough-going system of conceptions, and to bring all happenings back to cases of immutably valid law, is able to shake our faith in the rightness of principles." The phenomenal totality is expressed as the generalization of the reflex-action theory of mind (91-93). Their inter-relationships are pointed out on pp. 98-99.

14. See chapter 4, "Concrete Acts of Thinking," note ten.

15. See chapter 10 on truth and intentionality.

16. James never explored the relationship between individual organizing structures and their social conditions, despite the fact that the funded character of experience must be socially transmitted and therefore would presumably differ with membership in distinctive communities and larger social groupings.

17. See chapters 10 and 11 on knowledge and truth.

Chapter Four

1. For the introduction of these terms see EPS, 28 and 7, n3.

2. James says, for instance, "What the system pretends to be is a picture of the great universe of God. What it is — and oh so flagrantly! — is the revelation of how intensely odd the personal flavor of some fellow creature is" (PM, 24). For Lyotard, see *The Postmodern Condition* (Minneapolis: University

of Minnesota, 1984). For Foucault, see *Power/Knowledge: Selected Interviews and Other Writings,* ed. Colin Gordon, (New York: Pantheon Books, 1980).

3. See EPS, 393.

4. William R. Woodward, "Introduction," EPS, xv.

5. Woodward, EPS, xiv,ff. James usually denied this Kantian element in his thought but his position cannot be coherently formulated without acknowledging his own version of the Kantian explanation of "mental spontaneity" (see EPS, 47-52). What he actually objected to in "Kantian philosophy" is the neo-Kantian construal of mental spontaneity as denying that "the present sensation" has anything to do with the object (EPS, 48). He also understood Kant's synthesis of the manifold of sensation as another version of associationism and therefore also rejected it because of his own thesis of the dissociation of the phenomenal totality. Kant and Helmholtz were often linked together when he made this point, see PP,I, 493ff, PP,II, 908ff.

6. As was evident already in Woodward's definition of dissociation, James uses 'representation,' 'idea,' 'general character,' and 'properties' interchangeably. James is not interested in settling terminological disputes stemming from different philosophical traditions, but in going behind them to give a concrete description of the process by which a "partial character," however symbolized, is first distinguished from a phenomenal totality and then used as a mediating sign in rational thinking.

7. As was mentioned in the last chapter, James never clearly rethought his reliance on the empiricist assumption of a direct access to the being of things and his insistence that we pre-select according to aspects imaginatively created. The origins and consequences of this indecisiveness over whether we abstract or invent the perceived characteristics of a phenomenal totality are discussed in chapter 6, "Natural History Methodology."

8. Although this passage is found verbatim in PP,II, 969, as part of chapter 22 on "Reasoning," other parts of the article are also paraphrased in chapter 13 on "Discrimination and Comparison," where he talks about "the baby, assailed by eyes, ears, nose, skin, and entrails at once, feels it all as one great blooming, buzzing confusion" (PP,I, 462).

9. This analysis is the concrete basis for what James later formalizes in his radical empiricism as his thesis of pure experience. It also enters into his theory of interpretation in such central metaphors as the one in which he explains how we discriminate aspects of a handful of beans thrown on a table (see VRE, 346, n7).

10. According to Oliver Sacks and Robert Wasserman, Hermann von Helmholtz analyzed color constancy in *Physiological Optics* (1856-7) as a special act "of 'perceptual judgment' required to make a stable world from a chaotic sensory flux, a world that would not be possible if our brains merely reflected passively the ever-changing input that bathed our receptors. There is thus in Helmholtz, even though he is seen as the great successor of the Newton and Young tradition, something that departs radically from the naturalistic tradition, in that it assigns an *active* role to the organism and to

the brain." Furthermore, the thesis that the living processes of perception go beyond any algorithm to a judgment involving meaning is central to Helmholtz's *On the Sensations of Tone*, 1863, translated, Dover, 1954. "The Case of the Colorblind Painter," *The New York Review of Books*, 34(Nov. 19, 1987), 30 and 31, n7. James called Helmholtz's *Physiological Optics* "immortal," and drew on it in developing his own position (EPS, 47). For his misapprehension of its 'Kantian' aspect, see note five above.

11. Although we may not be conscious of them at the time, such unknown aspects of our environment can, of course, have a profound influence on what we do experience. See James's distinction between "the front-door-way" and "the back-door-effects" (PP,II, 1223-1226).

12. See PP,II, 952, footnote.

13. James puts it even more strongly: "We mutilate the fulness [sic.] of S's reality" (PP,II, 959).

14. Such a view of essentialism is still defended in *Studies in Essentialism*, vol. 11, Midwest Studies in Philosophy, Peter A. French, Theodore E. Uehling and Howard K. Wettstein, eds. Essentialism is defined in the publisher's announcement for the book as "a metaphysical view dating back to Aristotle...[which] holds that some objects, no matter how they are described, have essences — that is, they have, essentially or necessarily, certain properties without which they could not exist or be the things they are."

15. James situates interests primarily in individuals and only secondarily in social, political, or economic systems. He points out the conditions which link knowledge with power but does not indict any particular class or system, since the problem is endemic to concrete acts of reasoning. Dewey, Marxists, and feminists have all identified particularized centers of power and therefore extended the Jamesian critique to specific instances.

16. For an explanation of this process developed by John Dewey, see *The Influence of Darwin on Philosophy*, title essay, (New York: Henry Holt & Co., 1910).

17. This connection of rationalism with religious belief is argued more extensively by Nietzsche. See, for instance, *Genealogy of Morals, The Gay Science, Beyond Good and Evil*.

18. See, for example, EPS, 32 and 37.

19. Rorty, *After Philosophy*, 60.

20. See Hans Seigfried, "Transcendental Experiments (II): Kant and Heidegger," *Hermeneutic Phenomenology: Lectures and Essays*, Joseph J. Kockelmans, ed., (Washington D.C.: University Press of America, 1988), 123-156 and his "Nietzsche's Radical Experimentalism," *Man and World*, 22(1989), 485-501.

21. Rorty, *After Philosophy*, 53.

Chapter Five

1. See C. I. Lewis, "A Pragmatic Conception of the A Priori," *The Collected Papers of Clarence Irving Lewis*, John D. Goheen and John L. Mothershead, Jr., eds., (Stanford University Press, 1970). For Sandra B. Rosenthal's latest clarification of this issue see "The Pragmatic A Priori: Lewis and Dewey," *The Southern Journal of Philosophy*, 25:1(Spring 1987), 109-121.

2. In Perry's formulation: "James's voluntarism is so insistent and so characteristic that one is tempted to place it on a plane of equality with his empiricism, and to interpret the movement of his thought as a rivalry and oscillation between the two." But he thinks that James's commitment to empiricism is deeper. However, in Perry's explanation of empiricism we can realize that it already includes a synthesis of the two aspects in a concrete analysis of being human: "His [experimentalist] empiricism lies in the fact that he accepts a verdict imposed from without through the medium of sensibility; but he submits proposals, and these proposals he first contrives by an act of will... In forming and trying hypotheses the mind is not only active, but interested." Furthermore, "intellectual rigorism" is impossible, since we must always "believe more than can be empirically proved," and since pragmatic philosophers renounce appeals to a priori proofs, they "must admit that extra-empirical belief has *no* theoretical proof. There remains only the practical or moral test appropriate to activity in general" (TCW, I, 454-456).

3. For a further development of James's concept of agency see my "Hodgson's Influence on James's Organization of Experience," *Pragmatism Considers Phenomenology*, 187-202.

4. This becomes an important part of John Dewey's philosophy and he develops this notion further. See, for instance, his discussion of 'awareness' in "The Construction of the Good," *The Quest for Certainty* (New York: Minton, Balch and Co., 1929), 254-286.

5. Josiah Royce, *The Religious Aspect of Philosophy*, (Boston, 1885), 316-17, 357.

6. See also Max H. Fisch, "Alexander Bain and the Genealogy of Pragmatism," *Journal of the History of Ideas*, 15 (June 1954), 413-444.

7. Compare James's insistence on the cognitive function of analogy with the recent findings by J. Allan Hobson and Robert W. McCarley that dream associations are metaphorical and analogical and may reflect how the brain and memory work when we are awake. Sharon Begley, "The Stuff That Dreams are Made Of," *Newsweek*, (August 14, 1989), 41-44.

8. James said that since "the mind is at every stage a theatre of simultaneous possibilities," the aesthetic activity of the mind, which is more obvious in art and ethics, can illuminate the epistemological process (EPS, 50-51). But because he later eliminated the passages demonstrating the epistemological relevance of these early findings when he selected from among them some to include in *Principles*, the continuity of his thought was once again obscured.

Chapter Six

1. The interested character of all organizations of experience is also a premise of feminist epistemologies. For a recent defense of this premise see Susan Bordo, *The Flight to Objectivity: Essays on Cartesianism and Culture* (State University of New York Press, 1987).

2. John Dewey picked up this revolutionary potential from James and developed it further. See "The Reflex Arc Concept in Psychology," *The Psychological Review*, 3(July 1896), 357-370. Reprinted in Jo Ann Boydston, ed., *John Dewey: The Early Works*, Vol. 5: 1895-1898, (Carbondale: Southern Illinois University, 1972), 96-109.

3. William R. Woodward says that the "fruitful tension" between James's emphasizing the physiological foundation of the problem of freedom and determinism and also insisting on the need for existential choice "was lost when behaviorists developed one side of James's theory of action and existentialists pursued the other." "Introduction," EPS, xxxvii.

4. See PP,I, 219, 225, 227, 228, 231-240. These passages were discussed in chapter 3, section 3.

5. Parts of "The Feeling of Effort" were scattered through chapter 26 of *Principles*, called "Will," but the section beginning with the title, "No Conscious Dynamic Connection Between the Inner and Outer Worlds," up to the sentence, "A little natural history becomes here necessary," was not among them (see EPS, 399-400). The fragment left out, which I have been discussing in the last three paragraphs, explicitly explores the differing relationship to reality that obtains between natural history and metaphysics. Its absence from *Principles* has helped to obscure some of his crucial presuppositions and has contributed to conflicting interpretations of his work.

6. James shares with Peirce this belief in an independent reality which can only be known in the indefinite future, although it may be correctly believed in earlier. See, for instance, *Collected papers of Charles S. Peirce*, ed. Charles Hartshorne and Paul Weiss, (Harvard University Press, 1960), 5.311. Peirce is also unable to satisfactorily explain how his scholastic realism and phenomenology can be consistently maintained in light of his semeiotic of interpretation.

7. This deliberate turn away from a scholastic refinement of concepts and logical relations to experiential reflections and praxis is what made the pragmatic movement both revolutionary and, later, a stumbling block for those philosophers who — under the pressure both of professionalization and of a positivistic understanding of science — decided to specialize in language and conceptual analysis.

8. See James, "Brute and Human Intellect," EPS, 1-36.

9. See my "Vagueness and the Adequacy of Concepts," *Philosophy Today*, 26(Winter 1982), 357-367.

10. James derived these "technical terms" of 'focal object' and 'marginal object' from the British biologist and philosopher, Lloyd Morgan (TT, 21).

11. Appendix I of *Essays in Radical Empiricism*, pp. 257-258, seems to contradict this, but not if seen in context in the chapter, "The Experience of Activity," pp. 79-95, as explained further on in this text.

12. Peirce, for example, also believed in exact observation and pure description: "The first and foremost" faculty of the phenomenologist is that "of seeing what stares one in the face, just as it presents itself, unreplaced by any interpretation.... What we have to do, as students of phenomenology, is simply to open our mental eyes and look well at the phenomenon and say what are the characteristics that are never wanting in it (CP 5.41-42).

13. Henry James, ed., *The Letters of William James*, vol. I, (Boston: The Atlantic Monthly Press, 1920), 266.

14. James, "Louis Agassiz," MS, 3-16.

15. This recalls T. H. Huxley's admonition to Charles Kingsley: "Sit down before the facts as a little child, be prepared to give up every preconceived notion, follow humbly wherever and to whatever abyss nature leads, or you will learn nothing." Quoted by Stephen J. Gould, "Between You and Your Genes," *New York Review of Books*, 31(August 16, 1984), 38.

16. Feminists have brought this pragmatic insight back into wide discussion. Just one example out of many: "What feminists have to contribute is the insistence that subjectivity and context *cannot* be stripped away, that they must be acknowledged if we want to understand nature and use the knowledge we gain without abusing it." Ruth Hubbard, "Some Thoughts about the Masculinity of the Natural Sciences," *Feminist Thought and the Structure of Knowledge,* Mary McCanney Gergen, ed., (N.Y.: New York University Press, 1988), 10.

17. See MT, 26, n8. Likewise, James's main objection to the "Kantian machine-shop" explanation of space is that he has "no introspective experience of mentally producing or creating space." He mistakenly takes as assertions of temporal succession a transcendental explanation of the conditions necessary to explain the fact of the synthetic unity of perceptions. He does agree that we experience such a unity. He concurs with Kant that "the higher parts of mind...interweave the space-sensations with intellectual relations," but he takes the Kantian explanation to be an assertion that "one moment of passive inextensive sensation" is "succeeded by another of active extensive perception," rather than being grasped immediately as a synthesis (PP,II, 905).

18. Thayer, for instance, interprets James as being anti-intellectual and distrusting of science. He says James cannot see the significance of scientific method. *Meaning and Action*, 422.

19. Theodore W. Schick, Jr. still defends realism in much the same way when he argues against Davidson's and Rorty's verification theory of meaning that "from that fact that there is no reliable way of telling whether or not something is the case, it neither follows that it is not the case nor that it is unreasonable to believe it is not the case." "Rorty and Davidson on Alternate Conceptual Schemes," *Journal of Speculative Philosophy*, 1:4(1987), 301.

20. Dewey recognized this more clearly than James did and his unflinchingly drawing the humbling conclusions of our radical finiteness and temporality still bothers those who seek a certitude in our truth claims that goes beyond what we can justifiably claim. See, for instance, Schick Jr.'s complaints about Dewey "moving 'truth' to the ideal limit of inquiry," and thereby depriving us of the comfort of believing that our specific truth claims are just true in some unqualified sense. Schick Jr., "Rorty and Davidson," 308.

21. This section is taken from section four of "James's Reconstruction of Ordinary Experience," *The Southern Journal of Philosophy*, 19:4(Winter 1981), 509-513.

22. George Santayana did not grasp the centrality of creativity to James's thought, but understood enough of it to disagree, thinking it too unabashedly materialistic. "Free will, a deep moral power contrary to a romantic indetermination in being, he endeavored to pack into the bias of attention — the most tempermental of accidents. He insisted passionately on the efficacy of consciousness and invoked Darwinian arguments for its utility." "Brief History of my Opinions," George P. Adams, ed., *Contemporary American Philosophy*, vol. 2, (New York: Russell and Russell, 1962, orig. 1930), 252.

23. Compare Calvin O. Schrag's similar thesis in regard to the continental phenomenological tradition in *Radical Reflection and the Origin of the Human Sciences* (W. Lafayette: Purdue University Press, 1980), x-xi.

24. In "Two Dogmas of Empiricism" W.V.O. Quine apparently holds this Jamesian position: "But in point of epistemological footing the physical objects and the gods differ only in degree and not in kind. Both sorts of entities enter our conception only as cultural posits. The myth of physical objects is epistemologically superior to most in that it has proven more efficacious than other myths in working a manageable structure into the flux of experience." *From a Logical Point of View* (New York: Harper Torchbooks, 1963), 44. But later, in his review of Nelson Goodman's *Ways of Worldmaking*, for instance, he objects strenuously to the parity of 'worlds,' including the aesthetic, and wants to stop at "physical theory." Taking back his own earlier formulation, he contrasts physical theory, somehow no longer mythical, with "tenuous metaphor[s]" — the "other worlds" of Goodman and, I would add, of James. Like many before him, Quine falls back into translating pragmatic efficacy into metaphysical exclusivity. *New York Review of Books*, 25 (November 23, 1978), 25.

25. See Nietzsche's remarks about "active interpretation" being mistaken for mere "conceptual translation," *The Will to Power* (New York: Vintage Books, 1968), nos. 604-608, pp. 327-328.

26. Dewey, "Emerson — The Philosopher of Democracy," Jo Ann Boydston, ed., *John Dewey: The Middle Works*, Vol. 3: 1903-1906 (Carbondale: Southern Illinois University, 1977), 185.

27. For Nietzsche's admiration for Emerson see Kaufmann's introduction to *The Gay Science* , "Emerson," 7-13.

28. Kaufmann, Introduction, 8.

29. James, "Absolutism and Empiricism," *Mind*, 9(1884), 285.

30. "Absolutism and Empiricism," 286. Dewey develops this appeal to feeling as disclosive of reality under the rubric of 'awareness.' See sections three and four of "Does Reality Possess Practical Character?" (1908), *John Dewey: The Middle Works*, vol. 4: 1907-1909, (Carbondale: Southern Illinois University, 1977), 132-141.

31. For more details of James's Darwinism see my "Extending the Darwinian Model: James's Struggle With Royce and Spencer," *Idealistic Studies*, 14(September 1984), 259-272. See also James's "Great Men and Their Environment," WB, 163-189.

32. This third meaning of seeing-as is developed in two essays in *Talks to Teachers:* "On a Certain Blindness in Human Beings" and "What Makes a Life Significant." See also my "Pragmatism, Feminism, and Sensitivity to Context," in *Who Cares?*, Mary M. Brabeck, ed., (New York: Praeger, 1989), 63-83.

Chapter Seven

1. For instance, John J. McDermott says that James reverses the usual order of philosophic reading, which is often obscure and technically demanding at first and then becomes progressively easier to understand: "On reading James, however, the first response is one of elation at the apparent simplicity and elegance of the literary style. It is only after several readings that the philosophical depth and complexity begin to emerge." *Classical American Philosophy*, John J. Stuhr, ed., (N. Y.: Oxford University Press, 1987), 105.

2. Henry James, ed., *Letters*, II, Appendix, 354-356. May 26, 1909 letter to "Miss S — ."

3. *Letters*, II, 355.

4. James accepts the traditional nineteenth century distinction of sex roles and always speaks of philosophers as men. His insistence on the dangers of rationalism and his reconstruction of philosophy as a harmonious weaving of order out of chaos, however, easily lend themselves to feminist appropriation.

5. *Letters*, II, 355.

6. James, "A Pluralistic Mystic," EPH, 172-190. See also 276ff.

7. On James's popularity as a lecturer, see Thayer, "Introduction," (PM, xvi-xvii).

8. James, "A Great French Philosopher at Harvard," EPH, 166-171. See also p. 276.

9. *Letters*, II, 356.

10. Ibid., 355-56.

11. Ibid., 281.

12. Not until the current wave of development of feminist theory has sympathetic interpretation been reaffirmed as central to hermeneutics. Its

affinities with Jamesian theory can be recognized despite the sexist presuppositions evident in the quote.

13. Ignas K. Skrupskelis refers to these same passages as part of his argument that James continued and corrected the empiricist tradition of Locke and Hume by incorporating developments in physiology and psychology that had been made in the intervening years (78-79). This explanation seems plausible, especially in regard to how James saw his own contribution. But it is incomplete and inadequate to explain the full scope of his reconstruction of the philosophical tradition. James did not just incorporate new discoveries of fact, but used them to develop original concrete and hermeneutical analyses. "The 'Principles' as a Heartier 'Essay Concerning Human Understanding,'" DeArmey & Skousgaard, eds., *The Philosophical Psychology of William James*, 73-94.

14. This is developed in chapter 12, "Why Metaphysics?," and only summarized in this paragraph.

15. Russell, Ayer, Suckiel and Myers, for instance, all interrogate the Jamesian texts to make them answer a set of problems formulated from a different philosophical angle of vision and so do not attempt to reconstruct the original textual context. James himself points this out in regard to Russell. See Thayer, *Meaning and Action*, 520.

16. Levinson says that as a graduate student he was shocked to discover the lack of critical analyses of James's classic work on religion (vii). I came across his book only after having written the first draft of this one and was pleasantly surprised to find out that his analysis provides independent corroboration for the radical empiricist hermeneutical approach sketched out in this section. See *The Religious Investigations of William James*, Part II, 71-167.

Chapter Eight

1. See PP,II, 970 and PU, 68.

2. Compare this with Friedrich Nietzsche's similar comments on aphorisms: "In the mountains the shortest way is from peak to peak: but for that one must have long legs. Aphorisms should be peaks — and those who are addressed, tall and lofty." *Thus Spoke Zarathustra*, Walter Kaufmann, trans., (New York: The Viking Press, 1966), 40.

3. See, for instance, EPS, 11 and VRE, 406.

4. This and the following two paragraphs are taken from my "Vagueness and the Adequacy of Concepts, *Philosophy Today*, 26(Winter 1982), 362-363.

5. Edward Manier, *The Young Darwin and His Cultural Circle* (Dordrecht, Holland: D. Reidel, 1978), 172. See also the footnote on page 228 to Mary Hesse (1964), "The Explanatory Function of Metaphor," 157-177.

6. Nietzsche, *On the Genealogy of Morals*, Walter Kaufmann, trans., (New York: Vintage Books, 1969), 23.

7. PU, 187, note 71.4. This is developed in detail in "The Help given by Association by Similarity," PP,II, 970-983, "Different Orders of Human Genius," PP,II, 984-993. See also WB, 52, EPS, 29-37.

8. This metaphor of a handful of beans on a table is also developed in a 1907 letter to Dickinson S. Miller, which can be found in Henry James, ed., *The Letters of William James*, vol. 2, (Boston: Atlantic Monthly Press, 1920), 295-296.

9. Only the excesses of the complementary passions of simplification and clarification are criticized, not their worth. He praises our simplifying drive to unify the chaos, for instance, in a simile: "Our pleasure at finding that a chaos of facts is at bottom the expression of a single underlying fact is like the relief of the musician at resolving a confused mass of sound into melodic or harmonic order" (EPH, 35).

10. James, *Letters*, II, 326.

11. The lengthy sentence that follows reflects the rhythm of speech rather than of writing and reminds us that the spoken word is paradigmatic for James.

Chapter Nine

1. I think Levinson is correct that "James wavered between the panpsychism of the personal idealists and a naturalism of a Deweyan sort for the rest of his life." *Religious Investigations*, 177. In chapter 5 of *William James's Philosophy* Marcus Peter Ford argues that James's "panpsychism is never systematically developed nor is it very sophisticated. Nonetheless, he is a panpsychist" (6). (Amherst: University of Massachusetts, 1982), 75-89.

2. For James's final reflections (1910) on how his radical empiricism is a philosophy if understood in his reconstructed, 'eulogistic' sense of "the *only complete kind of knowledge*,...knowing life in its full thickness and activity," and is not a philosophy if understood in the traditional, one-sided sense of a rational defense of transconceptual, absolute reality, see CER, 497-499.

3. McDermott points out the discrepancy of these two views of James as to the relation between radical empiricism and pragmatism and suggests without further elaboration that "acceptance of a radically empirical doctrine of relations is necessary if the pragmatic method is to prevail" (ERE, xxxvi-xxxvii).

4. Flower points out that despite James's claim that pragmatism and radical empiricism were independent, they "are difficult to disentangle; parts of *Pragmatism* (1907) duplicate *Essays in Radical Empiricism* (1912)." Although one can distinguish pragmatism as "a theory about the dependence of meaning and belief on experience, while Radical Empiricism is an account of the nature and content of experience[,]...given the background of the *Psychology*, with its account of experience, we are not surprised to find that in

James's own case they are thoroughly interrelated." Flower and Murphey, eds., *A History of Philosophy*, 662, 673.

5. See PM, 5, 6, 34ff, 120, 154 n5.18, n6.2; MT, 4, 71, 93.

6. See my "The Philosopher's 'License'": William James and Common Sense," *Transactions Charles S. Peirce Society*, 19(Summer 1983), 273-290.

7. PM, 11ff. Nietzsche says, for instance, that "philosophy is this tyrannical drive itself, the most spiritual will to power, to the 'creation of the world,' to the *causa prima*." See all of Part One, "On the Prejudices of Philosophers," *Beyond Good and Evil*, Walter Kaufmann, trans., (New York: Vintage Books, 1966), 16.

8. The appeal to the ordinary person and to the satisfaction of individual needs follows from James's concrete analysis of ordinary experience as constituted by ends-in-view or intentionality. Levinson explains this methodological aspect historically. James believed in "the doctrine of the vox populi [which was] so dominant in the National Period: God decided what course Providence would take and used the conflict [of the civil war] to clarify the nation's divine mission" (5). He traces James's earlier loyalty to the doctrine of the vox populi and his subsequent disillusionment in light of the "Philippine Tangle:" "Vox populi had run its gamut and failed. Ever the liberal, he believed that men's opinions were the predominant influence on social and historical change. But especially after the turn of the century, he became convinced that the educated classes must lead national opinion" (61, 241). See also *Religious Investigations*, 5, 40, 61, 241, 265.

9. Unless the radical consequences of James's criticism of metaphysics and reconstruction of it as an explanatory structure for his analyses of concrete experience are followed through, then one is stuck with James's misinterpretation of the relation of pragmatism to radical empiricism and can only conclude, with Suckiel, that his metaphysics of radical empiricism "represents a major shift in philosophical perspective for James," and that this shift cannot be reconciled with his pragmatist position. See Suckiel, *The Pragmatic Philosophy*, 11.

10. Heidegger, for instance, in his praise of openness to Being (the religious attitude) and hostility to autonomous individualism (the moral attitude), is still caught in this dualism originating in religious, metaphysical rationalism. See William J. Richardson's endnotes numbers 25-27 to Heidegger's "'Only a God can Save Us': The *Spiegel* Interview (1966) in *Heidegger: The Man and the Thinker*, Thomas Sheehan, ed., (Chicago: Precedent Publishing Co., 1981), 45-67.

11. The passages quoted in this paragraph are all taken from Nietzsche, "On the Afterworldly," *Thus Spoke Zarathustra*, Walter Kaufmann, trans., (New York: The Viking Press, 1966), 30-33.

12. See Nietzsche, *The Will to Power*, sections 13, 36, 552. Nietzsche's formula for nihilism and its overcoming are explained in my "Why Are Some Interpretations Better Than Others?" *The New Scholasticism*, 49: 2(Spring 1975), 157-161.

13. This theme of the basis of nihilism and its overcoming can be traced in Nietzsche, *The Gay Science*, sections 125, 277, 337.

Chapter Ten

1. This is not to say that parts of his program were not deeply influential on other philosophic movements. Bertrand Russell, for instance, acknowledges this influence in *A History of Western Philosophy*, where he says that he is convinced that William James was right in his doctrine of radical empiricism, which denied "that the subject-object relation is fundamental," and that James "would, on this ground alone, deserve a high place among philosophers." (New York: Simon and Schuster, 1946), 812.

2. See Rorty, *Consequences of Pragmatism*, xvii, ff.

3. See Thayer, *Meaning and Action*, 313. "For Wittgenstein often referred to James in his lectures, and for a time James's *Psychology* was the one book that he kept in his sparsely furnished rooms."

4. Karl Popper, for instance, attacks as 'psychologism' "the doctrine that statements can be justified not only by statements but also by perceptual experience" (94). I have no quarrel with his objection to the indubitable certainty claimed for our intuitions of the given or sense-data and arguments that "every statement has the character of a theory, of a hypothesis" because it includes interpretive symbols or ideas and therefore their veracity must be determined by experimental consequences. But then he contradicts his own thesis of the theory-ladenness of observation by claiming to be able to "distinguish sharply between objective science on the one hand, and 'our knowledge' on the other" (98). He privileges the standpoint of epistemology as somehow independent of social, biological, and cultural constraints. It is this latter claim to have escaped the psychologism of experience "linked with feelings of belief or of conviction" that puts him at odds with James's analysis (99). Karl Popper, *The Logic of Scientific Discovery* (New York: Harper & Row, 1968), 93-100.

5. Quoted in Thayer, *Meaning and Action*, 520.

6. Nietzsche also began his inquiry into truth by calling attention to the context and purpose of knowing. His explanation was developed along remarkably similar lines. See "On Truth and Lies in a Nonmoral Sense," (1873) in Daniel Breazeale, ed., *Philosophy and Truth* (New Jersey: Humanities Press, 1979), 77-97.

7. See my "The Philosopher's 'License': William James and Common Sense," *Transactions Charles S. Peirce Society*, 19(Summer 1983), 273-290.

8. See chapter 2, "Founding Level of Meaning," section four.

9. See H. S. Thayer, ed., *Pragmatism: The Classic Writings* (Indianapolis: Hackett, 1982), 57.

10. Thayer, *Pragmatism*, 27.

11. See, for historical truth, Carl Becker; for scientific truth, Feyerabend and Kuhn; for religious truth, Schleiermacher and Dilthey; for common sense truths, James, *Pragmatism*, chapter 5.

12. Thayer, *Meaning and Action*, 539ff.

13. This was pointed out by Perry, who found the claim in a 1907 letter by James to Charles A. Strong (TCW,II, 548, as referred to in MT, 205).

14. TCW,I, 799-800. He is commenting on MT, 23, n6.

15. In *The Works of William James*, for instance, Ignas K. Skrupskelis does not indicate in the Notes that James is responding to Brentano in either of the books where the excerpt occurs; see EPH, 211, and MT, 171. Wilshire discusses intentionality at length as it relates to Brentano, Husserl and James, but only in regard to *Principles*.. See *William James and Phenomenology: a Study of 'The Principles of Psychology'*, 150ff. James M. Edie explicitly follows Wilshire in restricting his discussion of intentionality to *Principles*. See *William James and Phenomenology*, 24ff.

16. See Franz Brentano, *Psychologie vom empirischen Standpunkt* (Vienna, 1874).

17. I am grateful to H. S. Thayer for pointing this out to me.

18. EPS, 142-167. Excerpted in PP,I, chapters 7, 9 and 12.

19. For the denial see such claims as: "In principle, then, as I said, intellectualism's edge is broken; it can only approximate to reality, and its logic is inapplicable to our inner life, which spurns its vetoes and mocks at its impossibilities" (PU, 130-131). For the continued and growing importance of 'totality' as horizon or fringe, see such statements as: "My present field of consciousness is a centre surrounded by a fringe that shades insensibly into a subconscious more" (PU, 130).

Chapter Eleven

1. Thayer, *Meaning and Action*, 539.

2. Ibid., 544; quotes MT, 80.

3. Ibid., 542; quotes MT, 128.

4. Ibid., 543.

5. See, for instance, ERE, 18-19.

6. See Aristotle, *On Interpretation*, I, 16a1-8.

7. See MT, 50. Rorty, *Philosophy and the Mirror of Nature*. James explicitly rejects conversation in Rorty's sense. See SPP, 67.

8. Norwood Russell Hanson, *Observation and Explanation* (New York: Harper Torchbooks, 1971), 15.

9. Rorty also picks up and develops James's distinction between the lower and upper case treatment of the great words of the Western tradition. See "Pragmatism and Philosophy," *After Philosophy*, 28.

10. Werner Heisenberg, basing his position on contemporary physics, comes to much the same conclusion: "Furthermore, one of the most important features of the development and the analysis of modern physics is the experience that the concepts of natural language, vaguely defined as they are, seem to be more stable in the expansion of knowledge than the precise terms of scientific language, derived as an idealization from only limited groups of phenomena.... Only through these precise definitions is it possible to connect the concepts with a mathematical scheme and to derive mathematically the infinite variety of possible phenomena in this field. But through this process of idealization and precise definition the immediate connection with reality is lost." *Physics and Philosophy*, (New York: Harper and Row, 1958), 200. But what Heisenberg locates in natural languages James attributes to the experiential level, a field of consciousness both bodily and psychical, which expresses itself in ordinary language, but is not reducible to it. Ordinary language is to fields of consciousness what theoretical language is to scientific experiment. The languages are both outgrowths of the experiential levels and constituent features of them.

11. Nicholas Rescher. *Methodological Pragmatism* (New York: New York University, 1977).

12. Rorty, *Consequences of Pragmatism*, 173-74. For second quote see Suckiel, *The Pragmatic Philosophy*, 12. See also Myers, *William James*, 96-97.

13. Thayer, *Meaning*, 160ff.

14. Ibid., 161.

15. Unpublished manuscript in the James archives in Houghton Library, Harvard University, bMs Am 1092.9, no. 4440. Now published in MEN, 11.

16. For a similar explanation of the evolutionary utility of rationality see Nietzsche, *The Will to Power*, sections 480 and 498. This is elaborated further in Hans Seigfried, "Law, Regularity, and Sameness: A Nietzschean Account," *Man and World*, 6:4(November 1973), 381-382.

17. See notes for "The Sentiment of Rationality," EPH, 366.

18. *Collected Papers*, 212, in Thayer, *Meaning*, 566, n16.

Chapter Twelve

1. Radical empiricism also includes other claims, such as the reality of relations and of process, because they are demonstrable aspects of experience.

2. Walter Boughton Pitkin, "A Problem of Evidence in Radical Empiricism" *Journal of Philosophy, Psychology, and Scientific Methods*, 3(1906), 645-50. See ERE, 185, n. 123.1.

3. This discussion of what constitutes 'critical' philosophy continues in the next chapter.

4. See John Dewey, *The Influence of Darwin on Philosophy*, (New York: Henry Holt, 1910).

5. That he meant to claim two real worlds all along can be gathered from his metaphors, such as the one given in chapter 8 above about the relationship of our sensible world as a watery medium to the ideal world as air above it which is explicated by saying that "both worlds are real, of course, and interact" (PM, 63).

6. Thayer, ed., *Pragmatism: The Classic Writings*, 133.

Chapter Thirteen

1. James had earlier explained that by critical pragmatism he meant the subordination of aesthetic to practical rationality (PM, 269, EPH, 138-139). He seemed to recognize that we must turn to appreciable differences in action to settle metaphysical disputes precisely because any other way is dogmatic. Yet he still appeals in his later writings to "the actual constitution of reality," and not only to that reality for us which is accessible in purposeful action. This appeal is hardly distinguishable from the old metaphysical dogmatism that critical philosophy threw out. The earlier claim was accompanied by a tirade against Kant, one which does not demonstrate a particularly good grasp of his position. This lack of understanding catches up with him in his later comments on critical philosophy in SPP.

2. See "The History," SPP, 198-207.

3. Sandra B. Rosenthal, *Speculative Pragmatism* (Amherst: University of Massachusetts Press, 1986), 93.

4. Eugene Fontinell, *Self, God, and Immortality: A Jamesian Investigation* (Philadelphia: Temple University Press, 1986).

5. Ibid., 9.

6. Ibid., 10.

7. Christine Ladd deftly captured the absurdity: "In fact, so devious and unpredictable was his [Peirce's] course that he once, to the delight of his students, proposed at the end of his lecture, that we should form (for greater freedom of discussion) a Metaphysical Club, though he had begun the lecture by defining metaphysics to be 'the science of unclear thinking.'" *Journal of Philosophy* 13(1916), 716f. Quoted in *Studies in the Philosophy of Charles Sanders Peirce*, Wiener and Young, eds., (Cambridge: Harvard, 1952), 291.

Chapter Fourteen

1. The chapters Perry posthumously published as *Essays in Radical Empiricism* do not exactly match the ones James originally planned to publish

together. This was mostly because James had already published some of the articles separately in *The Meaning of Truth*. His original list should be consulted by anyone seeking to reconstruct what he envisioned as his philosophy of radical empiricism. See ERE, 204.

2. For a full explanation of James's understanding of, and objections to, Kant, we have to wait for the publication and critical analysis of his running commentary on Kant's works. See SPP, 124, n14.6.

3. In this quote he is contrasting 'philosophical' to 'religious,' insofar as 'philosophy' means providing a reasoned basis for our beliefs, and is not using it in the traditional sense of a metaphysics of being.

4. Wohlgelernter, ed., *History, Religion, and Spiritual Democracy*, 231.

5. Towards the end of his life James summarized a series of lectures by Boutroux, emphasizing those aspects that clarified his own position. EPH, 166-71.

6. John Dewey, *Experience and Education* (New York: Collier Books, 1966), 43-44.

7. James, *Letters*, II, 295.

8. Frederick J. Down Scott, ed., *William James: Selected Unpublished Correspondence, 1885-1910* (Columbus: Ohio State University Press, 1986), 518.

9. Scott, *Letters*, 519.

10. Myers, *William James*, 310.

11. For a more detailed reconstruction of James's theory of pure experience see my *Chaos and Context: A Study in William James*, (Athens, Ohio: Ohio University Press, 1978), 38-53.

12. Myers, *William James*, 310.

13. James also incorporates this example into a footnote in VRE, 346, n7.

14. James, *Letters*, II, 295.

15. Ibid., 296.

Chapter Fifteen

1. Editors' introduction to "Jean-François Lyotard," *After Philosophy*, 68.

2. Richard Rorty, "Habermas and Lyotard on Postmodernity," Richard J. Bernstein, ed., *Habermas and Modernity* (Cambridge: The MIT Press, 1985), 174-175.

3. See Sarah Kofman, *Nietzsche et la métaphore* (Paris: Payot, 1972).

Conclusion

1. MEN, 11.

2. Harold Beaver, "The Endless Filament," *Times Literary Supplement* (May 6-12, 1988), 497.

Index

Consult also the topics, articles, and books listed in the contents, as they are not repeated in this index. Titles of works cited throughout the text are listed selectively.